This book describes how the Chinese government, between about 620 and 850, developed an official organization designed to select, process, and edit material for inclusion in official historical works eventually to be incorporated in an official history of the dynasty. The process is important because of the dependence of modern historians on the evidence contained in the official histories, and the consequent need to subject it to close critical scrutiny so that we can counterbalance the biases of its authors. There is no comparable work in any language, including Chinese.

Cambridge Studies in Chinese History, Literature, and Institutions
General Editor   Denis Twitchett

THE WRITING OF OFFICIAL HISTORY UNDER THE T'ANG

The Writing of Official History Under the T'ang

Denis Twitchett

Gordon Wu Professor of Chinese Studies, Princeton University

CAMBRIDGE
UNIVERSITY PRESS

Published by the Press Syndicate of the University of Cambridge
The Pitt Building, Trumpington Street, Cambridge CB2 1RP
40 West 20th Street, New York, NY 10011–4211, USA
10 Stamford Road, Oakleigh, Victoria 3166, Australia

First published 1992

Printed in the United States of America

Library of Congress Cataloging-in-Publication Data
Twitchett, Denis Crispin.
The writing of official history under the T'ang / Denis Twitchett.
p.   cm. – (Cambridge studies in Chinese history, literature,
and institutions)
Includes bibliographical references (p.   ).
ISBN 0–521–41348–6
1. China – History – T'ang dynasty, 618–907 – Historiography.
I. Title.   II. Series.
DS749.3.T95   1992
951'.017'072 – dc20   91–19735
CIP

A catalogue record for this book is available from the British Library.

ISBN 0–521–41348–6 hardback

Contents

v

Preface

I have been thinking about this book for a long time. Its inception goes back to 1950, when I began seriously to study the T'ang period, and the necessity for the closest possible critical examination of its rather meager sources became an everyday preoccupation. Later, like that of all historians of China of my generation, my interest in historiographical problems was greatly stimulated by the Conference on the Historians of China and Japan held at the School of Oriental and African Studies in London during the summer of 1956, one of the first, and still one of the best, of the specialized research conferences that have played such an important part in our academic life.

But, although I wrote some short studies on historiographical themes in the 1950s, the focus of my attention turned to other historical problems.[1] I returned to the study of historiography largely through an invitation to contribute to the Yale Seminar on Chinese and Comparative Historiography organized in 1970 and 1971 by my dear friend the late Arthur Wright. A short preliminary outline sketch for part of this volume, entitled "Some Notes on the Compilation of the T'ang Dynastic Record," was written in his gracious home at Sachem's Head and was one of the two papers I contributed to that stimulating seminar.[2]

Once again the pressures of other work distracted me from taking this study farther, and even from publishing my preliminary survey. Nevertheless, for the past quarter century, historiographical problems

1 See Denis C. Twitchett, "The Derivation of the Text of the *Shih-huo Chih* of the *Chiu T'ang-shu*," *Journal of Oriental Studies*, 3, no. 1 (1956): 48–62; "Chinese Biographical Writing," in W. G. Beasley and E. G. Pulleyblank, eds., *Historians of China and Japan* (London, 1961), pp. 95–114; "Problems of Chinese Biography," in Arthur F. Wright and Denis C. Twitchett, eds., *Confucian Personalities* (Stanford, 1962), pp. 24–39; "Chinese Social History from the Seventh to the Tenth Centuries: The Tunhuang Documents and Their Implications," *Past and Present* 35 (1966): 28–53.
2 The other, "Liu Fang: A Forgotten T'ang Historian," remains to be revised and published separately.

have necessarily been a recurrent theme throughout my graduate teaching, whatever its specific subject matter, and in 1982, largely thanks to the encouragement of Professor Wang Yuquan of the Academy of Social Sciences, Beijing, who was then a visiting professor at Princeton, I decided that it was time to set down some of my ideas on T'ang historiography in a more systematic form than had been done previously.

This book deals with only one aspect of T'ang historiography. It is an attempt to give as clear a picture as our sources allow of the institutional setting in which official histories were written, and to explore the varied implications of history writing practiced as both a bureaucratic and a political activity. It outlines, as far as that is possible for such a remote period, the limitations and pressures this system imposed on T'ang historians. And, lastly, it is an attempt to demonstrate how the T'ang historical sources that survive came to be written and how they are interrelated. Although many questions of detail must remain unanswered, for the evidence has long since been lost, the results should sensitize the scholar of traditional Chinese history to the fact that the massive and monumental writings produced by official historiography are by no means the seamless works they first seem to be.

I do not attempt to deal with the more fundamental and far subtler problems of T'ang historiographical theory, or with the complex and multilayered attitudes of T'ang scholars and writers to the past. These factors, too, must constantly be in the mind of the modern western historian writing about China. We approach China's past as twentieth-century scholars with our own theoretical conception of history, our own ideas about the relative importance of various issues and problems, and our own methodologies – all of which are products of our own culture and our own time. When we attempt to apply our type of historical investigation to the written record of China's past, we have first to try to understand the attitudes, biases, and limitations of the historians on whose writings we are forced to depend for our evidence, so that we can read them with the fullest possible understanding. We should do so remembering that just as their ideas and their way of writing history were determined by the times in which they lived, and should be understood in the light of the intellectual and institutional history of T'ang times, so our own approaches to the past – immediate, sophisticated, and clearly focused as they may seem to us – are equally ephemeral, facets of twentieth-century western thought and subject to ever changing fashions in the pursuit of history. If sometimes we feel frustrated that traditional Chinese historians paid little or no attention to subjects we currently view as crucial, we should at least pay them the courtesy of attempting to understand exactly what was expected of them and what they were trying to accomplish – to see the writing of history in their terms, to understand its raisons d'être and the way in which they themselves perceived their craft.

But these large concerns are subjects for another and quite different book; here I only touch upon them tangentially as they affected the procedures and the work of the official historians.

I must acknowledge the kindness of many friends and colleagues with whom I have discussed parts of this book. I would like, however, especially to express my warmest gratitude to David McMullen, Frederick W. Mote, and Wang Yuquan, each of whom read an earlier version of the entire draft with meticulous care, whose caution has saved me from some errors and rash speculations, and whose corrections and suggestions have materially improved the text.

Conventions

I employ the standard Wade-Giles romanization for Chinese with the single exception that the second Emperor Hsüan-tsung (reigned 846–59) is romanized "Hsiuan-tsung" to distinguish him from his more famous predecessor (reigned 712–56). This follows the convention employed in *The Cambridge History of China*, volumes 3 and 4. For Japanese, the standard Hepburn romanization is used.

Place names in hyphenated form are T'ang-period names. Modern place names are given unhyphenated, and the conventional standard "postal" spellings – for example, Peking, Canton, Kwangtung, Szechwan, Shensi – are used for place names of provinces and major cities that have been "naturalized" into the English language.

Dates are given in terms of the Chinese lunar calendar as in the original sources. Transcribing them into those of the western calendar would be pointless and would make reference back to the original sources unnecessarily difficult. Years are given in the western equivalent corresponding to the greater part of the Chinese year. Thus K'ai-yüan 14 is rendered as A.D. 726, although it actually corresponds to the period from 2 February 726 until 26 January 727. The translations of official titles are loosely based on the French renderings employed by Robert des Rotours. Charles O. Hucker's *Dictionary of Official Titles in Imperial China* appeared after the bulk of the book was already completed. Emperors are referred to throughout by their temple names (*miao-hao*).

In descriptions of books, I systematically render *chüan* as "chapter" and *pien* as "section" to avoid cluttering the text with transliteration.

Abbreviations

BMFEA	*Bulletin of the Museum of Far Eastern Antiquity*
BSOAS	*Bulletin of the School of Oriental and African Studies*
CTS	*Chiu T'ang shu*
CTW	*Ch'uan T'ang wen*
CWTS	*Chiu Wu-tai shih*
CYYY	*Chung-yang yen-chih yüan, Li-shih Yü-yen yen-chiu so chi-k'an*
HHS	*Hou Han shu*
HJAS	*Harvard Journal of Asiatic Studies*
HS	*Han shu*
HTS	*Hsin T'ang shu*
HWTS	*Hsin Wu-tai shih*
JAOS	*Journal of the American Oriental Society*
JESHO	*Journal of Economic and Social History of the Orient*
SJCCTLSY	*Sung jen chuan-chi tzu-liao so-yin*
SPTK	*Ssu pu ts'ung k'an*
SS	*Sui shu*
TCTC	*Tzu-chih t'ung-chien*
TFYK	*Ts'e-fu yüan-kuei*
THY	*T'ang hui yao*
TLT	*T'ang liu-tien*
TPKC	*T'ai-p'ing kuang-chi*
TPYL	*T'ai-p'ing yu-lan*
TT	*T'ung tien*
TTCLC	*T'ang ta chao ling chi*
TWT	*T'ang wen ts'ui*
WHTK	*Wen-hsien t'ung k'ao*
WTHY	*Wu-tai hui yao*
WYYH	*Wen-yüan ying-hua*

Part I
The bureaucratic apparatus

1
Introduction

The modern historian concerned with the earlier periods of Chinese history remains heavily dependent on the material contained in the standard dynastic histories. It is therefore essential for him to subject the texts of these works to the most rigorous critical scrutiny, for they are rarely the simple product of a single author or group of compilers that they appear to be at first sight. A first step in such a critical scrutiny must be an understanding, in the greatest possible detail, of the process by which the "normative" official historical record of a period came into being, in order to assess the ways in which the process of compilation influenced the final record. Failure to understand such technical matters can blunt our critical interpretation of the histories almost as much as failure to appreciate and make allowance for the conventional intellectual attitudes of official "Confucian" historiography or to understand which specific issues and political problems seemed of paramount importance to contemporary official historians.

This study provides such critical scrutiny of history writing in the T'ang period, and shows how changes in the historiographical process gave rise to marked variations both in the reliability and in the level of detail of the record for different reigns that are reflected in the surviving histories.

Critical investigation of T'ang historical sources is not, of course, anything new. Ssu-ma Kuang was, after all, engaged in just such an activity in the eleventh century when he compiled the critical notes on his sources, the *K'ao-i*, appended to his great history the *Tzu-chih t'ung-chien*, and Ch'ing historians did much invaluable work along the same lines. But their studies raise an interesting interpretative problem. Critical historians of the Ch'ing period, such as Chao I and Ch'ien Ta-hsin, who in the eighteenth century gave close attention to the compilation of the historical record under the T'ang, immediately understood the T'ang system, because the bureaucratic apparatus created to

3

compile the state record, and the general process of compilation the T'ang had created, had later become permanent features of Chinese government. Many professional historians through the centuries knew the system instinctively from having worked within it. But this heightened understanding based on an awareness of parallels with the official historiography of more recent periods was not without its dangers. Just as scholars brought up in the traditional educational and examination system of Ming and Ch'ing times tended to see the T'ang examination system in terms of their own times, and to read into it an importance, a place in society, a basis in Confucian orthodoxy, and a sophistication of method that it had not yet acquired, so the historiographical system has been taken as evidence of a highly complex, firmly established organization along the lines of that existing under later dynasties. In what follows, I try to show how, just as the T'ang examination system remained in a formative, flexible, and experimental stage by comparison with later practice, the machinery for state historiography was also still in the course of development and underwent considerable changes during the dynasty.

I shall first attempt to examine the various institutions that were involved in the compilation of the record, and to see what limits were put on the record by the circumstances under which its material was collected. Second, I shall examine in turn each of the categories of official historical record – the stages through which the official record was refined, selected, and edited – and show at which stages of the process specific types of materials were inserted.

Lastly, I shall venture some tentative hypotheses on how these institutional changes in the machinery and methods of historical compilation are reflected in our chief source for the period, the *Chiu T'ang shu*. This section was originally intended to give an analysis of the entire history, but the ongoing publication of a vast mass of previously inaccessible epigraphic material, both in China and Taiwan and in Europe, has made it premature to attempt such a study of the biographical section, much of which was intimately related to memorial inscriptions of various sorts. I have confined my detailed remarks to the annals and monographs.[1]

---

1 An example of the complex historiographical problems raised by this new material is provided in David McMullen, "The Death of Chou Li-chen: Imperially Ordered Suicide, or Natural Causes?" *Asia Major*, 3d ser., 2 (1989): 23–82.

2

The bureaucratic apparatus

Before the T'ang period, the composition of official history had been the concern of two separate groups of officials: the court diarists, responsible for keeping the day-by-day record of the activities of the emperor and the court, and the Office of Literary Composition, responsible for the actual writing of the national record. This division of functions continued under the T'ang but became far more complex.[1]

The court diarists

The existence of court diarists can be traced back to the dawn of Chinese recorded history. The diarists of T'ang times[2] saw themselves as the successors to the various recorders mentioned in the *Chou li*[3] and to the recorders of the left and of the right (*Tso-shih, Yu-shih*) mentioned in the *Li chi*[4] and in the *Tso chuan*.[5] According to a tradition generally

---

1 See *TT* 21, p. 124a; *TFYK* 554, p. 3b; Wang Ying-lin, *Yü hai* (Taipei, 1964) 48, p. 3b. The division of functions was first formalized under the Northern Chou (559–79). See Wang Chung-lo, *Pei-Chou Liu-tien* (Peking, 1979), vol. 1, p. 191.

2 See, for example, Liu Chih-chi, *Shih t'ung*, "wai-pien" 1, *Shih t'ung t'ung-shih* (Shanghai, 1978) 11, pp. 304ff.

3 The *Chou li* mentions four different categories of recorders, the *T'ai-shih, Hsiao-shih, Nei-shih*, and *Wai-shih*. See Edouard Constant Biot, *Le Tcheou-li; ou, rites des Tcheou* (Paris, 1851), vol. 2, pp. 104–20.

4 See *Li chi*, "Yü-ts'ao"; Seraphim Couvreur, *Li Ki ou mémoires sur les bienséances et les cérémonies* (Ho Kien Fou, 1913; reprint, Paris, 1951), vol. 1, pp. 678–9; James Legge, *The Li Ki, Book of Rites* (Oxford, 1885), vol. 2, p. 2. The T'ang commentary to *Li chi* identifies the recorder of the left with the *T'ai-shih* of the *Chou li*, and the recorder of the right with its *Nei-shih*.

5 *Tso-chuan* mentions the recorder of the left under Duke Hsiang, fourteenth year, and Duke Chao, twelfth year. See Seraphim Couvreur, *Tch'ouen-ts'iou et Tso tchouan; La chronique de la principauté de Lou* (Ho Kien Fou, 1914; reprint, Paris, 1951), vol. 2, p. 297; vol. 3, p. 207; James Legge, *The Chinese Classics, vol. 5, The Ch'un-ts'ew with the Tso Chuen* (London, 1872; reprint, Hong Kong, 1960), pp. 464, 641. There seems to be no early mention of the recorders of the right. William Hung, "A T'ang Historiographer's Letter

believed in T'ang times, the functions of these officials had been strictly distinguished, the recorder of the left having been responsible for noting down the emperor's actions, the recorder of the right for taking down his words. T'ang scholars believed that these two officials had produced distinct types of records from which had originated two separate genres of ancient historical writing. The Spring and Autumn Annals (*Ch'un ch'iu*) and the Tso Tradition (*Tso chuan*) were essentially concerned with the actions[6] of rulers, the traditional business of the recorders of the left, whereas the Book of Documents (*Shang shu*) and the Discourses of the States (*Kuo yü*) merely recorded their utterances, as had the diary kept by the recorder of the right.[7] This somewhat naive theory of a division of roles between the diarists and its connection with the origins of the earliest genres of historical writing does not bear very close examination, but the scholar-historians of T'ang times believed it and took it seriously as an ideal institutional arrangement to which they themselves tried to conform.[8]

In the period of division following the collapse of the Han the titles and organization of the court diarists underwent many changes.[9] The deliberate separation of the routine keeping of the Court Diary from the process of state-sponsored historical composition was finally formalized under the Northern Chou and under the Sui.[10] Under the Sui the com-

---

of Resignation," *HJAS* 29 (1969): 5–52, esp. 17–18, n. 18, suggests that the original meaning of *Tso-shih* was not "recorder of the left" but "assistant scribe" and that the term "recorder of the right" (*Yu-shih*) was a Han invention based on a misunderstanding of this original meaning. For a detailed discussion of these early recorders or annalists, and an attempt to make coherent sense of the relations between the recorders of the left and the right and the other titles mentioned in early literature, especially the *Chou li*, see Chin Yü-fu, *Chung-kuo shih-hsüeh shih* (Peking, 1962), pp. 3–19.

6 Although the *Tso chuan* is full of speech and dialogue, the Spring and Autumn Annals itself contains no direct speech whatever.

7 This division of functions between the different recorders, and the identification of their work with the Spring and Autumn Annals, on the one hand, and the Book of Documents, on the other, had already been made in the bibliographical monograph of Pan Ku's *Han shu*. See *HS* 30, p. 1715; *Han shu i-wen chih* (Shanghai, 1955), p. 13. However, *Pan Ku* reverses the respective functions ascribed to the recorders of the left and the right in the *Li chi*, the account usually followed by T'ang scholars.

8 See, for example, the response of Li Chi-fu (758–814) to Hsien-tsung's enquiries about the Record of Administrative Affairs (*Shih-cheng chi*) in the tenth month of 813, recorded in *THY* 64, p. 1109. See also the edict dated the ninth month of 817, and the memorial from the diarist Yü Ching-hsiu that followed its promulgation, in *THY* 56, pp. 962–3.

9 See *TLT* 8, pp. 23b–24a; *TT* 21, p. 124a; *TFYK* 554, p. 3b. These changes are set out in tabular form in Chin Yü-fu, *Chung-kuo shih-hsüeh shih*, pp. 88–9.

10 However, in early T'ang times this rule was not very strictly enforced. Under Kao-tsung, for example, Ku Yin, a professional historian who was one of the compilers of the Veritable Record for T'ai-tsung's reign and of the National History of the first two reigns, the *Wu-te Chen-kuan liang-ch'ao kuo-shih*, was appointed concurrently as a court

position of the national record was undertaken by a subdepartment of the Imperial Library (discussed later), as was responsibility for the calendar, while the keeping of the Court Diary became the responsibility of officials entitled *Ch'i-chü she-jen* on the staff of the Imperial Secretariat (*Chung-shu sheng*). At first the T'ang continued this practice,[11] but in 628 the diarists of the Secretariat were replaced by similar officials with the title *Ch'i-chü lang* serving in the Imperial Chancellery (*Men-hsia sheng*). This change presumably reflects the increasing prestige of the Chancellery at the expense of the Secretariat. In the period 656–61 the diarists attached to the Secretariat were also revived, and from this time onward the T'ang court maintained two parallel groups of official diarists, who theoretically divided their functions on the lines described in the *Li chi* and other early texts: The *Ch'i-chü lang* attached to the Secretariat were responsible for recording the emperor's actions, whereas the *Ch'i-chü she-jen* under the Chancellery recorded his words. The identification of these posts with the models provided by antiquity was made specific when first during the period from 662–70 under Kao-tsung, and again during the "Chou dynasty" under Empress Wu Tse-t'ien (690–705) the titles of many posts in the bureaucracy were changed to follow the ancient models of the *Chou li*. Under these reforms the diarists again became recorders of the left and of the right.[12]

Although the conception of the diarists' functions was an ancient one,

diarist and as a compiler of the National History at some time between 650 and 656. See *CTS* 73, p. 2600. Similarly, in the 670s, Li Jen-shih, while holding the post of diarist of the left (*Tso-shih*), also worked on additions to the unsatisfactory National History that had been completed in 659 under Hsü Ching-tsung. See *THY* 63, p. 1094; *CTS* 73, p. 2601; *Shih t'ung* 12, p. 373. During the reign of Chung-tsung (705–10) after the completion of the Veritable Record of Empress Wu's reign (*Tse-t'ien Shih-lu*) in 706, the assistant in the Historiographical Office, Wu Ching, who had been one of the compilers, was appointed court diarist (*Ch'i-chü lang*) and apparently continued to work as an official historiographer as before. See *CTS* 102, p. 3182.

11 On the court diarists under the T'ang, see *TLT* 8, pp. 23a–25a; *CTS* 43, p. 1845; *HTS* 47, p. 1208 (Robert des Rotours, *Traité des fonctionnaires et traité de l'armée* [Leiden, 1947], vol. 1, pp. 152–63) for the *Ch'i-chü lang*, and *TLT* 9, pp. 19a–20b; *CTS* 43, pp. 1850–1; *HTS* 47, p. 1212 (Rotours, *Fonctionnaires*, vol. 1, p. 187), for the *Ch'i-chü she-jen*. See also *THY* 56, pp. 961–5, and *TT* 21, pp. 123c–124a, for general discussion. The T'ang court was not alone in continuing the Sui practice. Their rival successor to the Sui in Hopei, Tou Chien-te, self-styled emperor of the Hsia Dynasty (617–21) employed as *Ch'i-chü she-jen* Wei Cheng, later to become famous as a minister and historian during T'ai-tsung's reign, who had fallen into his hands in 619. See *CTS* 71, p. 2546; *HTS* 97, p. 3868.

12 See *TLT* 8, p. 24b; *TLT* 9, p. 19b; *TT* 21, p. 124a; *TFYK* 554, p. 4a, and the other sources listed in n. 11. From 662 to 670 the *Ch'i-chü lang* in the Chancellery were given the title *Tso-shih* recorders of the left. They were again given this title under Empress Wu from 690 to 705. The *Ch'i-chü she-jen* under the Secretariat were entitled *Yu-shih*, recorders of the right, during these same periods.

7

the titles *Ch'i-chü she-jen* and *Ch'i-chü lang* were recent innovations.[13] These titles derived from the name of the Court Diary, the *Ch'i-chü chu*, for which they were responsible.[14] This title for the Court Diary, the "Diary of Activity and Repose," was a long-established one that can be traced back at least to Han times.[15] In the pre-Sui period of division the *Ch'i-chü chu* had been the standard chronological record compiled for each reign.[16]

After the middle of the seventh century the two pairs of diarists were

13 The title *Ch'i-chü she-jen* had first been established under the Sui and was subsequently taken over by the T'ang. The parallel *Ch'i-chü lang* were first established in 628. See *TLT* 8, p. 24a–b; *CTS* 43, p. 1845.

14 Until 628 it seems that the Office of Literary Composition (*Chu-tso chü*) actually composed the Court Diary, reducing the record kept by the diarists to a final polished form. See *CTS* 43, p. 1845.

15 The *SS* Monograph on Literature traces the Diaries of Activity and Repose back to the *Ch'i-chü chu* said to have been kept in the Inner Palace during the reign of Han Wu-ti (141–87 B.C.), and to that kept for Ming-ti of the Later Han (A.D. 57–75) by his empress née Ma. See *HHS* 10A, p. 410. The monograph also speculates that they may have originated as Inner Palace records kept by women scribes. See *SS* 33, p. 966; Chang-sun Wu-chi, *Sui shu ching-chi chih* (Shanghai, 1955), p. 49.

Modern scholarship rejects this account of the origins of the Diaries of Activity and Repose. Charles S. Gardner, *Chinese Traditional Historiography* (Cambridge, Mass., 1938), p. 88, disposes of the record connecting the diaries with Wu-ti's time, pointing out that the only evidence for this comes from a spurious text, the *Hsi-ching tsa-chi*. Hans Bielenstein, "The Restoration of the Han Dynasty: With Prolegomena on the Historiography of the *Hou Han shu*," *BMFEA* 26 (1954): 1–210, esp. 21–2, also disputes the idea that the diaries were kept by female clerks and makes the important observation that the context in which the diaries kept by Empress Ma in Ming-ti's reign are mentioned suggests that such records were already commonplace. A. F. P. Hulsewé, "Notes on the Historiography of the Han Period," in Beasley and Pulleyblank, *Historians of China and Japan*, p. 41, following Chu Hsi-tsu's "Han Shih-erh shih chu-chi k'ao," *Kuo-hsüeh chi-k'an* 2, no. 3 (1930): 397–409, points out that a more important origin of the later Court Diaries was the Recorded Notes (*chu-chi*) kept by the imperial astronomers of Han times. This same idea was already expressed in early T'ang times by Yen Shih-ku (581–645) in his commentary to the *HS* Monograph on Literature: It was repeated by Wang Ying-lin in *Yü hai* 48, p. 20a–b.

The *SS* account of their origin, however, was generally believed in T'ang times. See, for example, Liu Chih-chi, *Shih t'ung*, 11, p. 324, a passage that closely follows the account in the *SS* monograph, and Tu Yu, *T'ung tien* (*TT* 21, p. 124a). For a general discussion of the Court Diaries, see also Chu Hsi-tsu, "Han, T'ang, Sung *Ch'i-chü chu* k'ao," *Kuo-hsüeh chi-k'an* 2, no. 4 (1930): 629–40.

16 The *SS* bibliographical monograph (*SS* 33, pp. 964–66; *Sui shu ching-chi chih*, pp. 48–49) lists forty-four works in this category, the earliest of them dealing with the reign of the last Hou Han emperor, Hsien-ti (reigned 189–220). Some of them, like the *Chin Ch'i-chü chu* in 317 chapters by Liu Tao-hui and the *Hou Wei Ch'i-chü chu* in 336 chapters, were very large works indeed. No fewer than twenty-one of them dealt with various reigns of the Chin dynasty. The bibliographical monograph of *CTS* also lists twenty-six works in this genre, twenty-one of them relating to the Chin, as being included in the Imperial Library in 721. See *CTS* 46, pp. 1997–8; *T'ang shu ching-chi i-wen ho chih* (Shanghai, 1956), pp. 91–3.

of equal rank, holding the lower six rank upper division.[17] They were thus quite important officials, of equal standing with the under secretaries (*yüan-wai lang*) of the six executive boards. From Sui times onward, they had been classed as "officers in constant attendance" (*shih kuan*), that is, part of the emperor's personal retinue, as his ceremonial guard of honor (*i-chang*) was. The posts were also classified as "pure offices" (*ch'ing-kuan*), that is, offices reserved for men of notable family, proved rectitude, and high moral repute.[18] They were thus members of an elite group of officials, which included the higher-ranking grand counselors (*San-ch'i ch'ang-shih*) and counselors (*Chien-i ta-fu*) and the lower-ranking omissioners (*Pu-chüeh*) and remembrancers (*Shih-i*), all of whom were also on the staff of the Chancellery and Secretariat. All these officials, whose court functions were closely linked to the emperor himself, were expected to exercise criticism and a sort of moral censorship over the emperor's pronouncements and actions. They were allowed considerable freedom of speech to exercise this function and had influence far greater than their relatively low ranks would suggest.

The diarists were not expected to be mere passive observers, or high-class stenographers taking minutes of the court meetings. Like the remembrancers and omissioners, they were expected to remonstrate against policies they felt to be unwise or ill-considered, particularly when matters of historical precedent or analogy were involved. For example, in 727 the famous historian Wei Shu, then employed as a diarist, *Ch'i-chü she-jen* remonstrated successfully with the emperor for neglecting a long-established practice by not observing mourning and suspending the court as a mark of respect for the deceased former chief minister, Su T'ing.[19]

---

17 See *TLT* 8, p. 23a; *TLT* 9, p. 19a, etc. See also Chang Jung-fang, *T'ang-tai ti Shih-kuan yü shih-kuan* (Taipei, 1984).

18 See the manuscript table of official posts dating from the T'ien-pao reign period (742–56), discovered at Tun-huang and now in the Bibliothèque Nationale, *Fonds Pelliot Chinois Touen-houang* P. 2504, published in Yamamoto Tatsuro, Ikeda On, and Okano Makoto, eds., *Tun-huang and Turfan Documents concerning Social and Economic History*, vol. 1 (B), *Legal Texts* (Tokyo, 1978), p. 90 (Document XXII (4), section 23).

19 See *THY* 56, p. 962. Su T'ing died on either the fourth (according to *CTS* 8, p. 91), or the ninth (according to *TCTC* 213, p. 6778) day of the seventh month of 727. The incident is curiously omitted from Wei Shu's biographies. Because Wei was a protégé of Chang Yüeh, who had been removed from office as chief minister in the fourth month of 726, and then forced to retire in the second month of 727, Wei Shu may have been protesting on his patron's behalf about this slight offered to the memory of a statesman of unblemished reputation. Wei Shu's personal connection with Chang Yüeh continued: In the second month of 728 Chang Yüeh, though retired, was appointed to the Chi-hsien Academy and given overall responsibility for the National History on which Wei Shu was also engaged.

In 819, another diarist, P'ei Lin,[20] was exiled to a provincial post in disgrace for presenting a lengthy and scathing memorial attacking the emperor for his increasing reliance on alchemists and their elixirs, which ended with the following justification of his doing so:

I submit that since the *Chen-kuan* era there have been numbered among the Diarists of the Left and Right men such as Ch'u Sui-liang, Tu Cheng-lun, Lü Hsiang, Wei Shu and so forth, all of whom have given the utmost of their loyalty and sincerity, who have with all their hearts remonstrated with their emperors. Your petty servant has by error been placed among your majesty's retinue, and has received this post among the "officers in attendance," as one of your close attendants [*tsui-chin tso-yu*]. Since the *Tso chuan* says "The intimate officers of the King should devote themselves entirely to remonstrating with him," for an officer in close attendance on the emperor it is truly his fundamental duty to express himself to the throne with the utmost of loyalty and sincerity.[21]

Not every diarist measured up to this ideal. But it is important to remember, in the context of the didactic preoccupations of traditional Chinese historiography, that the basic material for the historical record, the Court Diary, was written not by mechanical reporters of what occurred but by officials holding posts with serious political and moral responsibilities, who saw themselves and were perceived by others as active participants in, and commentators on, state affairs. The introduction of moral criteria into the historical record was therefore not simply an element introduced in the later stages of the historiographical process when the historians were writing up a considered verdict on the events of a given reign. The application of Confucian[22] moral judgments

---

20 P'ei Lin (d. 838) has biographies in *CTS* 171, pp. 4446–50; *HTS* 118, p. 4287; and a brief note in *CTW* 713, p. 19a.

21 See *THY* 56, pp. 963–5; *TFYK* 546, pp. 17a–19a; *CTS* 171, pp. 4447–8. The incident is dated in the tenth month by *THY* 56, p. 963, and in the eleventh month by *CTS* 15, p. 471. Among other suggestions, P'ei Lin proposed that before the emperor took any elixir the alchemist who had compounded it should be made to ingest it for twelve months to prove whether it was efficacious. His concerns proved only too real. Two months later the emperor was dead, almost certainly poisoned by elixirs containing massive doses of mercuric salts compounded by an alchemist called Liu Pi. On this incident, see Joseph Needham, *Clerks and Craftsmen in China and the West* (Cambridge, 1970), pp. 317–19.

22 Although the histories made their judgments in the light of conventional Confucian ethical standards, not all historians were necessarily Confucians. For example, Li Ch'un-feng, the author of the Monographs on Astronomy, on the Calendar, and on Portents in both the Chin history and the Monographs on the Five Dynasties (later incorporated into the *SS*) who also served as an official historian in the early years of Kao-tsung's reign, was strongly influenced by Taoism and was the son of a noted Taoist scholar, Li Po. He, his son, Li Yen, and his grandson, Li Hsien-tsung, all served as astronomers royal in the seventh century. See *CTS* 79, pp. 2717–19; *HTS* 204, p. 5798. Under Hsüan-tsung a Taoist priest, Yin Yin (also read Yin An), was appointed in 737

10

to the recording of events began with the men responsible for the very first stage of the record.[23]

The identification of the diarists with the other "pure officials" in attendance is underlined, particularly in the eighth and ninth centuries, by the frequent promotion to diarist of men who had served as omissioner or remembrancer,[24] and by the frequent appointment of remembrancers, omissioners, grand counselors, and counselors to concurrent duties in connection with the compilation of the National History.[25] There was a high degree of specialization and professionalism in the careers of T'ang historians, and one aspect of such specialization was the regular transfer of officials between posts connected with historiography and the "pure" remonstrative posts that required a similar knowledge of precedents and exercise of moral judgment on events. Such a career track tended to keep the individual within the inner circle of court advisers. The record kept by the diarists was thus intimately connected with those in power and was almost exclusively concerned with events that affected the central administration.

The Office of Literary Composition

Until the early T'ang the composition of the dynastic record as distinct from the actual day-to-day recording of court events as they occurred had been the responsibility of the Office of Literary Composition (*Chu-tso chü*), a subdepartment of the Imperial Library (*Pi-shu sheng*).[26]

to the control of the Historiographical Office (as *chih Shih-kuan shih*) and even received a special dispensation to perform his duties wearing his Taoist religious robes. See *THY* 63, p. 1101; *HTS* 200, p. 5702.

23 The didactic purpose of the Court Diary is spelled out in the specification of the duties of the diarists given in *CTS* 43, p. 1845. These duties were of course defined in the section of the Statutes relating to the office, from which the passage in *CTS* derives.

24 For examples, see Sun Kuo-t'ung, *T'ang-tai chung-yang chung-yao wen-kuan ch'ien-chuan tu-ching yen-chiu* (Hong Kong, 1978), pp. 314–25, tables 2, 4, 5. These show that more than half (twenty-seven of fifty-one known cases) of the diarists whose careers are analyzed had previously served either as omissioner or as remembrancer. Table 6 (pp. 326–7) also shows that almost all the diarists, particularly after the end of the seventh century, were next promoted as under secretaries of one or other of the six boards. Of the sixty-one individuals whose careers are analyzed, all but eight were promoted directly into higher-ranking "pure offices" in the central government.

25 Such a combination of roles was, however, sometimes the object of protests. In 795, for example, P'ei Yen-ling objected to the appointment of one of the grand counselors as a compiler of the National History on the grounds of an implicit conflict of interest between the two offices. See *THY* 63, p. 1101.

26 For details on the Office of Literary Composition, see *TLT* 10, pp. 19b–23a; *CTS* 43, p. 1855; *HTS* 47, p. 1215 (Rotours, *Fonctionnaires*, vol. 1, pp. 207–8). See also *TT* 26, pp. 155c–156a; *THY* 65, p. 1123, and Li Hua, "Chu-tso lang t'ing pi chi," in *CTW* 316, pp. 5a–7b; *WYYH* 799, pp. 2b–4b. See also David McMullen, *State and Scholars in T'ang China* (Cambridge, 1988), p. 22.

The Imperial Library also controlled the Imperial Observatory (*T'ai-shih chü*), headed by the astronomer royal (*T'ai-shih ling*), the officer responsible for the calendar.[27] This officer had an ancient and intimate connection with the work of the historians[28] and continued to provide a variety of information for the historical record throughout the T'ang period.[29] The Office of Literary Composition was called the *Chu-tso ts'ao*, as under the Sui, until 621. Under the Sui it had employed two chief secretaries and eight assistant secretaries: the latter increased to twenty under Emperor Yang-ti. When the T'ang renamed the office *Chu-tso chü* in 621, its size was drastically reduced to two chief secretaries and four assistant secretaries. This reduction is inexplicable, because the T'ang government shortly after began an ambitious program of compiling standard dynastic histories for the Sui and the preceding dynasties in which the Office of Literary Composition played a leading role.[30] In 629, however, with the establishment of the Historiographical Office (*Shih-kuan*), the Office of Literary Composition ceased to have any direct formal responsibility for the compilation of the historical record,[31] although members of its staff, and also members of the staff of the Imperial Library, frequently appear among the lists of editors and compilers of historical works.[32] From 662 to 670 the office was renamed the *Ssu-wen chü*. In 738 the office was still further reduced in size, and by this time its functions were restricted to the composition of funerary

27 For details on the Imperial Observatory, see *TLT* 10, pp. 23a–34b. The descriptions given in *CTS* 43, pp. 1855–6, and *HTS* 47, pp. 1215–17 (Rotours, *Fonctionnaires*, vol. 1, pp. 208–17), describe the office after its complete reorganization in 758, when the Imperial Observatory (*T'ai-shih chü*) became the *Ssu-t'ien t'ai*, a large astronomical service totally independent of the Imperial Library. After 758 its director held equal rank with the director of the Imperial Library and controlled a staff of 138 ranking officials, with many assistants.

28 In the *Chou li* the *T'ai-shih* was responsible both for the historical record, astronomical observations, the calendar, and the various rituals marking the seasons. Under the Han the *T'ai-shih ling*, the "prefect grand astrologer," was likewise responsible for the calendar, arrangements for the appropriate dates for ritual observances, and recording omens and portents. See H. Bielenstein, *The Bureaucracy of Han Times* (Cambridge, 1980), pp. 19 and 163 (n. 61–62). Wang Yü-ch'üan, "An Outline of Central Government of the Former Han Dynasty," *HJAS* 12 (1949): 151, says that he kept the Court Diary. Bielenstein finds no evidence to support this, however.

29 See *THY* 63, p. 1089; *WTHY* 18, pp. 293–4. See also *TLT* 10, p. 26a, according to which at the end of every quarter the Imperial Observatory should record all the omens and portents it had observed and send these to the Chancellery–Secretariat so that they might be entered in the Court Diary. At the end of every year they should also make a separate comprehensive record to be sent under seal to the Historiographical Office, thus providing a double check on such information.

30 See William Hung, "The T'ang Bureau of Historiography before 708," *HJAS* 23 (1960–1): esp. 94–98.

31 See *THY* 65, p. 1123; *THY* 63, p. 1089; *TT* 21, p. 126c; *TLT* 9, p. 29b, commentary.

32 See Li Hua, "Chu-tso lang t'ing pi-chi," *WYYH* 799, p. 4a.

memorial inscriptions, the texts of prayers addressed to the spirits, and the liturgical texts employed in the state sacrifices.[33] Nevertheless, posts in the office, like all positions in the Imperial Library,[34] remained prestigious appointments for a man of literary talent and were a desirable step in the elite career of a "pure" court official.[35] Both the secretaries and the assistant secretaries were classified as "pure" officials (*ch'ing-kuan*).[36]

The Historiographical Office

The Historiographical Office (*Shih-kuan*) is said to have been established as a separate bureau in the palace in 629.[37] According to the *T'ang liu-tien* its duties were as follows:

The historiographers[38] [*shih-kuan*] are responsible for the compilation of the National History. They may not give false praise, or conceal evil, but must write a straight account of events. The portents of heaven, earth, sun and moon, the distribution of mountains and rivers, fiefs and cities, the precedence between junior and senior lines of descent, ritual and military affairs, changes of reward

33 See Li Hua, "Chu-tso lang t'ing pi-chi," *WYYH* 799, p. 4a. The reduction in the size of the office was probably the result of the growing influence under Hsüan-tsung of the Chi-hsien and the Han-lin academies, the scholars of which were increasingly used to compose state documents of all kinds. This further eroded the responsibilities of the Office for Literary Composition.

34 See Feng Yen, *Feng-shih wen-chien chi* (edition of Chao Chen-hsin, *Feng-shih wen-chien chi chiao-chu* [Peking, 1958]) 3, p. 16, which gives a first appointment as a collator (*chiao-shu*) or corrector (*cheng-tzu*) as an important stage in an elite career track for a man of literary talent.

35 Po Chü-i, supplemented by K'ung Ch'uan, *Po-K'ung liu tieh* (Taipei, 1969) 74, pp. 176–89, quotes a story about the historian-scholar Hsü Ching-tsung, who, upon being appointed secretary of the Office of Literary Composition, said to his kinsmen, "If a scholar-official does not serve in the Office of Literary Composition, there is no way to perfect his family's standing." Where this anecdote came from is unclear; it was not in Po Chü-i's original *Po-shih liu tieh shih lei chi* (Tapei, 1969) 21, p. 506, and was thus inserted by K'ung Ch'uan in the mid twelfth century.

36 See *Fonds Pelliot Chinois Touen-houang* P. 2504 (as cited in n. 18), p. 89, section 19; p. 90, section 23. The secretaries held the lower fifth rank, upper division; the assistant secretaries the lower sixth rank, upper division.

37 For details of the Historiographical Office, see *TLT* 9, pp. 28a–30b; *CTS* 43, pp. 1852–3; *HTS* 47, p. 1214 (Rotours, *Fonctionnaires*, vol.1, pp. 199–204). See also *THY* 63, pp. 1089–1104; *THY* 64, pp. 1105–14; *TT* 21, pp. 126c–127a.

38 The term *shih-kuan* is usually used as a general term for all officials engaged in the writing of history, irrespective of their rank and of the official bureau to which they were affiliated. However, it is also sometimes used in a more specialized sense meaning *The Historiographer*, that is to say the director of the National History, elsewhere known as the *Chien-hsiu Kuo shih* or *Chien Kuo shih*. See, for example, *CTS* 43, p. 1852; and *THY* 63, p. 1092, where Ch'ang-sun Wu-chi, the senior chief minister, is entitled *Shih-kuan T'ai-wei* in connection with the compilation of the National History and the Veritable Records for T'ai-tsung.

and punishment, between prosperity and decline, all should be first recorded. The historians should base themselves on the Court Diary [*Ch'i-chü chu*] and the Record of Administrative Affairs [*Shih-cheng chi*] to make a Veritable Record [*Shih-lu*], setting this out in chronological form and incorporating the principles of praise and blame. When this is completed it is to be stored in the official storehouse.[39]

Neither the *T'ang liu-tien* nor any other source gives a complement of regularly established posts in the office; they list only its staff of clerical assistants.[40] The official historiographers, the directors of the National History (*Chien-hsiu Kuo shih*) and the compilers (*Hsiu-chuan*), were in fact always appointed while concurrently holding other offices; exceptionally talented younger men could also be seconded from their substantive posts to work as assistants in the department (*chih-kuan*). During the early years of the reign of Hsüan-tsung (713–36) those compilers who were not already "officers in attendance" (*kung-feng*) in their substantive office were required to attend court daily, together with the court diarists. This practice ended late in 736 when Li Lin-fu became chief minister.[41] The senior historian sometimes held the title "in charge of the affairs of the historian officials" (*chih shih-kuan shih*).[42]

In 809, following a memorial from Chief Minister P'ei Chi, there was a systematization of the status of the members of the Historiographical Office. All officials who in their substantive office were entitled to attend court were to be appointed as compilers, while those who did not attend court were to be made assistants. The compiler with the highest-ranking substantive office was put "in charge of the affairs of the office" (*p'an kuan-shih*) as a sort of project manager.[43]

---

39 *TLT* 9, p. 296.
40 The exception is *HTS* 47, p. 1214, which lists four compilers (*hsiu-chuan*). This figure, however, almost certainly refers, like much else in the monograph on officials in *HTS*, to the situation at the end of the T'ang period. *CTS* 43, pp. 1852–3, merely lists the titles of the *Shih-kuan* (which here, from the commentary, refers to the director of the National History), the compilers (*hsiu-chuan*), and the assistants (*chih-kuan*). It says that compilers were first appointed during the T'ien-pao period (742–55) and were concurrent holders of offices in other bureaus who worked in the Historiographical Office, whereas those first entering the office were given the title of assistant.
41 See *HTS* 47, p. 1208.
42 For example, see *CTS* 102, p. 3184, which tells us that Wei Shu held this title from 730–9.
43 See *THY* 63, p. 1101, which dates the reform in the sixth month of 811; *CTS* 43, p. 1853, which confirms the year as 811; *HTS* 169, p. 5150, which is undated; and *CTS* 148, p. 3990, which dates it in the autumn of 809. The date given in *THY* 63 cannot be correct since P'ei Chi died on the thirteenth day of the fifth month of 811 (see *CTS* 14, p. 435), having been seriously ill since the end of 810 (see *CTS* 148, p. 3990). P'ei Chi's reform also attempted to regularize the titles of scholars in the Chi-hsien Academy. According to *HTS* 169, this reform was incorporated into the Statutes (*ling*).

14

Later in the eighth century there came to be a regular establishment of four compilers of the National History, but as late as 832 court opinion objected to the appointment of as many as four compilers, favoring only two or at most three compilers employed at any one time.[44] In 852, following a memorial from Cheng Lang, the number of compilers was permanently increased to four, each in theory responsible for one of the quarters of each year, while the position of assistant was abolished.[45]

The compilers' and assistants' concurrent offices give a clear indication of their place in the bureaucratic structure.[46] All these offices were prestigious "pure offices" reserved for the scholarly elite within the civil service, men of proved intellectual talent and impeccable family. The established offices and ranks of the compilers before Hsüan-tsung's time tended to be higher than in the second half of the dynasty, usually in the range from the seventh to the fourth rank, though a few, mostly under Hsüan-tsung, held basic posts of the third rank. After the accession of Su-tsung their basic offices were slightly lower, from the eighth to the fourth rank, and in the ninth century none held higher than the fifth basic rank. However, the type of basic appointment, "pure offices" in the elite stream of central offices, remained unchanged. The assistants, too, formed part of the same charmed circle. Their rank was very low, mostly in the ninth rank. But their basic posts, normally marshals (*wei*) of counties within the metropolitan administration, or posts of collator (*chiao-shu lang*) in the Imperial Library, were the most desirable of first appointments for a promising young man.

The compilers worked under the general supervision of one or more of the chief ministers who were designated director of the National History. There was normally a single director in charge of the National History. But there were exceptions to this rule. The greatest number of concurrent directors was in the early 650s, when there were six or seven acting simultaneously,[47] and in the first decade of the eighth century, when there were again several directors. Liu Chih-chi (661–721) sarcastically describes them as "nine shepherds for ten sheep."[48] After Hsüan-tsung's reign there was always a single director, except for the period from 788 to 800, when Te-tsung allowed the post to remain

---

44 See *THY* 63, p. 1102.
45 See *THY* 64, p. 1114; *HTS* 47, p. 1214.
46 See the materials conveniently tabulated in Chang Jung-fang, *T'ang-tai ti Shih-kuan yü shih-kuan*, pp. 253–69.
47 See the edict of 651, mentioning three names; *CTW* 11, pp. 22b–23b; *WYYH* 464, pp. 5b–7a. The edict of 653 presenting the subcommentaries to five Confucian canons mentions six, *CTW* 136, pp. 7b–9b, and another edict of 653 presenting the completed law code mentions seven, *CTW* 136, pp. 9b–12b.
48 See *Shih t'ung* 20, p. 591.

empty. In the confused days of the end of the dynasty, from 889 on, it became customary to appoint more than one director,[49] even though by then the functioning of the Historiographical Office was largely suspended, not least because the imperial archives and libraries had been completely destroyed or dispersed.[50]

According to Sung Min-ch'iu (1019–79), the post of director was one of a number of concurrent responsibilities distributed among the chief ministers. He claimed that the T'ang tradition was for the senior of the four chief ministers to be appointed concurrently as commissioner for the T'ai-ch'ing Palace, the Temple of Lao-tzu in Ch'ang-an: His colleagues were appointed, in order of precedence, as chief scholar (*ta hsüeh-shih*) of the Hung-wen Academy, director of the National History, and chief scholar of the Chi-hsien tien Academy.[51] The reality was less orderly than this ideal pattern.[52] It is unclear what period Sung Min-ch'iu refers to; presumably it is to very late T'ang, but I cannot identify any group of chief ministers to whom it applies, and there was never a set number of four chief ministers.

The director was, nonetheless, usually one of the junior chief ministers. He was also, like the historians under his charge, normally a member of the scholarly elite within the bureaucracy. After the An Lu-shan rebellion the great majority were examination graduates: By the ninth century almost every director had passed the *chin-shih* examination. Moreover almost half of them had, earlier in their careers, either served in the Historiographical Office or held office as diarists. They thus had professional experience of historical compilation.[53]

---

49 For details, see Chang Jung-fang, *T'ang-tai ti Shih-kuan yü shih-kuan*, pp. 47–58, and table, pp. 270–80.

50 See a memorial by Lo Kun, probably written either in 891 or 898, which suggests the establishment at the capital of a special agency, funded by the Palace Treasury, to buy books for the government and to make up for the destruction of the Imperial Library and the collections of the Three Academies. *CTW* 828, pp. 6a–7a; *WYYH* 694, pp. 15a–16a.

51 See Sung Min-ch'iu, *Ch'un-ming t'ui-ch'ao lu* (Shanghai, *Ts'ung-shu chi-cheng* edition, 1936) A, pp. 10–11.

52 See *HTS* 46, p. 1183. Wang Ying-lin (1223–96) also says that the Hung-wen Academy (which he mentions under the alternative name Hsiu-wen Academy), the Historiographical Office, and the Chi-hsien Academy were grouped together as the Three Academies (*san-kuan*), and that the system under which each was headed by a chief minister was established in 726. See *Yü hai* 165, p. 11a–b. The use of the term *san-kuan* in this unusual sense (it normally referred to the three principal schools in the Imperial University system) is confirmed by an address from Lo Kun to the "Chief Minister Director of the National History" dating from the 890s in which it is implied that these were the three major offices involved in the recording of history. See *WYYH* 653, p. 7a–b; *CTW* 828, pp. 7b–8b.

53 See the information tabulated in Chang Jung-fang, *T'ang-tai ti Shih-kuan yü shih-kuan* pp. 270–80. The increasing proportion of *chin-shih* among the chief ministers acting as

The post of director was usually, but not invariably, a purely nominal "political" appointment. All the actual writing was done by the compilers. However, the directors frequently interfered with their work, and the appointment of chief ministers to direct the office underlines the fact that the compilation of the historical record was thought of as one of the ongoing functions of government. Official historiography was as much a political as a scholarly activity.

The historians were not simply recorders of events. Like the court diarists, they were held to be the custodians of precedents and traditions. For example, in 717 Hsüan-tsung ordered the historians, in the months preceding the great seasonal sacrifices, to memorialize in detail about the ceremonies that ought to be carried out.[54]

Although the Historiographical Office had a somewhat anomalous and quasi-independent status, standing outside the regular bureaucratic hierarchy, it was attached for administrative purposes to one of the central ministries.[55] At first it was placed under the Chancellery, and its premises were next door to or to the north of the main[56] Chancellery

directors during the late T'ang may not be the result of deliberate policy but may simply reflect the steadily growing preponderance of men with a strong scholarly background among the highest court officials. The large number with historical experience does suggest conscious choice, however.

54 *THY* 64, pp. 1107–8.
55 See *TLT* 9, p. 28a; *CTS* 43, p. 1852; *HTS* 47, p. 1214, all of which show it as a subordinate bureau under the Chancellery. Hung ("The T'ang Bureau of Historiography before 708," p. 100) has questioned whether, at least in the earlier part of the dynasty, this was the case. However, his arguments are not conclusive, being largely based on the absence of confirmatory evidence, and in any case apply only to the seventh century. There is no doubt that the origins and early activities of the Historiographical Office remain obscure. However, by 663 the office is definitely mentioned by name. See *THY* 63, p. 1089. Hung's objection that in the tenth month of 670 (8 January 671 in the western calendar) an edict uses the term *Shih-ssu* rather than *Shih-kuan* (see *THY* 63, p. 1100, some texts of which write not *Shih-ssu* but *suo-ssu*, the "office responsible"; and *TTCLC* 81, p. 467) has little force, because the edict dates from a period of Kao-tsung's reign during which the names of all offices were changed to archaic forms, many of them ending in *-ssu*. The term *Shih-ssu* was thus probably (although this is unconfirmed by other evidence) the name used for the Historiographical Office from 662–70. The old names for offices were restored only on the twentieth day of the twelfth month of 670 (February 671 in the western calendar), some weeks after the edict in question had been promulgated. By the reign of Hsüan-tsung the office was certainly subordinated to the Chancellery, just as were the Chi-hsien Academy and the office responsible for the Urns for Communication with the Throne (*Kuei-shih yüan*). None of these bodies had a regular establishment of ranked posts, and their personnel, like the historians, held their substantive offices elsewhere.
56 The Chancellery and Secretariat had their main buildings inside the Palace City (Kung-ch'eng) close to the main audience halls. See Hiraoka Takeo, *Chōan to Rakuyō* (Kyoto, 1956), maps 19, 20. They also maintained Outer Offices (*wai-sheng*) in the outer Administrative City (*Huang-ch'eng*) on either side of the main street leading to the great gateway to the palace. See ibid., maps 17, 18.

PUBLIC BUSINESS AREA
OF THE
TA-MING PALACE

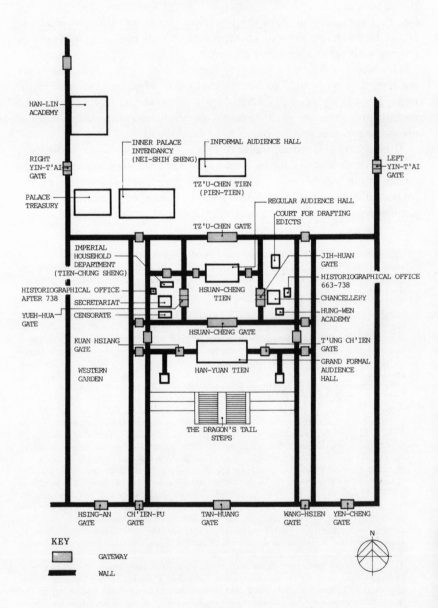

building in the palace. When, in 663, the Ta-ming Palace was rebuilt and became the permanent residence of the emperor and the site of the court assemblies, the premises of the Historiographical Office were placed south of the new Chancellery building.[57] There was also a branch Historiographical Office in the eastern capital, Loyang, where the court spent much of the late seventh and early eighth centuries. In the Loyang palace the historiographical office was sited next to the Secretariat building.[58] Later, as the Secretariat gradually replaced the Chancellery as the most important of the central ministries, the location of the Historiographical Office next to the Chancellery building in the Ta-ming Palace in Ch'ang-an became both inconvenient and inappropriate. In 737[59] Li Lin-fu, who was then chief minister and concurrently director of the National History, suggested that because the Secretariat was now the most crucial and important organ of government it would be appropriate if the Historiographical Office was moved. In response to a memorial from one of the historiographers, Yin Yin,[60] the office was moved into a building near the Secretariat that had formerly housed the Imperial Pharmacy.[61] Responsibility for the supervision of the Historiographical Office was also formally transferred to the Secretariat.[62]

Either the office was subsequently moved yet again or, in addition to its business office in the Ta-ming Palace and its branch office in Loyang,

57 See *THY* 63, p. 1089.
58 See *Shih t'ung* 11, p. 318. Hung suggests that this is evidence that at this time (circa 703) the Historiographical Office was not subordinate to either ministry but placed close to one or other of them for convenience. The two ministries were responsible for receiving all memorials and other documents addressed to the throne and for drafting and promulgating edicts. They were thus essential sources of documentation for the historiographers. Liu Chih-chi says that the premises of the office in Loyang were much superior to those in Ch'ang-an, and that the working conditions too were better there.
59 See *TT* 21, p. 127a; *CTS* 43, p. 1852. This date is wrongly given as 727 in *THY* 83, p. 1089, and as 732 in *HTS* 47, p. 1214. Both dates are impossible, because Li Lin-fu became chief minister only in late 736.
60 See n. 22 in this chapter.
61 See *TT* 21, p. 127a; *THY* 63, p. 1089; *CTS* 43, p. 1852. On the office's new location, see Hsü Sung (1781–1848), *T'ang liang ching ch'eng-fang k'ao* (edition of *Lien-yün-i ts'ung-shu*, 1848, reprinted in Hiraoka Takeo, *Chōan to Rakuyō*) 5, p. 4a, which says that their building was to the west of the Secretariat building and north of the Imperial Pharmacy. For the position of the Historiographical Office in Loyang, where it was also to the west of the Secretariat, see the anonymous *Ho-nan chih* (*Ou-hsiang ling-shih*, 1908 ed., reprinted in Hiraoka Takeo, *Chōan to Rakuyō*) 4, p. 2b. Hsü Sung's plan of the Ta-ming Palace (*Chōan to Rakuyō*, map 27, 1) shows the Historiographical Office to the west of the Chancellery, as does the modern reconstruction of the plan of the palace by Sekino Tadashi (1867–1935) (ibid., plan 29).
62 See *THY* 63, p. 1089; *HTS* 47, p. 1214. At this same time the compilers ceased to attend court together with the diarists, although they might do so by reason of their substantive office. See *HTS* 47, p. 1208.

it also kept at least some of its records in another building, for when the Historiographical Office and its records were burned during the An Lu-shan rebellion, it is said to have been in the little-used secondary Hsing-ch'ing Palace in the east of Ch'ang-an.[63]

The Palace Department of the Imperial Library

When at the beginning of T'ai-tsung's reign the new Historiographical Office was set up under the control of the Chancellery, it did not immediately take over all the responsibilities for historical writing formerly exercised by the Office of Literary Composition. A separate organization, the Palace Department of the Imperial Library (*Pi-shu nei-sheng*) is also said to have been set up in the palace, at the Secretariat.[64] This office, about which we have little information, seems

---

63 See *THY* 63, p. 1094.
64 See *THY* 63, p. 1091; *TFYK* 554, p. 4b; *TFYK* 556, p. 11a–b; *Yü hai* 121, pp. 31b–32a.
The text says that "The Palace Department of the Imperial Library was set up at the Secretariat [*yü Chung-shu*]." Whether this means it was located in the premises of the Secretariat, or that it was placed under its administrative control is unclear. Because the Imperial Library was an important organization quite independent of the Secretariat, the latter seems unlikely. According to Sung Min-ch'iu, *Ch'ang-an chih* (*Ching-hsün t'ang ts'ung-shu*, 1784 ed., reprinted [chapters 6–10 only] in Hiraoka Takeo, *Chōan to Rakuyō*) 6, p. 2a, it was set up in 629 and abolished "shortly afterward." Hung, "The T'ang Bureau of Historiography before 708, " pp. 96–8, has already pointed out that there is very considerable confusion here. First, the Imperial Library had already had a "Palace Department" (*nei-sheng*) since Sui times. See *SS* 58, p. 1413; *HTS* 98, p. 3887. Like the Secretariat and Chancellery and other ministries, the Imperial Library had offices both inside the palace compound, and in the Administrative City. The latter was called its "Outer Department" (*wai-sheng*), and its premises are shown on the fragmentary map of Ch'ang-an by Lü Ta-fang engraved on stone in Sung times and dated 1080 that survives in the P'ei-lin in Sian (see Hiraoka Takeo, *Chōan to Rakuyō*, map 2). The "Outer Department" had a book depository *shu-ko*, which was to the east of the business office of the director (*chien-yüan*). See *Ch'ang-an chih* 7, p. 4a. It also housed an elementary school for the children of the imperial family and very high ranking officials. See *THY* 35, p. 633. The "Outer Department" is mentioned as early as 618, and this would imply that the Palace Department also existed at the beginning of the T'ang. Certainly the Palace Department existed in 628 or 629, when Ching Po was sent there to work on the Sui history with Yen Shih-ku and K'ung Ying-ta. See *CTS* 189A, p. 4954; *HTS* 198, p. 5056. Second, there is some doubt whether in fact the work of the Palace Department on the histories of the preceding dynasties was in fact clearly separated from that of the newly founded Historiographical Office. It was not until some years later that the work on the T'ang Veritable Records was begun. Before that, what did the Historiographical Office do, if not work on the earlier periods? Reworking the Court Diaries into polished form would in itself hardly have justified a whole new organization and the Office for Literary Composition was already doing this. Third, there is the question why the work was to be done at the Secretariat building. The Imperial Library certainly had its own premises within the palace, although the site

20

to have been specially assigned responsibility for the compilation of the standard histories of the earlier dynasties, work on which had begun some years earlier[65] and which were a major preoccupation of T'ai-tsung. They first undertook the compilation of the histories of the "Five Dynasties" (the Northern Chou, Sui, Liang, Ch'en, and Ch'i), which were completed in 636.[66] Later, in 646, they were ordered to produce a

has never been identified. These buildings must have been rather large, simply to accommodate in scroll form the very large collection we know it to have held. Does the term "Imperial Library" here perhaps refer to the Office for Literary Composition, which was its main subsection responsible for historical writing? Officials from the Imperial Library, and also from the Heir Apparent's Library, had been engaged on the writing of the histories of earlier dynasties since 622. Some historians were already working at the Office for Literary Composition before 629. It seems that the innovation initiated in 629 was that a new coordinated program for the compilation of the earlier histories was put into motion, with the Imperial Library in charge, and that the work was perhaps accommodated in the building of the Secretariat, where some of the principal compilers held their substantive offices.

65 See *CTS* 73, p. 2597; *THY* 63, p. 1090. In the eleventh month of 621 Ling-hu Te-fen, then a court diarist, made an informal address to Kao-tsu reminding him that Standard Histories of the recent dynasties were lacking, and pointing out that although documents were available from the Liang and Ch'en dynasties in the South, and from the Northern Ch'i, there were many gaps in the records of the Northern Chou and the Sui. He urged that work be begun on these histories while people with direct experience of the period were still alive. After another decade the traces of these events would be irretrievably lost. A year later, on the twenty-sixth day of the twelfth month of 622, an edict appointed a team of historians to compile histories of the Wei, Northern Chou, Sui, Liang, Ch'i, and Ch'en dynasties. See *TTCLC* 81, pp. 466–7; *CTS* 73, pp. 2597–8. But although the work continued for several years, these histories remained uncompleted and work on them was suspended. See *THY* 63, pp. 1090–1.

66 See *CTS* 3, p. 45; *CTS*, 73, p. 2598; *THY* 63, p. 1091. See also Wu Ching, *Chen-kuan cheng-yao* (Harada Taneshige's variorum edition, *Jōgan seiyō teihon* [Tokyo, 1962]) 7, p. 218. This section is missing in most current editions of *Chen-kuan cheng-yao*, for example in the edition published by the Shanghai Ku-chi ch'u-pan she in 1978.
The histories commissioned under T'ai-tsung and now completed did not include a new history for the Northern Wei, although one had been begun in 622. This was excluded because there were already two histories of the period that were considered adequate, one the surviving *Wei shu* by Wei Shou (listed under the title *Hou Wei shu* in 130 chapters by the bibliographical chapter of *CTS* 46, p. 1990), and the other by Wei T'an (this probably refers to his *Wei Shu* in 107 chapters, listed in *CTS* 46, p. 1990, but may refer to his *Wei chi* in twelve chapters, listed in *CTS* 46, p. 1991; both works are lost). It was therefore thought unnecessary to compile the Wei history afresh. Not everybody agreed: Ling-hu Te-fen subsequently produced a *Hou Wei shu* of his own in 50 chapters. Yet another *Wei shu* in 100 chapters was written by Chang Ta-su, who was a compiler in the Historiographical Office during the 650s, and presumably wrote his book as a result of his dissatisfaction with the existing histories. See *CTS* 68, p. 2507. Both works were in the Imperial Library in 721. See *CTS* 46, p. 1990. Small fragments of each survived into Sung times: Wang Yao-ch'en, *Ch'ung-wen tsung-mu (Ssu-k'v ch'üan-shu chen-pien, pieh-chi* [Taipei, 1975]) 3 lists a single chapter of the annals of Wei T'an's history, and two chapters of the Monograph on Astronomy from that of Chang Ta-su as having been in the imperial collections in 1042, but lost by 1144.

new history of the Chin.[67] By the beginning of Kao-tsung's reign, however, responsibility for the compilation of the histories of earlier dynasties seems to have been transferred to the Historiographical Office.[68] In 656 the historiographers presented the newly completed monographs on the Five Dynasties (*Liang Sui Ch'i Chou Ch'en Wu-tai chih*) to the throne.[69] There is no further mention of the Palace Department of the Imperial Library as a separate office.

In T'ai-tsung's reign, moreover, members of the staff of the Imperial Library and of its subordinate bureaus, the Office for Literary Composition and the Imperial Observatory, the offices that traditionally had been responsible for the compilation of historical records, are still to be found not only on the editorial teams appointed for each of the histories of the earlier dynasties, but also among the compilers of the first official histories of the T'ang, such as the Veritable Records for the reign of Kao-tsu and for the first years of T'ai-tsung, completed in 643;[70] the Veritable Records for the last years of T'ai-tsung, completed in 650;[71] those for the first years of Kao-tsung, completed in 659;[72] and the first National History, completed in 656.[73] Although this arrangement may have been due in part to administrative convenience, in that each of these departments held some of the required documentation, the old involvement in historical compilation of various subordinate sections of the Imperial Library apparently continued for many years after the establishment of the Historiographical Office.

67 See *THY* 63, p. 1091; *TFYK* 554, p. 16a–b; *TFYK* 556, pp. 12a–13b; *TTCLC* 81, p. 467; *CTS* 73, p. 2598. This work was entrusted by Fang Hsüan-ling to a team of eighteen compilers led by Ling-hu Te-fen, who had been disgraced and removed from office shortly before, owing to his close involvement with the former heir apparent Li Ch'eng-ch'ien who had been degraded in 643. Ling-hu Te-fen had been the president of the heir apparent's Secretariat of the Right, a very important office in his administration. The work on the *Chin shu* seems to have been begun in 644 and completed in 646. The edict *ordering* its compilation is dated 646 in *TTCLC* 81, however, so the dates given elsewhere may possibly be incorrect.
68 It is also quite possible that the Palace Department of the Imperial Library and the Historiographical Office were not in fact completely separate entities at this time. Li Hua (see *WYYH* 799, p. 4a) says that the Historiographical Office was set up early in the reign of T'ai-tsung to undertake the histories of the five former dynasties, and that many of the historians appointed to it were secretaries from the Office of Literary Composition.
69 See *CTS* 4, p. 75; *TFYK* 554, p. 4b. *THY* 63, p. 1092, mistakenly writes the title as the *Liang Ch'en Ch'i Chou Sui Wu-tai shih*, not *chih*, but undoubtedly refers to the same work in thirty chapters. This book was originally an independent work, but was subsequently incorporated into the *Sui shu* to form its monographs.
70 See *THY* 63, p. 1092; *TFYK* 556, p. 12a. For further details, see *Chen-kuan cheng yao* 7, p. 219–20 (in Harada Taneshige's edition).
71 See *TFYK* 556, p. 14a.
72 See *THY* 63, p. 1093; *TFYK* 554, p. 16b; *TFYK* 556, p. 14a–b.
73 See *THY* 63, p. 1093; *TFYK* 556, pp. 14b–15a.

The diarists of the heir apparent

Under the T'ang, the heir apparent presided over his own administration in his official residence, the Eastern Palace, and held his own court assemblies at which he received petitions and issued orders. This administration, which was a sort of microcosm of the central government, was designed primarily to train and accustom the future emperor to the routines and procedures of his future role. His orders and acts, however, had real consequences. Among the officials of his Secretariat of the Left (*Tso Ch'un-fang*) were four grand secretaries (*Ssu-i lang*) who were expected both to act as the prince's moral censors and also to keep a record of the prince's performance of his ritual and administrative duties. This diary, the *Tung-kung chi-chu*, was forwarded to the Historiographical Office at the end of every year.[74]

The involvement of other offices

The offices discussed thus far were primarily responsible for the compilation of historical records and the writing of history. As we have seen, however, the Historiographical Office was a somewhat nebulous organization. Its personnel held no established ranks and all were concurrently employed in other posts. Various other offices thus became involved in the historiographical process from time to time as a result of the overlapping responsibilities of those of their staff members who held concurrent posts as historians. Often this seems to have been done by design, and official historians were appointed to substantive posts that were either connected in some way with their historical duties or were relative sinecures, so as to free most of their time for their work on the histories. Some career historians retained their concurrent posts in the Historiographical Office for many years while they were promoted through a series of substantive offices and, even when transferred to posts with no specific responsibilities for historical work, continued to work on official historical projects, sometimes with official authorization,

---

74 See *TLT* 26, p. 21a–b; *TT* 30, p. 173a; *CTS* 44, p. 1907; *HTS* 49A, p. 1293 (Robert des Rotours, *Traité des fonctionnaires et traité de l'armée* (Leiden, 1948), vol. 2, pp. 579–80); *Yü hai* 128, pp. 26b–27a. According to *HTS* there were only two of these grand secretaries. The posts were first established in 631. In the early years of the dynasty, these secretary-diarists were sometimes employed concurrently in compiling official histories. The posts were considered very prestigious and exceptionally "pure" offices. When Ching Po was appointed to one of these posts in 643, one of the chief ministers, Ma Chou, expressed his regret that he himself was of too high a rank to serve in the same office. See *CTS* 189A, p. 4954.

sometimes without. One example was Wu Ching (ca. 665–749), a long-term historiographer who continued to work on the National History even after he was disgraced and transferred to a series of provincial posts during Hsüan-tsung's reign.[75] Another was Ling-hu Huan. When in 789 he was exiled to Chi-chou in Kiangsi following the death of his patron Li Mi (722–89), he was allowed to take with him the Veritable Record of Tai-tsung, on which he had been working, so that he could complete it in his provincial post.[76] Another later case was that of Shen Ch'uan-shih (769–827), who was permitted to take with him the unfinished Veritable Record of Hsien-tsung's reign when he was posted as civil governor of Hu-nan in 823.[77]

Many of the official historiographers were also notable scholars who wrote extensively in other genres. Throughout the T'ang a great many of them not only held concurrent appointments in the Historiographical Office, but were at the same time also members of one or other of the academies in which the government maintained talented scholars whose services were at the disposal of the emperor. The academies were thus drawn into the process of historical compilation.

In the early years of the dynasty the most important of the academies were the short-lived Wen-hsüeh kuan attached to the household of the future T'ai-tsung when he was Prince of Ch'in[78] and the Hung-wen kuan. The Hung-wen kuan, founded in 621 under the name Hsiu-wen kuan, and renamed in 626, was attached to the Chancellery.[79] Like the Historiographical Office, and like the later academies, it had no fixed complement of scholars; its scholar-academicians (*hsüeh-shih*), auxiliary scholars (*chih hsüeh-shih*), and assistants (*wen-hsüeh chih-kuan*) had no fixed ranks and held their substantive offices elsewhere.[80] After T'ai-tsung ascended the throne in 626 he built up a substantial library at the academy, where he maintained a large group of gifted scholars with

---

75 See *CTS* 102, p. 3182; *HTS* 132, p. 4529.
76 See *CTS* 149, p. 4014.
77 See *CTS* 149, p. 4037; *HTS* 132, p. 4541.
78 See *THY* 64, p. 1117.
79 On the Hung-wen kuan, see *TLT* 8, pp. 41a–44b; *CTS* 43, pp. 1847–8; *HTS* 47, pp. 1209–10 (Rotours, *Fonctionnaires*, vol. 1 pp. 169–73); *TT* 21, p. 124c; *THY* 64, pp. 1114–5; also the wall record for the Chao-wen kuan by Ch'üan Te-yü, dated 807, *Ch'üan Tsai-chih wen-chi* (*SPTK* edition, Shanghai, 1936) 31, pp. 4b–6a; *WYYH* 797, pp. 5a–6a. See also McMullen, *State and Scholars in T'ang China*, p. 15. Unlike the other later academies, the Hung-wen kuan was not only a center for government-sponsored scholarly and literary work. It was also a school, with lecturers who taught a small group of students selected from among the sons of high-ranking metropolitan officials. These students were presented for a modified version of the *ming-ching* examination.
80 The titles given to these scholars grew more and more confused as time went on. A final attempt to regularize them was made in 823. See *THY* 64, p. 1116.

whom he regularly discussed state affairs.[81] A number of them were also engaged in the various historical projects of his reign.

The Hung-wen kuan was a permanent institution. Other less closely organized groups of scholars were also recruited from time to time to act as imperial secretaries and to assist in drafting state papers. During the 660s Empress Wu recruited such a group, known as the "scholars of the Northern Gate" (*Pei-men hsüeh-shih*), who acted as her confidential secretariat, and also compiled a long series of literary works under her name.[82] During Chung-tsung's reign the Hung-wen kuan fell into disrepute. On Jui-tsung's accession in 710 many of its scholars who had been associated with the discredited former regime were dismissed or degraded, and it was reorganized.[83] Its place as the chief center for important government-sponsored scholarship was taken by a new academy established by Emperor Hsüan-tsung in 718. This was at first called the *Ch'ien-yüan yüan* and was placed under the loose supervision of the Secretariat. It was renamed the *Li-cheng yüan* or *Li cheng-hsiu shu yüan* in 719, and in 725 became the *Chi-hsien yüan*, the "Academy of Assembled Worthies."[84] This new academy rapidly became the major center of

---

81 See *THY* 64, p. 1114; *THY* 57, p. 977. See also Liu Po-chi, *T'ang-tai cheng-chiao shih* (Taipei, 1954), pp. 92–6.

82 This group is first mentioned under this name in 675 (see *TCTC* 202, p. 6376) but were almost certainly already in existence as early as 666 (see *TFYK* 550, p. 3a; *THY* 57, p. 977). According to *TFYK* they ceased to be employed as drafting officials for state papers from 682 onward. They are last mentioned under the name of the "Scholars of the Northern Gate" in 688 (see *TCTC* 204, p. 6447).

83 See *THY* 64, p. 1115.

84 The best account of the *Chi-hsien yüan*, although it stops short at the An Lu-shan rebellion, is Ikeda On, "Sei Tō no Shūken'in," *Hokkaidō Daigaku Bungakubu kiyō* 19, no. 2 (1971): 47–98. This assembles a wide range of source material, including many quotations from Wei Shu's lost account of the academy, the *Chi-hsien chu-chi*, which are preserved in the late twelfth-century *Chih-kuan fen-chi* of Sun Feng-chi (1135–99), (reprint, Taipei, 1983) and in *Yü hai*. On Wei Shu's *Chi-hsien chu-chi*, see *HTS* 58, p. 1477; *Ch'ung-wen tsung-mu* 3, p. 25a; Ch'ao Kung-wu, *Chün-chai tu-shu chih (Yüan-pen)* (*SPYK* edition, Shanghai, 1936) 2B, p. 5a, *(Ch'ü-pen)* (Wan-wei pieh-tsang edition, Taipei, 1981) 7, p. 14a; Ch'en Chen-sun, *Chih-chai shu-lu chieh-t'i (Ssu-k'u ch'üan-shu chen-pen* edition, *Pieh chi*, vols. 150–1. Taipei, 1975) 6, pp. 4b–5a; *Yü hai* 48, p. 34a–b; *WHTK* 202, p. 1687c. See also Chao Shih-wei, ed., *Chung-hsing Kuan-ko shu-mu chi-k'ao* (Peking, 1932) 2, p. 20b. It is said to have been in three chapters by *HTS*, by *Ch'ung-wen tsung-mu*, and by *Chih-chai shu-lu chieh-t'i*; in two chapters by *Yü hai* (citing *Ch'ung-wen tsung-mu*) and *WHTK*, and in a single chapter by both recensions (the Yüan-chou and Ch'ü-chou versions) of *Chün-chai tu-shu chih*. The latter informs us that it was written in 756. Formal descriptions of the academy are to be found in *TLT* 9, pp. 22a–28a; *CTS* 43, pp. 1851–2; *HTS* 47, pp. 1212–13 (Rotours, *Fonctionnaires*, vol. 1, pp. 189–98); *TT* 21, p. 126c; *THY* 64, pp. 1118–21. The Chi-hsien yüan had its main premises in the Ta-ming Palace, immediately west of the Historiographical Office. It also had a building or buildings in the Hsing-ch'ing Palace in Ch'ang-an, and premises at the detached palace at the hot spring west of the capital, the Hua-ch'ing kung. There was also a branch of the academy in Loyang.

government-sponsored literary and scholarly activities. It built up a very large library and a great collection of paintings. Its scholars included most of the prominent writers and scholars of the time, and under its auspices they produced a flood of major works: bibliographies and catalogs, ritual compendiums, canonical commentaries, calendrical and legal works, literary collections, and encyclopedias.

There was also much historical activity at the academy, a large part of whose library consisted of historical works.[85] In 725, when it received the name Academy of Assembled Worthies, it was placed under the control of Chang Yüeh, who was then a chief minister and a compiler of the National History. He worked there on his "Veritable Record of the Reigning Monarch" (*Chin-shang Shih-lu*), in which work he was assisted by T'ang Ying, a young scholar of the academy.[86] Wu Ching, who had been an active historiographer since Empress Wu's reign, was also engaged as a scholar of the academy, where he worked both on the compilation of the official National History (*Kuo-shih*) and on his private chronological history of the T'ang entitled *T'ang Ch'un-ch'iu*.[87]

Wei Shu, a young man destined to become a major historian, was also appointed to the academy by his patron Chang Yüeh, and worked there on the National History and on various private historical projects.[88] So much historical work was going on at the Academy of Assembled Worthies that for a while in the late 720s it seemed that the status of the Historiographical Office was threatened. In the sixth month of 727 Li Yüan-hung, who had replaced Chang Yüeh as chief minister, memorialized the throne complaining that the work of Chang Yüeh and Wu Ching on the National History was causing important documents to be transferred from the Historiographical Office to the academy, with a serious risk of loss. Orders were issued that the historians working at the academy were to go to the Historiographical Office to consult their sources.[89] The academy remained important well into the ninth century, although its days of literary glory ended with the An Lu-shan rebellion,

---

85 See *THY* 64, p. 1119. In 731 the collection comprised 89,000 *chüan* of which 26,820 *chüan* were historical works. The library contained many old books, but the greater part were newly copied specially for inclusion in its collection. The academy suffered severe losses during the An Lu-shan rebellion. In 763 its chief scholar memorialized the throne asking that a reward of one thousand cash per volume be offered to replace works that had been stolen. See *TFYK* 50, p. 12a.
86 See *CTS* 97, pp. 3054–5; Wei Shu's *Chi-hsien chu-chi* as cited by *Yü hai* 48, pp. 4b–5b.
87 See *CTS* 102, p. 3182; *HTS* 132, pp. 4529–31.
88 See *CTS* 102, pp. 3183–5; *HTS* 132, pp. 4529–31.
89 See *THY* 63, p. 1099.

and members of the Historiographical Office continued to be concurrently engaged as scholars there.[90]

Occasionally, too, special personal arrangments were made to supplement the offical record. During the first half of Hsüan-tsung's reign, for example, his elder brother, Li Ch'eng-ch'i (679–741), the prince of Ning, who although banned from participation in court affairs had a profound understanding of politics, was given a special dispensation to prepare his own annual summary of events for presentation to the Historiographical Office. This was no formality but a serious work running to several hundred pages each year.[91]

Information reported from various administrative offices

It is often stated that the sources for the Veritable Records were almost exclusively the formal records of events and decisions at court incorporated in the Court Diaries, *Ch'i-chü chu*, and the Records of Administrative Affairs, *Shih-cheng chi*. However, it is important to remember that the Historiographical Office had many other sources of information. About those of a personal, informal nature we can only surmise. But a wide variety of governmental agencies and ministries were legally required to collect and to make regular returns of specific types of information directly to the Historiographical Office for incorporation in the dynastic record. The rules on this subject are as follows:[92]

Fortunate omens: The Board of Rites [*Li-pu*] should draw up a list of these and report them every quarter.

Heavenly portents: The Astronomer Royal [*T'ai-shih*][93] should report these together with his predictions and evidences of coming good fortune.

Appearance at court of tribute-bearing missions from foreign countries: Whenever such a foreign mission arrives the Court for Diplomatic Reception [*Hung-lu ssu*] should examine them on the natural conditions and customs of their country, on their dress, and the products brought as tribute, and on the distance and route by which they have come. These facts are to be reported together with the names of their leaders.

Changes in the musical scales and newly composed airs: The Court of Imperial

---

90 The historian Chiang I, for example, began his career in 781 or 782 as a clerical assistant (*hsiao-li*) in the academy at the recommendation of then Chief Minister Chang I. See *TFYK* 608, p. 28a–b; *HTS* 132, p. 4531.
91 See *CTS* 95, p. 3012.
92 *THY* 63, pp. 1089–90.
93 *WTHY* 18, p. 293, gives the responsible office as the Imperial Observatory (*Ssu-t'ien t'ai*), which replaced the *T'ai-shih chü* in 757.

Sacrifices [*T'ai-ch'ang ssu*] should draw up an account of those responsible, and of the words and music, and report it.

Establishment and suppression of Prefectures and Counties; the granting of marks of distinction to "filial and righteous families":[94] The Board of Finance [*Hu-pu*] should report such matters whenever they occur.

Changes in the laws, and decisions of cases involving new principles: The Board of Justice [*Hsing-pu*] should report these as they occur.

Good harvests, famines, flood, drought, locusts, hail, wind, and frost, together with earthquakes and the flooding of rivers: Whenever such things occur the Board of Finance [*Hu-pu*] and the local Prefecture and County should investigate the exact date, and report it together with an account of the relief measures taken to relieve the people.

Enfiefment of various types:[95] The *Ssu-fu*[96] should investigate and report on such events. Succession to a fief by inheritance need not be reported.

Appointment to office of senior officials in the various offices at the Capital together with Prefects, Governors-general, Protectors-general, Grand Commanders of Armies in the Field, and Deputy Commanders: All such appointments should be reported together with the text of the edict of appointment. In the case of civil officials the Board of Civil Office [*Li-pu*] should send in the report. In the case of military officers the Board of War [*Ping-pu*] should report.

Details of unusual evidences of good administration by Prefects and County Magistrates: If there is anything particularly outstanding of this sort the Prefecture responsible should report it, entrusting their report to the commissioner responsible for local merit assessments [*K'ao-shih*].

Eminent scholars, men of unusual ability, great men, retired scholars, righteous husbands and chaste widows:[97] Whenever there are exemplary persons of this sort in a Prefecture or County, without question whether or not they hold official rank, the authorities should investigate the truth of what they have heard, and each year record it and send this in, entrusting it to the commissioner responsible for the local merit assessments [*K'ao-shih*].

The deaths of senior officials employed in the various offices of the Capital: The office concerned shall ascertain the facts according to the individual's curriculum vitae and send it in.

The deaths of Prefects, Governors-general, Protectors-general, Deputy Com-

---

94 *WTHY* 18, p. 294, in place of "filial and righteous families" has "filial sons, obedient grandsons, righteous husbands, and chaste wives."

95 *WTHY* 18, p. 294, specifies the "enfiefment and establishment of ancestral temples in the empire."

96 The vague term *Ssu-fu* in the text of *THY* would normally refer to the various household administrations that were attached to each prince's fief. In the context, however, it seems rather more likely that it derives from a graphic error for *Ssu-feng*, the Department of Noble Fiefs, a subdepartment of the Board of Civil Office that was directly responsible for the nobility, as in *WTHY* 18, p. 294.

97 *WTHY* 18, p. 294, has a special section for "men of great virtue, unusual ability, great men, retired scholars, hermits who have lived for many years in the mountains, and writers."

manders of Armies in the field and below: The Prefecture or Army concerned should investigate the deceased's curriculum vitae [*li-chuang*] and send it in, entrusting it to a convenient envoy.

The fixing of Posthumous canonizations [*Shih*] of Princesses and Officials: The office of Merit Assessments [*K'ao-kung*] should record it, and send in the recommendation on the granting of a posthumous canonization [*Shih-i*] together with the Account of conduct [*Hsing-chuang*] of the individual.[98]

Attendance of Princes at court: The Court of the Imperial Clan [*Tsung-cheng ssu*] should investigate and report on this.[99]

All the above matters should be investigated and reported to the Historiographical Office as they occur by the responsible authority specified in the appropriate section. If the Historiographical Office discovers any matter which is appropriate for inclusion in the record, but not analogous with the matters specified above, it may send an official communication directly requesting information about it. Any place receiving such a communication should make enquiries in accordance with the schedule of requests, and make its report within a month.[100]

It is far from clear how seriously this system was enforced. There is ample evidence, for example, that the Historiographical Office actually did receive the Accounts of Conduct and the recommendations on posthumous canonization for deceased high officials. Population and tax figures reported by the Board of Finance were certainly sent in and included in the record. The responsibility of the astronomer royal for calendrical information was also taken seriously and was specifically mentioned among the duties of his post in the *T'ang liu-tien*.[101]

After the An Lu-shan rebellion, this system for reporting information fell into disorder and disuse. In 779–80 the historians requested that it be revived.[102] There is, however, no means of checking whether this was actually done. The system certainly fell into disuse during the latter decades of the T'ang and during the political confusion of the Liang dynasty (907–23). In 924, under the new Later T'ang dynasty (923–36),

---

98 *WTHY* 18, p. 294, does not mention princesses, and also adds a note that the deceased's family is permitted to submit an Account of Conduct.

99 *WTHY* 18, p. 294, also makes the Court of the Imperial Clan liable for reporting the activities of members of the imperial clan employed in office, and for the ceremonies attending the weddings of imperial princesses.

100 See *THY* 63, p. 1090. Compare the slightly more detailed version of these arrangements given in a memorial from the Historiographical Office under the Later T'ang in 924 describing the "old precedent of our dynasty"; see *WTHY* 18, pp. 293–4. The Later T'ang considered themselves a continuation of the T'ang, and the "old precedents" were those in force during the T'ang.

101 See *TLT* 10, p. 26a.

102 See *THY* 63, p. 1090.

the revived Historiographical Office memorialized the throne, asking that all official documents and reports be sent in to the office as had been done under the T'ang.[103]

Thus there existed throughout the T'ang dynasty a group of court diarists and other officials responsible for the collection of information and the keeping of a court record. There were also official historiographers with the ongoing responsibility for transforming this material into a polished history of the dynasty, and for writing the histories of earlier periods. But these arrangements remained fluid and changed repeatedly during the course of the dynasty. The organization for producing the historical record had by no means yet reached a final form such as was to be achieved under later dynasties.

103 See *WTHY* 18, pp. 293–4. On this attempt to revive the Historiographical Office, see Wang Gungwu, "The *Chiu Wu-tai Shih* and History writing during the Five Dynasties," *Asia Major*, n.s., 6, no.1 (1957): 1–22; Chin Yü-fu, "T'ang-Sung shih-tai she kuan hsiu-shih chih-tu k'ao," *Kuo-shih-kuan kuan-k'an* 1, no. 2 (1948): 6–18.

Part II
The compilation of the historical record

3

Introduction

It is, of course, common knowledge among scholars that the Standard Histories were only the end product of a long and complex process of compilation, recompilation, and editing. The outline of this process is well known. The record began with the Court Diaries (*Ch'i-chü chu*) and the Administrative Record (*Shih-cheng chi*), the material which was successively compiled into a Daily Calendar (*Jih-li*) for each year, then into a Veritable Record (*Shih-lu*) for each reign, into a full-scale National History (*Kuo shih*) of the reigning dynasty, and finally after the dynasty had fallen and had been replaced by its successor into the Standard History (*Cheng shih*) of its period.

The Standard History comprised two essential components: the basic annals (*pen-chi*) and the biographies (*lieh-chuan*), the latter including entries on various foreign peoples. In most cases, they also included monographs (*chih*) on specific historical topics, mainly ritual and administrative, and in exceptional cases might also include table (*piao*) of various sorts. Each of these sections underwent a rather different process of compilation. The political narrative that eventually became the basic annals of the Standard History had normally been through each of the successive stages of compilation mentioned and, as the definitive record of each reign's achievements, was subjected to the most careful scrutiny. The biographies of individuals were normally inserted for the first time at a rather late stage of the process when they were incorporated into the chronological framework of the Veritable Record, after the notice of their subject's death. They were usually derived from commemorative writings by private individuals. When later the National History or Standard History was compiled, they were removed from the chronological record, selected, and grouped together according to the overall plan of the compilers in the *lieh-chuan* section. The National History was a work in the "composite form" (*chi-chuan*), comprising the basic annals and biographies essential to a Standard History, and usually also contained

33

monographs on specific topics. Those were written afresh at the time of the work's compilation, the material being mostly extracted from the Veritable Records.[1] The sections of the *lieh-chuan* dealing with foreign peoples were also added when the National History was compiled.

The existence during the T'ang of this complex and continuous process of recording the functions of government, along with the establishment of offices specially charged with these duties and of routines for carrying them out effectively, gives an overall picture not dissimilar to that of official historiography in later dynasties. Many scholars have assumed that this whole complex machinery came into existence early in the T'ang period, and that an impersonal, rather mechanical system for the collection and processing of information was then set up and continued to function smoothly. In this historiograhical "production line," the influence of the individual historian was supposedly reduced to the minimum. The eloquent complaints of T'ang historians caught up in the inevitable personal frustrations facing any creative scholar working in such a formal apparatus help to strengthen this impression.

I shall now look at the evidence about each of the stages of compilation in turn, to see how far the system was in fact firmly established and operational in T'ang times.

1 For important earlier studies on the various stages of compilation, see the following: (1) Chu Hsi-tsu, "Han, T'ang, Sung *Ch'i-chü chu* k'ao," pp. 629–40; (2) Tamai Zehaku, "Tō no Jitsuroku senshū ni kansuru ichi kōsatsu," included in his *Shina shakai keizai shi kenkyū* (Tokyo, 1943), pp. 415–28 (originally published in *Keijō teidai shigakkai hō* 8, 1953); (3) Lo Hsiang-lin, "*T'ang shu* yüan-liu k'ao," *Kuo-li Chung-shan Ta-hsüeh Wen-shih hsüeh Yen-chiu so yüeh-k'an* 2, no. 5 (1934): 53–114; (4) Chao Shih-wei, "Shih-lu k'ao," *Fu-jen Hsüeh-chih* 5, nos. 1–2 (1936): 1–55. (5) Chin Yü-fu, "T'ang Sung shih-tai she kuan hsiu-shih chih chih-tu k'ao," pp. 6–18; (6) Bernard S. Solomon, *The Veritable Record of the T'ang Emperor Shun-tsung* (Cambridge, Mass., 1955), pp. xxiii–xxxi. (7) L. S. Yang, "The Organization of Chinese Official Historiography: Principles and Methods of the Standard Histories from T'ang Through the Ming Dynasty," in Beasely and Pulleyblank, *Historians of China and Japan*, pp. 44–59; (8) Ch'en Kuang-ch'ung, "T'ang Shih-lu tsuan-hsiu k'ao," *Liao-ning Ta-hsüeh hsüeh-pao* 3 (1978): 45–59.

4
The Court Diaries
(*Ch'i-chü chu*)

The Court Diaries were the only official record that was compiled continually throughout the dynasty. We have already seen that they were written by the court diarists, the *Ch'i-chü lang* and *Ch'i-chü she-jen* who were part of the emperor's regular retinue. They kept a full record of what went on at the formal court assemblies.

The *Ch'i-chü lang* are responsible for recording the models provided by the emperor's acts, to fulfill the functions of the Recorder in charge of noting events. The system for recording events is that events shall be arranged by the day, the days organized into months, the months by the seasons, the seasons by the year. They must record the cyclical day for the first days of the month, so as to place in correct order the calendrical succession. They must record the canons and rituals, the words and objects employed, so as to scrutinize institutions, to record promotions, marks of distinction and rewards to encourage the good, and punishments and degradations to give warning to the evil. At the end of each quarter, their record is to be sent for use in the National History.... Each quarter [their record] is to be made into a scroll and sent to the Historiographical Office.[1]

The *Ch'i-chü she-jen* is responsible for compiling and recording a historical account of the Emperor's utterances. His edicts [*chih*], decrees [*kao*] and pronouncements [*te-yin*] are to be recorded according to the same system as his acts, so as to record the shortcomings and excellencies of his administration.[2]

It is clear that they were expected to record the emperor's acts and words in court, but we must attempt to be more precise about what was actually recorded. Curiously, although we are rather fully informed about the functioning of government during this period, there is considerable confusion about the various types of court assemblies and the emperor's daily routine.

1 See *TLT* 8, p. 23a.　2 See *TLT* 9, pp. 19a–20a.

It oversimplifies matters considerably to talk of the "court," for there were in fact various types of court assembly, held in different places, attended by different persons, and conducted with different levels of formality and ritual. This is not the place to attempt to clarify this very complicated subject.[3] The court was held daily at dawn in one or other of the halls in the palace. In the Ta-ming Palace, where the emperor normally resided and held court after 663, the great outer hall, the *Han-yüan tien*, seems rarely to have been used, and the court assembly was usually held in one of the two inner halls. Behind the *Han-yüan tien* was a great enclosure in front of the principal audience hall, the *Hsüan-cheng tien*. This was used for the regular daily court assembly (*Ch'ang-ch'ao* or *Ch'ang-ts'an*) and was known also as the Regular Court (*Cheng-ya*). Behind the *Hsüan-cheng tien* was yet another great audience hall, the *Tzu-ch'en tien*. Here the emperor held court on the first and fifteenth of every month. On these days the emperor would give the order to "instruct the ceremonial guard to enter the chamber" (*huan-chang ju-ko*), and the guards who had been stationed as normally in the *Hsüan-cheng tien* came into the inner hall followed by the officials who had been "awaiting audience" with them. In the *Tzu-ch'en tien*, the ceremonial was much relaxed, and the court assembly there was commonly known as the "informal court" (*Pien-tien*). In time the term "entering the chamber" (*ju-ko*) came to be used as the name of this less formal court meeting.

Even the more ceremonious court assemblies seem to have been conducted with rather less than perfect decorum. Particularly after the An Lu-shan rebellion there are repeated memorials from the censors asking that courtiers be punished for running into the hall, jostling for their places, eating, laughing, chattering, and squabbling, not keeping their ranks, being improperly dressed, holding their tablets of office askew, or taking the opportunity to visit the nearby Chancellery and Secretariat for social calls without having any business there.[4] There are also continual complaints of ministers not attending court.[5]

---

3 The account that follows is largely derived from a memorial addressed by Li Ch'i to the newly enthroned Ming-tsung of the Later T'ang in 926 (see *HWTS* 54, pp. 617–18) and from a lengthy note written in 1136 by the Sung author Yeh Meng-te (1077–1148), *Shih-lin yen-yü* (Peking, *T'ang Sung shih-liao pi-chi ts'ung-k'an* edition, with the critical notes of Yü-wen Shao-i, 1984) 2, pp. 19–20.

4 See, for example, the edict of the eleventh month of 791 cited in *THY* 24, p. 465, and the memorial from the Censorate dated the twelfth month of 807 cited in *THY* 24, p. 467.

5 For example, in the fourth month of 796 the Censorate complained that none of the vice-presidents, chief secretaries or undersecretaries of the Board of Civil Office, the Board of War, or the Board of Rites had attended court for the past five months, on the pretext that they were busy with the exminations. See *THY* 24, p. 466. A similar complaint was voiced in the sixth month of 827. See *THY* 24, p. 468.

It would appear that after the An Lu-shan rebellion the regular daily audience in the *Hsüan-cheng tien* fell into disuse, and the Regular Audience (*Ch'ang-ch'ao*) was held only on the odd days of the month. The bulk of the officials never in fact saw the emperor, whose decisions were taken in *Tzu-ch'en tien* in the presence only of his highest officials and regular attendants, and then conveyed to the other officials where they waited in the main audience hall. The old ceremonial of summoning them to the presence in "the chamber" (*ju-ko*) was not revived until Ching-tsung's time (825–7). From this time on the officials again had audiences on the first and fifteenth of the month, and this "informal audience" gradually became more and more important. After the Ch'ien-fu period (874–9) the daily audience was abandoned altogether, and the officials in general only attended court twice a month.

It is difficult to talk of the "court," because the arrangements changed radically in the latter part of the dynasty. The question is still further complicated by the fact that, even when the system of the daily court was in full operation, the same persons did not attend court every day. The daily court, although the texts speak of the "hundred officers" or the "crowd of officials," was attended by a minority of the metropolitan officials; the head officials of the principal offices of state, holding the fifth rank and above, together with the palace censors responsible for court protocol, the various "officers in attendance" from the Chancellery and Secretariat, the officers responsible for court ritual from the Court of Imperial Sacrifices (*T'ai-ch'ang ssu*), and the executive under secretaries (*Yüan-wai lang*) of the twenty-four departments of the six boards. The highest-ranking military officers attended court once every three days; the middle-ranking military, once every five days. On the first and fifteenth of the month, all active officials in the capital were expected to attend. Once a quarter all the students of the imperial schools in the capital also had audience.

The diarists always attended the court as "officers in attendance" and kept a record of all the proceedings. But at least one source specifies that they were to attend and take a record only of the regular court assembly in the *Cheng-tien* (that is the *Hsüan-cheng tien*), where the formal business of receiving memorials and promulgating edicts was conducted. Here, when the emperor promulgated an edict, the diarist was supposed to prostrate himself at the steps of the throne, and then retire to write down what he had heard. But in fact they consulted with the officers of the Chancellery and Secretariat to confirm the actual text, which the latter had themselves drafted, and much of their work must have consisted of assembling the documents relating to a court meeting. It is not certain whether the diarists attended the less formal court meetings in the *Tzu-ch'en tien*. It seems that sometimes they did so but that often they did not. This matter is of some significance because after the middle of the dynasty the regular daily audience declined in importance, and more and more business was actually conducted in the *Tzu-ch'en tien*.

Much more important, however, was the fact that they attended only the proceedings of the formal court assembly. Even at the beginning of the dynasty, many of the most important decisions were taken by the emperor and his chief ministers, who met regularly with him after the court assembly was finished. As the dynasty progressed, less and less real business was conducted in open court, and the need for a record of the informal consultations between the emperor and his chief ministers became more and more essential. The Court Diary, *Ch'i-chü chu*, was a full record of the emperor's actions and decisions only insofar as these were conducted through the regular bureaucratic channels in open court. The more government came to be conducted in private, the less full and reliable a record the diarists provided of the actual conduct of government, and the more urgent the need for a supplementary record of administrative action became.

Ta-T'ang ch'uang-yeh ch'i-chü chu

One work with the title Court Diary (*Ch'i-chü chu*) survives intact from the T'ang period. This is the *Ta-T'ang ch'uang-yeh ch'i-chü chu*, in three chapters, by Wen Ta-ya.[6]

Wen Ta-ya[7] was the son of Wen Chün-yu, a fairly well-known scholar-official under the Northern Ch'i and Sui who had retired to his family home near T'ai-yüan on the grounds of ill-health when it became apparent that the Sui regime was on the verge of collapse, and died shortly

---

6 See *CTS* 46, p. 1998; *HTS* 58, p. 1471; *CTS* 61, p. 2360; *TFYK* 560, p. 5a; *Yü hai* 48, pp. 26b–27a; *WHTK* 194, p. 1641a; *Ch'ung-wen tsung-mu* 3, p. 17a; Chao Shih-wei, *Chung-hsing Kuan-ko shu-mu chi-k'ao* (Peking, 1933) 2, p. 12b; *Chün-chai tu-shu chih* (*Yüan-pen*) 2A, p. 10a (*Ch'ü-pen*, 5, p. 10b); *Chih-chai shu-lu chieh-t'i* 4, p. 36b; Chi Yün, (*Ch'in-ting*) *Ssu-k'u ch'üan-shu tsung-mu ti-yao* (Shanghai, 1934) 47, pp. 1027–8. Editions in *Chin-tai pi-shu*; *Hsüeh-chin t'ao-yüan*; *Ou-hsiang ling-shih*; *Shan-yu ts'ung-shu*; *Ts'ung-shu chi-ch'eng*; *Pi-ts'e hui-han*; *Ssu-k'u ch'üan-shu chen-pen*. The best edition is that in Miao Ch'üan-sun's *Ou-hsiang ling-shih*.

7 For Wen Ta-ya's short biographies, see *CTS* 61, pp. 2359–60; *HTS* 91, pp. 3781–2. See also Woodbridge Bingham, "Wen Ta-ya: The First Recorder of T'ang History," *JAOS* 57 (1937): 368–74; Lo Hsiang-lin, "*Ta-T'ang ch'uang-yeh ch'i-chü chu* k'ao-cheng," included in his *T'ang-tai wen-hua shih* (Taipei, 1955), pp. 1–28, esp. 5–8; Niu Chih-kung, "Wen Ta-ya yü *Ta-T'ang ch'uang-yeh ch'i-chü chu*," *Shih-hsüeh shih yen-chiu*, 1983, no. 1: 54–58.

after. Three of his sons became closely involved with the T'ang founder, Li Yüan, during his rise to power; Wen Ta-ya was the oldest. As a young man he had achieved a reputation as a scholar and had served under the Sui in the household of the heir apparent and in the Imperial Library. At the end of Yang-ti's reign, probably in 616 or 617, he retired from office and returned home to observe mourning for his father. When Li Yüan, the future Kao-tsu, raised his rebellion against the Sui at T'ai-yüan in 617, both Wen Ta-ya and his younger brother Wen Ta-yu, who was also living at home, joined the T'ang cause and became intimate members of Li Yüan's entourage. A third brother, Wen Yen-po, was serving on the staff of Lo I, the Sui commander at Yu-chou (modern Peking), and later came over with him to the T'ang camp.[8] All three brothers rose to important offices after the T'ang replaced the Sui royal house in 618. Wen Yen-po (584–637) eventually became a chief minister under T'ai-tsung in 636, and one of his sons became the consort of Kao-tsu's daughter, the Ch'ien-chin princess; Wen Ta-yu was a vice-president of the Secretariat before his early death shortly after 618; and Wen Ta-ya himself became president of the Board of Rites after T'ai-tsung ascended the throne in 626.[9]

Wen Ta-ya was thus a member of a family that was intimately involved in the events of the T'ang founding and whose members played important roles at the early T'ang court. He was an eyewitness to events from the first T'ang uprising until Li Yüan seized the throne and established his new dynasty. From the beginning of the march on the Sui capital, he had served on Li Yüan's staff as the administrator of his secretarial staff (*Chi-shih ts'an-chün*).[10] Later, when Li Yüan took the

---

8 See *CTS* 61, p. 2360.
9 Wen Ta-yu has brief biographical notices in *CTS* 61, p. 2362; *HTS* 91, p. 3783, Wen Yen-po in *CTS* 61, pp. 2360–2; *HTS* 91, pp. 3782–3. Probably Yen-po was his style (*tzu*), and Ta-lin his personal name (*ming*). Wen Ta-ya was styled Yen-hung and Wen Ta-yu Yen-chiang. *Hsin T'ang shu* informs us that Yen-po's style was Ta-lin, but it is probable that the compilers of *HTS* read their sources carelessly and confused his personal name and style. See Bingham, "Wen Ta-ya," p. 370, n. 3. This is confirmed by his tomb inscription by Ou-yang Hsün, "Ta T'ang ku T'e-chin Shang-shu yu P'u-yeh, Shang chu-kuo, Yü-kung kung Wen kung mu-chih," item 57 in Mao Han-kuang and Lu Chien-jung, eds. *T'ang-tai mu-chih-ming hui-pien* (Taipei, 1984), vol. 1, pp. 256. Wen Yen-po was the author of a collection of outstanding edicts, the *Ku-chin chao-chi* in thirty chapters. See *HTS* 58, p. 1473.
10 The secretarial staff, *Chi-shih*, was used by the future Kao-tsu not simply to "record events," as some scholars have assumed, but also to handle his correspondence. For example, see Wen Ta-ya, *Ta-T'ang ch'uang-yeh ch'i-chü chu* (*Ou-hsiang ling-shih* edition) 2, p. 9a; *CTS* 53, p. 2221, where Wen Ta-ya, as head of the *Chi-shih*, answered a letter addressed to Li Yüan by the rival rebel Li Mi.

throne for himself, Wen Ta-ya was one of the small group of advisers who arranged the ceremonies of abdication for the Sui child-emperor and for the accession of Kao-tsu.

The *Ta-T'ang ch'uang-yeh ch'i-chü chu* is his record of these events.[11] Its importance as an independent source was already appreciated by Ssu-

---

11 There is some confusion about the date of this work. It is mentioned under the title of the extant version in Wen Ta-ya's *CTS* biography, but not in his *HTS* biography. *TFYK* 560, p. 5b, says that "At the beginning of the Chen-kuan period Wen Ta-ya became president of the Board of Rites and wrote the *Ch'uang-yeh ch'i-chü chu* in three chapters." Both biographies confirm that he was promoted to president of the Board of Rites after T'ai-tsung's accession, so this account would suggest that the book was written after 626. However, the extant editions give the author as "Wen Ta-ya, Founding Duke of Lo-p'ing Commandery, Grand Pillar of State, and President of the Board of Works in the Provisional administration of Shan-tung." The provisional administration of Shan-tung (*Shan-tung ta hsing-t'ai*) was one of the regional administrations established to bring order to disturbed regions of the empire during the pacification campaigns of Kao-tsu's reign. That for Shan-tung was the provisional administration set up to control the newly conquered territories of Ho-nan, and placed under the command of Li Shih-min, prince of Ch'in, the future T'ai-tsung. It was set up in the tenth month of 621. See *CTS* 2, p. 28; *CTS* 42, pp. 1909–11; *TCTC* 189, p. 5931. The president of its Board of Works was also responsible for the Board of Justice in the conquered territories. See *CTS* 42, p. 1809. The provisional administration was abolished a few days after the Hsüan-wu Gate coup, which brought T'ai-tsung to the throne in the sixth month of 626. See *CTS* 2, p. 20. (On these provisional administrations, see Rotours, *Fonctionnaires* vol. 2 pp. 708–9.) This would suggest that the *Ta-T'ang ch'uang-yeh ch'i-chü chu* was written between the end of 621 and 626, and not after T'ai-tsung's accession. Moreover, internal evidence in the text itself provides clear proof that it was written before 626, while Kao-tsu was still on the throne. This dating is confirmed by Sung Ta-ch'uan, "*Ta T'ang ch'uang-yeh ch'i-chü chu* ch'eng yü ho shih," *Shih-hsüeh shih yen-chiu*, 1985 no. 4: 57–66.

The date of composition after 626 given in *TFYK* 560 may be the result of confusion with another book by Wen Ta-ya. In another section of *TFYK* there is an undated passage saying, "Wen Ta-ya became president of the Board of Rites, and compiled the *Chin-shang wang-yeh chi* in six chapters." See *TFYK* 556, p. 14a. Bingham, "Wen Ta-ya," p. 372, assumed that this refers to the *Ta-T'ang ch'uang-yeh ch'i-chü chu* under an alternative title, and that the "present sovereign" of the title was Kao-tsu. However, if as *TFYK* says this work was written by Wen Ta-ya when he was president of the Board of Rites, the "present sovereign" must refer to T'ai-tsung, and it seems most likely that this was a different book by Wen Ta-ya, dealing with the earlier career of T'ai-tsung, under whom he had served in the Shan-tung provisional administration. The *Chin-shang wang-yeh chi* is listed as a separate book in the section of miscellaneous historical works (*Tsa-shih*) in *HTS* 58, p. 1467. See also *Yü hai* 48, pp. 26b–28a.

Yet another work by Wen Ta-ya is recorded among the works dealing with various government offices (*Chih-kuan*) in *HTS* 58, p. 1477, entitled *Ta Ch'eng-hsiang T'ang-wang Kuan-shu chi* (record of the officeholders under the great chief minister, the prince of T'ang) in two chapters. From the offices attributed to Li Yüan in the title of this work we know that it must have been written between the tenth month of 617 and his seizure of the throne in the fifth month of 618. This book must surely have had a close connection with the *Ta-T'ang ch'uang-yeh ch'i-chü chu*, but nothing of it survives to prove what this connection may have been.

ma Kuang, who cited it repeatedly in his critical notes to the *Tzu-chih t'ung-chien*, and is now widely recognized, although the work still awaits a full critical study.[12] Not only does it give an eyewitness account by a participant in the events described, almost certainly written during the reign of Kao-tsu (618–26),[13] but it enables us to counterbalance the bias written into the official record of the early T'ang by official historiographers working under T'ai-tsung and Kao-tsung, who were at pains to overemphasize the part played in the dynastic founding by Li Shih-min, the future T'ai-tsung, and to downplay the importance of his father Li Yüan as the leader of the original uprising so as to justify T'ai-tsung's subsequent usurpation of the throne.[14] It also provides an alternative account of many incidents.[15]

Of its authenticity and its importance as a historical source there can be no question. But it was not, however, a Court Diary in the normal sense. This is clear from the circumstances under which it was compiled. Li Yüan was still at the time of the events it describes a Sui official, not an emperor, and the work ceases with his assumption of the imperial throne. It is a private record, not an official work. A telling piece of evidence that in T'ang times it was not thought of as an ordinary Court Diary is the fact that in 721 it is listed as an independent work in the Imperial Library.[16] None of the subsequent official Court Diaries was so

---

12 On the *Ta-T'ang ch'uang-yeh ch'i-chü chu*, see the articles of Bingham and Lo Hsiang-lin cited earlier in n. 7. See also Fukui Shigemasa, "Dai Tō sōgyō kikyochū kō," *Shikan* 63 (1961): 82–94; Howard J. Wechsler, *Mirror to the Son of Heaven* (New Haven, 1974), pp. 16–27. See also an unpublished paper by the late Robert Somers, "The Historiography of the T'ang Founding," presented to the Yale Seminar on Chinese and Comparative Historiography in 1971.
13 See Fukui Shigemasa, "Dai Tō sōgyō kikyochū kō," pp. 85–6.
14 See subsequent discussion and Wechsler, *Mirror to the Son of Heaven*, pp. 16–27. Although Wen Ta-ya was a member of Li Yüan's original entourage, and the *Ta-T'ang ch'uang-yeh ch'i-chü chu* has been much used by modern revisionist historians as evidence supporting the future Kao-tsu's role as the real leader of the T'ang uprising against the Sui, it is worth remembering that Wen Ta-ya was also closely associated with Li Shih-min, the future T'ai-tsung, both before and after he usurped the throne in 626. The deliberate attempts to tamper with the record of the dynastic founding in T'ai-tsung's favor were made in the 640s and 650s, long after Wen Ta-ya's death. It remains curious, however, that T'ai-tsung, who in his later years was so obsessed with the record of his own career, did not suppress the *Ta-T'ang ch'uang-yeh ch'i-chü chu*. It would seem impossible that he would not have known of a work written by a close associate and included in the Imperial Library, and widely enough circulated for a copy to have later found its way to Japan.
15 See Lo Hsiang-lin, *T'ang-tai wen-hua shih* (Taipei, 1955), pp. 8–19; Fukui Shigemasa, "Dai Tō sōgyō kikyochū kō."
16 See *CTS* 46, p. 1998.

41

listed. They seem simply to have been stored as source material in the Historiographical Office.[17]

Another indication that the *Ta-T'ang ch'uang-yeh ch'i-chü chu* was an independent work, quite different from a normal Court Diary, is the fact that it was allowed to be taken to Japan, where it was listed in the late ninth-century catalog *Nihon koku genzai sho mokuroku* of Fujiwara no Sukeyo.[18]

Moreover, many of the compilers of catalogs from the eleventh century onward clearly felt that it was not a regular Court Diary.[19] The *Ch'ung-wen tsung-mu* places it among the "Miscellaneous historical works" (*Tsa-shih*) together with various other private accounts of the collapse of the Sui and the rise of the T'ang.[20] The *Chün-chai tu-shu chih* lists it as a "Chronicle history" (*Pien-nien shih*),[21] as do the eighteenth-century compilers of the *Ssu-k'u ch'üan-shu*.[22]

It thus does not provide us with a surviving example of a T'ang Court Diary, as is sometimes claimed; nor does it give us any picture of what the normal Court Diaries were like.

17 The *K'ai-yüan ch'i-chü chu* in 3,682 chapters, listed without author's name in *HTS* 58, p. 1471, was not a real work. The title almost certainly arises from a misreading by the *Hsin T'ang-shu* compilers of the account of the destruction of the Historiographical Office in *THY* 63, p. 1095. The "3,682 chapters of books" mentioned there as having been destroyed were "the various Court Diaries and other books" held in the office, not simply the Court Diaries for the K'ai-yüan period.

18 See Fujiwara no Sukeyo, *Nihon koku genzai sho mokuroku* 7, p. 109 (in Kariya Ekisai's edition in the *Nihon koten zenshū* [Tokyo, 1928]). The original edition mistakenly gave the title as *Wen T'ang ch'uang-yeh ch'i-chü chu*, an obvious scribal error.

19 It was classified among the Court Diaries by *CTS* 46, p. 1998, and *HTS* 58, p. 1471. *WHTK* 194, p. 1641a, also classifies it in the same way.

20 See *Ch'ung-wen tsung-mu* 3, p. 17a. Among the other works dealing with this period that survived into the eleventh century and were cited by Ssu-ma Kuang in the *Tzu-chih t'ung-chien k'ao-i* (Peking, 1956) were the following: (1) *Ho-Lo hsing-nien chi* in ten chapters by Liu Jen-kuei (602–85), written in Kao-tsung's reign and widely circulated in the late seventh century. This gave an account of the period from second month of 617 until the capture of Tou Chien-te in the seventh month of 621. See *Ch'ung-wen tsung-mu* 3, p. 16b; *Chün-chai tu-shu chih (Yüan-pen)* 2A, p. 10a (*Ch'ü-pen* 5, p. 10b); *CTS* 84, p. 2796. *HTS* 58, p. 1467, lists it under the title *Liu-shih hsing-nien chi* and gives its length as twenty chapters. (2) *Ta-yeh lüeh-chi* in three chapters by Chao I (see *Ch'ung-wen tsung-mu* 3, p. 16b. 3), *Sui-chi ko-ming chi* in five chapters by Tu Ju-t'ung (see *HTS* 58, 1467, which informs us that the author lived in the time of Empress Wu), and *Ch'ung-wen tsung-mu* 3, p. 16b. There are two further related works listed in *Ch'ung-wen tsung-mu* 3, p. 16b. The first, the *Ta-yeh shih-i* in ten chapters, is presumably the same as the *Ta-yeh tsa-chi* in ten chapters by Tu Pao listed in *HTS* 58, p. 1466, and *Chün-chai tu-shu chih* 2A, p. 18b. The second, entitled *Ta-yeh shih-i lu* in a single chapter by Yen Shih-ku, is otherwise unknown.

21 See *Chün-chai tu-shu chih (Yüan-pen)* 2A, p. 10a (*Ch'ü-pen*) 5, p. 10b.

22 See *Ssu-k'u ch'üan-shu tsung-mu ti-yao* 47, pp. 1027–8.

5

The Inner Palace Diary
(*Nei Ch'i-chü chu*) [1]

The Court Diary and Record of administrative Affairs dealt in considerable detail with the public acts of the emperor and of his administration. But there is nothing in the official histories to suggest that any formal record was kept of his personal life and activities in the palace.[2] Such a record would have been of move than minor importance, because the ruler spent the greater part of his time in the comparative privacy of his own quarters in the palace, where many important decisions were made on the basis of personal contacts with the imperial entourage.

A short work by the ninth-century writer Li Chün entitled *Sung-ch'uang tsa-lu*[3] gives, however, rather circumstantial details of how such a record came to be compiled during the reign of Hsüan-tsung:

---

1 This section was published as a separate article, Denis C. Twitchett, "The Inner Palace Diary (*Nei ch'i-chü chu*)," *T'ang Studies* 4 (1986): 1–9.

2 In this connection, it is worth remembering that the earliest mentions of the Court Diary, dating from the Han period, seem to refer not to a Court Diary in the later sense, but to a Palace Record kept by the ladies of the imperial household. See Chapter 2, n. 15. See also Wang Mao (1151–1213), *Yeh-ko ts'ung-shu* (Peking, *Hsüeh-shu pi-chi ts'ung-k'an* 1987) 15, p. 166.

3 See Li Chün, *Sung-ch'uang tsa-lu*, edition in *Chung-kuo wen-hsüeh ts'an-k'ao tzu-liao ts'ung-shu* (Peking, 1958), pp. 3–4. I am indebted to Dr. Wang Zhenping for drawing my attention to this important passage. The preface to *Sung-ch'uang tsa-lu* claims that it is a record of what the author remembered from his childhood, and various stories circulating among the court officials. *Ssu-k'u ch'üan-shu tsung-mu t'i-yao* 140, pp. 2890–1, notes that there is considerable confusion over both this work's title and its author. It appears variously as the *Sung-ch'uang lu*, *Sung-ch'uang hsiao-lu*, and *Sung-ch'uang tsa-lu* in Sung sources, and its author is given either as Li Chün or as Wei Chün. Modern editions all attribute it to Li Chün. There were several persons with this name recorded during the T'ang. The best known was a prominent provincial official with biographies in *CTS* 112, p. 3338; *CTS* 185B, pp. 4812–13; *HTS* 142, p. 4663, but he died in 720, before most of the incidents recorded in the book. Two other Li Chüns are listed in the genealogical tables of the imperial clan in *HTS* 72A, pp. 2525 and 2548. *CTW* 816, p. 3b, has an entry on yet another Li Chün, which merely says that he was a writer of Hsi-tsung's reign (873–88) and includes under his name only a single undated inscription for a temple in Nanking that the author claims as his family temple. Lu Hsin-yüan's *T'ang-wen shih-i* (reprint,

After Hsuan-tsung had for the second time pacified internal troubles in the Hsien-t'ien period [712–13],[4]...he paid especial attention to the Court Diaries *Ch'i-chü chu*. During the Hsien-t'ien and K'ai-yuan periods [712–741], Confucian scholars of broad erudition or pure and upright officials were always selected to fill [the posts of diarist]. If there was someone who could perfectly perform these duties, then even after ten or more years he would still wield his brush "by the dragon's head,"[5] clinging to [his duty] and not wishing to be discharged from it, so that although he might be promoted to be Principal Secretary of an important bureau, he would nevertheless continue concurrently to hold his post as diarist. From the first year of the Hsien-t'ien period [712][6] to the winter of the eleventh year of the T'ien-pao period [752][7] there were compiled 700 chapters of the Court Diary [*Ch'i-chü chu*] and 300 chapters of the Inner Palace Diary [*Nei Ch'i-chü chu*].

The Inner Palace Diary began from the spring of the second year of the K'ai-yuan period [714] when the Emperor paid a state visit to the mansion of

---

Taipei, 1962) 27, p. 26a, however, denies that the author of the preface to *Sung-ch'uang tsa-lu* was the person listed in *CTW* and suggests that he flourished in the early ninth century, during the reigns of Hsien-tsung and Mu-tsung (805–24).

In fact its contents show that it must have been written later, for some of its anecdotes deal with the reign of Wen-tsung (827–40) and it also mentions a correct prophecy of the death of Li Te-yü, who died in 850. Lu Hsin-yüan's suggestion about the supposed author's date is thus at least a quarter century too early. Perhaps the nearest that we can get to the truth is that Li Chün wrote this work in the second half of the ninth century, and there is thus no reason why he and the author listed in *CTW* could not have been the same person.

The issue of the work's title is even more complicated than the editors of the *Ssu-k'u ch'üan-shu* would have us believe. First, there has been confusion with a quite different work with a similar or identical title, the *Sung-ch'uang tsa-chi* (also sometimes called *Sung-ch'uang tsa-lu*) by Tu Hsün-ho, which is preserved in truncated form in *T'ang-tai ts'ung-shu* (*ch'u chi*) and elsewhere. Second, exactly the same work as Li Chün's *Sung-ch'uang tsa-lu*, with the omission of two sections and the addition of one other anecdote, but otherwise virtually identical and including the same preface, has also been preserved under the title *Chih-i chi*, also in a single chapter and also attributed to Li Chün, and this is included in the *T'ang-jen shuo-hui*, in the *T'ang-tai ts'ung-shu*, ser. 5, and in the *Wan-wei shan t'ang* edition of *Shuo-fu*. E. D. Edwards, *Chinese Prose Literature of the T'ang Period* A. D. *618–906* (London, 1937–8), vol. 2, pp. 227–8, has a note on this work, but wrongly states that it deals with events from the K'ai-yüan period and incorrectly assumes its author to have been the Li Chün who died in 720, as mentioned earlier. The *Chih-i chi* version of the story concerning the Inner Palace Diary and the prince of Ning is identical, save for a few variant characters, with that in *Sung-ch'uang tsa-lu*.

4 This refers to his coup against Princess T'ai-p'ing in the seventh month of 713.

5 *Ch'ih-t'ou kuan*: This is a term for the diarists, the *Ch'i-chü lang* and *Ch'i-chü she-jen* who stood, during the court assembly, by the sculptured heads of dragons ornamenting the stone balustrade of the great stairway, the "Dragon's Tail Steps" *Lung-wei tao*, leading to the imperial audience hall. For details and a diagram, see Rotours, *Fonctionnaires*, vol. 1, pp. 155–6.

6 This date is contradicted immediately thereafter, where it is given as 714.

7 This date, too, is problematical. A brief résumé of this first paragraph is also included in *T'ang yü lin* (Chou Hsün-ch'u, ed., *T'ang yü lin chiao-cheng*, Peking, 1987) 2, pp. 118–19. This version gives the date as the twelfth year (753). *Sung-ch'uang tsa-lu* itself gives the date below as the tenth year (751).

the Prince of Ning.[8] They discussed the family ritual observances of members of their family, and when it came to the correct order for musical performances, or what wine and food should be provided, the emperor never exclusively followed his own inclinations, but always deferred to the instructions of the Prince of Ning. The Emperor said, "Elder brother, you love to act the host, and I [*A-man*][9] simply respectfully play the principal guest." With this they were extremely happy and the feast came to an end.

Next day the prince of Ning leading [his brothers] the princes of Ch'i[10] and Hsueh[11] together memorialized the throne, "We have heard that the Court Diary must record the words and actions of the Son of Heaven. We, your subjects, fear that the Diarists of the Left and Right cannot gain [any knowledge of] how Your Majesty's conduct in the inner chambers of the Palace carries to perfection the rules of propriety for the common people, and have no means to enlighten the ten thousand generations to come. We therefore request that from this time onward myself and my brothers shall each in rotation wield the writing brush before the imperial presence[12] so that we shall be enabled to write a record of events wherever the emperor happens to be. At the end of each of the four seasons [this record], affixed with the vermillion seal and with our signatures, shall be forwarded to the Historiographical Office. It should be presented to the throne together with a memorial in accordance with the usage for histories of the outer court. Your subjects who clearly understand the multitude of affairs will maintain these responsibilities just like the Court Diarists [*ch'ih-t'ou kuan*]."

The Emperor composed an extremely respectful response to this memorial, which he wrote in *pa-fen* script on paper from Japan, consenting to all their requests.

---

8 The prince of Ning, Li Ch'eng-ch'i (679–741), Jui-tsung's eldest son, and thus Hsüan-tsung's eldest brother, was an important figure during the early reign of Hsüan-tsung. He had renounced his claim to the throne in favor of the future Hsüan-tsung in 710, after the coup against Empress Wei. In 711, the future Hsüan-tsung, embroiled in a fierce factional quarrel with Princess T'ai-p'ing, offered to resign as heir apparent in his favor but he declined to accept. Li Ch'eng-ch'i held a number of important posts, becoming president of the Court of Imperial Sacrifices from 721–6. The title given here is, strictly speaking, an anachronism, because he received the title prince of Ning only in 716. He remained on close friendly terms with the emperor, who, for instance, always paid a visit to his mansion on Ch'eng-ch'i's birthday, and regularly kept him supplied with rare food and drink from the palace.

9 *A-man* is said by the commentary to the *Sung-ch'uang tsa-lu* to have been the term used in the T'ang Inner Palace by the emperor to speak of himself.

10 The prince of Ch'i was Li Fan (d. 726, original name Li Lung-fan), the fourth son of Jui-tsung. Both he and his younger brother Li Yeh had assisted Hsüan-tsung in the coup against Princess T'ai-p'ing, which had brought him to power in 713, and like Li Ch'eng-ch'i were very intimate with the emperor. At this time he was the second tutor of the heir apparent.

11 The prince of Hsüeh was Li Yeh (d. 734, original name Li Lung-yeh), the fifth son of Jui-tsung, who was second protector of the heir apparent.

12 *Ch'eng* is followed by a missing character in the text of *Sung-ch'uang tsa-lu*. In *Chih-i chi* the missing character is *yü*.

From this time [until] the winter of the tenth year of the T'ien-pao period [751] the record thus compiled extended to 300 chapters, on the average with 50 sheets of yellow hemp paper forming one section [*pien*]; [they were mounted on] carved sandalwood rollers, and stored in sleeves [wrappers] of purple damask with a dragon and phoenix motif.

When the writing[13] was completed, the Prince of Ning requested that his own copy be placed in the storehouse for the histories [*shih-ko*]. The Emperor ordered that he be presented with wine and music, and a banquet was held for the attendant officials [*shih-ch'en*] at the Historiographical Office. The Emperor especially treasured this history, and therefore ordered that a large storehouse [*ta-ko*] be separately built to house it.

When An Lu-shan captured Ch'ang-an[14] on the advice of Yen [Chuang] and Kao [Shang], before he entered the Palace, he first had this storehouse set aflame with a thousand blazing torches, so that it was rapidly burned to ashes. Because of this only three or four parts out of a hundred of Hsüan-tsung's Veritable Record [*Hsüan-tsung Shih-lu*] could be put together, and as a result the accounts handed down [about the period] among the people are especially sparse.

None of this detail survives in any other source, as far as I am aware, and quite apart from its unique information about the Inner Palace Diary, the passage informs us that the destruction of the historical archives in 756, which I have already mentioned, was a deliberate act by An Lu-shan. There seems no reason to doubt its authenticity.

The existence of such an Inner Palace Diary, though not its name, is confirmed by the biography of Li Ch'eng-ch'i, prince of Ning, in the *Chiu T'ang shu*.[15] According to the biography, the prince, though barred from participation in court discussions, had a profound understanding of politics and was given special dispensation to prepare his own annual summary of events for presentation to the Historiographical Office. The record was said to run to several hundred pages annually. The *Chiu T'ang shu* gives the impression that it was a privileged individual's independent overview of court politics. However, because it is most unlikely that there were two different records in the writing of which the prince of Ning was involved, the *Sung-ch'uang tsa-lu's* account must refer to the same record, and makes it clear first that it dealt with subject matter not included in the regular Court Diary, and also that its compilation

---

13 This must, of course, refer to the first sections, not to the three hundred chapters eventually completed that are mentioned earlier.
14 This took place probably on the seventeenth day of the sixth month of 756. For details on the conflicting accounts of the date of the rebel capture of the capital, see Robert des Rotours, *Histoire de Ngan Lou-chan* (*Ngan Lou-chan Che tsi*) (Paris, 1962), p. 273, n. 4.
15 See *CTS* 95, p. 3012. See also *THY* 2, pp. 21–2.

was not simply a personal arrangement involving the prince of Ning but one in which other royal princes participated.

The Inner Palace Diary thus seems, at least during its initial period, to have been a joint record composed by the royal brothers. The compilers of the National History of 759–60, from which the *Chiu T'ang shu* biographies of Jui-tsung's sons directly derive, may well have deliberately omitted any record of the participation of Hsüan-tsung's younger brothers, Li Fan and Li Yeh, for political reasons. Both were serious intellectuals, well known for their deep interest in scholarly matters, but both became tainted by political scandals, the details of which are impossible to unravel. Li Fan was a well-known scholar, calligrapher, and bibliophile, and the center of a lively intellectual circle. In 720 a scandal involved him and his brother-in-law, P'ei Hsü-chi, in charges that they had been "improperly consulting prophetic writings" – a common euphemism for planning a coup against the throne. Various implicated persons were banished from court, although Li Fan himself was not punished and the emperor publicly declared his brotherly affection for him.[16]

Li Yeh was also well known for his scholarly interests, and had been director of the Imperial Library under Jui-tsung. In 725 a similar scandal implicated him, his brother-in-law Wei Pin, and a number of palace officials.[17] Once again the royal prince and his consort escaped without punishment and remained on cordial terms with the emperor, although Hsüan-tsung now began deliberately to curtail the power and freedom of action of the royal princes.[18] Li Fan lived until 726 and Li Yeh until 734, both honored and holding high offices to the last and both being granted the posthumous title of "heir apparent." However, their reputations had been compromised, and the fact that neither is mentioned by *Chiu T'ang shu* in connection with the compilation of Li Ch'eng-ch'i's Inner Palace Diary may well have been quite deliberate.[19]

After the death of Li Yeh in 734, only Li Ch'eng-ch'i survived, living

---

16 *CTS* 95, p. 3016; *HTS* 81, p. 3601; *TCTC* 212, pp. 6741–2.
17 See *CTS* 95, pp. 3018–19. *TCTC* 212, pp. 6741–2, incorrectly includes this in its entry for 720, together with the plot implicating Li Fan.
18 On these events, see Denis C. Twitchett, ed., *The Cambridge History of China* vol. 3 (Cambridge, 1979), pp. 370–4, 379–82.
19 It is noteworthy that *Sung-ch'uang tsa-lu* does not mention the remaining brother Li Ch'eng-i (later Li Wei), prince of Shen, the second of the five sons of Jui-tsung. He was the odd man out among the emperor's brothers, described as magnanimous and of outstanding presence, a great drinker and gourmand. He served in a series of important provincial posts until 720, when he was recalled to the capital, where he died in 724. See *CTS* 95, pp. 3015–16. In 714 when Li Ch'eng-ch'i presented his memorial, he was at his provincial post as prefect of Yu-chou (modern Peking) and not at court.

on until the eleventh month of 741, and during these last years, he must have been solely responsible for preparing the Palace Diary.[20] The account in *Sung-ch'uang tsa-lu* however, tells us that the Palace Diary did not end with his death in 741 but continued until 751 or 752. Who was responsible for it after Li Ch'eng-ch'i's death is unknown.[21]

The existence of this Palace Diary is of considerable historical interest, but it seems to have been an arrangement that arose out of the anomalous and potentially unstable situation in the imperial family during the early years of Hsüan-tsung's reign.[22] It was never revived, and the official histories refer to it only obliquely. Moreover, it can have had little influence on the surviving official record of Hsüan-tsung's reign, unless some of its information was incorporated into the draft

20 This suggests another possible reason for the omission of the names of Li Fan and Li Yeh from the *CTS* account. After 730 the historian Wei Shu, who was then in charge of the affairs of the Historiographical Office, and who later wrote the first draft of the National History covering the period, including the biographies of Hsüan-tsung's brothers, would have seen the Palace Diary annually in the course of his duties and would have associated it with Li Ch'eng-ch'i's name alone.

21 If indeed the Palace Diary came to an end in the winter of 752 this would have coincided with the death of the chief minister, Li Lin-fu, which produced a general political crisis. But the diary may well have ceased to be compiled for other reasons; probably the death of its principal compiler was one of them. After Li Ch'eng-ch'i died in 741, it must have been continued by a royal prince with access to the palace, and because all of the emperor's brothers were now dead, it was most likely to have been continued by one of the more senior of the twenty-three of Hsüan-tsung's sons who survived to maturity. (See *CTS* 107, p. 3258.) Two likely candidates died about the time when the Palace Diary came to an end. The first was the emperor's eldest son, Li Tsung, prince of Ch'ing, who, for reasons that remain obscure but most likely because he was childless, had always been passed over as a potential heir apparent. He died in 752, but in the fifth month, not in winter. See *CTS* 9, p. 226; *CTS* 107, p. 3258. *HTS* 82, p. 3606, incorrectly dates his death in 751. The second son, Li Ying, the former heir apparent, had been reduced to commoner status and subsequently forced to commit suicide in 737 as the result of his supposed implication in a trumped-up succession plot. See *CTS* 107, p. 3260; *HTS* 82, p. 3608; *THY* 5, p. 53. The third son, Li Yü, was currently the heir apparent, the future Su-tsung. As heir apparent he had his own official diarists and lived in a separate palace. The fourth son, Li Yen, prince of Ti, however, is another possible candidate. At the end of 752 one of his concubines became involved in dealings with a magician. A censor with whom the prince had quarreled discovered this and denounced him to the emperor, who had the prince imprisoned in the royal mews, where he died. See *CTS* 107, pp. 3260-1; *TCTC* 216, pp. 6196-7; *HTS* 82, p. 3608. We do not know the exact date of his death, or of the accusation against him, but Ssu-ma Kuang places it at the end of 752.

22 At the time when the Palace Diary was begun, the abdicated former emperor Jui-tsung was still alive. Moreover at court there was not only the emperor's elder brother, Li Ch'eng-ch'i, but also his uncle Li Shou-li whose claims to the throne had been promoted by the princess T'ai-p'ing before her death in 713. There had been no less than four successful coups during the previous decade, and in such an unstable situation Hsüan-tsung was forced to do all in his power to seek the cooperation and maintain the firm support and friendship of the senior members of the royal family with a viable claim to the succession.

National History compiled by Wei Shu in the 730s and 740s. It cannot have been used as a source by Liu Fang in writing up the events of Hsüan-tsung's reign for the National History of 759–60, because it had been deliberately destroyed in 756.

Appendix to Chapter 5

As we have seen, there was a tradition that in Han times the Court Diary had been kept by the ladies of the palace. Liu Chih-chi tells us in his *Shih t'ung*, completed in 710, that during the reign of Sui Wen-ti (581–604) his long-serving historian Wang Shao[23] proposed in a memorial that posts of lady historiographers (*Nü shih*) be reestablished after the model of antiquity, and that they should record the formalities of the Inner Palace and report these to the outer ministries. But Wen-ti declined his suggestion, and it was never put into force.[24] Liu Chih-chi ends his account of palace records kept by female scribes at this point, and had the institution existed in the seventh century, he would almost certainly have commented upon it. Nobody to my knowledge has doubted that by T'ang times the system was long dead.[25]

It is possible, however, that there is a reference to the existence of a palace record kept by the palace women in the *Chiu T'ang shu* biography of the remarkable Sung Jo-hsin (d. 820).[26] The daughter of Sung T'ing-fen, she was a member of a family with a strong tradition of Confucian learning, descended from the famous writer Sung Chih-wen (d. 712).[27] Sung T'ing-fen's sons were untalented, but he had five remarkable daughters to whom he gave a strict education not only in classical learning but also in writing poetry and rhymeprose. All five were accomplished writers by the time they reached maturity, and they made a pact never to marry but to devote themselves to writing.[28] In 788 they were recommended by a local official to Emperor Te-tsung, a great devotee of literature, who personally examined their work and recruited them all into the palace service. Te-tsung and later Hsien-tsung held them in the

---

23 This memorial is not mentioned in Wang Shao's biography in *SS* 61 or elsewhere in *SS*.
24 See *Shih t'ung* 11, p. 324.
25 The issue is confused because the same term, *nü-shih*, is also used for female scribes employed in the palace service in tasks having nothing to do with history.
26 See *CTS* 52, pp. 2198–9; also *HTS* 77, pp. 3508–9.
27 See *CTS* 7, p. 67.
28 The eldest daughter, Sung Jo-hsin, wrote a "Women's Analects," *Nü lun-yü*, in ten chapters to which Sung Jo-chao, the second daughter, added a commentary. See *HTS* 58, p. 1487. This book survives today, but only in a truncated version in a single chapter, included in *Shuo-fu* (Wan-wei shan t'ang version, *chüan* 70) and elsewhere.

highest esteem, especially the eldest sister, Sung Jo-hsin who, from 791 to her death, was "in charge of the 'records' [*chi-chu*], the registers and the accounts of the inner palace." Just what these "records" were is not clear, but they *may* have been some sort of Inner Palace Diary.

Sung Jo-hsin was almost certainly one of the two palace matrons (*Shang-kung*), as two of her younger sisters were later to be. The duties of these lady officals in T'ang times included responsibility for all the paper work in the imperial harem, but there is no specific mention of their keeping an Inner Palace Diary. *Chi-chu* in Jo-hsin's biography may refer only to "records" in a very general sense, but the same term is used for the heir apparent's diary.

After Jo-hsin's death in 820, the new emperor Mu-tsung appointed the second sister, Sung Jo-chao, to take over her duties and the post of palace matron.[29] Specifically said to have been extremely perceptive about politics, she had considerable influence with Hsien-tsung, Mu-tsung and Ching-tsung, besides enjoying great respect among the members of the royal family and their consorts. When she died in 825, she was buried with full official honors.[30]

Ching-tsung replaced her with a third surviving sister, Sung Jo-hsien, who continued to enjoy great favor under the literature-loving Wen-tsung, who valued both her literary skills and her shrewd advice on practical affairs. However, in 835 she became implicated in the bitter factional struggles that led up to the "Sweet Dew" incident.[31] As part of a plot to ruin Li Tsung-min, she was accused, together with Shen I, the consort of Princess Hsüan-ch'eng, Hsien-tsung's oldest surviving daughter, of having accepted bribes to persuade the emperor to appoint Tsung-min a chief minister. As a result of this scandal the emperor had her secluded in a mansion outside the palace and subsequently ordered her to commit suicide, a decision he later bitterly regretted. Many relatives of her brothers' were also implicated in this affair and banished to the far south. There is no proof of her guilt, and it seems likely that she was merely the victim of a trumped-up charge.

The Sung sisters were thus in charge of the inner palace for no fewer than forty-four years, and during that period they may possibly have been the keepers of a palace record of some kind.

29 *CTS* 16, p. 484, dates her appointment on the twelfth day of the seventh month of 821.
30 *CTS* 52, p. 2198.
31 For the details of this scandal, see *CTS* 52, pp. 2198–9; *CTS* 176, p. 4553; *CTS* 17b, p. 56; *HTS* 174, p. 5236.

6

The Record of
Administrative Affairs
(*Shih-cheng chi*)

The insufficiency of the *Ch'i-chü chu* as an adequate record of government business with its bare record of proceedings in open court, was felt very early. In the reign of T'ai-tsung (626–49), relations between the emperor and his chief ministers were unusually close, and many crucial decisions and discussions of policy took place during their private meetings, not in the full court assembly in the presence of the diarists. The need for a record of these deliberations was met by having one of the court diarists keep a record of these more private discussions. Under T'ai-tsung's successor, Kao-tsung, however, the emperor ceased to be the dominant force in decision making, and even the record of his meeting with his ministers provided no account of many important decisions. When the elder statesmen who had previously served his father died or were driven from office in the mid 650s, the new chief ministers, Hsü Ching-tsung and Li I-fu, wishing to conceal their blatant political manipulations, forbade the attendance of the diarists at the informal meetings of the chief ministers, which henceforth left no formal record.[1] From this time on, the diarists only "heard the instructions issued by

---

1 In one of the rare personal comments incorporated in his *Hui yao* (see *THY* 56, p. 961), Su Mien says, "In the Chen-kuan period, after the court withdrew each day, and T'ai-tsung deliberated with his chief ministers about affairs of state, he would order one of the diarists (*Ch'i-chü lang*) to take notes and compile a record. Because of this the Record of Administrative Affairs for the Chen-kuan period is to be praised for its completeness. But afterward, when Kao-tsung held court, he just sat gravely without speaking, while the officials simply memorialized when they wished to take formal leave or to report for duty in the capital. Later when Hsü Ching-tsung and Li I-fu exercised authority they frequently memorialized irresponsibly about affairs, and fearing that the historians would make a straightforward record of their shortcomings, requested that the diarists should withdraw following the guards, so that they should not be able to learn about the discussions of critical affairs. This subsequently became an established practice."

by the emperor in the presence of the guards and had no knowledge of the deliberations carried on after the withdrawal of the court." [2]

During the reign of Empress Wu, in 693 Chief Minister Yao Shou[3] memorialized the throne requesting that "since the emperor's instructions cannot go unrecorded" one of the chief ministers should be given the duty of keeping a record of what was said about important military and administrative affairs during the deliberations held after the court had withdrawn, and that this record should be called the Record of Administrative Affairs (*Shih-cheng chi*). It was to be sent under seal to the Historiographical Office at the end of each month.[4]

The *T'ang liu-tien*, *T'ang hui yao*, and Yao Shou's *Chiu T'ang shu* biography all state that the compilation of the *Shih-cheng chi* began from this time,[5] and many historians, beginning with Chao I[6] (1727–1814), have asserted that a Record of Administrative Affairs was regularly compiled from Yao Shou's time onward. However, in the 1930s Tamai Zehaku showed that this was probably incorrect and that there is evidence that the Record of Administrative Affairs was not continued beyond Yao Shou's period as chief minister.[7] The only evidence of their continued

2 See *THY* 63, p. 1104; *TLT* 9, pp. 19b–20a.

3 Yao Shou (632–705) was a grandson of Yao Ssu-lien, who had been a member of T'ai-tsung's *Wen-hsüeh kuan* and later a secretary in the Office for Literary Composition and a scholar of the Hung-wen Academy. Yao Ssu-lien had been responsible for the first National History of the T'ang and was also the chief compiler of the Liang and Ch'en dynastic histories, completed in 636, both of which were based on unfinished works of his father Yao Ch'a who had been an official historian under the Ch'en and the Sui. The family thus had a very strong historical tradition. See *CTS* 89, p. 2902; *HTS* 102, p. 3980.

4 See *TLT* 9, pp. 19b–20a; *THY* 63, p. 1104; *CTS* 89, p. 2902; *TCTC* 205, p. 6488; *HTS* 102, p. 3980.

5 See *CTS* 89, p. 2902; *THY* 63, p. 1104; *TFYK* 560, p. 9b; *HTS* 102, p. 3980. See also the memorial from the historiographers suggesting the revival of a Record of Administrative Affairs submitted under the Later Chin in 939, which also assumes that from Yao Shou's time on one of the chief ministers had regularly kept a Record of Administrative Affairs. See *WTHY* 18, p. 304; *CWTS* 78, p. 1033.

6 See Chao I, *Nien-erh shih cha-chi*, ed. Tu Wei-yün, 2 vols. (Taipei, 1974), 19, pp. 395–6.

7 The Treatise on the Bureaucracy of *HTS* (see *HTS* 47, p. 1208; Rotours, *Fonctionnaires* vol. I, p. 160) speaks of Yao Shou's record as follows: "But in general it gave prominence to that which was fine, and only recorded the good, so that the record of events did not correspond with reality. Shortly after the record was discontinued." A memorial by Li Chi-fu, dated 813, also refers to its abandonment. "When Yao Shou ceased to be chief minister, the record was discontinued." See *THY* 64, p. 1109. Yao Shou served twice as chief minister under Empress Wu, the first time from the eighth month of 692 until the ninth month of 693, the second time from the eighth month of 694 until the eighth month of 697. See *CTS* 6, pp. 1656–60; *HTS* 61, pp. 1656–60. The reference to the ending of the Record of Administrative Affairs with Yao Shou's dismissal as chief minis-

existence before the very end of the eighth century is a note in *T'ang liu-tien*[8] stating that they were one of the sources from which the Veritable Records was compiled.

By the end of the eighth century the keeping of the Record of Administrative Affairs had long been discontinued, and under Te-tsung there came the first of a series of attempts to revive it, provoked, there can be little doubt, by the increasing concentration of the administrative power in the hands of chief ministers, the growth of irregular "inner court" influences on government such as the eunuchs and the Han-lin scholars, and the general decline in influence of the regular bureaucracy and their representatives at court. In 796, following a memorial from Chief Minister Chao Ching, the old system by which one of the chief ministers kept a record of the deliberations between the emperor and his ministers was revived, but almost immediately Chao Ching died, and shortly thereafter[9] the records were once again abandoned.[10] At the most, they seem to have been continued for a short while by Chao Ching's fellow chief minister Chia T'an and by his colleague Ch'i K'ang[11] and to have been finally suspended when Ch'i K'ang was dismissed from office in the seventh month of 803.[12]

Another attempt to revive them took place under Hsien-tsung. In 813, the emperor himself questioned his chief minister and director of the National History, Li Chi-fu, about the Records of Administrative Affairs and asked why they had sometimes been kept and sometimes not. Li Chi-fu's answer, although it praises the records kept by Yao Shou and Chia T'an as "good history," gives an interesting set of reasons why such a record should *not* be provided to the historians:

ter may thus refer either to 693 or to 697, but the latter seems the more likely date of the two. The bibliographical chapter of *HTS* (see *HTS* 58, p. 1471) lists a *Shih cheng chi* in forty chapters by Yao Shou, but it is rather difficult to imagine precisely what this might have been. It was surely too long to have been the Record of Administrative Affairs kept by him as chief minister covering his relatively short period of five years in office.

8 See *TLT* 9, p. 29b.
9 Chao Ching died in the eighth month of 796.
10 See *THY* 56, pp. 962–3; *THY* 64, p. 1112; *TFYK* 560, p. 10a; *TPYL* 604, p. la–b.
11 See *THY* 64, p. 1109; *TPYL* 604, p. 1b.
12 Chia T'an was chief minister from the fifth month of 793 until his death in the tenth month of 805. Ch'i K'ang became chief minister in the ninth month of 800 and remained in office until 803. Li Chi-fu's memorial is the sole evidence that compilation of the Record of Administrative Affairs continued after Chao Ching's death. His grasp of historical details, however, seems to have been very shaky, in spite of his position as director of the National History. Elsewhere in the same memorial he speaks of Yao Shou as having been chief minister in the Yung-hui (650–56) period, forty years before the true date.

When we have received the emperor's opinion directly from him, but his orders have not yet been put into effect, they are to be called a state secret, and certainly may not be written down and conveyed to the Historiographical Office. If moreover there is any counsel given by the officials involved, it is not permissible that they themselves should make a record of it for transmission to the Historiographical Office. Yet when once the policy has been put into force, an imperial edict or instruction will have made it public, and the whole empire will have been informed about it.[13]

In 817 an edict was issued ordering that on every day when there was a court assembly, after the chief ministers and heads of bureaus had withdrawn, if there was any matter worthy to be recorded as providing an example to encourage or give warning (to later generations), the chief minister who had received the instruction was to convey it to the diarists of the left and right and have them compile a record according to the former precedent, which could be transmitted at the end of each quarter to the historiographers.[14]

This edict was issued as the result of a memorial from one of the diarists, Yü Ching-hsiu, which complained that for a century and a half the diarists had not taken a record of the confidential discussions held after the open court assembly and that during that period Records of Administrative Affairs had only occasionally been kept. However, the attempt to revive them was blocked by the chief ministers, who refused to report affairs to the diarists on the ground that they were secret matters. Once again the system was abandoned.[15]

Under Hsien-tsung's successor, Mu-tsung, yet another attempt was made in 821 to institute such a record, this time at the suggestion of Chief Ministers Ts'ui Chih (772–829) and Tu Yüan-ying (d. 832) and of the Chancellery and Secretariat. The record was to be entitled the *Sheng-cheng chi*. It was to be kept regularly and transmitted to the Historiographical Office under seal at the end of each year. But once again, although the memorial was approved, the new system was not put into practice.[16]

In the reign of Wen-tsung, too, there were renewed misgivings about the system of recording political events. In 831 yet another edict ordered the compilation of a Record of Administrative Affairs, the keeping of which was to be entrusted to an assistant from the Chancellery or Secretariat.[17] This move may have been connected with a memorial from Lu Sui, who had been ordered to revise the Veritable Record of Shun-tsung's controversial reign in an edict that complained that what

13 See *THY* 64, p. 1109; *TPYL* 604, p. 1b.
14 See *TTCLC* 81, p. 468.   15 See *THY* 64, pp. 1109–10; *TFYK* 560, pp. 8b–9a.
16 See *THY* 64, p. 1111; *CTS* 16, p. 489; *TPYL* 604, p. 2b.   17 See *CTS* 17B, p. 541.

the Veritable Records had reported on affairs in the palace during the reigns of Te-tsung and Shun-tsung had been based on incorrectly transmitted reports and could not be considered trustworthy history.[18] But this edict too can have had little effect. In 836, after the Sweet Dew incident, Wen-tsung revived the ancient practice of having the diarists attend and take a record of the informal (*ju-ko*) discussions between ministers and the emperor.[19] In 838, however, one of the chief ministers, Yang Ssu-fu, was again complaining that only matters discussed in the Regular Court (*Cheng-ya*) were being recorded, whereas no record was being kept of the informal discussions held in the "Informal Court," the *Pien-tien* (i.e. in the *Tzu-ch'en tien*).[20] The Chancellery and Secretariat once more requested the revival of the Record of Administrative Affairs.[21] But his fellow ministers disapproved, and once again it proved impossible to implement the scheme.[22]

Wen-tsung, however, was clearly sensitive to the need for a better record and did, in some cases at least, employ the diarists to take a record of the informal court meetings with his ministers. For example in 837 Chou Ch'ih (793–851) was appointed acting diarist (*chih ch'i-chü she-jen shih*) and regularly attended the meetings of the emperor with his chief ministers in the *Tzu-ch'en tien* to advise them on the appropriateness of measures under consideration.[23] This practice seems to have been later regularized.

Finally, during Li Te-yü's regime in 843, the Chancellery and Secretariat submitted yet another lengthy memorial on the subject,[24] the suggestions in which are said to have been put into practice. Certainly

---

18 See *CTS* 159, p. 4193; *THY* 64, p. 1112; *TFYK* 556, pp. 24b–25a; *TFYK* 562, pp. 10b–11a.
19 See *CTS* 17B, p. 572.
20 See *TFYK* 560, p. 10a–b. This complaint was not quite accurate. We have quite a number of records of discussions in the Tzu-ch'en tien preserved from 837. For a few random examples, see *TFYK* 562, p. 11a; *CTS* 172, p. 4485; *CTS* 173, p. 4491; *CTS* 173, p. 4506. A systematic search of the sources would certainly produce many more. Moreover in 837 the emperor had given a special audience to the diarists of the left and the right, P'ei Su and others, and the record of this meeting explains that they had been recording discussions with ministers since the previous year, and that consequently the record of administrative matters for the K'ai-ch'eng period (836–41) was far more detailed than for recent reigns. See *CTS* 17B, p. 572.
21 See *THY* 64, p. 1112.
22 See *TFYK* 560, p. 10a–b.
23 See *TFYK* 560, pp. 9b–10a; *HTS* 182, p. 5370. See also Tu Mu's memorial inscription for Chou Ch'ih, "Tung-Ch'uan Chieh-tu Shih chien-chiao Yu-p'u-ye chien Yü-shih tai-fu tseng Ssu-t'u Chou kung Mu-chih-ming," in *Fan-ch'uan wen-chi* (Shanghai, 1978) 7, p. 12a; *CTW* 755, p. 10a; *WYYH* 938, pp. 6b–7a. He was invited not simply to record the proceedings but to act as a consultant, if not as a full participant.
24 See *THY* 64, pp. 1112–13.

the Record of Administrative Affairs was still being kept in Hsiuan-tsung's reign, because when P'ei Hsiu became chief minister in 852[25] he complained in a memorial that the record of the ministers' deliberations in the Record of Administrative Affairs was unbalanced because the minister deputed to keep the record would give his own arguments in great detail, and merely summarize those of the other participants. He requested that each of the chief ministers should keep his own record of the proceedings and send it to the Historiographical Office, and this suggestion was put into effect.[26]

It is clear that, unlike the Court Diary, which was regularly compiled throughout the dynasty, the Record of Administrative Affairs was a much more irregular record, compiled only during a few brief periods, mostly at times when much official business was decided by the chief ministers in private rather than in open court, and when there was widespread concern that there should be a reliable record of these pro-ceedings. It was kept by various officers during the course of the dynasty, but unlike the Court Diary, which was kept by nominally impartial diarists, it was usually compiled, for reasons of preserving secrecy, by one of the actual participants in the deliberations it recorded.

By the late eighth and ninth centuries even had the Record of Admin-istrative Affairs provided a full account of ministerial consultations, there would still have been important areas of decision making that would have gone unrecorded. By the ninth century the emperors in-creasingly relied on their private secretaries and on consultation with their eunuch counselors. All these activities of "secret" government left no formal record; and this, as much as the often reiterated antieunuch bias of the official historians, largely accounts for our serious lack of full information about the actual functioning of the late T'ang government. The problem was, of course, compounded by the open hostility between the scholar–official historians and the eunuchs, who in at least one instance are known to have made strenuous efforts to have the record changed in their favor.

No example of a Record of Administrative Affairs survives.

---

25 P'ei Hsiu, who had served as a compiler in the Historiographical Office in Wen-tsung's reign, became chief minister either in the fourth month (according to *CTS* 188, p. 630) or in the seventh month (according to *HTS* 63, p. 1732; *TCTC* 249, p. 8051) of 852.
26 See *HTS* 182, p. 5371. This incident is not mentioned in P'ei Hsiu's *CTS* biography, *CTS* 177, pp. 4593–4.

7

The Daily Calendar
(*Jih-li*)

The Daily Calendar (*Jih-li*) was a chronological record prepared as a first stage in correlating and combining into a single work the information from the Court Diary, the Record of Administrative Affairs, and other sources previously mentioned, in preparation for the eventual compilation of the definitive Veritable Record of each reign. The compilation of this type of Daily Calendar was, however, a late development, having been begun only in 805, following a suggestion by the then director of the National History, Wei Chih-i.[1]

We know little about the official *Jih-li* although a small part of that for the T'ien-yu period (904–7), the *T'ien-yu jih-li*, survived into the Southern Sung.[2] Those of the reigns from Hsiuan-tsung on seem to have been lost early on. When in 891, after the Huang Ch'ao rebellion, P'ei T'ing-yü was ordered to compile the Veritable Records for Hsiuan-tsung's reign, "not a single character survived of the *Ch'i-chü chu* and *Jih-li* of the preceding forty years."[3]

The question of the Daily Calendar is further complicated by the existence of a number of private works with the same title, *Jih-li* or the title "Calendar," *li*. A work that was apparently representative of this genre and was very widely read among the official class in the mid ninth century was the *Chiang-shih Jih-li* written by Chiang I (747–821), a compiler in the Historiographical Office under Te-tsung and Hsien-tsung. This was subsequently continued by his sons Chiang Hsi and

---

1 See the *Hui yao* as cited in *Yü hai* 47, p. 28a; *THY* 63, p. 1097; *TCTC* 236, p. 7621. The memorial was dated the sixth day of the ninth month, less than one month after Hsien-tsung's succession. The regnal title is wrongly given as "Chen-yüan" by *THY* 63. It should read "Yung-chen."

2 See *Yü hai* 47, p. 28a. This cites a passage from the *Chung-hsing Kuan-ko shu-mu* (compiled 1174) saying that one chapter of this work still survived, and that Ou-yang Hsiu had been of the opinion that, although it was incomplete, it was certainly a genuine T'ang text.

3 See P'ei T'ing-yü's preface to the *Tung-kuan tsou-chi* as cited in *CTW* 841, pp. 3b–4a.

Chiang Shen, who were also in turn appointed as official historians. Chiang I's *Chiu T'ang shu* biography[4] tells us that "In the capital it was said that there was no official family that did not possess its copy." Two other works of this type cited by Ssu-ma Kuang in the *Tzu-chih t'ung-chien k'ao-i* are the *Niu-Yang jih-li* by Liu K'o[5] and its continuation, the *Hsü Niu-Yang jih-li* by Huang-fu Sung,[6] which dealt with the factional struggles of the 820s and 830s.[7]

The reason why these *Jih-li* of individual authors became so influential in the ninth century may be that the original memorial of 805 by Wei Chih-i had suggested that *each* official historiographer should draw up his own individual *Jih-li*. These were to be collated, corrected, and verified at the Historiographical Office at the end of the month, and then sealed and locked away, inscribed with the historian's name, in preparation for the compilation of the Veritable Record. One of the reasons given for the proposal was that the historians had been accustomed to writing in their own homes, so that no copy existed in the Historiographical Office itself. The historiographers were now forbidden to keep their *Jih-li* in their private homes.[8] As in the case of the other products of official historians, with the single exception of the Court Diaries, this attempt at preserving confidentiality was a complete failure. The *Jih-li*, which circulated so freely under the names of individual historians, were presumably for the most part private copies of their original drafts.

T'ang li and Hsü T'ang li

The most famous and influential T'ang historical work with the title "calendar" was the *T'ang li* of Liu Fang, comprising forty chapters.[9] This

---

4 See *CTS* 149, p. 4029; *HTS* 132, p. 4535; *Yü hai* 47, p. 28a.
5 Cited in *TCTC* 242, p. 7823. See *HTS* 59, p. 1543, where it is listed among the "hsiao-shuo"; *Chih-chai shu-lu chieh-t'i* 7, p. 7a, where it appears among the "chuan-chi." It is said to have comprised a single chapter, and to have dealt with the affairs of Niu Seng-ju and Yang Yü-ch'ing. It is also said to have had a preface by Huang-fu Sung.
6 This work is not listed in the *HTS* bibliographical chapters.
7 Miao Ch'üan-sun (1844–1919) collected the extant quotations of these two works in his *Ou-hsiang ling-shih* (1896), but not enough remains to give any very clear picture of the works as a whole.
8 See *THY* 63, p. 1097.
9 On Liu Fang's *T'ang li*, see *HTS* 58, p. 1460; *Ch'ung-wen tsung-mu* 3, p. 8a; Chao Shih-wei, ed., *Chung-hsing Kuan-ko shu-lu chi-k'ao* 2, p. 7a–b; *Chün-chai tu-shu chih (Yüan-pen)* 2A, pp. 9b–10a (*Ch'ü-pen* 5, p. 10a); *Chih-chai shu-lu chieh-t'i* 4, p. 21b; *Yü hai* 47, p. 27a–b; *HTS* 132, pp. 4535–6. See also E. G. Pulleyblank "The *Tzyjyh Tongjiann Kaoyih* and the Sources for the History of the Period 730–763," *BSOAS* 13 (1950): 459–60. *Ch'ung-wen*

work was quite different from those already discussed. It was a full chronological history of the T'ang from Li Yüan's original uprising at T'ai-yuan to 778. It was the work of Liu Fang, a prominent official historian who served as a member of the Historiographical Office for forty or more years and had been responsible for the National History (*Kuo shih*) completed in 759–60. Briefly banished to Ch'ien-nan (modern Kweichow) in 760–2, he had met Hsüan-tsung's influential eunuch confidant Kao Li-shih, who was banished at the same time to the same area. Liu Fang learned from him many details of politics and palace affairs during Hsüan-tsung's reign, which he recorded and later incorporated into his privately compiled *T'ang li*, which was written during Tai-tsung's reign, and probably completed in the early 780s under Te-tsung.[10]

Liu Fang was not the only official historian to compile his own private chronicle history. His predecessors as compilers of the National History, Wu Ching and his own close friend Wei Shu, had both written similar works.[11] There was a preference for the chronological form of history (*pien-nien shih*) among many eighth-century scholars and historians, who preferred, for example, Hsün Yüeh's (148–209) *Han chi* over the more famous *Han shu* of Pan Ku (32–92), written in the composite form (*chi-chuan*) that later became obligatory for standard dynastic histories. Other late eighth- and early ninth-century writers compiled private histories of the T'ang in similar form.

Although after his brief banishment Liu Fang continued working in the Historiographical Office until Te-tsung's reign, he was never apparently involved in further work on the National History, but employed

---

tsung-mu 3, p. 8a, also lists as a separate work a *T'ang li mu-lu* in a single chapter. This is noted as missing in 1144. Ssu-ma Kuang, in the *k'ao-i* to *TCTC* 189, p. 5921, also cites a *T'ang li nien-tai chi*, which may also be connected with Liu Fang's work. The date of the completion of the original *T'ang li* is not known exactly. According to the *Chung-hsing Kuan-ko shu-lu* as cited in *Yü hai* 47, p. 27b, the *T'ang li* covered the history of the dynasty from Li Yüan's uprising in 617 until the eighth month of 778. The latest of the very numerous citations in Ssu-ma Kuang's *K'ao-i* is dated from the third month of 775. There is one isolated citation under the eighth month of 814, but this must come from the continuation, the *Hsü T'ang li*. See *TCTC* 239, p. 7705. By 814 Liu Fang himself had already been dead for about thirty years. The compilation of *T'ang li* must then have been completed in the early years of Te-tsung's reign, probably in the early 780s. On the quotations preserved in the *Tzu-chih t'ung-chien k'ao-i*, see Taniguchi Akio, "Kyū Tō sho to Shiji Tsugan kōi hikareru Tōreki ni tsuite no ichi shitan," *Kagoshima joshi tanki daigaku kiyō* 15 (1980): 85–90.

10 See *CTS* 149, p. 4030; *HTS*, 132, p. 4536.
11 See for Wei Shu's work *HTS* 58, p. 1461: for Wu Ching's book *HTS* 132, p. 4529; *HTS* 58, p. 1461.

on other projects. Hence the knowledge gained from Kao Li-shih was never incorporated in the official record, but in his private chronological history.[12]

The *T'ang li*, at the time of its completion, was criticized by contemporary scholars, especially by the Confucians, who claimed that Liu Fang's use of moral judgment ("praise and blame") was unacceptable.[13] Nevertheless, the book soon won wide acceptance. In the early years of Hsiuan-tsung's reign, the emperor ordered an official continuation to be undertaken by the Historiographical Office. When in the eleventh century Ssu-ma Kuang produced his *Tzu-chih t'ung-chien*, it was one of the major sources he and his collaborators used. His textual notes, the *Tzu-chih t'ung-chien k'ao-i*, cite it as an authority no less than 167 times, more often than any work except *Chiu T'ang shu* and the various *Shih-lu*. It is cited frequently to resolve differences in dating between the *Chiu T'ang shu* and the Veritable Records, but also on a host of substantial issues. Not surprisingly, its dates usually coincide with those given in *Chiu T'ang shu*, for this incorporated verbatim the National History Liu Fang had also written.[14] There is also a report that it was widely used by the compilers of *Hsin T'ang shu*.[15] The *T'ang li* not only remained an authoritative account of the T'ang down to Tai-tsung's reign in China. By the end of the ninth century it had been taken to Japan, where it was used as a source by several historians during the Heian period.[16]

---

12 Even this did not include all he learned from Kao Li-shih. In Li Te-yü's *Tz'u Liu-shih chiu wen* (preface 834) are recorded a number of incidents about which he had heard from Liu Fang's son, the ritual expert Liu Mien. His father had omitted these stories from the *T'ang li* because they were either too dangerous or were accounts of supernatural events. On the *Tz'u Liu-shih chiu-wen*, see *HTS* 58, p. 1468, which lists it in a single chapter. It was cited as a source in Ssu-ma Kuang's *Tzu-chih t'ung-chien k'ao-i* on four occasions all relating to events in Hsüan-tsung's reign from 713–56. A probably abridged version of the book survives and is included in a great many *ts'ung-shu*, in some cases under the title *Ming-huang shih-ch'i shih*. The best edition is that of Yeh Te-hui (1864–1927), accompanied by text critical notes (*k'ao-i*) in a separate chapter, which is included in his *T'ang K'ai-yüan hsiao-shuo liu chung* (1911) and in the *Tzu-yüan hsien sheng ch'üan shu* (1935).

13 See *HTS* 132, p. 4535.

14 See for example the sample of early T'ang cases cited by Taniguchi Akio, "*Kyū Tōsho to Shiji Tsugan kōi hikareru Tōreki ni tsuite no ichi shitan*," pp. 85–90.

15 See Pulleyblank, "The *Tzyjyh Tongjiann Kaoyih*," p. 460, n. 4.

16 On the importance of the *T'ang li* in Japan, see Ota Shōjirō, "*Tōreki ni tsuite*," in *Yamada Takao tsuioku shigaku gogaku ronshū* (Tokyo, 1963), pp. 99–128, an extremely thorough and well-documented study that assembles more than thirty fragments of the *T'ang li* culled from a wide variety of medieval Japanese sources. See also Uematsu Yasukazu, "*Tōreki to Tōroku*," in *Iwai Hakase koki-kinen Denseki ronshū* (Tokyo, 1961), pp. 284–90.

Hsü T'ang li[17]

By the mid ninth century the *T'ang li* was apparently so influential a model that Emperor Hsiuan-tsung (846–59) ordered a continuation of Liu Fang's private history as a state-sponsored project, undertaken by the Historiographical Office under the direction of the director of the National History. It continued Liu Fang's history down to the death of Hsien-tsung in 820 in thirty chapters.[18] The director of the project was Ts'ui Kuei-ts'ung, who had become ad hominem chief minister and concurrent director of the National History in 850. He was himself an experienced historian who had served as a compiler in the Historiographical Office in Wen-tsung's reign. The actual compilers were Wei Ao, Li Hsün, Chiang Chieh, Chang Yen-yüan, and Ts'ui Yüan, who were ordered to divide the period between them and continue the record to the end of Hsien-tsung's reign. Wei Ao is known to have been appointed a compiler in the Historiographical Office and a Han-lin scholar by Chou Ch'ih (under whom he had previously served in the provinces) when Chou became a chief minister in the fifth month of 848. Chiang Chieh was also a compiler, and a member of a notable family of historians. He was a son of Chiang I, the author of the *Chiang-shih jih-li* mentioned earlier. The others are unknown.[19]

Like the *T'ang li* itself, the *Hsü T'ang li* survived into the Sung period. However, it seems never to have acquired an equal reputation. Ssu-ma Kuang only cites it once, in an entry for 814, and does so under the title of *T'ang li*.[20]

17 See *HTS* 58, p. 1460; *THY* 63, p. 1098; *TFYK* 556, p. 25b; *CTS* 176, p. 4573; *Yü hai* 47, p. 27b; *HTS* 132, p. 4535; *CTS* 18B, p. 632; *CTS* 163, p. 4262; *THY* 36, pp. 662–3.
18 Its length is variously given as thirty chapters in *CTS* 176, p. 4573; *THY* 63, p. 1098, *TFYK* 556, p. 25b; as twenty chapters in *Hui yao* as cited in *Yü hai* 47, p. 27b; or as twenty-two chapters in *CTS* 18B, p. 629, *HTS* 58, p. 1460; and Chao Shih-wei, ed., *Chung-hsing Kuan-ko shu-mu chi-k'ao* 2, p. 7a–b; *Chih-chai shu-lu chieh-t'i* 4, p. 22a. According to the *Chung-hsing Kuan-ko shu-mu*, as cited by *Yü hai* 47, p. 27b, a continuation of Liu Fang's *T'ang li* had previously been undertaken by Ts'ui Hsüan but had never been completed. This account may well result from a confusion with Ts'ui Hsüan having, when serving as chief minister in 853, presented to the throne the *Hsü Hui yao*, the continuation of Su Mien's *Hui yao* that had been compiled by Yang Shao-fu, Hsüeh Feng, Ts'ui Yüan, and Cheng Yen.
19 See *HTS* 58, p. 1640; *HTS* 132, p. 4535.
20 See *TCTC* 839, p. 7705, where it is cited under eighth month of 814, by which date Liu Fang was probably dead for almost thirty years.

8
Biographies

The largest part of any Standard History is taken up by *lieh-chuan* – literally, "connected traditions" or "connected accounts" – a section that is largely made up of biographical entries on notables of the period, but that also includes accounts of foreign peoples and their relations with the dynasty. Unlike the monographs (*chih*) and tables (*piao*), which might or might not be included, the *lieh-chuan* were, together with with the basic annals, a fundamental section of any history in the "composite" annal-biography (*chi-chuan*) form.

There is already a good deal of literature, including two previous studies of my own, dealing with the problems and special features of Chinese biography, in particular with those relating to the biographies included in the histories.[1] This is not the appropriate place to go into further detail on these important general issues in Chinese historiography, but a number of points need to be repeated as background before discussing the way in which the biographies that formed such an important component of T'ang official historical writing came into being.

First, the *lieh-chuan* chapters in a Chinese history in the composite form were not designed simply as a succession of separate biographies of individuals, each focusing on the personality and life of the individual per se, even though the modern reader often uses these sections of the histories as a convenient substitute for a biographical dictionary of the period. The *lieh-chuan* were part of the larger plan of the history, designed to flesh out with illustrative examples the bare bones of the chronicle provided by the Basic Annals and to give the reader details about a representative sample of people who not only played important

---

1 See Twitchett, "Chinese Biographical Writing," in Beasley and Pulleyblank, *Historians of China and Japan*, pp. 95–114; "Problems of Chinese Biography," Wright and Twitchett, *Confucian Personalities*, pp. 24–39; Peter Olbricht, "Die Biographie in China," *Saeculum* 8 (1957): 224–35. Also see Burton Watson, *Ssu-ma Ch'ien, Grand Historian of China* (New York, 1958), pp. 120–30.

roles in the events of the period but would, taken together, exemplify and illuminate the overall character of the era as the historian conceived it.

To this end, apart from a few exceptionally important figures the biographies are linked together in groups. Some of them are included in "collective biographies," explicitly so labeled; such groups as empresses, the sons of individual emperors, imperial relatives by marriage, eunuchs, good officials, oppressive officials, loyal and righteous officials, exemplars of filiality and friendship, Confucian scholars, literary figures, recluses, and model women. Each of these chapters or groups of chapters begins with a preface outlining the significance of the group as a whole and consists mostly of short notices dealing with figures who were noteworthy in this particular function but who played no part, or at best minor roles, in public affairs. The biographies of politically more important persons are also grouped together by category, although the chapters in which they appear are not specially titled: The chief ministers of a given reign, financial experts, generals, and officials involved in scholarship or ritual will be gathered together by period in such a way as both to express an implicit judgment on their collective character and to contrast the ways in which as individuals they fulfilled their primary role. These ideas are summarized and made explicit in the historian's "comment" appended to each chapter and encapsulated in highly formal terms in his "judgment" (*tsan*).[2]

Second, the biographies included in the *lieh-chuan* were not biographies in our sense at all. They made no attempt at a full portrait of their subject, or even at a rounded account of all his activities. They described an individual's performance of a specific function or role. They were part of a larger political history, and the individuals they describe were included in that history either because they exemplified some form

2 At the end of most chapters of *CTS* there are two summary comments. The first, "the comment," is introduced by "The historian says..." (*Shih-ch'en yüeh*) or "The historian's opinion is..." (*Shih-ch'en lun-yüeh*), very occasionally giving the historian's name. The second, written in four-character phrases in an archaic lapidary style modeled on the *Book of Documents* and usually rhymed, is entitled *tsan*. This term is often translated as "eulogy," but I prefer to adopt Burton Watson's rendering, "judgment," because the *tsan* as often expresses criticism as it does praise. The "historian's comments" are modeled directly on those in *Shih-chi* where they are introduced by "The Grand Historian says..." (*T'ai-shih kung yüeh*), but similar remarks are also interspersed in the much earlier *Tso chuan* and *Kuo yü* where they begin "The gentleman says..." (*Chün-tzu yüeh*). The term *tsan* originated with Pan Ku's *Han shu*. (See Watson, *Ssu-ma Ch'ien, Grand Historian of China*, p. 132.)

There are no "historian's comments" either to the monographs (*CTS* 21–50), or to the "collective biographies" (*CTS* 51–52; 183–93). These chapters have prefaces in which the historians make their opinions clear. The monographs also have no "judgments."

of official activity or because the historian could give in the context of the subject's biography a coherent articulated account of some train of events that would have been impossible to accommodate in the strict chronological framework of the basic annals, or because their lives added telling detail to or illuminated some aspect of the history of the dynastic polity. The people selected as the subjects for a biographical entry qualified either because their careers were of political importance in the broadest sense, or because they had performed some notable function related to the political order, or because they had contributed to the moral order that was believed to be the outward manifestation of the fundamental ethical character of the regime. The Confucian scholars and literary men who were included, for example, provided evidence of the intellectual climate of the time, which for a traditional Confucian historian was directly related to its government and served as an indicator of the moral qualities of its ruler.

Third, the *lieh-chuan* were considered as of secondary importance when contrasted with the annals (*pen-chi*). Historians writing about these matters in T'ang times repeatedly made the analogy between the annals and the Spring and Autumn Annals (*Ch'un ch'iu*) on the one hand, and between the biographies and the three commentaries to the Spring and Autumn Annals (*Ku-liang, Kung-yang, and Tso chuan*) on the other – with the obvious implication that the annals were of primary importance, the biographies of secondary standing. The difference was underlined by a difference in form: the annals, like the Spring and Autumn Annals, were "chronological" history (*pien-nien*); the biographies, like the *Tso chuan*, were "causally linked" history (*lieh-shih*).[3]

Many T'ang historians, moreover, distrusted the composite annal-biography form of history altogether, preferring, for example, Hsün Yüeh's purely chronological *Han chi* over Pan Ku's composite *Han shu* as an account of the western Han period. In several cases they themselves wrote annalistic histories similar to Hsün Yüeh's work as replacements or alternatives for the Standard Histories of various periods,[4] including

3 The most coherent account of those attitudes by a T'ang author is in Liu Chih-chi's *Shih t'ung*. See *Shih t'ung* 6, pp. 46–51 "lieh-chuan," esp. p. 46.
4 For chronicle-style histories of earlier dynasties written by T'ang authors, see the appropriate sections of *CTS* 46, pp. 1990–3; *HTS* 58, pp. 1459–61; *Ch'ung-wen tsung-mu* 3, pp. 6a–8a. Three well-known examples (all long since lost) that survived into the Sung were (1) the *Wei tien* in thirty chapters by Yüan Hsing-ch'ung (653–729), a chronological history of the Northern (Topa) Wei (*CTS* 102, p. 3177; *Ch'ung wen tsung-mu* 3, p. 7a–b); (2) The *San-kuo tien-lüeh* in thirty chapters by Ch'iu Yüeh (d. 713), a chronological history of the regional states of the late sixth century before the emergence of Sui (*CTS* 190 B, p. 5015; *Ch'ung wen tsung-mu* 3, pp. 7b–8a, according to which, by 1131, chapters 21–30 were lost); and (3) the *Chin Ch'un-ch'iu lüeh* in twenty chapters by Tu Yen-yeh

the T'ang itself.[5] Such an attitude also implied a negative assessment of the relative value of biographies. This meant that it was thought necessary to devote less care and less serious critical attention to the source material that went into the compilation of biographies and to their writing than was required in the case of the basic annals.

So much for the general rationale behind the *lieh-chuan*, which formed such a large part of of every major history; for example, they occupy three-quarters of the chapters of the existing *Chiu T'ang shu*. We must now turn to the more immediate problems. What was the source material upon which the official historians based their biographies? How and on what criteria did they decide who was eligible for inclusion? How were the biographies they selected finally edited and incorporated into the official record?

Later dynasties, beginning with the Later T'ang, not only maintained an ongoing process of compiling and editing biographies designed for the eventual dynastic history of their period but also assembled collections of biographies that were sometimes published as separate works.[6]

(dates unknown: *Chün-chai tu-shu chi* says he was a corrector in the Imperial Library under the Sui, not T'ang; his name is given as Tu Kuang-yeh in *Chung-hsing Kuan-ko shu-mu* as cited in *WHTK* 193, p. 1631b). *CTS* 46, p. 1992; *HTS* 58, p. 1460; *Ch'ung wen tsung-mu* 3, p. 7a, which gives its length as thirty chapters; *Chih-chai shu-lu chieh-t'i* 4, p. 20b–21a; *Chün-chai tu-shu chih* (fu chih) 5A, p. 17a, which omits *lüeh* from the title; *WHTK* 193, p. 1631b. Chang Ta-su, an official historian under Kao-tsung wrote a *Sui hou lüeh* in ten chapters (*HTS* 58, p. 1460). The official historiographer Wu Ching also wrote short histories of the Liang, Southern Ch'i, Ch'en, Northern Chou, and Sui. See *CTS* 102, p. 3182. *HTS* 58, p. 1458, lists these under "Standard Histories" but this is certainly wrong, as they were far too short to be works in this form, and they were almost certainly written in chronicle form.

5 Several prominent official historians wrote histories of the T'ang in chronicle form: Wu Ching wrote a *T'ang Ch'un-ch'iu* in thirty chapters (*CTS* 102, p. 3185; *HTS* 58, p. 1461); Wei Shu a *T'ang Ch'un-ch'iu* also in thirty chapters (*CTS* 102, p. 3185; *HTS* 58, p. 1461); Liu Fang a *T'ang li* in forty chapters covering the dynasty down to 779 (*HTS* 58, p. 1460; *HTS* 132, pp. 4535–6). The last named survived into the Sung and was used as an important source by Ssu-ma Kuang in writing *Tzu-chih t'ung-chien*. Even under the T'ang its standing was such that under Hsiuan-tsung a continuation entitled *Hsü T'ang li* was undertaken as an official project of the Historiographical Office and completed in 851. See Chapter 7 for details. There were also similar works written by scholars not connected with the Historiographical Office; Lu Ch'ang-yüan (d. 798) wrote a *T'ang Ch'un-ch'iu* in sixty chapters (*HTS* 58, p. 1461); Ch'en Yüeh a massive *T'ang t'ung-chi* in one hundred chapters, which depicted the whole dynasty down to the end of Mu-tsung's reign in 824 (*HTS* 58, 1461; *Ch'ung wen tsung-mu* 3, p. 8a; *Chih-chai shu-lu chieh-t'i* 4, p. 22a, by which time only the first forty chapters, ending in 692, survived; *WHTK* 193, p. 1632a). Chai Lu (d. 861) also wrote a *T'ang-ch'ao nien-tai chi* in ten chapters (*HTS* 58, p. 1461; *Ch'ung wen tsung-mu* 3, p. 8b, which notes that it was lost by 1131).

6 The first collection of this sort seems to have been the *Chuang-tsung lieh-chuan* or [*Hou*] *T'ang kung-ch'en lieh-chuan* in thirty chapters presented to the throne in 934. See *TFYK* 557, p. 7a. See also Wang Gung-wu, "The *Chiu Wu-tai shih* and History Writing during the Five Dynasties," pp. 1–22, esp. 10–12.

This was not done under the T'ang. The individual biographies in T'ang times were written by the compilers or assistants of the Historiographical Office usually, but not always, soon after the subject's death and were subsequently incorporated into the Veritable Records, normally being inserted at the end of the month during which the individual had died. The biographies included in the Veritable Records were thus written and inserted as separate individual items, not grouped together in categories. This rearrangement would be done later, first when they were selected and arranged to fit into the overall design of the National History, and again when eventually they were incorporated into the dynastic history. Some historians did write sets of biographies, grouped for didactic reasons, but did so as private scholars,[7] not as part of their official duties.

There is no question that the members of the Historiographical Office wrote the final version of these biographies, but as with the other sections of the history, they did not begin writing ab initio. They based their work on existing documentation. For the chronological accounts of events that made up most of the Veritable Records, the historians could depend on the products of the bureaucratic apparatus already described; on the Daily Calendar, produced in their own office after 805; and on the Court Diaries and the Records of Administrative Affairs – all of which were already compiled in chronic form – and they could supplement these from the wide variety of routine reports forwarded to the Historiographical Office by various ministries. For the biographies, they were forced to rely on sources over which there was much less official control.

In theory the Historiographical Office, when writing the biography of an official, had access to a mass of detailed information. The Board of Civil Office (*Li-pu*) kept full personal dossiers on all serving officials, which gave details of their families, listed their methods of entry onto the roll of officials, gave all their successive appointments, and included all their annual assessments of performance in office. On the death of a high-ranking member of the bureaucracy, the Department of Merit Assessments (*K'ao-kung ssu*), one of the four subordinate bureaus of the Board of Civil Office, had the responsibility of receiving and verifying an

---

7 For example Chiang I wrote a seventy-chapter record of T'ang chief ministers, *Ta T'ang tsai-fu lu*; sets of biographies of the scholars of the future T'ai-tsung's Wen-hsüeh Kuan Academy, *Ch'in-fu shih-pa hsüeh-shih*; of the twenty-four heroic ministers of T'ai-tsung whose portraits were displayed in the Ling-yen Pavilion, *Ling-yen ko kung-ch'en* and a set of biographies of historians, *Shih-kuan chuan*. See *CTS* 149, p. 4028; *HTS* 58, p. 1467.

Account of Conduct (*hsing-chuang*), a sort of extended curriculum vitae for the deceased, and forwarding this to the Historiographical Office.[8]

These Accounts of Conduct were of the utmost importance in the writing of official biographies, and it is thus essential to understand exactly what they were, and how they came to be written. An Account of Conduct was not simply a bid for posthumous fame, a claim to have the deceased's life included in the official history. It served a double purpose. Of perhaps more immediate consequence, it was also the evidence presented to the authorities in the hope that the deceased might be granted canonization with a posthumous designation (*shih*) or a posthumous office of high rank. These would give him an officially recognized posthumous standing that would be reflected both upon his family and upon his lifetime associates, and might also bring more tangible rewards in the shape of the right of his descendants to hereditary entry onto the roll of officials.[9]

The Account of Conduct and the justification statement requesting the granting of a posthumous designation (*shih-i*) based on it were composed by neither the historians nor the staff of the Department of Merit Assessments. The Account of Conduct was supposed to be written either by the deceased's sons or other junior relatives, by his disciples, or by his former official subordinates – all of whom were closely acquainted with him. They were expected to send the Account of Conduct to the authorities within a year of his death, and preferably before his interment.[10] The Department of Merit Assessments then examined the Account of Conduct and verified its contents from the records of the Board of Civil Office.[11] They had to complete their scrutiny within a month, and to ensure that the Account of Conduct should "only indicate the facts and record the truth, in straightforward words. The traces of both good and evil should all be set down in accordance with the facts." If the Account of Conduct failed to meet these criteria, it was to be rejected. If it was accepted, they were to forward the document both to the Historiographical Office and to either the Court of Rituals (*Li yüan*) or the erudit scholars (*Po-shih*) of the Court of Imperial Sacrifices

---

8 On the Department of Merit Assessments, see *TLT* 2, pp. 45a–55a; *CTS* 43, pp. 1822–4; *TT* 23, p. 136a–b; *HTS* 46, pp. 1190–2 (Rotours, *Fonctionnaires*, vol. 1, pp. 59–71).

9 See the various documents included in *THY* 79, p. 1455; *THY* 80, pp. 1487–9.

10 This was according to strict classical precedents for the granting of a posthumous designation. See Tjan Tjoe Som, *Po hu t'ung* (Leiden, 1949, 1952), vol. 2, p. 369. On the canonization of deceased officials under the T'ang, see McMullen, *State and Scholars in T'ang China*, pp. 11, 19–20.

11 See *TLT* 2, pp. 50b–51a; *THY* 79, p. 1455.

(*T'ai-ch'ang ssu*).[12] The latter then had a further month to determine an appropriate posthumous designation, should the deceased be found eligible for canonization. Their decision was incorporated in a statement of justification (*shih-i*), which was normally written by one of the erudit scholars. For the final decision,[13] the case was presented to the Central Bureau (*Tu-sheng*) of the Department of State Affairs (*Shang-shu sheng*).[14] When an appropriate posthumous designation for the deceased had been determined the Court of Imperial Sacrifices was expected to notify the Historiographical Office, enclosing a copy of their statement of justification (*shih-i*).[15]

The Department of Merit Assessments was not only responsible for examining Accounts of Conduct but also for verifying the contents of all private funerary writings and memorial inscriptions, family biographies (*chia-chuan*), the texts for memorial stelae (*pei*), funerary odes (*sung*), and eulogies (*lei*).[16] The department was a small office, with a very small staff of only six ranked officials, a principal secretary (*lang-chung*), two

---

12 The Court of Rituals (*Li yüan*) is not mentioned as a formal office in the descriptions of the organization of the Court of Imperial Sacrifices in *TLT* 14, *CTS* 44, *TT* 25, or *HTS* 48. It is however mentioned frequently in memorials and edicts concerning the granting of posthumous designations dating from the late eighth and ninth centuries, when various positions within the court were established or discontinued. These positions were not ranked offices, but were concurrent duties fulfilled by officials holding their substantive offices elsewhere, like those in the Historiographical Office or in the various academies. See *THY* 65, pp. 1135–7. According to an item dated 854, by that time the *Li yüan* was virtually controlled by the four erudit scholars (*Po-shih*) of the Court of Imperial Sacrifices. See *THY* 65, p. 1137. These very influential experts on ritual and precedent were responsible, according to *TLT* 14, pp. 16b–17b; *TT* 25, pp. 147c–148a; *TT* 104, p. 551a; *CTS* 44, p. 1873; and *HTS* 48, p. 1241, for the selection of appropriate posthumous designations.

13 The granting and choice of a posthumous designation was often hotly disputed. The sections on posthumous designations (*shih*) in *T'ung tien* (*TT* 104, pp. 551a–552c) and in *T'ang hui yao* (*THY* 79, pp. 1455–80, 1487) cite many examples of objections (*po-i*) being raised by members of different offices against a posthumous designation proposed by the Court of Imperial Sacrifices, and the Central Bureau of Department of State Affairs would often ask the Court of Imperial Sacrifices to reconsider, or to offer a second opinion (*ch'ung-i*), which was usually written by another of the erudit scholars. *T'ang wen ts'ui* 44 includes a number of statements of justification (*shih-i*) cited in full. In some cases – for example, those of Kuo Chih-yün (*TWT*, pp. 730–2) and of Lü Yin (*TWT*, pp. 726–9) – it gives the original brief, an objection, and the erudit's reply to the objection.

14 See *THY* 80, pp. 1488–9. These rules had been established by an edict in 763, and were incorporated in the Regulations (*Ko*) of 791. They were repeated by edicts in 810 and again in 819, in which year the whole system seems to have come under close scrutiny.

15 See *THY* 80, pp. 1488–9.

16 See *TT* 23, p. 136a, according to which this responsibility was laid upon the Department of Merit Assessments in 670. See also *HTS* 46, p. 1190. Neither *TLT* 2 nor *CTS* 43, both describing the situation around 737, mentions this.

under secretaries (*yüan-wai lang*), and three low-ranking business managers (*chu-shih*) with a clerical staff of less than fifty. Their responsibilities, however, were extremely onerous and extended far beyond the scrutiny of Accounts of Conduct and funerary memorial writings. They were responsible primarily for the annual assessments of conduct in office (*k'ao*) of all the seventeen thousand members of the bureaucracy and, until the 736 reform that transferred responsibility to the Board of Rites, also for the conduct of the official examinations. In the context of these far more pressing duties, the scrutiny of Accounts of Conduct cannot have been more than a very cursory affair, probably entrusted to one of the office's clerks, for the department must have had hundreds of Accounts of Conduct and epitaphs submitted for its inspection each year. They did the best they could to ensure that the Accounts of Conduct and these other funerary writings did not make any errors in describing the deceased's official career, or make any unfounded and improper claims on behalf of their subject, and they subsequently forwarded these documents to the Historiographical Office.

There were strict formal rules governing the persons for whom Accounts of Conduct should be compiled. Their preparation was mandatory only for all serving officials of the third rank and above, and for titular officials holding the first and second ranks.[17] Accounts of Conduct were thus automatically compiled only for the tiny superelite of officials who achieved the third rank – about two hundred officials out of a total of seventeen thousand in the whole bureaucracy at any one time. The formal rule thus covered only a small fraction of the bureaucracy, even when allowance is made for the rather widespread granting of high-ranking nominal and honorific offices. However, it is clear, for example, from a memorial presented in 819 that Accounts of Conduct, while required only in the case of high-ranking officials, might also be prepared and submitted for lower-ranked officials, and even for persons without office and of lowly status if it was considered that they were in some way exemplary or had some special claim to distinction.[18]

In the case of high-ranking officials the persons officially responsible for compiling the Account of Conduct were described as the deceased's "assistants" (*tso-li*), a term that was perhaps deliberately vague, and

---

17 See *THY* 79, p. 1455; *TLT* 2, p. 50b (commentary). This passage probably derives from the Statutes or Ordinances. In *THY* it is introduced as "The old system was..." (*chiu chih*), which usually indicates a rule that had been incorporated in the *Wu-te* Statutes of 624. The *TLT* citation is probably from the Statutes of 719.
18 See *THY* 80, p. 1488. The same exception is clearly envisioned in *TLT* 2, p. 51a.

probably included any of his subordinates in office.[19] This rule, however, never seems to have been strictly observed. We know from a memorial submitted in 810 by the Department of Merit Assessments that Accounts of Conduct were being written by persons other than the deceased's "assistants."[20] In the case of persons of low rank or of men without office, the Account of Conduct was composed by his sons or younger brothers, by other family members, by disciples, by former associates, or even by the local officials of his home district. Moreover, the Account of Conduct might never pass through the scrutiny of the Department of Merit Assessments at all. In an edict of 737 Hsüan-tsung ordered the sons and grandsons of deceased officials who had accomplished noteworthy services since the beginning of his reign to draw up accounts of their conduct, and send these in directly to the Historiographical Office.[21]

These details would suggest that the compilation of Accounts of Conduct was by no means so rigidly controlled as might at first appear. But whether the rules were observed or not, and whatever the individual circumstances, the Account of Conduct was never drawn up by an objective official or by an official historian but was written by somebody with a personal, official, or family relationship with, and intimate knowledge of, the deceased. It was in normal cases, but not always, checked by the Department of Merit Assessments and finally delivered to the Historiographical Office, where, if its subject was declared worthy of inclusion in the historical record, it became the main source material for the historian responsible for producing his official biography.

Although the Historiographical Office used them as source material, Accounts of Conduct, like epitaphs, were not considered by the historians as reliable, authoritative evidence to be considered on the same footing as the contents of the Court Diary. As early as the beginning of the eighth century Liu Chih-chi criticized the National History (*T'ang shu*) compiled by Niu Feng-chi for having been based largely on unreliable Accounts of Conduct.[22] The situation remained unsatisfactory throughout the T'ang period and beyond. A memorial submitted by the

---

19 The term *tso-li* is used in *TLT* 2, p. 50b. However in *TT* 104, p. 551a, in *THY* 79, p. 1455, and in a memorial dated 810 cited in *THY* 80, p. 1488, the term is written *tso-shih*. A memorial dated 819 also cited in *THY* 80, p. 1488, uses the term *ku-li*. All these terms are clearly not references to specific officials but mean "former subordinates" or "former employees." See Twitchett, "Chinese biographical writing," p. 104, n. 23.

20 See *THY* 80, p. 1488.

21 *TTCLC* 81, p. 468, edict dated fifth day of the fifth month of 737.

22 See *Shih t'ung* 12, p. 373.

historians under the Later T'ang in 933 succinctly summarizes their misgivings:

The great majority of Accounts of Conduct are written by disciples and former subordinates (of the deceased). They contain a great deal of meaningless ornament and literary flourishes. We request that Accounts of Conduct submitted in the future shall be in all cases straightforward accounts of real achievements, and should not be empty ornament and flowery style.[23]

Nor were these problems of florid ornament and lack of substance confined to the Accounts of Conduct themselves: They also affected the biographies written for the Veritable Records that were based on them. In 812 Emperor Hsien-tsung complained that the biographies in the Veritable Record of Su-tsung, which he had been reading, were "all empty words and baseless praise," and he ordered his own historians to keep to the facts and avoid this sort of literary embellishment.[24]

The problems were not simply stylistic. Many epitaphs and Accounts of Conduct not only were exercises in florid composition but also incorporated conventional fictitious incidents and actions designed to show the deceased in a model role.[25] Many of these were quite unfounded in fact. The following memorial presented in the fourth month of 819 by the famous writer Li Ao, then a compiler in the Historiographical Office,[26] gives us a vivid, if perhaps somewhat exaggerated, picture of the problems:

I your subject, without possessing any ability, have received by error the duty of wielding the brush in the Historiographical Office, with the writing of the record as my responsibility. The duties of the historian are to encourage good and to reprove evil, to express opinions in just speech with a straight brush, to record the merit and virtue of our divine dynastic house, to write down the deeds and accomplishments of the loyal and sage [ministers], to make a record of the shameful conduct of evildoers and sycophants, that may be handed down for ever.

---

23 See *WTHY* 18, p. 304.
24 See *THY* 64, p. 1109.
25 This problem was actually covered by an article in the Statutes on Mourning and Funeral Rites (*Sang-tsang ling*). See *Po-shih liu-t'ieh shih-lei chi* 19, p. 23b; *Po-K'ung liu-t'ieh* 66, p. 14b, which reads "The texts of all memorial inscriptions (*pei-chieh*) should be factual records. They must not be adulterated by the addition of laudatory embellishment." Cf. Niida Noboru, *Tōryō shūi* (Tokyo, 1933), p. 832. However, little notice was taken of this law.
26 See Li Ao, *Li Wen-kung chi* (*SPTK* edition, Shanghai, 1936) 10, pp. 75a–77b; *CTW* 634, pp. 6a–8b. *THY* 64, p. 1110; *TFYK* 559, pp. 11a–12a; and *TPYL* 604, pp. 1b–2a, give slightly abbreviated versions. The memorial is dated only in *THY*. *TFYK* gives Li Ao's rank as erudit scholar in the Imperial University and concurrently compiler in the Historiographical Office.

I submit that it is now fifteen years since Your Majesty came to the throne. In the first year of the reign Hsia-chou was pacified: In the second year Shu was pacified and [Liu] P'i executed: In the third year Chiang-tung was pacified and [Li] Ch'i executed. Chang Mao-chao subsequently gained I and Ting: In the fifth year Shih Hsien-ch'eng was captured and control was regained over Tse, Lu, Hsing, and Ming prefectures. In the seventh year T'ien Hung-cheng came and resumed regular tribute from the six prefectures of Wei-po province. In the twelfth year Huai-hsi was pacified and [Wu] Yüan-chi executed: In the thirteenth year Wang Ch'eng-tsung [once again] presented the tax revenues from Te and Ti prefectures, while the Board of Civil Office again made appointments to Ts'ang and Ching prefectures: In the fourteenth year Tzu-Ch'ing was pacified, Li Shih-tao executed, and control regained over twelve prefectures. For military successes based on divine policy, there has been no monarch to equal Your Majesty in restoring his dynasty since ancient times; yet no veritable record of Your surpassing virtue and great accomplishments has been written since the beginning of the Yuan-ho period,[27] and the historians have not yet recorded either those loyal subjects and sage ministers whose reputation and virtue make them exceedingly worthy to serve as examples, or those rebels and bandits whose infamous behavior is equally worthy to stand as a warning. The historians have simply omitted these and not yet written them. Your servant truly fears [the consequences of] this, and therefore without making any assessment of his own capabilities wishes to force himself to repair this lack.

Now the traces of individual men's lives, unless they be extremely good, or excessively evil, are something that ordinary people have no means of knowing about. The old rule was that [the historians] interviewed other persons to inquire [about their subjects], and took the Accounts of Conduct or the justification statements written in support of posthumous canonization for the deceased and used these as source material on which they might rely.

However, those who nowadays compose "Accounts of Conduct," if they are not actual disciples [of the deceased] are his former subordinates. There is none of them who does not falsely interpolate examples of his benevolence and righteousness, his observance of propriety and his wisdom, or tell lies about his loyalty, respectfulness, graciousness, and kindness. In some cases in speaking of their grand virtues and great achievements they exaggerate them and make them even more glorious; in others they represent their adherence to the correct way and their straight opinions as though even after their death they would be incorruptible, and never tell the facts in a straightforward way. Thus good and evil become confused, and cannot be clearly perceived.

Those like Hsü Ching-tsung, Li I-fu and Li Lin-fu were all evil subjects, yet if their disciples and former subordinates had been allowed to compose accounts of their conduct, they would not have pointed to the true facts, but would falsely have added that they had followed the way, and had been loyal and trustworthy,

27 This is evidence that, even as late as the early ninth century the idea that a Veritable Record might be written for a reigning monarch was not to be considered inappropriate.

72

so that they would have been ranked in place of such as Fang Hsüan-ling, Wei Cheng, or P'ei Yen, who truly accomplished great things.

They do this not because they are intentionally mendacious, but only because they wish to give an empty reputation to those from whom they once received favors.

Moreover those who compose these texts, are not in the category of true Confucian disciples or writers like [Ssu-ma] Ch'ien or [Yang] Hsiung: They devote themselves to ornament, forgetting the truth. They drown in verbiage, and abandon principle. Thus in their composition they lose the ancient style of the six canonical books, while in their recording of events they cannot produce true records like the work of historian [Ssu-ma] Ch'ien. If this is not the case, then their language is so mean and crude that they are unable to express themselves fully. Because of this the facts [they record] lose authority, while the [mode of] expression destroys the [underlying] principle, and thus the Accounts of Conduct are unfit to be accepted as credible. Were we to ensure that in dealing with affairs [their writers] wrote the truth, and did not embellish it with empty words, then men would know what was true and what was false. If this were so, then even if disciples and former subordinates wrote [the Accounts of Conduct] they could not embroider them by adding untrue incidents designed to show the subjects' goodness or virtue.

I now request that those composing Accounts of Conduct shall be required not to make false records of instances of benevolence, righteousness, observance of propriety, wisdom, loyalty, respectfulness, graciousness, and gentleness, or of supreme virtue of great achievements, correct speech, and correct conduct, [nor to couch these] in luxuriant compositions that cannot achieve credibility. They should only indicate facts and record the truth, straightforwardly writing down their words. The traces of good and evil should all be recorded in accordance with the facts, so that they are sufficient for the writer to feel satisfied. If they were set to write an account of Wei Cheng, they would only record the words of his admonitions, which would be enough of themselves to prove him to have been upright and true.[28] If they were to make an account of Tuan Hsiu-shih they would just record his using the seal of the Court of Agriculture sideways to send orders after the rebel forces, or his striking [the rebel] Chu Tz'u with an ivory tablet of office, acts that were enough in themselves to prove him to have been loyal and heroic.[29]

Those who now compose Accounts of Conduct fail to indicate such matters,

---

28 On Wei Cheng, see Wechsler, *Mirror to the Son of Heaven*.
29 On Tuan Hsiu-shih, see *CTS* 128, pp. 3583–8; *HTS* 153, pp. 4847–53. Tuan was a famous general who had formerly been a powerful military governor in the northwest. In 783 he was in Ch'ang-an serving as president of the Court of Agriculture when in the emperor's absence Chu Tz'u seized the palace and rebelled. Tuan managed to recall a rebel force sent to capture the emperor in Feng-t'ien, sending orders after them stamped with his seal set sideways so that the rebels could not tell who had ordered their recall. Later, when Chu Tz'u tried to induce him to join the rebels he took the tablet of office of one of the other plotters and furiously struck and cursed Chu Tz'u before being killed by the rebel troops.

but all sing the praises [of their subject] with insubstantial verbiage. Thus they would omit Wei Cheng's [actual] admonitions, but add praise of his correctness and uprightness, would make no mention of Tuan Hsiu-shih's [specific] heroic deeds, but add their praise for his being a loyal hero. All are like these. How can such accounts be thought worthy evidence? If the Department of Merit Assessments sees that an Account of Conduct does not follow this rule, they must not accept it. Only if it does follow these guidelines may they send it down to the Court of Imperial Sacrifices, and also communicate it to the Historiographical Office. After the Court of Imperial Sacrifices has settled on a posthumous name they should also send a communication to the Historiographical Office enclosing their statement of justification. If this is done the words of the Accounts of Conduct, even if they cannot yet be considered reliable in every respect, will be as different from those [of the present time], which are falsely embellished with lies and totally without substance, as a mountain is higher than a swamp.

When the historian records the events [of a man's life], he must trace them "from beginning to end." But if, following the old practice, the Account [of Conduct] is nothing but empty words, this will leave the Historiographical Office without anything upon which they can depend!

I therefore humbly beg that [the suggestions in] your subject's memorial be promulgated, and the Department of Merit Assessments be made to observe [them]. Your subjects require to know the true facts, and we thus dare to set out our opinions, lightly risking the awesome might of Heaven. Respectfully presented.

An edict gave assent to this memorial.

Many of the episodes interpolated in Accounts of Conduct and epitaphs to which Li Ao refers were not simple fiction but were drawn from a well-established repertory of formulaic passages and conventional episodes, which Herbert Franke, in a perceptive study published forty years ago, characterized as *topoi*.[30] They had a long history, many of them going back to Ssu-ma Ch'ien's *Shih chi* and even to the *Tso chuan*. They were of course widely recognized by educated men for what they were, attempts to link the deceased with some ideal model drawn from antiquity, rather than descriptions, even in the most oblique and metaphorical sense of his actual conduct or character.

The falsity of many of the Accounts of Conduct and Epitaphs was not simply a cause of concern for the historians, for whom it had serious professional implications, but was a matter of public notoriety. In 805, the young poet Po Chü-i wrote the following satirical poem, "Setting Up a Memorial Stele," ridiculing many of the epitaphs and memorial inscriptions of his time:

30 See Herbert Franke, "Some Remarks on the Interpretation of Chinese Dynastic Histories," *Oriens* 3 (1950): 113–22.

His achievements already forgotten,
The very text now crumbling;
Only a stone to be seen among the hills
His memorial stele standing beside the path.

The deeds in his eulogy sound like T'ai-kung;
His recorded virtues just like Confucius.
If sheer number of words could make one noble
These thousand characters are worth a fortune!

What sort of man was he who wrote the text?
When he put brush to paper he imagined
He wanted only to gratify the foolish
Not considering that worthy men would simply laugh.
But, is it merely that the wise will scoff?
This will pass on misleading facts to later ages.
Ancient stone, its characters masked in grey moss
How should one know these words would shame their subject?

I have heard that in Wang-chiang County
Magistrate Ch'ü looked after helpless widows;
In office practiced humane government,
But his fame was never heard in the Capital.
When he died he wanted to be buried in his native place,
But the common people blocked his way at the fork in the road,
Clung to the shafts so that he could not be sent back,
And kept his body for burial there on the banks of the Yangtse.
Down to this day, when they speak his name
Men and women alike shed tears....
Nobody set up a round memorial stele for him!
The local people's memory of his deeds was enough.[31]

For all their notorious imperfections, Accounts of Conduct and the related epitaphs and memorial inscriptions remained the principal sources for the biographies included in the Veritable Records and subsequently reorganized in the *lieh-chuan* sections of the National Histories and the Standard History.[32] Though subject to successive scrutiny by the Bureau of Merit Assessments, the Court of Imperial Sacrifices, and finally the members of the Historiographical Office, whose staff rewrote them, these accounts remained basically the work of writers who had stood in a close personal relationship with their subject: family

---

31 *Po Chü-i chi* (Peking, 1979) 2, p. 33.
32 For a very detailed study of the relationships between the biographies and funerary inscriptions of an individual, see Robert des Rotours, *Les inscriptions funeraires de Ts'ouei Mien (673–739), de sa femme née Wang (685–734) et de Ts'ouei Yeou-fou (721–780)* (Paris, 1975).

members, professional associates, disciples, or even well-known writers commissioned by the family, sometimes writing for payment.[33]

That the historiographers were willing to depend on this type of privately compiled material should remind us first of all that they subscribed to the view mentioned previously that biographies were somehow less authoritative and less important than the annals sections of their histories. But it also suggests that the Accounts of Conduct that they accepted can by no means always have been as fundamentally flawed, mendacious, and lacking in real substance as the quoted criticisms might suggest. Sufficient examples of *hsing-chuang* survive to prove that many, and probably the majority, were sober, substantial, and reliable works. Moreover, all official historians were by virtue of their profession skilled prose writers, and they themselves frequently wrote Accounts of Conduct, memorial inscriptions, and epitaphs for relatives, friends, or colleagues.[34] Hence they were intimately familiar with all the required literary conventions. If twentieth-century western readers can with a little experience easily pick out the literary hyperbole and the semifictitious interpolations of *topoi* they and contemporary educated readers would have automatically recognized them for what they were and discounted them as records of hard facts. It is also worth remembering that the historians would normally have received the Account of

33 For an example of a famous T'ang writer who was paid handsomely for writing *chia-chuan, mu-chih ming,* and *pei* inscriptions, see Li Hua's biography *HTS* 203, p. 5776. Li Chao, *T'ang kuo-shih pu* (Shanghai, 1957) B, p. 41, tells us that "whenever a great official died, people seeking to write his epitaph would throng to his gate as if to a marketplace." It also relates an anecdote that shows that money could not always persuade a writer of integrity to write an epitaph for a man he considered unworthy. When the very powerful and immensely rich provincial governor P'ei Chün, who had a well-earned reputation for cruel harshness and rapacity, died in 811, his sons, wishing to ensure him a high posthumous reputation, approached Wei Kuan-chih (760–821) a well-known writer and a man famous for his strict principles and unblemished integrity, offering him an enormous gift in return for writing his epitaph. "I'd sooner die of starvation!" was Wei Kuan-chih's reply. This anecdote is repeated in Wei Kuan-chih's *HTS* biography, *HTS* 169, p. 5155.

34 The writers whose objections to the shortcomings of funerary memorial writing are cited here were no exception. Li Ao, for example, has more than thirty Accounts of Conduct, tomb inscriptions (*mu-chih ming*), epitaphs (*shen-tao pei*), and sacrificial prayers (*chi-wen*) among his collected writings: Po Chü-i too knew at first hand what he was writing about – his collected works include some thirty *mu-chih ming* and many other memorial writings, texts of sacrificial prayers, etc. Other writers were even more prolific: Ch'üan Te-yü (759–818), chief minister from 810 to 813 and a prominent prose writer, has no fewer than twelve entire chapters of the *Ch'üan T'ang wen* devoted to his tomb inscriptions, epitaphs, and Accounts of Conduct (*CTW* 496–507), numbering eighty-five in all, and wrote dozens of memorial prayers in addition. As his biography tells us, "Epitaphs were requested from him for eight or nine out of ten of the great nobles, generals and ministers famous in his day, and his contemporaries considered him the supreme master of his craft." See *CTS* 148, p. 4005.

Conduct for examination within months of the subject's death. In the small and close-knit world of the court and of high-ranking officials, to which both the historians and most of their deceased subjects belonged, it would have been almost impossible for an Account of Conduct to have contained blatant untruths, especially about its subject's public life, and for these to pass into the official record, because the facts would have been common knowledge at court. The historiographer preparing to write a biography destined for the Veritable Record[35] read the Account of Conduct of a deceased prominent official with much the same insider's knowledge as a modern civil servant might possess when reading the newspaper obituary of some colleague with whom he had been both professionally associated and personally acquainted.

Even more crucial for the modern historian were the considerations that governed the choice, at every stage, of those persons held to be deserving of a biography. These criteria were effective in the Historiographical Office's initial decision whether a biography should be written on the basis of the deceased individual's Account of Conduct, subsequently in its decision whether it should be incorporated in the Veritable Record, and finally whether it should be included and where it should be placed in the National History or Standard History.

The essentially didactic intent behind the choice of persons to be provided with a biography was never more clearly expressed than in the following passage from the *Shih t'ung* of Liu Chih-chi, written in the early eighth century and completed in 710:

As long as the profession of historian is not cut off, and the bamboo and silk of their records survive, then even though a man himself has perished and disappeared into the void, his acts are as if they still survive, bright and clear as the stars of the Milky Way. As a result later scholars can sit and open the wrappers and boxes [holding the histories] and encounter in spirit all the men of antiquity; without leaving their own homes they can exhaust [the lessons of] a thousand years. When they read about a worthy exemplar they think of emulating him. When they read of an unworthy one, they inwardly examine themselves, just as refractory sons were struck with fear when the Spring and Autumn Annals were completed, and the acts of the regicide minister were

---

35 It is clear from the memorial by Li Ao cited earlier that the normal expectation was that biographies would already have been prepared for various prominent people during Hsien-tsung's reign and been ready for incorporation in the Veritable Record, which would be written after the emperor's death, and that the Historiographical Office had been delinquent in failing to do this. The expectation was then that biographies would be ready to hand for insertion at the appropriate place when the Veritable Record was eventually compiled, and that they would not all be written by the compilers of the Veritable Record at the time of its completion.

written down by the time the "Southern Historian"[36] arrived. If deeds and words are recorded in such a way, they will encourage good and reprove evil in such a way.[37]

This sort of statement, that the *lieh-chuan* ought to provide a sort of compendium of moral examples, of patterns of good and evil conduct, giving details of the actions of outstanding and extraordinary persons rather than simple accounts of routine careers, recurs over and over again in T'ang writing. It was an immemorial principle that all history should provide men with a "mirror" of the past, in which they might discern the lessons of human experience, and find models with which to confront their own actions.[38] The purpose of biographies, like that of the Accounts of Conduct or of memorial inscriptions, was to provide posterity with models for emulation. It was this, not the systematic recording of the routine details of an ordinary or conventional career, however high the rank of the deceased, that was supposed both to inspire the composition of the "biography" and the choice of what incidents should be included in it and also to dictate the choice of those individuals worthy of having a biography.

Perhaps the clearest single statement of the accepted theory on the selection of subjects for biographies is the following opinion written by Lu Sui[39] commenting on the fact that when Yüan Shao, a military governor of Ho-yang, had died in 805 no biography had been completed for the record.[40]

36 This is a reference to *Tso chuan*, Duke Hsiang, twenty-fifth year; see Legge, *Ch'un-ts'ew*, pp. 514–15. The Nan Shih was the "southern historiographer" of the state of Ch'i, who later became for historians the archetype of the fearless recorder of the truth. Ts'ui Shu murdered his lord, the duke of Ch'i. When the grand historiographer (*T'ai-shih*) attempted to record the deed, Ts'ui Shu had him executed: Two of his brothers subsequently suffered the same fate. The "southern historiographer" then set out to the capital to set the record straight, but on his way to the court found that the record had already been entered by another of the grand historiographer's sons. Nan Shih is taken by some commentators to be a name rather than a title. I follow Legge and Couvreur here. In either case, Nan Shih became the ideal model of a fearless recorder of the truth.
37 See *Shih t'ung* 11, p. 303. See also E. G. Pulleyblank, "Chinese Historical Criticism: Liu Chih-chi and Ssu-ma Kuang," Beasley and Pulleyblank, *Historians of China and Japan*, p. 144.
38 The "mirror" image of the recorded past goes back into high antiquity: See *Odes* (Shih ching) 235, 6, "In [the record of] Yin you should see as in a mirror that Heaven's high charge is hard to keep"; *Odes* 255, 8, "The mirror for Yin is not far off, it is the times of the Lord of Hsin." See Arthur Waley, *The Book of Songs* (London, 1938), pp. 251, 254.
39 See *THY* 64, p. 1108: *CTW* 482, pp. 18b–19b.
40 Yüan Shao died in the ninth month of 805. There was probably more to the omission of Yüan Shao from the historical record than pure historiographical theory. His appointment as military governor of the strategically crucial Ho-yang command was one of the very first acts of Shun-tsung's controversial reign (*CTS* 14, p. 405). His death followed

Wherever a man's meritorious achievements are not enough to warrant their being handed down to posterity, and where his goodness or wickedness had been insufficient to serve as an example, even though he had been a rich and powerful person [the Historian] should merely record his death in the appropriate place. T'ao Ch'ing, Liu She, Hsü Ch'ang, Hsüeh Tse, Chuang Ch'ing-ti, and Chao Chou were all Great Ministers of the Han, who ranked in nobility with the Feudal Lords, yet the historian considered that they were just ordinary persons who had merely filled their office honestly and conscientiously and who had done nothing in particular to achieve fame or reputation for meritorious services, and so he did not devote a biography to any of them. On the other hand in the cases of Po I, Chuang Chou, Mo Ti, Lu Lien, Wang Fu, Hsü Chih, and Kuo T'ai all either remained commoners to the end of their days, and established their fame by resigning from their state, or cultivated their virtue and wrote books, or propounded marvels and resolved perplexities, or held fast to the Way and averted calamities. They were thus given biographies in the same category as the Duke of Chou, the Duke of Shao, Kuan-tzu and Yen-tzu. Thus among the rich and noble there are some who should be denied [biographies] while among the poor and humble there are others who should be expanded upon. Confucius said, "The Duke Ching of Ch'i had a thousand teams of horses, but on the day of his death the people could think of no good deed for which to praise him. Po I and Shu Ch'i starved at the foot of Mount Shou-yang and yet the people sing their praises down to this very day."[41] This being the case, why should the scholar whose purpose is set and who wishes to provide illumination to posterity pay attention to nobility and rank? When rich and powerful persons have accepted responsibilities and gained positions of power, and yet still cannot hand down any example to posterity, this is because their virtue was not cultivated and they paid little attention to righteousness and much to temporal profit.

Sometime between 807 and 810, shortly before Lu Sui wrote this statement, Po Chü-i in one of his satirical "New Yüeh-fu" poems, "The Blue Rock," expressed a similar view about the sort of people he considered truly deserving of a monument:

less than a month after Shun-tsung's abdication (*CTS* 14, p. 406), and he may well have been denied a biography because of his close association with the discredited regime of Wang Shu-wen and Wang Pi during Shun-tsung's brief reign.

It appears at first glance that Lu Sui's memorial was written at the time of Yüan Shao's death. But Lu Sui is described as a historian (*shih-ch'en*) by *THY* 64, and his biography makes it clear that at the time of Yüan Shao's death he was serving in a minor provincial post in the Yangtze Valley. He seems first to have been appointed a compiler in the Historiographical Office shortly after 810, possibly in the aftermath of the purge of the Historiographical Office undertaken by Li Chi-fu in the fourth month of 811 (*THY* 64, p. 1108), and then to have continued to hold this post throughout the rest of Hsien-tsung's reign, concurrently serving successively as omissioner, court diarist, and under secretary of the Department of Honorific Titles in the Board of Civil Office. See *CTS* 159, p. 4191. The opinion thus must have been written after 810. It is impossible to be more specific about its date.

41 See *Analects (Lun yü)* 16, 12; Waley, *The Analects of Confucius*, p. 207.

A blue rock cleft from the mountains of Lan-t'ien,
Hauled to Ch'ang-an on linked wagons.
The masons grind and polish it, but what should it be used for?
Since the stone cannot say, let me speak for it.

I do not want to be used
For the Spirit Path Tablet before the tomb of some man,
Whose fame will be extinguished before the earth is dry on his
    grave.
I do not want to be used
For the Tablet of Virtuous Deeds beside the avenue of some official,
Engraved with empty sentiments, not with real fact.

I would like to be made into memorials for Lord Yen and Lord
Tuan[42]

Engraved with their titles: Grand Commandant and Grand
Preceptor.[43]
Inscribe these two tablets with the substance of steadfast sincerity,
To record the qualities of heroic loyalty of these two men.
Loyal hearts, rocklike, unshakable as mountain crags.
Constant till death, rocklike, unmovable as towering peaks.
As if one could see the time when the one rained angry blows on
    Chu T'zu,[44]
Or when the other shouted curses and insults at [Li]
Hsi-lieh.[45]

---

42 Lord Yen was Yen Chen-ch'ing, and Lord Tuan was the same Tuan Hsiu-shih already
   cited in the memorial of Li Ao. Both were loyal martyr-heroes who died during the
   provincial rebellions of the early years of Te-tsung's reign.
43 Yen Chen-ch'ing was created grand preceptor of the heir apparent (*T'ai-tso T'ai-tzu
   T'ai-shih*) in 781. See *CTS* 128, p. 3595. Tuan Hsiu-shih was posthumously appointed
   grand commandant (*T'ai-wei*) in an edict of the second month of 784. See *CTS* 128,
   pp. 3587–8; *CTS* 12, p. 340.
44 See n. 27 in this chapter.
45 When Li Hsi-lieh first rebelled in 782, Chief Minister Lu Ch'i, who bore a grudge
   against the aged Yen Chen-ch'ing, persuaded the emperor to send him to an almost
   certain death as an envoy to the rebel's camp in an attempt to win Li Hsi-lieh back to
   the imperial cause. There he steadfastly heaped curses and insults on Li Hsi-lieh, in
   the face of the threats of his followers, and was mistreated and imprisoned before
   eventually being murdered in 784. For details of this incident, see his biographies *CTS*
   128, pp. 3589–97; *HTS* 153, pp. 4854–61.
      Yen Chen-ch'ing is particularly interesting as a case study of T'ang biographical
   writing: Not only does he have biographies in both Standard Histories, but a very full
   Account of Conduct and his epitaph also survive. According to his biography (*CTS* 128,
   p. 3596), when under threat of death at Li Hsi-lieh's camp he also wrote his own
   epitaph (*mu shih*) and his own sacrificial prayer (*chi-wen*). His official Account of
   Conduct written by his cousin Yin Liang, "Yen Lu-kung hsing-chuang," is appended to
   his collected works *Yen Lu-kung wen chi* (*SPTK* edition) 14; and is included in *CTW* 514,
   pp. 9a–26b. It also circulated as a separate book. It is presumably the same as the
   Yen-shih hsing-chuang in a single chapter mistakenly attributed to Yin Chung-jung in

On each inscribe his name and posthumous titles
Set one on the mountain height and the other in the water's depths,
So that, even though mountains change places with valleys, their
memorials alone will survive,
So that, even when their bones are changed to dust, their fame will
never die.

And for evermore make those who are neither brave nor loyal
On seeing these memorials change their ways, and take them as
    their models.
Model themselves on them;
And be fired to serve their ruler![46]

Similar expressions continued even after the fall of the T'ang. In 933, the Historiographical Office of the Later T'ang memorialized the throne as follows:

Now we request that none of the Accounts of Conduct that have been forwarded to the Historiographical Office...shall be held entitled to be included in the compilation if their subjects have neither rendered [any noteworthy] service to the state, nor done any virtuous deed for the people, but [whose Accounts of Conduct] contain only a record of their petty talents and insignificant skills, so that there is nothing that can be transmitted to posterity as an example. Ever since there were histories written in the form of annals and biographies, successive ages have all had their historians, and all have kept to a fixed system which may not be relaxed.[47]

Any attempt to select biographies on the grounds that they would provide models for emulation or warning examples was necessarily highly subjective, and presupposed a preexisting and generally accepted repertory of ideal types of personal behavior that would provide reference points. The overt attempts that were made to fit every selected biography into a stereotype or into an ideal formal frame of reference, attempts that were often made quite specific in the historians' personal comments and the judgments attached at the ends of biographies, were not isolated phenomena, confined to historiography, but represented a

---

HTS 58, p. 1484, and the work with the same title listed as in two chapters in *Ch'ung-wen tsung-mu* 4, p. 18b, where it is said to have been already lost in 1131. *Ch'ung-wen tsung-mu* 4, p. 18b, also lists a *Yen-kung chuan* in two chapters, which may have been the same work under a variant title. See also Pulleyblank, "*Tzyjyh Tongjiann K'aoyih*," p. 472, n. 1. Yin Liang also wrote a single-chapter *Yen-shih chia-chuan*, which was a biography of Yen Chen-ch'ing's cousin Yen Kao-ch'ing. See *HTS* 58, p. 1484. Yen Chen-ch'ing's epitaph, by the official historian Ling-hu Huan, "Kuang-lu tai-fu, T'ai-tzu t'ai-shih, Shang-chu-kuo, Lu-chün K'ai-kuo kung Yen Chen-ch'ing mu-chih-ming," also survives and is included in *CTW* 394, pp. 11a–19b.

46 Hiraoka Takeo and Imai Kiyoshi, eds., *Haku-shi monshū* (Kyoto, 1971–3) 4, pp. 69–71; *Po Chü-i chi* 4, p. 74.
47 *WTHY* 18, p. 303.

deep-rooted and widespread attitude to the individual and his role. It was also of great significance in other areas of T'ang official life. The assessment of the performance of each T'ang official conducted annually by his superiors was couched in highly formal four-character set phrases descriptive of the ideal virtues required in an incumbent of the post.[48] Every Palace Examination proclaimed the specific combination of virtues that it attempted to find in the successful candidates.[49] Likewise the discussions of suitable posthumous designations (*shih*) for the canonization of deceased officials ranged around formal codified prescriptions that defined the personal qualities required in any person thought eligible to be granted a given posthumous canonization.[50] Prescribed roles, archetypes, and identification with set models were all-pervasive in the ways in which educated men in T'ang times thought about personality and human behavior. The linkage between biographies, Accounts of Conduct, and these deeply ingrained modes of thought is underlined by the fact that the responsibility for monitoring the annual assessments of officials, for the conduct of examinations, for the granting of posthumous canonizations,[51] and for the scrutiny of Accounts of

48 See *TLT* 2, pp. 46b–47b; *CTS* 43, pp. 1823–4; and *HTS* 46, pp. 1190–1, for the system of assessment by "excellences" (*shan*) and "perfections" (*sui*). These formed a section of the Statutes on Assessment (*K'ao-k'o ling*), Articles 3 to 33 in Niida's reconstruction. See Niida Noboru, *Tōryō shūi*, pp. 332–6; cf. also Rotours, *Fonctionnaires*, vol. 1, pp. 59–63; Robert des Rotours, *Le Traité des examens*, (Paris, 1932) pp. 50–55.

49 See the lists of palace examinations and their titles included in *THY* 76, pp. 1386–96; *TFYK* 645, pp. 10b–20b. Even these very extensive lists are far from complete.

50 On the system of posthumous canonization, see *TLT* 2, p. 50b; *TLT* 14, p. 16b; *TT* 104, pp. 550c–552c. On its practice, see the very copious material collected in *THY* 79–80, pp. 1455–87, which provides the definitions of character and conduct required for the granting of each posthumous designation. Sometimes it includes several alternative definitions. These model descriptions derived from an extensive list of special works on posthumous canonizations, mentioned in *TLT* 14, p. 17b; *CTS* 44, p. 1873. In particular the section entitled *Shih-fa* of the *Chou Kuan* and the section (now lost) with the same name in *Ta Tai Li chi*, with its commentary by the Han scholars Hsün K'ai and Liu Hsi (*SS* 32, p. 921; *CTS* 46, p. 1983), had great authority. Also mentioned was a work entitled *Shih-fa* in 2 chapters by the early Chin erudit scholar and expert on ritual Chang Ching (see *Chin shu* 20, pp. 618, 627); the *Shih-fa* in 5 chapters by the Liang scholar Ho Ch'ang (*SS* 32, p. 921), and the *Hsin Shih-fa* in 3 chapters by his nephew, Ho Ch'en (*CTS* 46, p. 1983), which was in use in T'ang T'ai-tsung's reign (*Liang shu* 38, p. 540). There was also a large compilation by Shen Yüeh (414–513) entitled *Tsung-chi Shih-fa* in 165 chapters (*TT* 14, p. 17b; *CTS* 44, p. 1873) and a more modest work in 10 chapters by the same author, the title of which is given as either *Shih-li* (Shen Yüeh's biography in *Liang shu* 13, p. 243; *CTS* 46, p. 1983) or as *Shih-fa* (*SS* 32, p. 921). On *Shih-fa* in general, see also Ku Yen-wu, *Jih chih lu* (Kuo-hsüeh chi-pen ts'ung shu edition, Shanghai, 1937) 14, pp. 84–85 (commentary of Lei Hsüeh-ch'i). See also McMullen, *State and Scholars in T'ang China*, pp. 11, 19–20.

51 In the case of posthumous canonizations, a statement of justification (*shih-i*) was nominally presented by the erudit scholars (*Po-shih*) of the Court of Imperial Sacrifices (*T'ai-ch'ang ssu*).

Conduct and epitaphs all fell upon a single office – the Department of Merit Assessments, which formed part of the most prestigious of all the ministries, the Board of Civil Office.

In the selection of individuals for biographies, however, intention and performance were very different issues. Whatever the historiographical orthodoxy of the time, whatever his own high moral stance, the historian was a serving official at court, surrounded by powerful and potentially dangerous men. It took considerable strength of mind and courage for an official historian, even for the director of the National History, who was himself almost always a chief minister, to exclude from the record the biography of any deceased person who had recently held high office, whose relatives and friends remained influential, and whose partisans might well still be in positions of power. Particularly when a biography was to be written shortly after the death of its subject, high rank gave an official a much better than even chance of selection, irrespective of his moral standing and his merits in the light of received theories about the writing of history.

As a result a great many of the biographies of high-ranking officials included in the *Chiu T'ang shu* are simply matter-of-fact descriptions of unremarkable careers in which a modern reader will find no models of outstanding behavior, and very little that could be thought inspiring.[52] However, such biographies are, to us, all the more valuable as historical evidence; for they give us some picture of what the ordinary, middle-of-the-road bureaucrat's career was like, something with which the T'ang historian was so familiar that it would never have occurred to him that it might be specifically worth recording. Even further from his mind was the idea that such routine details might be of far more interest to an unimaginably alien posterity such as ourselves than the examples of the Confucian virtues and morality that loomed so large in the traditional conceptions of history.

52 It is worth bearing in mind, when reading traditional biographies that seem little more than a skeleton curriculum vitae of successive offices that to the "insider" reader envisaged by the official historians, that is to future members of the same bureaucratic structure, every step in such a career had its meaning and significance. A T'ang official's curriculum vitae, even when stripped of contextual detail, could be read meaningfully by a near contemporary, just as we can read between the lines of an obituary of some member of our own profession, or interpret the details in a job application. See Twitchett, "Problems of Chinese Biography," pp. 31–2. Only recently have modern historians of the T'ang come to realize the importance of understanding career patterns, and their task has been made much easier by the labors of Sun Kuo-t'ung, whose massive *T'ang-tai chung-yang chung-yao wen-kuan ch'ien-chuan t'u-ching yen-chiu*, gives us an invaluable analysis of the career structures of T'ang officials.

9

Histories of institutions, historical encyclopedias, and collections of documents

The formal institutionalization of history writing in the early T'ang led to an increasing professionalization of history, a concentrated effort to write history that was didactic not only in the broadest sense, as embodying the moral–ethical lessons the past had to offer to all educated men, but also in a narrower sense, providing those involved in the governance of the empire with a rich body of precedents and examples. This aspect of official historiography was dealt with some thirty years ago by Etienne Balázs[1] in an important study in which he summed up the motivation of the state historians in a telling if exaggerated sentence: "History was written by officials for officials."[2]

Making the mass of material accumulated by the historians readily accessible to these potential specialist readers necessitated the rational categorization of information and the assemblage together of the documentation and decisions on specific subjects. The rational organization and categorization of knowledge was very much in fashion during the early T'ang. It can be seen in the grand-scale attempts to normalize and codify criminal and administrative law and ritual behavior: It can be seen in the huge state-sponsored genealogical compilations that tried to define a fixed social order.[3] It runs through the canonical scholarship

---

1 Etienne Balázs, "L'histoire comme guide de la pratique bureaucratique (Les monographies, les encyclopédies, les receuils de statuts)," in Beasley and Pulleyblank, *Historians of China and Japan*, pp. 78–94. Translated as "History as a guide to bureaucratic practise," in Etienne Balázs, *Chinese Civilization and Bureaucracy* (New Haven, 1964), pp. 129–49. This study was written for a conference held in London in 1956.
2 See Balázs, *Chinese Civilization and Bureaucracy*, p. 135.
3 On such writings the most accessible English source is Denis C. Twitchett, "The Composition of the T'ang Ruling Class: New Evidence from Tun-huang," in Wright and Twitchett, *Perspectives on the T'ang*, pp. 47–85.

of the period, with its attempt to bring order to the varied exegetical traditions that had emerged in the period of division; and it found expression in the various "encyclopedias" compiled in early T'ang, the works that the catalog of the imperial library of 720 classified as *lei-shih*,[4] "categorized matters." No fewer than twenty-two such works are listed,[5] among them the two earliest surviving works of this type, the *Pei-t'ang shu-ch'ao* in 160 chapters compiled under Yü Shih-nan (558–638) and completed under the Sui,[6] and the *I-wen lei chü* in 100 chapters compiled under Ou-yang Hsün (557–641) and presented to the throne in 624.[7] A third surviving example of the same genre is the *Ch'u-hsüeh chi* in 30 chapters compiled in the Chi-hsien Academy by Hsü Chien (659–729) and his colleagues and presented to the throne in 727.[8]

These books were not encyclopedias in our modern sense. They were designed not so much to organize knowledge and information as to provide a readily accessible collection of choice extracts from earlier literature and history that could be used by writers seeking examples of literary excellence and classical allusions. Among their different sections there were many that dealt with various aspects of "human affairs," and they thus classified a great deal of information on what we would consider historical and administrative topics. One very interesting link between them and history writing is that among the compilers of all three of these works,[9] and indeed among the compilers of the other early T'ang encyclopedias long since lost,[10] there were numbered many scholars whose primary reputations were as professional historians. Other official historians took part in the extensive codification of law and ritual under the first three emperors. This wide-ranging effort to

4 This category is renamed *lei-shu*, "categorized works," in *HTS* 59, p. 1564.
5 See *CTS* 47, pp. 2045–6.
6 See *CTS* 47, p. 2046; *HTS* 59, p. 1563.
7 See *CTS* 47, p. 2046; *THY* 36, p. 651; *HTS* 59, p. 1563; *TFYK* 607, pp. 9b–10a.
8 See *CTS* 47, p. 2046; *HTS* 59, p. 1563; *THY* 36, p. 658. Date given as 728 by Wei Shu's *Chi-hsien chu-chi* as cited in *Yü hai* 57, pp. 46b–47a; *Ta T'ang hsin-yü* 9, p. 145; *TFYK* 607, p. 13b.
9 Both Ou-yang Hsün (who worked on the *Ch'en shu* and was an acknowledged expert on early history; see *CTS* 189A, p. 4947) and Hsü Chien (who worked on the Veritable Record for Wu Tse-t'ien and on the National History *Kuo-shih* commissioned by Empress Wu in 703) were themselves engaged in work as official historians. Among the compilers of *Pei-t'ang shu-ch'ao* was Ling-hu Te-fen, who was employed as an official historian for most of his life. Of the dozen or so compilers of *I-wen lei chü* Ling-hu Te-fen and Ch'en Shu-ta worked on the *Chou shu*, while P'ei Chü worked on the *Ch'i shu*. The collaborators on the *Ch'u-hsüeh chi* included the famous professional historian, Wei Shu, and it was produced under Chang Yüeh, himself at the time involved in writing the *Chin-shang Shih-lu*, the Veritable Record for Hsüan-tsung's first years on the throne.
10 See the compilers of the various early T'ang encyclopedias listed in *HTS* 59, pp. 1562–3.

categorize and organize knowledge was thus an intellectual trend of the times and one in which many of the official historians were themselves directly involved.

In traditional historiography, collections of documentation on various aspects of administration had been provided in the monographs (*shu* or *chih*) of histories in the composite form. By the T'ang period there was an established, standard repertory of subjects that might be covered by monographs, and even a standard order of precedence in which these should be presented. These subjects covered ritual observances, rules of ceremonial propriety, ceremonial music and state liturgy, sumptuary rules governing costume and carriages, the calendar, records of portents conceived as supernatural "comment" on the exercise of authority, astronomy and astrology, the organization of the bureaucracy, administrative geography, state finance, law, waterways, and a bibliography (normally a catalog of the imperial library collection). As Balázs observed many years ago, in the course of time there was a tendency for more attention to be given to the rational "functional" topics, less to religious and ritual subjects. But this tendency begins only with the Sung. In the T'ang and pre–T'ang periods, those dynastic histories that included monographs followed closely the subjects covered by *Shih chi* and *Han shu*.

Ever since Ssu-ma Ch'ien had included monographs (*shu*) in his *Shih chi*, these had stood apart from other sections of the history. They were, in modern terms, "subject-oriented" history, each focusing upon a special field of government activity, and the governmental organizations that impinged upon it, and presenting the source material relative to its subject not simply in chronological order but in terms of broad causal relationships, even if these were not always fully articulated. Unlike the annals and the biographies, the obligatory components of an official history in the composite form, the monographs were an optional, if highly desirable, addition that added considerably to the standing of a history. Many of the histories compiled during the period of division did not include monographs – only the *Wei shu*, *Sung shu*, and *Nan Ch'i shu* have them – and the same is true of the various histories of earlier dynasties compiled by the official historians in early T'ang, of which only the *Chin shu* and *Sui shu* have monographs. Even as highly esteemed a history as the *Hou Han shu* of Fan Yeh (398–446), as originally written and as it still circulated in T'ang times,[11] had no monographs.

11 See *CTS* 46, p. 1989, which gives its length as only ninety-two chapters. Fan had planned to include ten monographs, but died before he had written them. Those included in modern editions were first incorporated in *Hou Han shu* in 1022, by simply adding to Fan Yeh's history the monographs originally written around 300 by Ssu-ma

The separateness of the monographs was further exemplified by the history of those included in the modern *Sui shu*. These were originally conceived of and written as a separate book, the *Wu-tai shih chih*, "The Monographs for the Histories of the Five Dynasties." Completed in 656, this work was originally independent of the *Sui shu*, which had been completed twenty years before in 636, and was designed to cover the history of the Sui and of the various sixth-century regimes that had preceded it both in north China (Northern Chou, Northern Ch'i) and in the south (Liang and Ch'en) in the form of a linked set of monographs. Its compilers were a totally different team from those who had worked on the annals and biographies of *Sui shu*, and the individual monographs were each allocated to a single specialist author, the names of whom in a few cases survive.[12] The monographs were attached to the *Sui shu* soon after their completion, and were certainly considered an integral part of it by the end of the seventh century,[13] but the original form of this work shows that early T'ang historians not only looked on the writing of monographs as a specialized task distinct from the compilation of the annals and biographies of a composite history but also were willing to think of them as a viable historical form in their own right.

Another feature set the monographs off from the remainder of a composite history. Ever since the *Han shu*, historians had felt free in these sections to extend their view beyond the narrow dynastic span and to present institutional development in the context of a longer time frame. Pan Ku's *Han shu* monographs, for example, had ranged back to high antiquity. They thus gave the historian writing a Standard History a place at which he could step back and present the achievements of the dynasty in comparison with those of earlier periods. The compilers of the two most important of the Standard Histories written in early T'ang times, the *Sui shu* and the *Chin shu*, also wrote their monographs with a broad historical perspective. Those included in the *Chin shu* range back into the Later Han and Three Kingdoms periods, while those of the present *Sui shu* deal not only with developments under the "Five

Piao (240–306) for his third-century history of the same period entitled *Hsü Han shu*. This had been in general circulation since the Liang period as a separate independent book with a commentary by the early sixth-century scholar Liu Chao, but large parts of it were gradually lost. By the eleventh century only the monographs survived. See Bielenstein, "The Restoration of the Han Dynasty," pp. 13–17. Liu Chih-chi, in the early eighth century, considered the *Hou Han shu* and *Hsü Han shu* as two separate books.

12 For a convenient summary, see the "Postface to the T'ien-sheng 2 (1024) printed edition of *Sui shu*" attached as an appendix to the Chung-hua shu-chü edition of *Sui shu*, pp. 1903–4.

13 This is shown by Liu Chih-chi's remarks in the *Shih t'ung* (see for instance *Shih t'ung* 3, p. 61).

Dynasties" of their original title, but covered events in the Eastern Chin, Sung, and Southern Ch'i as well, despite the fact that the already existing Standard Histories of Chin, Sung, and Southern Ch'i all included extensive monograph sections.

There was thus a long-standing tradition among official historians that, when writing monographs, they should deal in detail, and in a structured way, with a conventional repertory of specialized functions of government, and that they should do this in a long-term historical perspective not rigidly confined to the span of a single dynasty. They felt that the monographs had a special significance; Liu Chih-chi, for example, devoted the longest single section of the *Shih t'ung* to the subject of monographs, suggesting the elimination of some traditional subjects and the addition of new ones.[14] But they also tended to see the monographs as a type of composition quite distinct from the annals and biographies, for the production of which there were well-established official routines. They had thus been willing to undertake, as an official project, a large and important work, the *Wu-tai shih chih*, entirely in the form of a set of monographs.

During the eighth century official historians and private scholars alike began to develop new historical forms that would take still farther the specialized history whose methods and attitudes were implicit in the monographs, although, curiously, they rarely commented on the problems involved in the writing of monographs in the way that they constantly criticized the Court Diaries, the Veritable Records, and the various categories of biographical writing. Perhaps this may be explained by the fact that the writing of monographs was normally undertaken only at the time a major National History was commissioned and even then was confined to a few specialists, whereas *every* official historian was involved in one stage or another of the compilation of annals and biographies.

These sections of the histories did not come into being incrementally, as did the annals and biographies. They were written afresh by the historians when a National History or a Standard History for a defunct

---

14 See *Shih t'ung*, pp. 56–80. Liu Chih-chi suggested the elimination of three of the traditional subjects for monographs. The first of these was bibliography; this was in any case very different from the other monographs, in that they were essentially catalogs of books in the Imperial Library during the period and gave no information on historical changes. Second came the monographs on astronomy, which was a technical rather than a historical subject (one wonders how many contemporary scholars, not to mention modern historians, could understand these chapters), and third came the monographs on portents, the importance of which he downplayed. He also suggested new subjects – clans, cities, and articles offered as tribute. None of these suggestions was ever acted upon in later histories. But it is interesting to see that for new subjects such as these, Liu Chih-chi saw the monograph as the appropriate form.

dynasty was compiled, using only the documentation that had been collected by the Historiographical Office, but not any earlier draft stage of official compilation. It is not clear whether any of the National Histories compiled before Hsüan-tsung's time included monographs. Those drafts written during his reign and the National History completed by Liu Fang in 759–60 certainly did so, and during Hsüan-tsung's reign some members of the staff of the Historiographical Office were certainly engaged in writing monographs for the draft National History just when the new genres of "institutional history" began to appear. The connection is self-evident.

Although no official attempt was made to update or revise the monographs included in the National History compiled by Liu Fang in 758–60 after the comparatively minor revisions of Yü Hsiu-lieh and Ling-hu Huan in the 760s, work on specific and apparently independent "monographs" continued after the National History's final completion, as personal projects of individual historians, some of them scholars employed in the Historiographical Office.

In 764, Tai-tsung's dominant chief minister, Yüan Tsai (d. 777), who was concurrently both director of the National History and senior scholar of the Chi-hsien Academy, suggested that the scholars of the academy be ordered to undertake a major historical work covering all successive dynasties in the form of a series of monographs. This work, the name of which is given variously as the *T'ung chih* or the *Li-tai shu chih*, seems never to have been completed; at least there is no record of its completion or presentation to the throne.[15] We do know, however, that the various monographs were each entrusted to a specialist in its field. We know for instance, that Kuei Ch'ung-ching, a noted expert on ceremony and ritual, was given personal responsibility for the Monograph on Ritual Observances (*Li-i chih*).[16] Another monograph from this series may possibly have been the Revised Monograph on Administrative Geography compiled by K'ung Shu-jui (730–800), a well-known expert on geography who was a court diarist and briefly a compiler in the Historiographical Office in the 760s.[17] However, it seems more likely that this revised monograph was written later, as an independent book, when Kung Shu-jui served again in the Historiographical Office for a much longer period under Te-tsung.[18]

Other independent books in monograph form were written in late T'ang times. The bibliographical chapters of *Hsin T'ang shu* list a Mono-

---

15 See *CTS* 149, p. 4016; *TFYK* 556, p. 19b; *Yü hai* 57, p. 41b.
16 See *CTS* 149, p. 4016; *TFYK* 556, p. 19b; *TFYK* 607, p. 13b.
17 See *CTS* 192, pp. 5130–1; *HTS* 196, p. 5610.   18 See *HTS* 196, p. 5610.

graph on Ritual (*Li chih*) extending to ten chapters, written by Ting Kung-chu (769–832), who served as a scholar in the Chi-hsien Academy and later, under Wen-tsung in 828, became academician expositor in waiting (*Shih-chiang hsüeh-shih*) in the Han-lin Academy.[19]

Even more interesting is the Monograph on the Examination System (*Hsüan-chü chih*) in ten chapters attributed to the late eighth-century scholar-official Shen Chi-chi (no dates).[20] The examinations had never been the subject of a monograph in any dynastic history or in the National History. Until the Sui there had been no examination system, and until the eighth century they were of comparatively minor importance. Even Liu Chih-chi had not included the examinations in his proposals for new monograph subjects. But by the 780s the situation was completely altered, and the examinations were a major factor both in the function of government, and the lives of the ruling elite. Shen Chi-chi, who served briefly as a compiler in the Historiographical Office from 779 to 781 and wrote the *Chien-chung Shih-lu*, was certainly conscious of the vital and rapidly growing importance of the examinations, which by the late eighth century had become the only acceptable entrance to an elite career for young scholars.[21] His monograph (the precise date of which is unknown) was written at about the same time as his friend Tu Yu was also making the examinations one of the major subdivisions of his administrative encyclopedia, the *T'ung tien*.[22]

During the late eighth century and the ninth century, a series of other works relating to the examinations was written, which also reflects their ever growing importance in the life of the scholarly elite. Some seem to have been simple lists of graduates. Others give the detailed regulations for the examinations and selection procedures, or the subjects set in different years by different examiners.[23] Shen Chi-chi's lengthy mono-

---

19 See *HTS* 57, p. 1434; *CTS* 188, p. 4937; *Yü hai* 57, p. 41a.
20 See *HTS* 58, p. 1477. For Shen's biography, see *CTS* 149, pp. 4034–7; *HTS* 132, pp. 4538–40.
21 See his lengthy essays cited in *TT* 17, pp. 101a–103a, and *CTW* 476, pp. 15a–25a. These may very well have some connection with his monograph.
22 Note the very extensive quotations of his views that Tu Yu incorporated in *T'ung tien's* section (*TT* 13–18) on examinations and selection.
23 The most important of these seem to have been listed in *HTS* 58, p. 1485; (1) the *T'ang Hsien-ch'ing teng-k'o chi* in five chapters by a "Mr. Ts'ui" otherwise unidentified, with a preface by Chao Tan, briefly military governor of Fu-fang in 835; (2) the *T'ang teng-k'o chi* in two chapters by Li I, whose preface, preserved in *CTW* 536, pp. 5a–6a, is dated 792; and (3) the *K'o-ti lu* in sixteen chapters by Yao K'ang, a *chin-shih* of 820. (According to Ch'en Chen-sun, this work was only partly written by Yao K'ang, who completed the eleven chapters down to the end of Mu-tsung's reign. The other five chapters were added later by an unknown hand. See *WHTK* 198, p. 1663a.) (4) A similar work, the *Chu-chia k'o-mu chi* in thirteen *chüan* was completed in 856 by Cheng Hao, a court diarist, very noted examiner and consort of an imperial princess under

graph survived into the Sung period[24] and it seems very probable that it was available to Ou-yang Hsiu and his colleagues when they wrote the first monograph on the examinations to appear in a standard dynastic history, that in the *Hsin T'ang shu*.

At least one T'ang official historian experimented with the production of tables (*piao*), another form of historical compilation that had been included in the *Shih chi* and *Han shu*, but which had been abandoned and in disfavor since the time of Pan Ku. The compilers of the *Chin shu*, for instance, rejected the tabular form, which would have been a convenient and natural way of dealing with the complexities of the many petty regimes of the fourth century. At the beginning of the eighth century, Liu Chih-chi dismissed the tabular form in a few scornful sentences in his *Shih t'ung*.[25] In the years after the An Lu-shan rebellion, however, the official historian Liu Fang compiled a series of Tables of Chief Ministers, the *Ta-T'ang tsai-hsiang piao*, in three chapters,[26] and these may have been used by the compilers of *Hsin T'ang shu* who reintroduced tables, including a Table of Chief Ministers, to the Standard Histories on a grand scale.

Histories of specific offices

During Hsüan-tsung's reign there was a sudden vogue for the compilation of accounts of various government offices, some of them descriptive histories, others collections of traditions and precedents. These were mostly written about scholarly offices, or "pure offices" (*ch'ing-kuan*), appointment to and service in which signified an official's acceptance as a member of the scholarly elite within the bureaucratic service.

One of the first such works was a collection of notes on the Censorate, the power base of the aristocratic scholarly elite under Hsüan-tsung, entitled *Yü-shih t'ai tsa-chu*, compiled in five chapters during the later years of Kao-tsung's reign by Tu I-chien.[27] Two further histories of the Censorate were written under Hsüan-tsung, the *Yü-shih t'ai chi* in twelve

Hsiuan-tsung who died in 859 or 860. This work covered the whole dynasty down to 847. The facts about these four books, all of which were lost in Sung times, are very confused. See *Chih-chai shu-lu chieh-t'i* 7, pp. 11b–12a, *WHTK* 198, p. 1663a. There were many Sung and later attempts to compile such lists. See the preface to Hsü Sung's excellent *Teng-k'o chi k'ao* (*Nan-ching shu-yüan ts'ung-shu* edition, 1888) of 1838.

24 It is cited both in T'o-t'o, *Sung shih* (Peking, 1977) 203, p. 5101, and in *Chung-hsing Kuan-ko shu-mu* (see *Yü hai* 117, p. 12a). Both sources list it as having three, not ten, chapters.

25 See *Shih t'ung* 7, pp. 53–54.

26 See *HTS* 58, p. 1478.

27 See *HTS* 58, p. 1477; *CTS* 190A, p. 4999; *Yü hai* 57, p. 38a.

chapters by Han Wan[28] and another work with the same title in ten chapters by the official historian Wei Shu.[29] Yet another shorter work on the Censorate, the *Yü-shih t'ai ku-shih* in three chapters was completed during Te-tsung's reign by Li Kou.[30]

Liu K'uang, the eldest of Liu Chih-chi's sons, who after his father's death became a compiler in the Historiographical Office in the 720s, produced a work on the Board of Civil Office, the *T'ien-kuan chiu-shih*, in a single chapter.[31] The official historian Wei Shu also wrote an account of the Chi-hsien Academy, the *Chi-hsien chu-chi*, in three chapters,[32] extensive sections of which are preserved in quotations in the *Yü hai* and elsewhere.[33]

Writings in the same genre continued into the ninth century. One office that, largely because of its literary prestige, was the subject of a whole series of works was the Han-lin Academy. The first of these was a single-chapter book entitled *Han-lin yüan ku-shih* completed in 786 by Wei Chih-i (dates unknown),[34] a precociously talented young *chin-shih* graduate who had become a Han-lin scholar the previous year, while still in his early twenties, and who would later be ruined in 805 as a result of his involvement with the Wang Shu-wen clique during Shun-tsung's brief reign. A series of linked works on the Han-lin Academy was written at the end of Hsien-tsung's reign and during the short reigns of his successors, Mu-tsung and Ching-tsung. In 819 Li Chao completed his *Han-lin chih*, in a single chapter.[35] In 820 or 822 Wei Ch'u-hou (773–828) produced the *Han-lin hsüeh-shih chi*, also in a single chapter.[36] This same work was also inscribed in the Han-lin Academy as a "wall inscrip-

28 See *HTS* 58, p. 1477; *Ch'ung-wen tsung-mu* 3, p. 25a; *Chün-chai tu-shu chih* (*Yüan-pen*) 2B, p. 5a–b; *Chih-chai shu-lu chieh-t'i* 6, p. 4a–b; *WHTK* 202, p. 1687c; *Yü hai* 57, p. 38a.
29 See *HTS* 58, p. 1477; *Yü hai* 57, p. 38a–b.
30 See *HTS* 58, p. 1477; *Ch'ung-wen tsung-mu* 3, p. 25a; *Chih-chai shu-lu chieh-t'i* 6, p. 4b.
31 See *HTS* 58, p. 1478.
32 See *HTS* 58, 1477; *Ch'ung-wen tsung-mu* 3, p. 25a; *Chün-chai tu-shu chih* (*Yüan-pen*) 2B, p. 5a–b; *Chih-chai shu-lu chieh-t'i* 6, p. 4b; *Yü hai* 48, p. 34a–b; *WHTK* 202, p. 1687c.
33 These fragments are collected together in Ikeda On's "Sei Tō no Shūken'in," pp. 47–98.
34 See *Yü hai* 51, pp. 30b–31a; *Chih-chai shu-lu chieh-t'i* 6, p. 5b. Text is included in *Chih-pu-tsu chai ts'ung-shu* collection 13. See also Ts'en Chung-mien, *Lang-kuan shih-chu t'i-ming hsin k'ao-ting* (Shanghai, 1984), pp. 386–92, for detailed comments.
35 Text included in *Chih-pu-tsu chai ts'ung-shu*, ser. 13. For very extensive commentary, see Ts'en Chung-mien, *Lang-kuan shih-chu hsin k'ao-ting*, pp. 195–500. For a French translation and commentary, see F. A. Bischoff, *La forêt des pinceaux: Etude sur l'académie du Han-lin sous la dynastie des T'ang, et traduction du Han lin tche* (Paris, 1963), pp. 25–6; *HTS* 58, p. 1478; *Chün-chai tu-shu chih* (*Yüan-pen*) 2B, p. 5b–6a; *Chih-chai shu-lu chieh-t'i* 6, p. 5a. Li Chao was also the author of the *T'ang kuo-shih pu*, a supplement to the National History that survives.
36 See *WHTK* 202, p. 1688a; *Chih-chai shu-lu chieh-t'i* 6, p. 5b. Text in *Chih-pu-tsu chai ts'ung-shu*, ser. 13.

tion" (on this genre, see subsequent discussion) and survives under the title *Han-lin yüan t'ing pi-chi*[37] as well as in its form as an independent work. In 821 Yüan Chen (779–831), then holding the post of Han-lin academician recipient of edicts as well as very high court offices, composed another wall inscription, the *Ch'eng-chih hsüeh-shih yüan chi*,[38] which also survives under the title *Han-lin Ch'eng-chih hsüeh-shih t'ing pi-chi*,[39] an inscription for the Court of the Recipients of Edicts within the academy.[40] Some years later this inscription had become illegible and defaced, and in 837 Ting Chü-hui produced yet another single-chapter work revising and updating Yüan Chen's record. This was entitled *Ch'ung-hsiü Ch'eng-chih hsüeh-shih pi-chi*.[41] All this series of works has survived,[42] and the most important single work among them, Li Chao's *Han-lin chih*, has been integrally translated.[43]

These were not, however, the only late T'ang works devoted to the Han-lin Academy. There was also a single-chapter work entitled *Han-lin sheng shih*, the date and author of which are unknown,[44] a *Han-lin nei-chih*, also in a single chapter and also by an unknown author,[45] and a work on the old rules of the academy, the *Han-lin hsüeh-shih yüan chiu-kuei*, also in a single chapter, by Yang Chü, a Han-lin scholar and vice-president of the Board of Civil Office under Chao-tsung in 902 or 903.[46] The first of these works survived at least until late Sung times,[47] the last still survives today.[48]

It should not be surprising that the Han-lin Academy attracted so much attention. It was the unrivaled prestige office for the scholarly elite within the bureaucracy from the 780s on, an office entirely staffed

---

37 See *WYYH* 797, pp. 6a–7b.
38 See *Yü hai* 51, p. 31a, citing *Chung-hsing Kuan-ko shu-mu; Chih-chai shu-lu chieh-t'i* 6, p. 5a–b; *WHTK* 202, p. 1688a. Text in *Chih-pu-tsu chai ts'ung-shu*, ser. 13.
39 See *WYYH* 797, pp. 7b–8b.
40 The *Ch'eng-chih hsüeh-shih* (academician recipient of edicts) was a post established in 805 for the senior academicians. See Bischoff, *Forêt*, pp. 12, 75.
41 See Bischoff, *Forêt* pp. 28–9; *WHTK* 202, p. 1688a; *Chih-chai shu-lu chieh-t'i* 6, p. 6a. Text in *Chih-pu-tsu chai ts'ung-shu*, ser. 13.
42 They are reprinted together in *Chih-pu-tsu chai ts'ung-shu*, ser. 13; and elsewhere.
43 See n. 40.
44 See *Chün-chai tu-shu chih (Yüan-pen)* 2B, p. 6a. *WHTK* 201, pp. 1680c–1681a; *WHTK* 202, p. 1688a; *Sung shih* 203, p. 5102, attribute it to Chang Chu (or Chang Ch'u-hui). His dates are unknown.
45 See *HTS* 58, p. 1478. It is attributed to Li Chao in *Sung shih* 203, p. 5102.
46 See *HTS* 58, p. 1478; *Ch'ung-wen tsung-mu* 3, p. 25b; *Chih-chai shu-lu chieh-t'i* 6, pp. 5b–6a; *Sung shih* 203, p. 5102.
47 They were included, together with the works already cited and some Sung works on the Han-lin Academy in the *Han-lin Ch'ün-shu* in three chapters, listed in *Chün-chai tu-shu chih (Yüan-pen) Fu-chih* 5A, p. 25a–b.
48 It is included in *Chih-pu-tsu chai ts'ung-shu*, ser. 13.

with highly educated writers. This engendered a powerful *esprit de corps* among its members. But even more than this, the Han-lin Academy itself was an anomaly within the structure of government; it had no place in the hierarchy of offices and was not even listed in the Digest of Laws (*Liu-tien*); its members, for all their very real political importance and close links to the throne, held no formal rank (except for the nominal sinecures they held in other departments). By Hsien-tsung's reign it was under heavy pressure from the eunuchs. Its unquestioned prestige was based entirely on the achievements of its members, and these works were an affirmation of this collective achievement. It is surely no accident that they were almost all written in the academy's political heyday, between the reigns of Te-tsung and Wen-tsung.[49]

The other works mentioned all deal with other "pure" offices that were the exclusive preserve of the scholarly elite, the Censorate, the Chi-hsien Academy, and the Board of Civil Office. Like the works on the Han-lin Academy, their compilation was intended to record the detailed history of government offices whose incumbents were expected to practice and profess publicly the shared values of this scholarly elite – values that were equally shared by the official historians who were themselves members of this elite of letters. Moreover, several of their authors were also official historians; Wei Shu, Wei Ch'u-hou, and Liu K'uang were all compilers in the Historiographical Office; Wei Chih-i was a court diarist and later director of the National History. Finally, to underline the celebratory nature of these writings, all the authors except Liu K'uang seem to have served as members of the office about which they were writing. These writings were a form of institutional history, but of a highly specialized type, written by members of an elite office for their colleagues and successors, in an attempt to record for posterity both the achievements of their predecessors and the traditions and procedures of the office in which they were so proud to have served.[50]

49 The wall inscription repaired by Ting Chü-hui omits the names of those who had served in the Han-lin Academy before 779 (see Bischoff, *Forêt*, p. 28). Although the academy had existed since Hsüan-tsung's reign, it was only in Te-tsung's time that it developed into the most prestigious imperial secretariat.

50 Another work that may have been of a similar kind is the *Chung-t'ai chih* in ten chapters attributed to Li Ch'üan. This was presumably a work on the Department of State Affairs (*Shang-shu sheng*) for which Chung-t'ai was an alternative epithet. See *HTS* 58, p. 1484; *Sung shih* 203, p. 5111; *Chün-chai tu-shu chih* (*Yüan-pen*) 2B, p. 5b; *WHTK* 202, p. 1687b; *Yü hai* 57, p. 40a–b. Li Ch'üan was active in the 830s and served at one time as deputy civil governor of Ching-nan province. See *CTW* 361, p. 8a. He wrote a number of works on military strategy, for which see *Sung shih* 207, pp. 5278–9, and 5282. The most notable of these was a military chronicle entitled *K'un-wai ch'un-ch'iu* in ten chapters, which is listed in *HTS* 58, p. 1466, and *Sung shih* 203, p. 5096 (it is also listed in *Sung shih* 207, p. 5282). He also wrote a commentary on *Sun-tzu*. See *HTS* 59, pp. 1551–2; *Sung shih* 207, p. 5282; *Chün-chai tu-shu chih* (*Yüan-pen*) 3B, p. 18a; *Yü hai* 140,

Office inscriptions

Another form of institutional writing that seems to have begun in the reign of Hsüan-tsung but later became more and more common was the wall inscription, written for public display in a specific government office (*t'ing pi chi*). In late T'ang times, these had developed into a separate literary genre. The *Wen-yüan ying-hua* anthology, compiled in the last years of the tenth century, includes no fewer than ten chapters of such inscriptions devoted to offices ranging from the Hall of Deliberation of Governmental Affairs (*Cheng-shih t'ang*) of the Secretariat–Chancellery down to the lowly offices of county registrars and marshals.[51] The great majority of these (they were clearly selected on literary and stylistic grounds rather than on account of their contents) was composed by authors living in the post–An Lu-shan period and the early ninth century.

I have been able to find no inscriptions of this sort predating Hsüan-tsung's accession. However, a short entry in Feng Yen's *Feng-shih wen-chien chi* gives evidence that they were already common in the first years of his reign and also suggests that they were a T'ang innovation:

The premises of the one hundred bureaus of the court all have their wall inscriptions. They set out the ranks of the offices and record their establishment, together with a list of those selected and appointed to them in chronological order. If we seek the reasons for composing them, [their officers] wish to record the historical experience of former administrators, so as to bring out those things in it that their future successors should ardently strive after. Hence in the form in which such inscriptions are to be composed value is to be set upon careful detail and classic elegance: they must be neither careless [in fact] nor ornate [in style].

However, recently those who have written such inscriptions often set down unfounded hyperbole, giving exaggerated praise to men's talents and singing the praises of their achievements and ranks so that they completely lose the original intention of recording events.

Mr. Wei's *Liang ching chi* says "The secretaries [lang-kuan] profusely write wall inscriptions to record the successive selections and appointments, entry and leaving of office, within their own bureau and this has gradually become the accepted custom." This being the case the origins of wall inscriptions seem to

---

pp. 12b–13a. Li Ch'üan was also a Taoist recluse, writing under the names Shao-shih shan jen, Ta-kuan tzu, and Ta-kuan shan jen. *HTS* lists several of his writings under the categories Tao-chia (*HTS* 59, pp. 1520–1) and Wu-hsing (*HTS* 59, p. 1558); *Sung shih* also lists several more writings in these categories (206, pp. 5247, 5258). For other details, see Piet van der Loon, *Taoist Books in the Libraries of the Sung Period* (London, 1984), pp. 84, 139, 141, 144.

51 See *WYYH* 797 to 806, p. 3b.

have begun from our present dynasty, first in the major ministries [t'ai-sheng], and later spread to the offices of local government.[52]

Feng Yin's book was completed in the last years of Te-tsung's reign, probably in 800.[53] By that time we have ample surviving evidence that, as he says, such inscriptions were widespread. But the citation enables us to see that the practice may have begun very much earlier. "Mr. Wei" is the historian Wei Shu, and the *Liang ching chi* is his *Liang-ching hsin-chi*, which was completed in 722. Only a single chapter of this work survives,[54] and this does not contain the passage quoted by Feng Yen. But the citation is good evidence that such inscriptions were already commonplace by the early years of Hsüan-tsung.

Perhaps they were not yet highly regarded as a literary form, worthy to be preserved among their author's works, and were simply left forgotten on their office walls. The examples that survive from later in the dynasty are certainly polished literary compositions, which in most cases have probably been preserved only in a truncated form by removing the lists of the incumbents of offices, which of course had great importance for the members of the office but no general literary interest. They normally provide a short history of the institution, listing its changes of name and function, and a description, couched in terms of Confucian moral virtues rather than practical details, of the duties and responsibilities of the officials serving within it. The inscriptions would, when in place, usually have been accompanied by lists of previous incumbents with their dates of appointment and transfer; they were, in fact, rather like the "Honor Boards" displayed in a traditional English school hall.

One early example that probably antedates Wei Shu's comment by a few years is the *T'ai-yüeh ling pi-chi*, the wall inscription for the office of the director (*ling*) of the Office of Imperial Music (*T'ai-yüeh shu*), a most important subordinate office of the Court of Imperial Sacrifices (*T'ai-ch'ang ssu*), written by Liu Chih-chi's extraordinarily gifted eldest son, Liu K'uang. This was a far more extensive and discursive piece than any of the later surviving examples, a lengthy composition in three chapters that circulated as a separate book.[55] It remained extant at least until the beginning of the Yüan, and possibly later.[56] Sections of it, including its lengthy preface and table of contents, are cited in the *Yü hai*, and it is possible that it was an important source for *Chiu T'ang shu's*

---

52 See *Feng-shih wen-chien chi chiao-chu*, p. 37. A later version of this entry is in *T'ang yü lin* (Chou Hsün-ch'u, ed., *T'ang yü lin chiao-cheng*, Peking, 1987) 8, p. 686.
53 See Chao Chen-hsin's introduction to the *Feng-shih wen-chien chi chiao-chu*.
54 See Hiraoka Takeo, *Chōan to Rakuyō*, vol. 1, pp. 15–40.
55 See *HTS* 57, p. 1436; *Yü hai* 105, pp. 21a–23a.
56 See Chiao Hung's *Kuo-shih ching-chi chih* of 1590, as cited in *Ming-shih i-wen chih p'u-pien fu-lu* (Peking, 1959), vol. 2, p. 823b.

Monograph on Music (discussed later). There is no clear evidence from the surviving quotations that it included a list of incumbents, but it otherwise went into very great detail about court music.

Apart from this exceptional work, the earliest surviving examples of wall inscriptions seem to be those by Chang Yüeh's protégé Sun Ti (d. 760 or 761),[57] among whose surviving writings are wall inscriptions for the offices of the president of the Board of Civil Office (*Li-pu shang-shu*)[58] and of the vice-president of the Court of Diplomatic Reception (*Hung-lu shao-ch'ing*).[59] Sun Ti was a compiler in the Chi-hsien Academy from 733, where he would have been a colleague both of Liu K'uang and Wei Shu. He was both a fine writer of rescripts and a very successful examiner (in 734–5). One of the *chin-shih* he passed in 735 was the historian Liu Fang; another was the famous essayist Li Hua (ca. 710 – ca. 767), who wrote a wall inscription for the Hall of Government Affairs (*Chung-shu cheng-chih t'ang*), where the chief ministers held their deliberations,[60] and ten other surviving wall inscriptions for various local government offices,[61] some of them quite humble in status. A somewhat unlikely author of a work in this category was the poet Li Po (701–62), who also composed a wall inscription for a county magistrate's office in Shantung.[62] In the post–An Lu-shan period, there was a flood of writings in this genre. Many of them are of considerable historical interest.

There is certainly plenty of evidence to support Feng Yen's contentions that by his time such writings were commonplace, and that the habit had long spread from the prestigious offices of central government down to the yamens of county magistrates and even the offices of their lowly marshals and registrars.

Like the more extensive books dealing with the history of individual offices, these wall inscriptions were partly an expression of corporate pride among the incumbents of an office: but they were also rudimentary exercises in institutional history, and expressions of a common conception of the corporate identity of its officials.

Collections of edicts and memorials

Another long-established form of documentary compilation primarily designed not as a historical source but to provide models and precedents

---

57 Biographies: *CTS* 190B, pp. 5043–4; *HTS* 202, p. 5759.
58 See WYYH 798, p. 1b; *CTW* 312, pp. 8a–9a.
59 See *WYYH* 799, p. 2a; *CTW* 312, p. 9b.
60 See *WYYH* 797, pp. 4a–5a; *CTW* 316, p. 1a–2a; *TWT* 72, p. 1162.
61 See *CTW* 316, pp. 2a–3a; *WYYH* 798–801, 804; *TWT* 72–73.
62 See CTW 350, pp. 1a–2a; *WYYH* 804, p. 5b–6b; Li Po, *Li T'ai-po chi* (Shanghai, 1938) 28, p. 99.

for drafting official documents and to serve as an anthology of exemplary legislation for the instruction of a more general official readership was represented by collections of edicts and decrees. These were nothing new in T'ang times. The Imperial Library collection in 720 contained several such collections dating from the Chin (265–420) and Liu Sung (420–79) periods.[63]

Similar collections continued to be made under the T'ang, none of which have survived. The earliest of these were collections of model edicts from all periods. T'ai-tsung's favorite minister, Wen Yen-po (574–637), produced a *Ku-chin chao chi* in thirty chapters,[64] and somewhat later Empress Wu's supporter Li I-fu (614–66), who had served as one of the compilers of the *Chin shu* and in 651 became a director of the National History, together with the official historian Hsü Ching-tsung edited an even larger collection, the *Ku-chin chao chi* in one hundred chapters.[65]

This latter collection was compiled at the same time as the court scholars were engaged in producing a series of massive literary anthologies, the *Wen-kuan tz'u-lin*, completed in a thousand chapters in 658,[66] the *Lei pi* in 630 chapters, completed in 661,[67] and the *Yao-shan yü-ts'ai* in five hundred chapters, presented to the throne in 663.[68]

---

63 See *CTS* 46, pp. 1998–9, where they are classed under *Lieh-tai ku-shih*, "precedents," unlike collections from the T'ang, which are listed as *Tsung-chi*, "general anthologies."

64 *CTS* 47, p. 2078; *HTS* 58, p. 1473. *CTS* classifies this and the following item among "general anthologies" (*Tsung-chi*), not as in *HTS*, under a special category of "edicts" (*chao-ling*). This special category seems to have been an innovation in the *HTS* bibliography.

65 *CTS* 47, p. 2078; *HTS* 58, p. 1473.

66 *CTS* 82, p. 2764; *CTS* 47, p. 2077; *THY* 36, p. 656, *TFYK* 607, p. 12b. Edited by Hsü Ching-tsung, Liu Po-chuang, and others.

67 *CTS* 4, p. 82; *THY* 36, p. 657; *CTS* 82, p. 2764; *CTS* 47, p. 2046; *HTS* 59, p. 1563. Edited by Hsü Ching-tsung and others. According to *CTS* 47 it comprised four hundred chapters; according to *CTS* 4 and *HTS* 59, four hundred chapters plus a four-chapter table of contents.

68 *THY* 36, p. 657; *TFYK* 607, p. 13a; *HTS* 59, p. 1562. Compiled by Hsü Ching-tsung and others. The circumstances of the *Yao-shan yü-ts'ai*'s compilation are very interesting. It was undertaken not at the orders of Kao-tsung, but of his heir apparent, Li Hung, who asked to set up his own group of twenty academicians in the Ch'ung-hsien kuan with whom he studied the *Ch'un chiu*, *Tso chuan*, and *Li Chi*. In 661 several members of his household; Hsü Ching-tsung, his adviser (*T'ai-tzu pin-k'o*); Hsü Yü-shih (miswritten by *TFYK* as Hsü Wei-shih), his mentor of the right (*Yu Shu-tz*u); the vice-president of the Chancellery, Shang-kuan I, Yang Ssu-chien, secretary of the heir apparent's Secretariat; and others were ordered to produce the 500-chapter *Yao-shan yü-ts'ai*. This was presented to the throne and Hsü Ching-tsung and the other compilers were given promotions and rewarded proportionally with gifts of silk. See *TFYK* 258, p. 14a–b; also the heir apparent's biography in *CTS* 86, pp. 2828–9. The compilers' names are given by *HTS* 59, p. 1562, as Hsü Ching-tsung, Meng Li-chen, Kuo Yü and Ku Yin (both scholars of the Ch'ung-hsien kuan), and Tung Ssu-kung, diarist of the left. Kuo

Another very large anthology, the date of whose completion is unknown, but the compilers of which were almost the same as those who produced the *Yao-shan yü-ts'ai*, was the *Fang-lin yao-lan* in three hundred chapters.[69] Encyclopedic scholarship and anthologies on a monumental scale were thus in the air at the time and enjoyed lavish royal patronage. Many of the scholars engaged in these compilations were also active historians, several of them working on the production of the Veritable Records and the National History.

The collections of model edicts may also have had some connection with the works written for the guidance of future rulers during the midseventh century by (or more probably in the name of) successive emperors. The first of these was the *Ti-fan* comprising thirteen sections (*pien*) in four chapters written by T'ai-tsung in 649 as an injunction for his heir apparent, the future Kao-tsung,[70] which still survives. Some years after his accession to the throne, Kao-tsung followed his father's example and wrote two essays on the roles of ruler and subjects entitled *Yüan-shou ch'ien-hsing wei-ch'eng ku-kung chieh* and *Ku-kung lun*, and ordered Hsü Ching-tsung and his colleagues to provide them with a commentary. This work was completed in 657[71] and circulated under the title *T'ien hsün*, in four chapters. The work as a whole is long lost, but some fragments appear to have been recovered from Tun-huang (manuscript P. 5523).[72]

Later, collections came to be made of the model edicts promulgated under the various T'ang emperors. At the end of the seventh century,

---

Yü had taught the heir apparent the *Tso chuan* and *Li Chi* (*CTS* 86, p. 2828). Hsü Ching-tsung, Ku Yin, and Hsü Yü-shih were all historians, involved in compiling the Veritable Records and National Histories of the period. According to *THY* 36, p. 657, the completed book was presented to the throne in 663 by the then president of the Board of Finance, Tou Te-hsüan (who was in charge of a palace examination that summer; see *CTS* 4, p. 84). It was accepted and placed in the book depository (*shu-fu*). *CTS* 4, p. 84, confirms the date of its presentation as in the second month of 663.

69 See *HTS* 60, pp. 1621–2. The *Fang-lin yao-lan* in 300 chapters was put together by almost an identical team: Hsü Ching-tsung, Ku Yin, Hsü Yü-shih, Shang-kuan I, Yang Ssu-Chien, Meng Li-chin, Yao Shou (also a historian, who later began the compilation of *Shih-cheng chi*), Tou Te-hsüan, Kuo Yü, Tung Ssu-kung, and Yuan Ssu-ching. See *HTS* 60, pp. 1621–2. *HTS* also mentions two further works in the same genre: *Li-cheng wen yüan*, 20 chapters (*HTS* 60, p. 1621); and *Wen Kuan tz'u-lin*, 1,000 chapters, compiled by Hsü Ching-tsung and Liu Po-chuang (*HTS* 60, p. 1621), four chapters of which have survived in a Japanese manuscript copy.

70 *CTS* 47, p. 2026; *HTS* 59, p. 1512; *THY* 36, p. 656, dates its completion to 649. *Yü hai* 28, p. 26a–b. Edition in four chapters with extensive commentary in *Ying-yin Wen-yüan ko Ssu-k'u ch'üan-shu* (Taipei, 1983); edition in two chapters with a shorter commentary and collation notes by Lo Chen-yü in *Tung-fang hsüeh-hui ts'ung-shu*, first series.

71 See *CTS* 47, p. 2026; *HTS* 59, p. 1512; *THY* 36, p. 656, and the fuller version of *Hui yao* cited in *Yü hai* 28, pp. 26b–27a; and *Yü hai* 30, p. 1b.

72 See Wang Ch'ung-min, *Tun-huang ku-chi hsü-lu* (Peking, 1958), pp. 188–9.

Hsüeh K'o-kou (director of the Imperial Library, 689–90) compiled a *Sheng-ch'ao chao chi* in thirty chapters, presumably assembling the edicts issued under Empress Wu.[73] The bibliographical chapters of *Hsin T'ang shu* list anonymous compilations of the edicts by Hsüan-tsung, the *Ming-huang chih-chao* in a single chapter,[74] and of those issued by Hsien-tsung, the *Yüan-ho chih chi* in ten chapters.[75]

A particularly interesting work in this category was the ten-chapter *Hsieh hsüan* compiled during 838 to 841 by the diarist and Han-lin expositor in waiting, Wang Ch'i (760–847), in which he noted down the verbal instructions given by Wen-tsung to palace envoys, that is to the eunuchs, on doubtful issues.[76]

Various other works are included by the *Hsin T'ang shu* among the category of edicts,[77] but nothing is known of their contents, and none seems to have survived the T'ang period.

We have no clear idea of the content of these works or of their organization. The single large-scale work of this type dealing with the T'ang that we have at our disposal is not a T'ang compilation but an early Sung work, the *T'ang ta chao ling chi*, in 130 chapters, begun by Sung Shou (991–1040) and completed by his son Sung Min-ch'iu (1019–79), whose preface is dated 1070.[78] Sung Min-ch'iu was a prolific official historian who, besides working on the Court Diaries and on the Sung Veritable Records and *Hui yao*, was one of the collaborators on the *Hsin T'ang shu*, and was earlier responsible for a belated compilation of Veritable Records for the last T'ang emperors, for whom such records had never been written under the T'ang. Although the *T'ang ta chao ling chi* was compiled privately, not as an official project, Sung Min-ch'iu certainly had at his disposal all the resources both of the Sung imperial libraries and the Historiographical Office, and also Sung Shou's great personal library. It often cites documents in a more complete form than that preserved in such other sources as *T'ang hui-yao*, *T'ung tien*, or *Ts'e-fu yüan-kuei*. It is, therefore, an important source for the modern

73 *CTS* 185A, p. 4788; *HTS* 197, p. 5622; *CTS* 47, p. 2079; *HTS* 58, p. 1473. *CTS* 47 gives the author's name as Hsüeh Yao.
74 *HTS* 58, p. 1473.
75 *HTS* 58, p. 1473.
76 *HTS* 58, p. 1473; *CTS* 164, p. 4281; *HTS* 167, p. 5118.
77 *HTS* 48, p. 1473: They include an anonymous *T'ang te-yin lu* in thirty chapters; a *T'ai-p'ing Nei-chih* in five chapters; a *T'ang chiu-chih pien-lu* by a Mr. Fei in six chapters; a *Ni chuang chu chih* in ten chapters; and the *Wang-yen hui-tsui* in five chapters of Ma Wen-min, who is otherwise unknown.
78 On this work, which remained in manuscript until 1918, see Rotours, *Traité des examens*, pp. 95–96; and the excellent anonymous preface to the typeset edition published by Shang-wu yin-shu kuan in 1959.

historian of the T'ang. It seems to bear no direct relation, however, to the collections of imperial edicts assembled during T'ang times.

General encyclopedic works on government

The works listed so far dealt with single, limited aspects of government, or with individual government offices, or were simple collections of documents. But the eighth century also saw the appearance of a number of major works intended to give an overall historical account of government and its institutions. The first of these is rarely considered as a historical work at all, the *T'ang liu-tien*, whose title is often rendered as the "Institutes of the T'ang" or the "Digest of T'ang law."

T'ang liu-tien

The *T'ang liu-tien*, comprising thirty chapters, was completed in 738 and presented to the throne by Chief Minister Li Lin-fu in 739.[79] The compilation of the *Liu-tien* as a normative work on government institutions, was first entrusted by Hsüan-tsung to the scholars of the Chi-hsien Academy in 722. The emperor personally laid out its six main rubrics, which were modeled on the regulations for the six ministries in the *Chou li*:[80] the Canon of Government (*li-tien*), the Canon of Instruction (*chiao-tien*), the Canon of Propriety (*li-tien*), the Canon of Punishments (*hsing-tien*), the Canon of Administration (*cheng-tien*), and the Canon of Affairs (*shih-tien*). At first the work was entrusted to Lu Chien, a court diarist (*ch'i-chü she-jen*),[81] but under his direction nothing seems to have been done. When Chang Yüeh took over the academy in 725, he gave the *Liu-tien* project to Hsü Chien, but after another year the work had still not even been planned. At this time Hsü Chien and the other scholars of the academy were overwhelmed with other large and more urgent projects.[82] Chang Yüeh then ordered five other members of the

---

79 See *HTS* 58, p. 1477a, translated in Robert des Rotours, "Le *T'ang Lieou tien* décrit-il exactement les institutions en usage sous la dynastie des T'ang?" *Journal Asiatique* 263 (1975): 184; *Ta T'ang hsin yü* 9, p. 145; *Ch'ung-wen tsung-mu* 3, p. 25a; *Chih-chai shu-lu chieh-t'i* 6, pp. 2a–3a; *Chün-chai tu-shu chih (Yüan-pen)*; 2B, p. 7a *Ch'ün-shu k'ao-so* 19, p. 9a; *Yü hai* 51, pp. 25b–27a; *WHTK* 202, p. 1687a–b; *Ssu-k'u ch'üan-shu tsung-mu t'i-yao* 79, pp. 1667–9.

80 See *HTS* 58, p. 1477, from which the following account is largely extracted. See Biot, *Le Tcheou-li; ou, rites des Tcheou*, p. 20.

81 For Lu Chien's biography, see *HTS* 200, p. 5704.

82 At this time they were commissioned to prepare the great ritual compendium that became the *K'ai-yüan li*. Hsü Chien was its chief compiler, under Chang Yüeh. They were also extremely busy with the preparation for the Feng and Shan ceremonies on Mount T'ai in 726.

academy to take part in the compilation: Wu Chiung, who had produced the catalog of the imperial libraries in 721; the official historian, Wei Shu; Yü Ch'in; Hsien I-yeh; and Sun Chi-liang. They drew up the plan, which the surviving work follows, of rearranging a digest of the administrative laws embodied in the Statutes (*ling*) and Ordinances (*shih*) on a framework of the contemporary administrative structures that formed the T'ang equivalent of the six ministries of the *Chou li*. The work dragged on for years under successive chief ministers: Hsiao Sung took charge of the academy in 731 and added new scholars to the team working on the *Liu-tien*: Liu Cheng-lan, Hsiao Sheng, and Liu Jo-hsü. When Chang Chiu-ling succeeded him as head of the academy, he added Lu Shan-ching. Most of the work was by now completed, but when Chang Chiu-ling fell from power in 737, his erstwhile colleague as chief minister, Li Lin-fu, who was now in undisputed control of the government, took over the project and added yet another compiler, Yüan Hsien. The book was finally completed in 738 and presented to the throne by Li Lin-fu in 739.[83] Its promulgation was ordered, but for some time at least the completed work was kept in the academy and not immediately circulated.[84] By the late eighth century, however, it had become a widely consulted, convenient, and authoritative digest of administrative law.[85]

However, important as its function as a legal handbook may be, what is interesting in the present context is not so much the *Liu-tien* itself, but its commentary, to which the name of Li Lin-fu is usually attached. This commentary, besides adding explanatory detail and additional extracts from the Statutes and Ordinances, provides a history of each office, linking it to the offices that had performed a similar function in earlier dynasties, and giving details of changes in the nomenclature, rank, and numbers of its established officials under the early T'ang. It thus offers, in fragmented form, a very detailed history of the changing structures of government under the T'ang, and links these changes to

83 On *TLT* see Rotours, *Traité des examens*, pp. 99–102; Niida Noboru, *Tōryō shūi*, pp. 61–6; Tamai Zehaku, "Dai Tō Rikuten oyobi *Tsūten* no Sō kampon ni tsuite," *Shinagaku* 7, no. 2 (1934): 61–79; and 7, no. 3 (1934): 83–103 (reprinted in his *Shina shakai keizaishi kenkyū* [Tokyo, 1943]); Naitō Kenkichi, "Tō rikuten no kōyō ni tsuite," *Tōhō gakuhō (Kyoto)* 7 (1938): 103–34 (reprinted in the author's *Chūgoku hōseishi kōshō* [Tokyo, 1963], pp. 64–89); Yen Keng-wang, "Lüeh lun T'ang liu-tien chih hsing-chih yü shih-hsing wen-t'i," *CYYY* 24 (1953): 69–76; Rotours, "Le T'ang Lieou tien décrit-il exactement les institutions en usage sous la dynastie des T'ang?" pp. 183–201; McMullen, *State and Scholars in T'ang China*, p. 183.
84 See Wei Shu's *Chi-hsien chu-chi* as cited in *Yü hai* 51, pp. 25b–27a. However, Liu Su's *Ta T'ang hsin yü* (Peking, 1984) 9, p. 143, says; "It is in circulation until today." *Ta T'ang hsin yü* was written in 807.
85 See the evidence presented in the studies by Yen Keng-wang and Naitō Kenkichi mentioned in n. 83.

the history of institutions in pre-T'ang times. Although it reads as a dry and mechanical listing of formal changes, this historical commentary in fact represents a great deal of careful research on the part of the compilers and remains very useful.

While the *Liu-tien* was in the last stages of compilation, or shortly after its completion, another work was being written that attempted to provide a general history of government institutions in a far more sophisticated and ambitious form. This was Liu Chih's *Cheng tien*.[86]

Cheng tien

Liu Chih, who died shortly after 758, was the fourth son of the great official historian Liu Chih-chi, and two of his elder brothers, Liu K'uang and Liu Su, served as compilers in the Historiographical Office during Hsüan-tsung's reign. He completed his *Cheng tien* in thirty-five chapters in the late 730s or the 740s.[87] But Liu Chih himself, although he was a serving official, wrote the *Cheng tien* as a private author, not as a member of a government commission. Nor did he write it as a factual, objective record of various offices like that attached to the *Liu-tien*. The *Cheng tien* seems to have been an ambitious political treatise, cast in a historical form that, for the most part, was modeled on the subjects of the traditional monographs and drew its material from a wide range of sources, both historical and nonhistorical.

Liu Chih was one of the earliest members of the group of mid and late eighth-century political thinkers who are sometimes referred to as Neo-Legalists but are better described as statecraft writers. The Neo-Legalist label is not particularly illuminating, but it does firmly identify Liu Chih as one of a group of scholars and officials (he was briefly to hold high office and great influence among the emperor's

---

86 Liu Chih's *Cheng tien* was not the first T'ang period book with this name. The official historian Li Yen-shou, best known as the author of the *Nan shih* and *Pei shih*, and one of the compilers of the *Chin shu* and the Monographs for the History of the Five Dynasties *Wu-tai shih chih* had presented a thirty-chapter work with this name, also referred to as the *T'ai-tsung Wen huang-ti Cheng-tien* or *T'ai-tsung cheng-tien*, to the throne early in Kao-tsung's reign. In 680, long after Li Yen-shou's death, Kao-tsung again read this work and admired both its style and substance so much that he ordered copies to be made for the Palace Library (where it was still preserved in 720) and for the heir apparent. It is referred to on this occasion simply as the *Cheng tien*. See *THY* 36, p. 657; *CTS* 73, pp. 2600–1; *HTS* 102, p. 3986. *CTS* 46, p. 2008, lists it under works on ceremonial usage (*i-chu*) with the full title *T'ai-tsung Wen huang-ti Cheng-tien* in thirty chapters; *HTS* 58, p. 1467, includes it as *T'ai-tsung Cheng-tien* under the category of miscellaneous histories (*tsa-shih*). It was quite clearly a book about T'ai-tsung's conduct of government, quite different in nature to Liu Chih's work.

87 See *CTS* 147, pp. 3982–3; *HTS* 166, pp. 5089–90.

entourage following Su-tsung's usurpation of the throne in 756) who believed that history was essentially a matter of changes in social and political institutions and in the practice of government, and who thus attempted to write a new type of didactic history slanted toward these practical institutional factors, rather than toward the ethical lessons of Confucianism.

We know little about Liu Chih's career,[88] and his *Cheng tien* was lost long before the end of the T'ang period.[89] But it has nevertheless remained very influential, simply because of its incorporation into the surviving *T'ung tien* of Tu Yu.

T'ung tien

Tu Yu (735–812) enjoyed a highly successful political career,[90] but he was equally important and perhaps more influential as a political thinker.[91] He was deeply influenced by Liu Chih, and while serving in a provincial post at Yang-chou in the mid 760s he took the *Cheng tien* and expanded it into a massive treatise of his own, the *T'ung tien*, which extended to no fewer than two hundred chapters.[92]

88 He has very brief biographical notices in *CTS* 102, p. 3174; *HTS* 132, p. 4524; and *CTW* 372, pp. 18b–19a.

89 It is not included in *Ch'ung-wen tsung mu* or the *Sung shih* bibliography. Its inclusion in the *HTS* bibliography does not give clear proof that it existed in the eleventh century: The title was probably taken by its compilers from Liu Chih's biography. We know of three other works by Liu Chih: a military treatise, *Chih-ko chi*, in seven chapters (see *CTS* 102, p. 3124; *HTS* 132, p. 4524; *HTS* 59, p. 1551); a set of political proposals from his period in power, 756–8, *Chih-te hsin-i*, in twelve chapters (*CTS* 102, p. 3124; *HTS* 132, p. 4524); and a *Chih-yao* in three chapters (*CTS* 102, p. 3124). His few extant prose writings are in *CTW* 372, pp. 19a–26a. One long passage from the *Cheng tien* is cited in *THY* 47, p. 830, in its section on "feudalism" (*feng-chien*). See also *T'ang-wen shih-i* 22, pp. 3a–4a.

90 See *CTS* 147, pp. 3978–83; *HTS* 166, pp. 5085–90.

91 See Edwin G. Pulleyblank, "Neo-Confucianism and Neo-Legalism in T'ang Intellectual Life, 755–805," in Arthur F. Wright, ed., *The Confucian Persuasion* (Stanford, 1960), pp. 77–114, esp. 97–99; Kanai Yukitada, *Tōdai no shigaku shisō* (Tokyo, 1940); Naitō Torajirō, "Ni-ts'e i-tao," in *Kanō kyōju kanreki kinen Shinagaku ronsō* (Tokyo, 1930), pp. 5–8; Cheng Ho-sheng, *Tu Yu nien-p'u* (Shanghai, 1934); Tamai Zehaku, "Dai Tō Rikuten oyobi *Tsūten* no Sō kampon ni tsuite," in *Shinagakū* 7, no. 2 (1934): 61–79 and 7, no. 3 (1934): 83–103, reprinted in his collected essays, *Shina shakai keizai shi kenkyū*, pp. 429–61; Ke Chao-kuang, "Tu Yu yü chung-T'ang shih-hsüeh," *Shih-hsüeh shih yen-chiu*, 1981, no. 1: 9–23; Tseng I-fen, "Lun *T'ung-tien* tzu chu," *Shih-hsüeh shih yen-chiu*, 1985, no. 3: 1–10.

92 See *CTS* 147, pp. 3982–3; *HTS* 166, pp. 5089–90; *CTS* 13, p. 395; *THY* 36, p. 660; *HTS* 59, p. 1563; *Ch'ung-wen tsung-mu* 6, p. 13b; *Chün-chai tu-shu chih Yüan-pen* 3B, p. 23a–b; *Ch'ün-shu k'ao-so* 18, p. 9b (quoting *Chung-hsing Kuan-ko shu-mu*); *Yü hai* 51, pp. 27a–28b; *WHTK* 201, p. 1681a; *Ssu-k'u ch'üan-shu tsung-mu t'i-yao* 81, pp. 1695–6; *TT* original preface to the first draft by Li Han, and the memorial accompanying its presentation to the throne.

The importance of Tu Yu as a political thinker, and as the major figure among the statecraft thinkers of the late eighth and early ninth centuries, has been most admirably described by Pulleyblank in what remains, after a quarter century, the most important single study in any language of mid T'ang political ideas. There is no need here to go into any further analysis of Tu Yu's thought.

The *T'ung tien*, which remains a most important source for T'ang historians, was the model for a long series of institutional histories. Sequels to the *T'ung tien* itself, and adaptations of its form, were written in later dynasties, often as officially sponsored projects by official historians. However, authoritative as the *T'ung tien* was later to become, like the *Cheng tien* on which it had been modeled, it was originally a highly individual private history, a polemical work that propounded Tu Yu's own vision of human history dominated by administrative, organizational, and institutional factors.

The *T'ung tien* was completed and presented to the throne in 801, but its textual history was very complex. Large sections of it were not written by Tu Yu at all, but were taken over integrally from Liu Chih's much earlier *Cheng tien*. Another very large section of thirty-five chapters (106–140) was taken directly from the official ritual code, the *K'ai-yüan li*, completed in 732. This latter section is clearly identified, and its text can be verified since the *K'ai-yüan li* itself survives in full. But the clear differentiation between what was originally included in Liu Chih's *Cheng tien* and what was subsequently added by Tu Yu is impossible.[93]

Even Tu Yu's own part in the work, however, presents the modern reader with further critical problems. We know from Li Han's preface[94] that an original first draft was completed sometime between 766 and 771, while Tu Yu was serving at Yang-chou on the staff of his patron Wei Yüan-fu, military governor of Huai-nan.[95] The eighteenth-century historian Wang Ming-sheng (1722–98) believed that the writing of *T'ung tien* was begun in 766,[96] but both the Japanese scholar Tamai Zehaku, in his study of *T'ung tien*,[97] and Tu Yu's modern biographer

93 Wang Ming-sheng, in his *Shih-ch'i shih shang-chüeh* (Shanghai, 1937, reprint, 1959) 90, p. 1004, gives a perhaps exaggerated impression of the part *Cheng tien* played in the completed *T'ung tien*. Any such attempt is pure conjecture.
94 *TT*, original preface, p. 3a–b.
95 Wei Yüan-fu became governor of Huai-nan in the intercalary sixth month of 768 (see *CTS* 11, pp. 289–96) and held the office until his death in the eighth month of 771 (see *CTS* 11, p. 298). Tu Yu had, however, served on his personal staff when he was governor of Che-hsi (from 765 to 768) and for some years before this when he was prefect of Hua-chou, Jun-chou and Su-chou. See Cheng Ho-sheng's *Tu Yu nien-p'u*, p. 42–4.
96 See Wang Ming-sheng, *Shih-ch'i shih shang-chüeh* 90, p. 1003.
97 See Tamai Zehaku, *Shina shakai keizai shi kenkyu*, p. 446.

Cheng Ho-sheng, writing in the 1930s,[98] rejected this date in favor of 768. This original draft dealt with the whole history of human institutions from the earliest times down to the end of Hsüan-tsung's reign in 756.

Tu Yu later added supplementary material dealing with important developments subsequent to this date, mostly in the double-column commentary, but also in some places in the main text. These additions seem to have been inserted piecemeal at various dates. Toward the end of his life, when he was himself serving as military governor of Huai-nan,[99] with his headquarters at Yang-chou, where he had begun the *T'ung tien* some thirty years before, he completed the book and sent it to Ch'ang-an to be presented to the throne. There is conflicting evidence on the date of its presentation, which is given variously as 794,[100] 801,[101] and 803.[102] Modern scholars since the time of Wang Ming-sheng[103] have all accepted 801 as the correct date of its presentation and explain the date 803 as a product of confusion with the date when Tu Yu returned to the capital and presented to the throne his shorter work on statecraft entitled the *Li-tao yao-chüeh*[104] in ten chapters, now lost, which is thought to have been a summary version of *T'ung tien* dealing with substantive issues in government and administration.[105]

98 Cheng Ho-sheng, *Tu Yu nien-p'u* p. 49.
99 He served as governor from the twelfth month of 790 (see *CTS* 13, p. 368) until the third month of 803 (see *CTS* 13, p. 397).
100 This date is given in the memorial presenting *TT* to the throne (included at the beginning of some Sung editions, though omitted in the *Shih T'ung* edition), and also by *Yü hai* 51, pp. 27a–28a, citing *Chung-hsing Kuan-ko shu-mu*.
101 See *CTS* 13, p. 395, which dates it in the tenth month of 801, and says that he sent an envoy to court from Huai-nan to present it.
102 See *THY* 36, p. 660. This gives the date as the second month of 803. On the twenty-third of this same month, Tu Yu returned to the capital from his provincial governorship in Huai-nan (*CTS* 13, p. 397; *TCTC* 239, p. 7600).
103 See Wang Ming-sheng, *Shih-ch'i shih shang-chüeh* (Shanghai, 1937) 90, pp. 1001–5; this was written in 1787.
104 This explanation was developed by Naitō Torajirō.
105 On *Li-tao yao chüeh*, see *HTS* 59, p. 1537; *Ch'ung-wen tsung-mu* 5, p. 14b. *Yü hai* 51, pp. 28b–29a. Wang Ying-lin still had this book available to him in the thirteenth century. He cites it in his *K'un-hsueh chi-wen* and in *Yü hai* cites both Tu Yu's preface, which confirms that it was a summary of *TT*, divided into thirty-two or thirty-three sections, (*p'ien*), "giving details of the most important policies of ancient and modern times that are appropriate to be implemented in our age," and also the memorial of presentation to the throne, dated to the eighteenth day of the second month of 803, which gives a breakdown of its contents: Sections 1–3 dealt with state finance; 4 with the examination and selection of officials; 5 with ritual and instruction; 6 with the feudal system and the prefecture–commandery system; 7 with the military; 8 with frontier defense; 9 and 10 with opinions on the different institutions of ancient and modern times. It also stresses that it dealt with substantive issues, not theoretical counsel such as that in the Sui author Li Wen-po's *Chih-tao chi* or *Li-tao chi* (on which see *HTS* 59, p. 1532, where it is listed under Legalist works).

Even after this, further minor changes seem to have been made to the text, some during Tu Yu's lifetime (he died in 812) and possibly made by his own hand, others after his death.

Thus the current versions of *T'ung tien*, leaving aside the long section taken integrally from the *K'ai-yüan li*, contain the following layers of text and information: (1) the *Cheng tien* of Liu Chih, originally written in the late 730s or 740s; (2) Tu Yu's original systematic supplement to that work, giving an overall picture of developments down to the end of Hsüan-tsung's reign in 756 (this was written in 768–71); (3) Tu Yu's additional material relating to events after 756, the latest relating to 795 (this material was added, probably piecemeal at various dates, after the compilation of the first draft in 771 and before the final version of the book was presented to the throne in 801); (4) minor subsequent emendations and additions that were inserted, both by Tu Yu and by other, unknown hands (some of these date from as late as 820).

The sections that formerly were part of the *Cheng tien* were certainly written before Liu Fang's National History and may possibly have taken much of their material on the T'ang from either the Wu Ching or Wei Shu draft National Histories, which were lodged in the Historiographical Office where two of Liu Chih's brothers were employed. The first draft of *T'ung tien* by Tu Yu may just possibly have utilized Liu Fang's National History, though it does not seem very likely that a copy would have been available to him in Yang-chou, far from the capital. His later additions dealing with events during the reigns of Su-tsung, Tai-tsung, and Te-tsung must have derived from a variety of other, unknown sources. The extracts on Su-tsung may possibly have come from the Veritable Record of his reign, which was compiled before 777. The material on Tai-tsung and Te-tsung's reigns cannot have come from such a source, because the Veritable Records of these reigns were completed *after* the *T'ung tien*.

Hsü T'ung tien

T'ung tien's material thus effectively comes to an end with the T'ien-pao reign period in 756, and there is only a haphazard scattering of information from the 770s and early 780s, mainly incorporated as commentary. Systematic coverage of the period from 756 to the end of the Five Dynasties in 960 was subsequently included in an official continuation, the *Hsü T'ung tien*, originally commissioned by Sung T'ai-tsung in the Shun-hua period (990–5) and completed by Sung Pai and others in 1001.[106]

---

106 The compilation of a continuation of *TT* was first ordered by Sung T'ai-tsung during the Shun-hua (990–5) period, when Su I-chien (958–96), a Han-lin scholar, was

We are told that it covered the period from the Chih-te reign period of the T'ang (from 756) until the end of the Five Dynasties in 960. It consisted of two hundred chapters, together with a two-chapter table of contents.[107] The work was criticized for its repetitiousness and was not widely circulated. It was still in existence in the twelfth century,[108] but it has not survived.[109] Funakoshi Taiji has recently assembled the extensive fragments, mostly on administrative geography, that survive in quotation.[110]

T'ung tien was finally completed at a time, at the end of the eighth century, when other works of a similar type were being written.[111] The most important of these, the *Hui yao*, was also to found a genre of

ordered to undertake the work. He was shortly afterward transferred and the compilation abandoned. In the tenth month of 1000, the director of the National History, Li Hang (947–1004), requested that the work be begun again, and an edict was issued ordering Sung Pai (936–1012) and Li Tsung-o (965–1013) to undertake the compilation. They requested that Shu Ya (940–1009), Yang I (974–1020), Li Wei (n.d.), Shih Chung-li (972–1049), and Jen Sui (n.d.) be appointed co-compilers, with Tu Hao (938–1013) as reviewer. See *Hsü Tzu-chih t'ung-chien ch'ang-pien* 47, p. 1029; *Yü hai* 51, p. 34a–b. The work was very speedily completed, in less than a year, and presented to the throne in the ninth month of 1001. Sung Pai and the other compilers were given the customary feast and gifts, and the work was placed in the Palace Library (*Pi-ko*). See *Hsü Tzu-chih t'ung-chien ch'ang-pien* 49, p. 1073.

107 See *Ch'ung-wen tsung-mu* 6, p. 13b; *Chih-chai shu-lu chieh-t'i* 5, p. 155. *Yü hai* 51, p. 34b, gives an exact breakdown of its contents, which shows that it included far more on finance, examinations, the bureaucracy, and administrative geography, and much less on ritual, than the *T'ung tien* itself, although its major subdivisions remained identical.

108 It was included in the bibliographical monograph of the *San-ch'ao kuo-shih* (1030), which listed the books in the Imperial Libraries as of 1015. This entry was incorporated in *Sung shih* 207, p. 5299. It is also mentioned in *Chung-hsing Kuan-ko shu-mu* of 1178 as cited in *Shan-t'ang ch'ün-shu K'ao suo* 18, p. 9a. See also *WHTK* 201, p. 1681b. The table of contents is listed as a separate work in the *Pi-shu sheng hsü-pien-tao ssu-k'u shu-mu* of 1145 (see *Sung-shih I-wen-chih, pu, fu-pien* [Shanghai, 1957], p. 348).

109 It should not be confused with the later work still existing under this title, which was written following an imperial order in 1767.

110 See Funakoshi Taiji, *Sō Haku Zoku Tsūten shūhon fu kaidai* (Tokyo, 1985).

111 One work that may possibly have been a similar compilation on government is the *Li tien* (Canon of Government) in twelve chapters, attributed to P'ei Ch'eng in *Yü hai* 51, p. 29a. Wang Ying-lin cites it from *Hui yao*, but the modern *THY* does not mention this title, only the presentation in the eighth month of 795, of another work by P'ei Ch'eng, then Director of Studies in the Kuo-tzu chien, the *Sheng-yü Yüeh-ling*, also in twelve chapters. See *THY* 36, p. 659. This book is listed in *HTS* 59, p. 1538, as an agricultural calendar. Te-tsung's Basic Annals (*CTS* 13, p. 382) also records its presentation under the same date, together with a *Li tien* (Canon of Ritual) in twelve chapters. It is easy enough to see how such a confusion of titles might have arisen, but it is impossible to determine which *Li tien* is the correct title. None of the titles attributed to P'ei Ch'eng is listed in any of the Sung bibliographical sources, and presumably none survived into the eleventh century.

historical writing that would become a permanent part of the repertoire of forms employed by official historians.[112]

Hui yao

The *Hui yao* of Su Mien and Su Pien[113] was quite different from *T'ung tien* in a number of ways. It was limited to the institutional history of the T'ang, not the whole of recorded history. It was a collection of documents in forty chapters without overt editorializing, except for twenty or so comments that are clearly marked as expressions of the author's views.[114] It had no explicit didactic intention, and it was carefully divided into a complex yet eminently rational set of sections and subsections covering every conceivable aspect of institutions and government policy. It was a true administrative encyclopedia, a conveniently arranged body of documents that could easily be used as a reference book by a reader seeking the main documents regarding some particular office or issue in government.

It was, according to all the bibliographers of Sung times, written by Su Mien, but according to the text of the book itself it was the work of Su Mien and Su Pien, two of three brothers (the third was named Su Kun), who were all well known as Confucian scholars.[115] The youngest brother, Su Pien, was a famous book collector, and his library of twenty thousand *chüan* was said to have ranked in size only after the imperial collections and the library of the Chi-hsien Academy. Su Pien had a successful

---

112 There are also indications that there was some relationship between the *T'ung tien* and the *Hui yao*. See Hanabusa Hideki "Kai-yō ni tsuite," *Shinagaku kenkyū*, special issue no. 11 (1954): 5–6.

113 See *THY* 36, p. 660; *CTS* 189B, p. 4977; *HTS* 103, p. 3993; *HTS* 59, p. 1563; *Chih-chai shu-lu chieh-t'i* 5, p. 33b; *Sung shih* 207, p. 5294 (which also lists Su Mien's *Ku-chin kuo-tien* in one hundred chapters, a title otherwise unknown); *Chün-chai tu-shu chih (Yüan-pen) hou-chih* 2, p. 19a; *Yü hai* 51, p. 32b; *WHTK* 207, p. 1681b. The summary surviving version of *Ch'ung-wen tsung-mu* 6, p. 13b, lists two books entitled *Hui yao*, each in forty chapters. These may have been two copies, but are more probably the *Hui yao* and *Hsü hui yao*. It then lists (p. 14a) *THY* in one hundred chapters, and then yet another *Hui yao*, this time in thirty chapters. This was most probably the *Wu-tai hui yao*. All are listed as "encyclopedias" (*lei-shu*).

114 These comments are clearly separated from the text and begin "Mr. Su (Su-shih) says ..." or "Mr. Su's opinion or 'critique' (*Su-shih I, Su-shih po-i*) says...," and in a few places "Su Mien says..." They range from detailed questions of historical accuracy and dating to substantial discussion of issues.

115 See *THY* 36, p. 660; also *Yü hai* 51, p. 32b. See also Hanabusa Hideki, "Kai-yō ni tsuite," pp. 4–5, which points out that the author's comments, most of which are introduced by "Mr. Su says..." (*Su Shih yüeh...*), are in two cases written "Su Mien says..." (*Su Mien yüeh*), and one of these (*THY* 3, p. 28) is confirmed by a quotation in Ssu-ma Kuang's *K'ao-i (TCTC* 213, pp. 6772–3).

official career until his involvement in a heated dispute at court over the correct order of precedence of certain offices led to the disgrace and banishment of all three brothers.[116] It seems that it was after this that the *Hui yao* was compiled. When it was finally presented to the emperor in 804 or 805,[117] the names of the authors were given as Su Pien, then prefect of Hang-chou, and Su Mien.[118]

It is said in one late source that Su Pien and Su Mien did not start this work ab initio but, as Tu Yu had done, continued an existing book, the title of which is given as *Kuo-ch'ao ku-shih*.[119] The identity of this work is not clear, but it may refer to a book listed in *Hsin T'ang shu*'s bibliographical monograph as the *Kuo-ch'ao chiu-shih* in forty chapters.[120]

The *Hui yao* proved such a convenient and useful form of history that in the reign of Hsiuan-tsung, the Historiographical Office was ordered to produce an official sequel to it, the *Hsü Hui yao*.

Hsü Hui yao

The *Hsü Hui yao*[121] comprised forty chapters. Compiled by a large team of scholars – Yang Shao-fu,[122] Hsüeh Feng,[123] Ts'ui Yüan,[124] Cheng Yen,[125]

---

116 See *CTS* 189B, p. 4977.
117 Rotours, *Traité des Examens*, p. 92, gives the date of the *Hui yao* as 804, citing Edouard Chavannes and Paul Pelliot, "Un traité manichéen retrouvé en Chine," *Journal Asiatique*, ser. III, 1 (1913): 262, n. 2. Rotours is, however, in error. This note does *not* date the *Hui yao* precisely: It says simply that it went up to 804, and was compiled at the beginning of the ninth century. There is no record of the precise date of its completion or its presentation to the throne in the *CTS* Basic Annals or elsewhere. *THY* 36, p. 660, records its presentation, but without an exact date, in a chronological listing of presentations of books to the throne, between that of *TT* in 803, and the presentation of a commentary to the *Ch'un ch'iu* and a work on statecraft entitled *Chün-ch'en t'u-i* by Lu Chih, who died early in 805, as did Su Pien. This would confirm its date of completion roughly at 803–4.
118 See *THY* 36, p. 660. See also *Yü hai* 51, p. 32b (commentary).
119 *Yü hai* 51, p. 32b.
120 See *HTS* 58, p. 1485. The work is otherwise unknown. It is listed there without an author, but it follows immediately after another work with a similar title, *Kuo-ch'ao chuan-chi*, in three chapters, by Liu Su (yet another of Liu Chih-chi's sons, an official historian in the T'ien-pao period [742–56] and an elder brother of Liu Chih), and, although his name is not repeated, it *may* well also have been by the same author, as is commonly the case in the *HTS* bibliography. It is unlikely to refer to the short *T'ang-ch'ao ku-shih* in three *chüan* by Ts'ui Yin-ju, listed as missing in *Pi-shu sheng hsü ssu-k'u shu-mu* (reprinted in *Sung-shih i-wen chih pu tu pien* Shanghai, 1957), p. 443.
121 See *CTS* 18B, p. 632; *CTS* 163, p. 4262; *THY* 36, pp. 662–3; *HTS* 59, p. 1563; *Yü hai* 51, pp. 32b–33a; *Chih-chai shu-lu chieh-t'i* 5, p. 33b; *Chün-chai tu-shu chih (Yüan-pen)*, *hou-chih* 2, p. 19a; *WHTK* 207, p. 1681b. See *CTS* 163, p. 4262.
122 Yang Shao-fu was a son of Yang Wu-ling (753–830) a precocious scholar who became a *chin-shih* at the age of seventeen and played an important role in the politics of the reigns of Hsien-tsung and his successors. One of his other sons, Yang Ssu-fu was chief

P'ei Te-jung, Chou Fu-min, Hsüeh T'ing-wang,[126] Yü Kuei, and Yu Ch'iu[127] – it was presented to the throne in 853 by Chief Minister and Director of the National History Ts'ui Hsüan.[128]

This sequel seems to have followed strictly the original plan of the *Hui yao*, adding under each rubric material dealing with the period from the reign of Te-tsung down to 851 or 852.[129] Because the compilers were working with the full resources of the Historiographical Office at their disposal, it was much more detailed than the *Hui yao*, which had dealt with the period down to the late eighth century.[130]

The fact that the Historiographical Office was willing to take over as an official project a genre that had originated as an innovation by private individuals shows that this new form was considered both important and convenient. As we shall see later, in discussing the monographs of *Chiu T'ang shu*, future historians would find the *Hui yao* and, above all, the *Hsü Hui yao* rich sources for the writing of institutional history.

Moreover, the compilation of *Hsü Hui yao* in 853 permanently gave the *Hui yao* form the dignity and authority of official historiography. In the Five Dynasties period we find the *Hui yao* and *Hsü Hui yao* cited as authoritative official sources of record for the T'ang, together with

minister from 738–40. Shao-fu was a *chin-shih* graduate who later became chief secretary of the Secretariat. The Yangs were a scholarly lineage: Four of Shao-fu's own sons and six of his nephews became *chin-shih* and all achieved high court office.

123 Hsüeh Feng was a *chin-shih* of 841, and a protégé of Ts'ui Hsüan, who, when he became chief minister in 849, had Hsüeh made an assistant in the Hung-wen Academy. See *CTS* 190C, p. 5079.

124 Ts'ui Yüan was also a compiler of the *Hsü T'ang li* completed in 851.

125 Cheng Yen was the top *chin-shih* graduate in 844. See *Teng-k'o chi k'ao* 22, p. 11b.

126 P'ei Te-jung, Chou Fu-min, and Hsüeh T'ing-wang are otherwise unknown.

127 Yü Kuei and Yü Ch'iu were brothers, members of a lineage notable both for its scholarship and its Confucian tradition. They were great-grandsons of the official historian Yü Hsiu-lieh, who worked on the National History in the 760s. Their grandfather Yü Su was one of the two sons of Yü Hsiu-lieh to serve as Han-lin scholars: Their father Yü Ao was a *chin-shih* graduate who held high court ranks under Hsien-tsung and served as vice-president of the Chancellery in 824. Yü Kuei and Yü Ch'iu were among the four sons of Yü Ao who became *chin-shih*. See *CTS* 149, pp. 4010–11; *HTS* 104, p. 4009.

128 Ts'ui Hsüan served as chief minister from 840 to 855. He was also the senior scholar of the Hung-wen Academy, in which Hsüeh Feng and Ts'ui Yüan were assistants (*chih*). He is known to have been a close friend and associate of Yang Shao-fu. See *HTS* 160, p. 4974.

129 See *THY* 36, p. 663; *Yü hai* 51, p. 33a.

130 It is difficult to precisely date when *Hui yao* ended and *Hsü hui yao* began. One piece of evidence is to be found in *THY* 87, p. 1591 (line 13), where the text deals with the establishment in 799 under Li Ch'i of a tax on travelers, which is said to "have begun from this date," implying that it was still in force. These taxes were in fact abolished in 807. See Denis C. Twitchett, "The Derivation of the Text of the *Shih-huo Chih* of the *Chiu T'ang-shu*," *Journal of Oriental Studies* 3, no. 1 (1956): 48–62, esp. 53–4.

the National History.[131] Under the Sung the regular systematic compilation of *hui yao* would became a major function of the official historiographers.[132]

The adoption of this new genre by the official historians in 853 should be seen in its broader historical context. The beginning of the reign of Hsiuan-tsung saw an attempt to bring about a dynastic revival that deserves more careful historical scrutiny than it has so far received. One part of this minor dynastic "restoration" was a series of novel scholarly projects. Two of these were legal compilations: The first was a new codification of the legislation embodied in edicts issued during recent reigns, the *Ta-chung hsing-fa tsung-yao ko-hou ch'ih*[133] in sixty chapters, completed in 851. This was followed by a rationalized rearrangement of the whole body of codified law in accordance with the basic structure of the Code, the *Ta-chung hsing-fa t'ung-lei* in twelve chapters, completed in 853.[134] This quite novel and convenient form of codification was imitated under the Sung and later dynasties.

Another set of new works related to the examination system. Lists of examination graduates and examination topics were compiled.[135] These attempted to establish and define the new scholarly elite within the bureaucracy, much as the great state-sponsored genealogies of the seventh and early eighth centuries had tried to define the old aristocracy.

Historical works played an important part in this revival of imperially sponsored scholarship. In 851 two works were presented to Hsiuan-tsung by Yao K'ang, supervisor of the heir apparent's household: one a huge *T'ung shih* in three hundred chapters, which arranged and categorized, in a manner similar to *T'ung tien*, all the important edicts, laws, and policy decisions from ancient times to the end of Sui, and the other a

---

131 See, for example, *WTHY* 12, p. 203, where it is cited in a Southern T'ang memorial dated the first month of 928 from the Secretariat–Chancellery as authority for a change in the public holiday celebrating Lao-tzu's birthday, which had been reduced from three days to one day in 841. Both *Hsü hui yao* and *Hui yao* are cited as authoritative in a memorial from the Secretariat–Chancellery dated 942 in *CWTS* 149, p. 1991, and *Hui yao* in a memorial dated 955 from the president of the Court of Imperial Sacrifices cited in *CWTS* 143, p. 1913.

132 See T'ang Chung, *Sung Hui yao yen-chiu* (Shanghai, 1931); Wang Yün-hai, *Sung Hui yao chi-kao k'ao-chiao* (Shanghai, 1986), pp. 1–4; and the summary by Sudō Yoshiyuki in *Ajia rekishi jiten* (1962), vol. 5, p. 335. There were eleven successive *Hui yao's* compiled under the Sung.

133 See *CTS* 50, p. 1256; *TFYK* 613, p. 7a; *HTS* 58, p. 1497. *Ch'ung-wen tsung-mu* 4, p. 2b, lists it as missing in 1133.

134 See *CTS* 50, p. 2156; *CTS* 18B, p. 628, which records its presentation in 851, has confused this work with the *Ta-chung hsing-fa tsung-yao ko-hou ch'ih*. The correct date is given in *CTS* 18B, p. 631. See also *CTS* 177, p. 4607, the biography of its chief compiler, Liu Yüan, the vice-president of the Board of Justice.

135 See n. 23 in this chapter.

ten-chapter summary of this entitled *Ti-wang cheng-t'ung*. Both were largely concerned with institutional matters.[136] The official historians meanwhile continued their normal routine, completing the Veritable Records for Wen-tsung in 854,[137] and revising those for Hsien-tsung, to replace the politically biased new version that had been introduced in 843 by Li Te-yü and his historians. They were also ordered to undertake, as official projects, continuations of two major private histories that had enjoyed wide praise. The first was the *Hsü T'ang li*, a continuation of Liu Fang's *T'ang li*, the private chronological history of the T'ang completed under Te-tsung.[138] The second was the *Hsü Hui yao*. The decision to undertake these two projects gives us a feeling that, as in the case of the new reorganized digest of penal law, there was both a dissatisfaction with existing official forms and a willingness to adopt and experiment with new improved methods of presentation in the interest of rational arrangement and convenience of reference. In both cases the new forms were to have lasting influence.

Neither the *Hui yao* nor the *Hsü Hui yao* survives in its original form. But their substance has been preserved for us in a work completed at the beginning of the Sung period, the *T'ang hui yao* of Wang P'u (922–82), which remains one of our most important sources for T'ang history.[139]

---

136 See Twitchett, *Cambridge History of China*, vol. 3, pp. 673–74; *THY* 36, p. 662. Neither work seems to have survived into the Sung: they are not listed in the *HTS* bibliography. On Yao K'ang, whose name is mistakenly written Yao Ssu-lien, out of confusion with the eminent seventh-century historian, by *THY* 36, but is cited in its correct form in a quotation from the original *Hui yao* in Yü hai 47, p. 9a–b, see Ch'en Kuang-ch'ung, "Chi wan-T'ang shih-chia Yao K'ang ho Ch'en Yüeh," *Shih-hsüeh shih yen-chiu* 1984, no. 2: 51–54.

137 See *THY* 63, p. 1098; *TFYK* 554, p. 35b; *CTS* 18B, p. 632.

138 See *THY* 63, p. 1098; *TFYK* 556, p. 25b; *CTS* 163, p. 4262; *THY* 36, pp. 662–3.

139 Wang P'u's *THY* has not been transmitted either in its original form or in its entirety: The book is cited frequently by Yü hai (usually as *Hui yao*), and it is clear that Wang Ying-lin (1223–96) used a text very different from the present book. It is unclear whether he was in some cases quoting an earlier recension of *THY*, or the original *Hui yao* and *Hsü hui yao*. Hu San-hsing (1230–? *chin-shih* 1256) also used a different text, which he once cites under the title *T'ang-shu hui yao*. He may there be referring to another work, although this title is otherwise unknown. The *THY* was not printed until the eighteenth century. The entry in *Ssu-k'u ch'üan-shu tsung-mu ti-yao* 81, pp. 1696–7, which is also appended to the *Wu-ying tien* edition, which was its first printing, notes that the book had only been transmitted in manuscript, and that the text contained many errors and interpolations: These problems were particularly serious in chapters 7–10. The *Ssu-k'u ch'üan-shu* used a manuscript copy from the personal library of the Hangchow bibliophile Wang Ch'i-shu (1728–99), which still exists in the National Central Library, Taipei. It bears seals that show it was once in the possession of Ts'ao Jung (1613–85) a famous collector of Sung and Yüan books. Another similar manuscript exists in the National Central Library, Taipei. These two manuscripts were recently the subject of a study by Shimada Tadao, "Zai Taihoku Kokuritsu Chūō Toshokan shōhon *Tōkaiyō* ni tsuite," in *Takigawa Masajirō Hakase Beiju*

T'ang hui yao

T'ang hui yao comprises one hundred chapters. It was completed and presented to the throne by Chief Minister and Director of the National History Wang P'u at the beginning of 961.[140] It was ordered to be stored in the Historiographical Office, and its compilers were rewarded as convention demanded.[141] Both it and its sister work, the *Wu-tai hui yao*, completed two years later in 963,[142] were certainly compiled very hurriedly. Wang P'u, then the director of the Historiographical Office, and his collaborators seem simply to have conflated the *Hui yao* and *Hsü Hui yao*, section by section. Sometimes the joins still show.[143] Although Wang P'u and his compilers claimed to have "collected together ma-

kinen ronshū: Ritsu-ryō-sei no shomondai (Tokyo 1984), pp. 669–89. Yet another manuscript of very similar type was formerly in Lu Hsin-yüan's (1834–94) Pi-Sung lou library, and had once been in the collection of the seventeenth-century painter and calligrapher Tan Chung-kuang. This is now in the Seikadō Bunko collection in Tokyo.

There are also three old manuscripts in the Pei-ching T'u-shu kuan and three more in the Shang-hai t'u-shu kuan. One of those in Peking is an incomplete Ming copy, the other two from early Ch'ing; of the three manuscripts in Shanghai, one is also probably of Ming date, according to the taboo characters observed. See Cheng Ming, "T'ang hui-yao ch'u t'an," in Chung-kuo T'ang-shih hui lun-wen chi (Hsi-an, 1989), pp. 167–82.

These manuscripts are all clearly related: The chapters mentioned as interpolations by the Ssu-k'u editors have been filled out and replaced with a variety of non related texts. Chapter 7, for example, appears to have been made up from long quotations of Po-hu t'ung; chapter 8 is a large section of the Ma-shih Nan T'ang-shu, describing many events that took place years after the compilation of THY. These chapters probably represent a missing fascicle of an early manuscript that has been supplemented to disguise the loss by copying out the chapter headings taken from the THY table of contents, followed by an appropriate amount of text taken from some other work. In the late eighteenth century, probably at the time the work was copied for the Ssu-k'u ch'üan-shu, these missing chapters were "reconstructed" from genuine T'ang sources. Unfortunately we do not know by whom this was done. These reconstructions were included in the Wu-ying tien edition, and in modern editions deriving from this, the supplemented sections (and their sources) are clearly indicated. The reconstruction was conscientiously done, but these reconstructed chapters have no historical value.

140 See Hsü Tzu-chih t'ung-chien ch'ang-pien 2, p. 39; Ch'ung-wen tsung-mu 6, p. 14a (lei-shu); Sung shih 207, p. 5299 (lei-shih); Chung-hsing Kuan-ko shu-mu (in Sung shih i-wen chih, pu, fu-pien edition), p. 530; Chün-chai tu-shu chih (Yüan-pen) hou-chih 2, p. 19a; Chih-chai shu-lu chieh-t'i 6, p. 14a; Yü-hai 51, pp. 32b–33a; WHTK 201, p. 1681a–c (ku-shih); Ssu-k'u ch'üan-shu tsung-mu t'i-yao 81, pp. 1696–7 (cheng-shu).

141 See Hsü Tzu-chih t'ung-chien ch'ang-pien 2, p. 39, dated the chia-tzu day of the first month of 961. Yü hai 51, p. 33a, gives the dates as the ting-wei day of the same month.

142 On WTHY see Chün-chai tu-shu chih (Yüan-pen) 3B, p. 23b. Ssu-k'u ch'üan-shu tsung-mu t'i-yao 81, p. 167, is in error when it states that WTHY was presented to the throne in 961 together with THY. In fact Wang P'u and his colleagues produced WTHY subsequently, and presented it to the throne on the chia-yin day of the seventh month of 963. See Hsü Tzu-chih t'ung-chien ch'ang-pien 4, p. 97; Yü hai 51, p. 33a.

143 See n. 85 in this chapter.

terials on the reigns of Hsiuan-tsung and his successors," their only new contributions seem to have been a few desultory items of information dealing with events subsequent to 853, most of which they may well have taken from *Chiu T'ang shu*, which had been completed in 945.

As a result of this process of compilation the material in the *T'ang hui yao* varies considerably in richness and density from period to period. Almost all of the information on the early T'ang down to 758 in the original *Hui yao* of Su Mien and Su Pien seems to have been taken from the National History. It is not particularly detailed. The origins of the *Hui yao's* materials relating to the next reigns are more difficult to pinpoint. The documentation on the reign of Su-tsung probably came from the Veritable Record of his reign. But the material on Tai-tsung and Te-tsung must have been collected independently, because when the *Hui yao* was compiled the Veritable Record for Tai-tsung's reign was still in the hands of its author's family and had not yet been presented to the throne,[144] while that for Te-tsung, who was still the reigning emperor, had, of course, not yet been compiled.[145]

The *Hsü Hui yao's* compilers, working in the Historiographical Office with all its resources at their disposal, almost certainly extracted a large part of its material for the reigns of Te-tsung, Shun-tsung, Hsien-tsung, Mu-tsung, and Ching-tsung from their completed Veritable Records and, for the reign of Wen-tsung, that of Wu-tsung, and the first years of Hsiuan-tsung', from the drafts and materials destined for their Veritable Records under preparation in the Historiographical Office.[146] In spite of Wang P'u and his colleagues having claimed to have collected together materials on the reigns of Hsiuan-tsung and his successors,[147] when they amalgamated the two books to form the extant *T'ang hui yao* in the mid tenth century, they seem to have made no systematic effort to complete the account beyond 852–3, and with a few trifling exceptions, the book contains virtually nothing from the last half century of the dynasty. The result is an uneven distribution of material in the *T'ang hui yao*. The period to 758 is adequately covered, and the

---

144 It was completed by Ling-hu Huan in Chiang-hsi some time after 789. After his death in 805, his son presented it to the throne, either in 807 or 808. See *CTS* 149, p. 4014; *CTS* 14, p. 421; *THY* 63, p. 1097; *TFYK* 556, p. 20a.

145 The *Te-tsung Shih-lu* was compiled only in 810. See *THY* 63, p. 1097; *TFYK* 556, pp. 20a–21b; *CTS* 14, p. 432.

146 The *Wen-tsung Shih-lu* was presented to the throne in the next year, 854, and must already have been in an advanced stage of preparation. See *THY* 63, p. 1098; *CTS* 18B, p. 132; *TFYK* 554, p. 35b. The Veritable Records for Wu-tsung's reign were not completed until the 870s, and for this period the historians probably used the Daily Calendars (*Jih-li*).

147 *Hsü Tzu-chih t'ung-chien Ch'ang-pien* 2, p. 39.

material is similar to that in the *Chiu T'ang shu,* which came from the National History. The coverage of the period from 758 to 800 is fuller than that of the earlier period and more complete in many respects than that in *Chiu T'ang shu.* The coverage of the period from 800 to 852 is full indeed, and markedly better than that of *Chiu T'ang shu.* The period after 852 is not systematically covered at all, only a few random items being included.

Like the *Hsü Hui yao,* the *T'ang hui yao* and *Wu-tai hui yao* were undertaken by official historians in the Sung Historiographical Office. Wang P'u, their principal compiler, was director of the National History. Their compilation tells us that by the beginning of the Sung the *hui yao* form had become an accepted format for official historical writing. Moreover, its relationship to the standard forms of history was now quite changed. *Hui yao* and *Hsü Hui yao* had been compiled under the T'ang as supplementary works dealing with a period for which the National History and its monographs had stopped short with Su-tsung's reign. The *T'ang hui yao* was compiled as an official work supplementing the *completed* dynastic history of the T'ang period, which had been presented to the throne sixteen years before in 945. Its compilation thus affirmed the idea that *hui yao* were now a standardized form of official historical writing, complementary to the old, established forms such as the Veritable Records or the Standard Histories, and with their own special purpose. Under the Sung the compilation by the Historiographical Office of successive *hui yao* continued, side by side with more traditional work on the successive Sung Veritable Records and National Histories.

It thus seems that from the ninth century onward the writing of institutional history in the form of collected documents gradually became a specialized activity of the official historians. This work was, however, isolated from the cumulative process of compiling a standard dynastic history through the stages of Court Diary, Veritable Records, and National History, the essential motive of which was moral judgment on court politics and the administration of the empire. In the newly adopted *hui yao* form the official historians, though still not free of the compulsion to make implicit judgments, began to compile truly "professional" history "by bureaucrats for fellow bureaucrats," designed almost exclusively to provide a body of precedent in Balázs's sense. We should not, however, exaggerate this change. Although such histories appear at first sight to be "problem-oriented" in a modern sense and certainly provide a convenient collection of evidence for modern historians of institutions, in their own way the *hui yao* were as innocent of any deliberate attempt on the part of their authors to establish and elaborate upon causal relationships as were the Basic Annals; it is only their categorization of documents and their concentration on a single subject at a time that provides them both with a focus and a natural, chronological "story line."

It is perhaps significant too that this form of "professionalized" institutional history emerged as a full-fledged form of official history writing under the Sung just when the mainstream of historical scholarship, official and private alike, was increasingly coming under the dominance of Confucian ideologues, who gradually came to look on history more as a philosophical avocation than as the production of an accurate historical record of events.

In this connection it is worth looking beyond the T'ang period to the compilation of the *Ts'e-fu yüan-kuei,* perhaps the richest single source for T'ang history, and certainly the most important source for the history of the Five Dynasties.

When the early Sung emperors, after the long and difficult process of stabilization and reunification was finally completed, began to sponsor great imperial collaborative works through which they could exercise their patronage over the scholarly elite, they commissioned a series of massive official compilations, the great literary enterprises known to later scholars as the "Four Great Books of the Sung Dynasty" (*Sung-ch'ao ssu ta shu*).[148] Of these, the *T'ai-p'ing yü-lan,* ordered in 977 and completed in 983, was a literary encyclopedia on the old model;[149] the second, the *T'ai-ping kuang-chi,* commissioned in 977 and completed in 978, was a huge compendium of classified extracts from the extensive fictional or semifictional literature of the pre-T'ang, T'ang, and Wu-tai periods.[150] The third was the *Wen-yüan ying-hua,* a very large literary anthology conceived as a continuation of the *Wen-hsüan,* ordered in 982 and completed in 987.[151]

The fourth, the *Ts'e-fu yüan-kuei,* was an afterthought. Commissioned by Chen-tsung in 1005, and completed in 1013, it is an enormous historical encyclopedia extending to a thousand chapters.[152] It covers the whole sweep of history to the end of the Five Dynasties in 960. But it was a historical encyclopedia of a new and different kind. Where the *Hui yao*

148 See Kuo Po-Kung, *Sung ssu ta shu k'ao* (Shanghai, 1937).
149 See John W. Haeger, "The Significance of Confusion: The Origins of the *T'ai-p'ing yü-lan*," *JAOS* 88 (1968): 401–10.
150 See Yeh Ch'ing-ping, "Yu kuan *T'ai-p'ing kuang chi* te chi-ko wen-t'i," in K'o Ch'ing-ming and Lin Ming-te, eds., *Chung-kuo ku-tien wen-hsüeh yen-chiu ts'ung-k'an: Hsiao-shuo chih pu* (Taipei, 1977) 2, pp. 11–44.
151 See Hanabusa Hideki, "*Bun'en eiga* no hensan," *Tōhō gakuhō (Kyoto)* 19 (1950): 116–35.
152 The best work on *Ts'e-fu yüan-kuei* to date is the symposium volume Liu Nai-ho, ed., *Ts'e-fu yüan-kuei hsin-t'an* (Cheng-chou, 1983).

and *T'ung tien* had arranged their material according to straightforward, practical institutional criteria, *Ts'e-fu yüan-kuei,* although it is very broadly organized according to the basic functions of government, is broken up into an extremely complicated series of thirty-one sections (*pu*) and 1,106 subdivisions (*men*), which relate to a highly subjective scheme of moral assessments of events and individuals' actions. Each section has a substantial preface, and each subsection an introduction followed by documents and extracts arranged in chronological order.[153]

Although it was printed soon after its completion, *Ts'e-fu yüan-kuei* was strangely neglected by historians until the nineteenth century, when the richness of its contents began to be generally recognized. For example, Ssu-ma Kuang and his team of compilers working on the *Tzu-chih t'ung-chien* never once cite it in the *K'ao-i,* although it must have been available to them. Partly this neglect must be ascribed to its huge and unwieldy bulk (it was the second-largest work incorporated in the *Ssu-k'u ch'üan-shu,* the late eighteenth-century imperially sponsored collection of all the works considered worthy of preservation for posterity, exceeded in size only by the all-inclusive rhyming dictionary *P'ei-wen yün-fu*), but the main reason was probably its subjective and inconsistent arrangement, which made it inconvenient for reference.

Unlike *T'ung tien* and *Hui yao,* each of which developed a long series of continuations and sequels, *Ts'e-fu yüan-kuei* remained without descendants or imitators. This was largely because it was an unhappy attempt to mix institutional history designed to provide practical lessons for bureaucrats, with more general and more traditional moral didacticism. Such an attempt may have been in harmony with the general intellectual trends of the early eleventh century, but as a history it proved a practical failure. The writers of institutional histories, official and private alike, reverted to the plans of *T'ung tien* and of the *Hui yao.*

153 These essays are themselves of considerable intrinsic value for the study of historiography in early Sung times.

10

The Veritable Records
(*Shih-lu*)

In later dynasties the Veritable Records were the most important and prestigious products of official historiography, the authorized official account of each individual emperor's reign, and most historians have treated the T'ang *Shih-lu* as though they were exactly analogous to those of later dynasties. It is sometimes forgotten, however, that they were in fact a T'ang innovation. Works under the title *Shih-lu* had been compiled under the minor northwestern dynasty of Western Liang (400–23),[1] and for certain reigns under the Liang (502–57) in southern China,[2] but the T'ang was the first major dynasty to compile a Veritable Record systematically for each successive reign.

---

1 The bibliographical monograph of *SS* mentions the *Tun-huang Shih-lu* in ten chapters by Liu Ching (*SS* 33, p. 963). *CTS* 46, p. 2001, lists a work of the same title in twenty chapters by Liu Yen-ming. *HTS* 58, p. 1462, also lists the same work in twenty chapters and gives its author as Liu Ping. Liu Ping and Liu Yen-ming (d. ca. 440) are the same person (Yen-ming is his style). See his biographies in *Wei shu* 52, pp. 1160–1, and in Li Yen-shou, *Pei shih* (Peking, 1974) 34, pp. 1267–9, both of which say that he was the author of a *Tun-huang Shih-lu* in twenty chapters.
2 Three Veritable Records from the Liang seem to have survived in Sui and early T'ang times. (1) The bibliographical monograph of *SS* lists a *Liang Huang-ti Shih-lu* in three chapters by Chou Hsing-ssu (d. 521) and adds a note that it dealt with the affairs of Liang Wu-ti's reign. It can in fact only have dealt with Wu-ti's early years, because the author died in 521. See *SS* 33, p. 960. Chou Hsing-ssu's biographies in Yao Ssu-lien et al., *Liang shu* (Peking, 1973) 49, pp. 607–98, and Li Yen-shou's *Nan shih* (Peking, 1975) 72, pp. 1779–80, included the *Huang-ti Shih-lu* among his writings but give no number of chapters. *CTS* 46, p. 1997, lists it as in three chapters, *HTS* 58, p. 1471, as in two chapters, probably a copyist's error. (2) The *SS* also lists a *Liang Huang-ti Shih-lu* in five chapters by Hsieh Wu, a secretary of the Secretariat under the Liang, and adds a note that it recorded the events of Yüan-ti's reign. See *SS* 33, p. 961. The same work is listed without an author's name in *CTS* 46, p. 1997. *HTS* 58, p. 1471, also lists it, giving as author Hsieh Hao, presumably a copyist's error for Hsieh Wu. (3) The *SS* also includes a *Liang T'ai-ch'ing lu* in eight chapters, without any author's name. See *SS* 33, p. 960. This is given the title *Liang T'ai-ch'ing Shih-lu* in eight chapters in *CTS* 46, p. 1997, and is listed under the same title but in ten chapters by *HTS* 58, p. 1471. Neither source gives an author's name.

Under later dynasties a Veritable Record normally was not compiled until a reign was over and a retrospective summary of events was possible, but in early T'ang several Veritable Records of the early part of a reign were written while the same emperor was still on the throne. The first Veritable Records were ordered in 640 by T'ai-tsung, who demanded to see what the historiographers were recording about his own reign. Veritable Records were later prepared for the early years of the reigns of Kao-tsung, Empress Wu, and Hsüan-tsung, while these sovereigns were still occupying the throne. In fact, until the mid eighth century, every emperor except for Chung-tsung and Jui-tsung, neither of whom reigned for more than a few years, commissioned Veritable Records for the first part of his own reign.

These Veritable Records were in every case ordered for a political purpose. T'ai-tsung ordered the Veritable Record for the first years of his reign after the death of his dethroned father Kao-tsu, in a period when there was a growing problem over the succession. Kao-tsung's first Veritable Record was compiled following the crisis surrounding the replacement and subsequent murder of Empress Wang by Empress Wu and the sweeping political changes that ensued. Empress Wu commissioned the Veritable Record covering her own early years in power after 683 when in 690 she was on the point of overthrowing the T'ang imperial house and setting up a dynasty of her own. Hsüan-tsung's first Veritable Record was probably compiled following his performance of the supreme Feng and Shan sacrifices, celebrating a peak of dynastic power. Clearly in the first half of the T'ang a Veritable Record was not yet simply the history of a past reign.[3]

The compilation of a Veritable Record was not simply a routine rewriting of the official record but was in every case a major and deliberate political act. In the case of the Veritable Record of a past reign the compilation might be ordered by the succeeding emperor almost immediately upon his accession, but it might often be delayed until a more propitious time. Here again, the practice was changed greatly during the course of the dynasty. In early T'ang (until the An Lu-shan rebellion) the Veritable Record was always completed soon after a sovereign's death or abdication. In contrast to this, only one of the Veritable Records for the nine T'ang emperors from Su-tsung to Wu-tsung

---

3 A memorial (translated in Chapter 8 of the present volume) presented in 819 by Li Ao, then a member of the Historiographical Office, suggests that a Veritable Record might properly have been undertaken during the lifetime of the ruling emperor, Hsien-tsung, to record his achievements in restoring the dynasty. See Li Ao, *Li Wen-kung chi* (*SPTK* edition) 10, pp. 75a–77b; *CTW* 634, p. 6b. Thus even in the ninth century a Veritable Record for a ruling monarch was still very much a possibility.

(from 756 to 846) was completed within five years of the emperor's death. Those for the reign of Tai-tsung, for example, were finally presented to the throne no fewer than twenty-eight years after his death, and most of the others took between ten and twenty years before they were completed. Moreover, in the second half of the T'ang only two Veritable Records were even completed during the reign of the succeeding emperor. It is worth drawing a comparison with later periods, when the procedures of official historiography were more firmly established. The far more detailed and complex Veritable Records of Ming times were in almost every case completed within five years of the end of a reign, and never took more than a decade to compile.

That the compilation of every Veritable Record had political implications will become clear as we examine each in turn. That they were considered to be important political statements, offering a coherent judgment on the events of a recent reign with implications for contemporary politics, is equally clear from the way in which they were subjected to repeated revision, editing, and rewriting. We know some details about the Veritable Records produced for sixteen reigns. In seven cases at least these were rewritten and revised, in some cases several times, because of dissatisfaction with the original versions. In a number of cases it is quite obvious that the revision was necessitated not because the Veritable Record was considered defective as an accurate depiction of events, but because its political bias no longer coincided with the interests of those now in power.

Unlike many of the other categories of historical record with which I have dealt so far, examples of which do not survive, we have, in the Veritable Records of Shun-tsung's reign (*Shun-tsung Shih-lu*), preserved in Han Yü's collected works, an actual example of the genre. Although, as we shall see, there has been much controversy over which particular recension of the Veritable Record of this short but highly controversial reign we actually possess, this work, which has been integrally translated into English,[4] does give us a clear picture of what a Veritable Record was like, a picture borne out by many quotations from other T'ang Veritable Records surviving elsewhere.[5]

The Veritable Record was the first stage in the writing of the dynastic record where a systematic attempt was made to "write history," to give a balanced judgment, and to produce an overall picture of the reign by applying the principles of "praise and blame." Its director was normally one of the chief ministers. In some cases he clearly exerted strong

---

4 See Solomon, *The Veritable Record of the T'ang Emperor Shun-tsung.*
5 Notably in the *Tzu-chih t'ung-chien K'ao-i.*

pressures on the compilers to produce a politically acceptable account of the period. Its authors were "the historians" (*shih-kuan*), not the court diarists. When their work was completed, it was formally presented to the throne, and the historians involved in its compilation would be lavishly rewarded, promoted, and sometimes given noble titles and presented with special imperial letters of commendation. Moreover, the Veritable Record was lodged in the Imperial Library; none of the earlier stages of compilation was so honored. It was also considered a part of the "National History."

The earlier stages of compilation were contemporary records, written down piecemeal as events took place. The Veritable Record digested all the previous records to produce a chronologically arranged history, which would later become the main source for the Basic Annals (*pen chi*) of each reign in the National or Standard History. It also included biographies of prominent men, which would later provide source material for the biographical sections (*lieh-chuan*) of the dynastic history.

Unlike the situation in more recent dynasties, when the Veritable Records were considered confidential, the T'ang Veritable Records seem to have been widely circulated. The emperors themselves sometimes demanded to see what was being written about their own conduct of government.[6] We know that copies of the first Veritable Records were prepared for the heir apparent and for the other royal princes, and that high-ranking officials were allowed to have their own personal copies made. Liu Chih-chi in the autobiographical chapter of his *Shih-t'ung* claims that by his seventeenth year his reading of history had extended to the "Veritable Records of our own dynasty."[7] Copies circulated in the provinces. In 848 the government issued orders to all prefectures and local administrations to search for copies of a revised Veritable Record of Hsien-tsung's reign that had been compiled and circulated under Wu-tsung and was now, because of its political implications, ordered to be withdrawn in favor of the original version, which had been presented to the throne in 830.[8]

Copies of some Veritable Records were even taken abroad. There are references to and quotations from the "Veritable Records for Kao-tsu"

---

6 On the confidentiality of the record, see the memorial of Wei Mu cited in *TFYK* 554, p. 27a–b, and the discussion between Wen-tsung and the diarist Cheng Lang, *TFYK* 554, pp. 26b–27a.

7 See *Shih t'ung* 10, p. 288.

8 See *TFYK* 556, p. 22a; *TFYK* 562, p. 11a–b; *THY* 63, p. 1098.

and the "Veritable Records for T'ai-tsung" in various Japanese works written during the Heian period.[9] In the late ninth century the Japanese bibliography *Nihon koku genzai sho mokuroku* of Fujiwara no Sukeyo, compiled between 885 and 897, lists the "Veritable Records for Kao-tsung" and two other unidentifiable "T'ang Veritable Records."[10]

The following are the Veritable Records known to have been compiled during the T'ang period.

The T'ang Veritable Records

I. *Kao-tsu Shih-lu*

Twenty chapters. Compiled by Ching Po and revised by Hsü Ching-tsung under the direction of Fang Hsüan-ling.[11]

According to *Chung-hsing Kuan-ko shu-mu* as quoted by *Yü hai*, Kao-tsu's Veritable Record covered events from the beginning of the T'ang rebellion against the Sui and ended with the ninth year of the Chen-kuan period (635).[12] It was compiled together with that for the first years of T'ai-tsung's reign, at T'ai-tsung's own direct order. The two works taken together provided an "authorized version" of the dynastic founding and the consolidation of the new regime in the early years of

---

9 See Ota Shōjirō, "*Tōreki* ni tsuite," in *Yamada Takao tsuioku shigaku gogaku ronshū* (Tokyo, 1963), pp. 99–128.

10 The Veritable Record of Kao-tsung's reign is attributed to Wu Hsüan-chih and is said to have comprised sixty chapters. This recension of the Veritable Record for Kao-tsung is otherwise unknown. The two works entitled *T'ang Shih-lu*, both in ninety chapters, are attributed to Fang Hsüan-ling and Hsü Ching-tsung respectively. Neither is easily identifiable with any one of the known Veritable Records of early T'ang times, though from the dates of their compilers they must have dealt only with the reigns of Kao-tsu, T'ai-tsung, and possibly the early years of Kao-tsung.

11 See *CTS* 46, p. 1998; *HTS* 58, p. 1471; *Yü hai* 48, p. 2a–b; *WHTK* 194, p. 1641a–b; *Ch'ung-wen tsung-mu* 3, p. 10b; *Chün-chai tu-shu chih* (*Yüan-pen*), *hou-chih* 1, p. 14a (*Ch'ü-pen* 6, p. 4a); *Chih-chai shu-lu chieh-t'i* 4, p. 37a. This latter notes that "the title at the beginning of present editions says 'Edited at imperial order by the Director of the National History, Hsü Ching-tsung,'" but the title of chapter 11 says, "Compiled at the Imperial Order by the Grand Master of Works, Fang Hsüan-ling." Ch'en Chen-sun could not explain this discrepancy. If this was the case, it would suggest that Hsü Ching-tsung not only participated in editing Ching Po's original work but that he himself later produced a revised edition. He became director of the National History only in 657. See also the quotation from *Chih-chai shu-lu chieh-t'i* in *WHTK* 194, p. 1641b.

12 This presumably means that it recorded not only the reign of Kao-tsu but also his life after the usurpation of the throne by T'ai-tsung, until the former's death in 635.

123

T'ai-tsung's reign.[13] T'ai-tsung was conscious of the image of his reign that was to be transmitted to posterity. In 639 he asked Ch'u Sui-liang, who had just been appointed state counselor (*Chien-i tai-fu*) and concurrently given charge of the Court Diary (chien chih *Ch'i-chü chu*), to show him what the diarists were recording about his own actions and was refused on the grounds of historical precedent. In 640 he once again remarked to Fang Hsüan-ling that he could not understand why since ancient times rulers had not been permitted to see what was being written by the state historians about their own times and he ordered that a record be compiled so that he might take heed of any warnings it contained.[14] The two resulting works were to be the first of the T'ang Veritable Records.

The Veritable Records of Kao-tsu's reign, in twenty chapters, and those of T'ai-tsung's own first years, the "Veritable Records of the Reigning Sovereign" (*Chin-shang Shih-lu*, see IIA), also in twenty chapters, were presented to the throne on the sixteenth day of the seventh month of 643 by the grand director of Works (*Ssu-k'ung*), Fang Hsüan-ling; the chief secretary of the Chancellery, Hsü Ching-tsung; and the chief secretary of the Office of Literary Composition, Ching Po.[15] We are told that they produced the Veritable Records by summarizing the "National History" (*kuo shih*, here presumably meaning the Court Diary) into chronological form.[16]

The emperor had Ch'u Sui-liang read it aloud to him; he began with the auspicious omens that had accompanied the emperor's birth. T'ai-tsung was so deeply moved that he lost his composure and ordered that the scrolls be accepted and sent to the Imperial Library. He also ordered

13 They seem deliberately to have overemphasized the role of T'ai-tsung in the dynastic founding, and to have played down that of his father. Their interpretation of events was carried over into the two Standard Histories of the T'ang, and into the *TCTC*. That their account was a propagandistic fabrication is clear from Wen Ta-ya's "Diary of the Dynastic Founding" (*Ta T'ang ch'uang-yeh ch'i-chü chu*) written during Kao-tsu's reign, and also from many passages in biographies included in *CTS* that clearly prove Kao-tsu's predominant role. On Wen Ta-ya's "Diary of the Dynastic Founding," which still survives, see the previous discussion in Chapter 4. On the bias introduced into these early Veritable Records, see Wechsler, *Mirror to the Son of Heaven*, pp. 14–27. See also Bingham, "Wen Ta-ya: The First Recorder of T'ang History," pp. 368–74.

14 See *Chen-kuan cheng-yao* 7, pp. 218–20.

15 See *THY* 63, p. 1092; *CTS* 66, p. 2461; *CTS* 82, p. 2761; *CTS* 189A, p. 4954; *HTS* 198, p. 5656.

16 See *Chen-kuan cheng yao* 7, p. 220. Just what this means is far from clear, because the Court Diary and the Records of Administrative Affairs were already in chronological form. The only other possibility is that the "National History" refers to a thirty-chapter history by Yao Ssu-lien, which had been roughly drafted in annal–biography form shortly after T'ai-tsung's accession. This work is mentioned by Liu Chih-chi. See *Shih t'ung* 12, p. 373. It can have dealt only with Kao-tsu's reign.

that a copy be given to the heir apparent and one to each of the imperial princes, and that those of the metropolitan officials of the third rank and above who wished to have a copy made for themselves were to be permitted to do so.[17]

However, other sources suggest that its reception was not entirely straightforward. According to Wu Ching's *Chen-kuan cheng yao*, when the emperor read its account of the Hsüan-wu gate coup, which had brought him to the throne, he objected and had it rewritten. He objected not to the recording of the events themselves but to the fact that they had been shrouded in obscure language. He asked that because his deeds (the murder of his brothers and usurpation of his father's throne) had been done for the good of the state and for the benefit of all mankind, they should be recorded straightforwardly without any attempt to conceal them.[18]

IIA. *Chin-shang Shih-lu*

(Later renamed *T'ai-tsung Shih-lu*.) Twenty chapters. Compiled by Ching Po (and possibly Ku Yin)[19] under the direction of Fang Hsüan-ling.[20]

This was compiled together with the Veritable Records for Kao-tsu between 640 and 643, when both works were presented to the throne. See the previous entry for details and references. According to Ching Po's *Chiu T'ang shu* biography,[21] it covered events down to the fourteenth year of the Chen-kuan period (640). It is elsewhere described as having been reliable and detailed.[22] Its account was, however, later changed and falsified by Hsü Ching-tsung, probably after its incorporation into the *Chen-kuan Shih-lu* in 654.

---

17 See *THY* 63, p. 1092.

18 See *Chen-kuan cheng yao* 7, pp. 219–20; *TCTC* 197, p. 6203. On these early Veritable Records, see Wechsler, *Mirror to the Son of Heaven*, pp. 22–7. I disagree, however, with his contention that in this instance T'ai-tsung was asking the official historians to *falsify* the record relating to his rise to power, although clearly he was determined to interfere with the way in which the historians had described events.

19 Ku Yin's name is written "Ku Ssu" in *Yü hai's* quotation from *HTS*. The character "yin" was tabooed under the Sung, as part of the personal name of the dynastic founder, and in this instance was replaced by its synonym "ssu." Ku Yin is mentioned as a compiler of the *Chin-shang Shih-lu* only by *HTS*, which has almost certainly confused this with his work on the later *Chen-kuan Shih-lu*. Ku did not become a member of the Historiographical Office until after 650. See *CTS* 73, p. 2600.

20 See *CTS* 46, p. 1998, *HTS* 58, p. 1471; *Yü hai* 48, p. 2a–b; *WHTK* 194, p. 1641b.

21 See *CTS* 189A, p. 4954. His biography in *HTS* 198, p. 5656, mentions his work on the *Kao-tsu Shih-lu* only, but as it says the work extended down to 640, it must imply that he was also involved in the compilation of the *Chin-shang Shih-lu*.

22 See *CTS* 82, p. 2764; *HTS* 223A, p. 6338.

IIB. *Chen-kuan Shih-lu*

(Also called *T'ai-tsung Shih-lu*.) Forty chapters. Compiled by Ku Yin under the direction of Chang-sun Wu-chi.[23]

This work combined the *Chin-shang Shih-lu* with twenty additional chapters dealing with the period from 641 to the fifth month of 649. *T'ang hui yao* and *Ts'e-fu yüan-kuei* say that it was completed and presented to the throne on the twenty-third day of the intercalary fifth month of 650 by Grand Commander in Chief (*T'ai-wei*) Chang-sun Wu-chi.[24] There is something wrong with this date; Chang-sun Wu-chi was not appointed director of the National History until 651,[25] and there was no intercalary fifth month in 650. There was such a month in the fifth year of the Yung-hui regnal period, 654, at which date Chang-sun Wu-chi was still grand commander in chief and now also director of the National History. He would have been unlikely to have presented the Veritable Record in 650, although he might possibly have done so in his already unquestioned role as the senior statesman at court. I would therefore suggest that it was most probably completed in 654 rather than in 650.[26]

The actual compilation was the work of Ku Yin, who was appointed a court diarist and concurrent compiler of the National History at some unspecified date during the Yung-hui period (650–6), and Ching Po, who was at this time secretary of the Office for Literary Composition and also a compiler.[27] After its completion[28] Ku Yin was rewarded with promotion in rank and appointment as a scholar of the Hung-wen Academy. Another scholar rewarded at the same time was Sun Ch'u-yüeh, a chief secretary in the Secretariat who later served with Hsü Ching-tsung as chief minister from 664–5.[29]

---

23 See *CTS* 46, p. 1998; *HTS* 58, p. 1471; *Yü hai* 48, pp. 2b–3a; *WHTK* 194, p. 1641b; *Ch'ung-wen tsung-mu* 3, p. 10b (listed as missing in 1144); *Chung-hsing Kuan-ko shu-mu chi-k'ao* 2, pp. 12b–13a; *Chün-chai tu-shu chih (Yüan-pen), hou-chih* 1, pp. 14b–15a (*Ch'ü-pen* 6, p. la); *Chih-chai shu-lu chieh-t'i* 4, p. 37a–b.
24 See *THY* 63, p. 1092; *TFYK* 556, p. 14a; *Yü hai* 48, pp. 2b–3a, citing *Hui yao*.
25 See *CTS* 65, p. 2454.
26 Scribal confusions between *yüan nien* and *wu nien* are not uncommon.
27 According to *CTS* 189A, p. 4955, and *HTS* 198, p. 5656, Ching Po was also a compiler of this Veritable Record, under the title *T'ai-tsung Shih-lu*, although none of the bibliographical entries mention his name. See also *HTS* 223A, p. 6338. He also participated at this time in the compilation of the major work on the Western Regions entitled *Hsi-yü t'u-chih* compiled in sixty chapters under Hsü Ching-tsung's direction and completed in 658.
28 See *CTS* 73, p. 2600; *HTS* 102, p. 3985.
29 See *CTS* 81, p. 2758.

IIC. *T'ai-tsung Shih-lu*

Compiled (or edited) by Hsü Ching-tsung.[30]

The Veritable Record of T'ai-tsung's reign surviving in the eleventh century and used by Ssu-ma Kuang in compiling the *Tzu-chih t'ung-chien* is identified by him, in one instance at least,[31] as "Hsü Ching-tsung's *T'ai-tsung Shih-lu*." None of the bibliographical sources attributes the *T'ai-tsung Shih-lu* to Hsü Ching-tsung as either director or compiler. Both his biographies, however, tell us that he twisted the facts and cut and changed the text of the Veritable Records of Kao-tsu and T'ai-tsung that had been compiled by Ching Po, and that these changes were considered very serious.[32] The *Hsin T'ang shu* passage mentions this in the context of his being in charge of the "National History," and it thus may very well refer to the inaccuracies and falsifications introduced by Hsü Ching-tsung into the first National History (*Kuo shih*) of 656. However, the term "National History" is so frequently used in a vague sense to refer to all the activities of the Historiographical Office, that it might equally well mean that Hsü was responsible for a "revision" of the Veritable Records for Kao-tsu and T'ai-tsung, perhaps after he became director of the National History.

Early in Kao-tsung's reign Hsü was temporarily in disgrace. He was reinstated in 652 as president of the Court of Imperial Insignia, and concurrently both a scholar of the Hung-wen Academy and a compiler in the Historiographical Office, which posts he retained until the tenth of the eighth month of 657, when he became president of the Chancellery and concurrently director of the National History.[33] He was thus serving in the Historiographical Office at the time when the *Chen-kuan Shih-lu* was presented to the throne (assuming that this was in 654, as sug-sted, rather than in 650) and could have taken a part in its compilation. Equally, he was director during the subsequent period when a "revision" of which we have no surviving evidence might well have been carried out under his orders. Whether or not he was responsible for a revised edition of the Veritable Records for T'ai-tsung's reign, there is no doubt

---

30 See *TCTC* 183, p. 5718; *WHTK* 194, p. 1641b; *Chih-chai shu-lu chieh-t'i* 4, p. 37a–b.
31 See *TCTC* 183, p. 5718, *K'ao-i.*
32 See *CTS* 82, p. 2764; *HTS* 223A, p. 6338.
33 See *CTS* 82, p. 2763; *HTS* 223A, p. 6338. The precise date of his appointment is given in *CTS* 4, p. 77, as the tenth day, and in *TCTC* 200, p. 6305, as the fifteenth day of the eighth month.

that he was responsible for seriously tampering with the records for the whole early T'ang period, at least down to 658.[34]

IIIA. *Huang-ti Shih-lu*

(Later entitled *Kao-tsung Shih-lu*.) Thirty chapters.[35] Compiled under the direction of Hsü Ching-tsung; Hsü Yü-shih,[36] vice-president of the Secretariat; Li Ch'un-feng,[37] astronomer royal; Yang Jen-ch'ing and Ku Yün,[38] chief secretaries of the Office for Literary Composition; and Ling-hu Te-fen.[39]

According to *T'ang hui yao* and *Ts'e-fu yüan-kuei* this Veritable Record covering the first years of Kao-tsung's reign, from his accession in 649 to the third year of the Hsien-ch'ing period (658), was compiled by imperial order following the completion of the first National History (*Kuo shih*) in 656 and was completed and presented to the throne on the fifth day of the second month of 659. It comprised twenty chapters, and together with the National History provided an account of the dynasty's history extending to one hundred chapters.[40] After its completion, some of the directors, and the sons of others, were granted noble titles as a reward for their work on the Veritable Record.[41]

Both *T'ang hui yao* and *Ts'e-fu yüan-kuei* continue their accounts of the completion of these Veritable Records by quoting remarks made by Kao-tsung expressing his dissatisfaction with Hsü Ching-tsung's work. These remarks would appear at first glance to have been made at the time of the Veritable Record's being presented to the throne. However,

---

34 On Hsü Ching-tsung's notorious dishonesty as a historian, see *CTS* 82, pp. 2761–5 (esp. 2763–4); *HTS* 233A, pp. 6335–9 (esp. 6338); *THY* 63, pp. 1093–4; *TFYK* 556, pp. 14b–15a; *TFYK* 562, pp. 8b–9b; *TFYK* 562, p. 14a–b. Liu Chih-chi scornfully dismissed his work on the National History as having sometimes falsified facts to satisfy those currently holding power, sometimes doing so out of personal spite, and generally failing accurately to apportion praise and blame. See *Shih t'ung t'ung-shih* 12, p. 373. See also Wechsler, *Mirror to the Son of Heaven*, pp. 23–7; R. W. L. Guisso, *Wu Tse-t'ien and the Politics of Legitimation in T'ang China* (Bellingham, Wash., 1978), pp. 9–10.
35 See *CTS* 46, p. 1998; *HTS* 58, p. 1471; *Yü-hai* 48, p. 3b.
36 See *CTS* 59, p. 2330; *HTS* 90, p. 3771.
37 See *CTS* 79, pp. 2717–19; *HTS* 204, p. 5798.
38 His name is written Ku I in *TFYK* 556, p. 14b.
39 See *CTS* 73, pp. 2596–9; *HTS* 102, pp. 3982–4.
40 See *THY* 63, p. 1093; *TFYK* 556, p. 14b; *CTS* 73, p. 2599.
41 See *THY* 63, p. 1093; *TFYK* 556, p. 14b; *CTS* 73, p. 2599. Hsü Ching-tsung's son Hsü Hsüan was made baron of Hsin-feng County; Ling-hu Te-fen's son was promoted to duke of Peng-yang County; Hsü Yü-shih was enfiefed as duke (or baron, according to the Sung print of *CTS*) of Ping-en County; Li Ch'un-feng was enfiefed as baron of Ch'ang-lo County; Yang Jen-ch'ing was made Baron of Yü-hang County and Ku Yün's son Ku Hsü was appointed a state counselor.

as we may see from the personages involved and the offices they held, these events clearly took place many years later. The emperor's remarks were addressed to Liu Jen-kuei, who is given the titles of president of the Left Secretariat of the Heir Apparent (*T'ai-tzu tso shu-tzu*) and ad hominem chief minister. These titles were conferred on him in the twelfth month of 672, when he was also made director of the National History.[42] Li Ching-hsüan is also mentioned as vice-president of the Board of Civil Office and ad hominem chief minister, to which posts he had been appointed in the tenth month of 672.[43] Hsü Ching-tsung had died shortly before this, in the eighth month of that same year.[44] These events thus took place in the twelfth month of 672 or shortly thereafter.

The result of the emperor's dissatisfaction with the Veritable Record and of the discussions that ensued was that Liu Jen-kuei, Li Ching-hsüan, Ho Ch'u-chou, the vice-president of the Secretariat, and Kao Chih-chou,[45] the vice-president of the Chancellery, were ordered to collaborate in revising the history. They deputed the actual editing and revision to Li Jen-shih,[46] the diarist of the left. Li Jen-shih, however, died in office shortly thereafter, and the revision was thereupon abandoned. This revision of Hsü Ching-tsung's work was ordered "in the third month." This was almost certainly the third month of 673, because in the third month of 674 Liu Jen-kuei was no longer at court, having left in the previous month to compaign in Korea.

IIIB. *Kao-tsung hou-hsiu Shih-lu*

Thirty chapters. Its compilation was begun by Ling-hu Te-fen, whose original version ended with the Ch'ien-feng (666–8) period. Much later, in the early eighth century, it was continued and completed by Liu Chih-chi and Wu Ching.[47]

This work was clearly not the same as the *Huang-ti Shih-lu* (IIIA) presented to the throne in 659, in the compilation of which Ling-hu

---

42 See *CTS* 5, p. 97; *CTS* 84, p. 2795.
43 See *CTS* 5, p. 97.
44 See *CTS* 5, p. 97; *CTS* 82, p. 2764.
45 Kao Chih-chou's name is mistakenly written "Chou Chih" by *TFYK* 556, p. 15a.
46 On Li Jen-shih's career, see *CTS* 73, p. 2601; *HTS* 102, p. 3986.
47 See *HTS* 58, p. 1471; *Yü hai* 48, p. 3b; *WHTK* 194, p. 1641b; *Ch'ung-wen tsung-mu* 3, p. 10b (gives title as *Kao-tsung fu-hsiu shih-lu*); *Chung-hsing Kuan-ko shu-mu chi-k'ao* 2, p. 13a; *Chün-chai tu-shu chih* (*Yüan-pen*), *hou-chih* 1, p. 15a (gives its length as thirty chapters; *Ch'ü-pen* 6, p. 1b gives it as twenty chapters); *Chih-chai shu-lu chieh-t'i* 4, p. 37b. The latter notes that only nineteen chapters remained, eleven chapters having been lost.

Te-fen had also played an important part. Presumably the new "subsequently compiled" Veritable Record was a continuation and updating of this. Because Ling-hu Te-fen was permitted to retire on the grounds of old age in 662 and died in 666,[48] it must have ended with the very beginning of the Ch'ien-feng period, and must therefore have been completed some years *before* the revision of the Veritable Records for Kao-tsung's early years in 673 mentioned earlier. Perhaps, therefore, that revision was based not upon the Veritable Record as completed in 659 (IIIA) but on Ling-hu Te-fen's continuation of it (IIIB).

The biographies of Liu Chih-chi and Wu Ching do not mention their subsequent continuation and completion of this Veritable Record as reported in *Hsin T'ang shu*. Nor is there any record of the work's completion or presentation to the throne.

IIIC. *Kao-tsung Shih-lu*

Thirty chapters. Compiled by Wei Shu.[49]

Nothing further is known about this work, which may have been a revision of IIIB. It is listed among Wei Shu's various historical writings in his *Chiu T'ang shu* biography.[50]

IIID. *Kao-tsung Shih-lu*

Sixty chapters. Compiled by Wu Hsüan-chih.[51]

Nothing further is known of this work, which is not mentioned in any of the Chinese sources, but included in the late ninth-century Japanese catalog *Nihon koku genzai sho mokuroku* of Fujiwara no Sukeyo.[52]

IIIE. *Kao-tsung Shih-lu*

One hundred chapters. Compiled by Empress Wu Tse-t'ien.[53] Nothing further is known of this work.

---

48 See *CTS* 73, p. 259; *HTS* 102, p. 3984.
49 See *HTS* 58, p. 1471; *Yü hai* 48, p. 3b; *CTS* 102, p. 3185.
50 See *CTS* 102, p. 3185.
51 See *Nihon koku genzai sho mokuroku* (Kariya Ekisai's edition, 1928) 7, pp. 106–7.
52 Wu Hsüan-chih is presumably the same person as the Wu Yüan-chih noted as the author of the fifteen-chapter work on rhymes entitled *Yün ch'üan* listed in *HTS* 58, p. 1451. Both of Empress Wu's known brothers had personal names beginning with Yüan. It is therefore possible that he was a close relative belonging to the same generation as the empress.
53 Compiled by Empress Wu Tse-t'ien. See *CTS* 46, p. 1998; *HTS* 58, p. 1471; *Yü hai* 48, p. 3b.

IIIF. *Shu Sheng chi*

One chapter. Compiled by Empress Wu Tse-t'ien.[54]

This work is listed among the Veritable Records in the bibliographical chapter of *Chiu T'ang shu* and was thus almost certainly included in the Imperial Library in 721. Being so short it was unlikely to have been a Veritable Record, however, and is almost certainly the same as the *Ch'ien-ling Shu Sheng chi* by the Empress Wu preserved in a very badly mutilated form in *Ch'üan T'ang wen* and elsewhere.[55] This text was the memorial inscription composed by Empress Wu for Kao-tsung's mausoleum, and erected in 683 at the time of his burial.

Another text bearing this title also seems to have circulated as an independent work during the T'ang. Among the Tun-huang manuscripts are one short fragment entitled *Ta-T'ang Huang-ti Shu Sheng chi* forming part of the Tunhuang manuscript S. 4612[56] and another somewhat longer fragment forming part of manuscript S. 343.[57] It seems to bear no relation with Kao-tsung's memorial inscription.

IVA. *Sheng-mu shen-huang Shih-lu*

Eighteen chapters. Compiled by Tsung Ch'in-k'o.[58]

Tsung Ch'in-k'o was the son of a paternal cousin of Empress Wu who played a major role in encouraging her to usurp the throne and set herself up as sovereign. He is also said to have been the actual inventor of the new characters whose use was made compulsory in 690 as one of the symbols of her new regime.[59] His brief biographical notices[60] make no mention of his part in compiling the Veritable Records.

The title of this work shows that it was written between the eighteenth day of the fifth month of 688, when the empress assumed the style Sheng-mu shen-huang,[61] and the twelfth day of the ninth month

---

54 See *CTS* 46, p. 1998.
55 See *CTW* 97, pp. 12a–14b. It is also included in Wang Ch'ang, comp., *Chin-shih ts'ui-pien* (Ching-hsün t'ang edition, 1805) 60, pp. 5b–11a, and in Lu Hsin-yüan's *T'ang-wen hsü shih-i* 1, pp. 3b–7a.
56 Lionel Giles, *Descriptive Catalogue of the Chinese Manuscripts from Tunhuang in the British Museum* (London, 1957), p. 1, item 2.
57 This title is erroneously transcribed by Giles in his *Catalogue*, p. 202, item 6439. I am indebted to Beth McKillop of the British Library for sending me a copy of these manuscripts.
58 See *CTS* 46, p. 1998; *HTS* 58 p. 1471. Not included in *Yü hai*.
59 See *TCTC* 204, pp. 6462–3. See also Toyama Gunji, *Sokuten Bukō* (Tokyo, 1966), pp. 116–17.
60 *CTS* 92, p. 2971; *HTS* 109, pp. 4101–2.
61 See *CTS* 6, p. 119; *TCTC* 204, p. 6448.

of 690, when, after the establishment of her new Chou dynasty on the ninth, she assumed the new imperial title Sheng-shen Huang-ti.[62] According to *Ts'e-fu yüan-kuei*, the work was completed while Tsung Ch'in-k'o was serving as *Nei shih* president of the Secretariat.[63] He received this appointment on the twelfth day of the ninth month of 690.[64] Very shortly thereafter, he and his two younger brothers Tsung Ch'u-k'o and Tsung Chin-ch'ing were found guilty of malfeasance and banished to the far south, where Tsung Ch'in-k'o died.[65] His dismissal took place in the tenth month of 690.[66]

The *Sheng-mu shen-huang Shih-lu* was thus almost certainly compiled at the time of the establishment of Empress Wu's new regime, as an attempt formally to legitimize her rule after 684 and to lay the foundation for the new dynasty set up in 690. It was probably presented at the time of the empress's assuming the throne in her own right, or almost immediately thereafter.

IVB. *Tse-t'ien Huang-hou Shih-lu*

Thirty chapters. Compiled under the direction of Wu San-ssu, grand counselor of the left, Wei Yüan-chung, president of the Secretariat, and Chu Ch'in-ming, president of the Board of Rites, by the historians Hsü Yen-po, the vice-president of the Court of Imperial Sacrifices, Liu Chung, the deputy director of the Imperial Library, Ts'ui Jung, the vice-rector of the Imperial University, and Ts'en Hsi and Hsü Chien, chief secretaries in the Secretariat.[67]

This first version of the Veritable Record for the whole of Empress Wu's reign was ordered in the twelfth month of 705.[68] It was thus not commissioned immediately after the coup of the twenty-fifth day of the first month of 705, which forced the eighty-year-old empress to abdicate, but following her death on the twenty-sixth day of the eleventh month. By this time, the group of ministers who had engineered the coup had

---

62 See *CTS* 6, p. 121; *TCTC* 204, p. 6467.
63 See *TFTK* 556, p. 16b.
64 See *CTS* 6, p. 121. *HTS* 109, p. 4102, mentions the appointment without date. The table of chief ministers in *HTS* 61, p. 1654, incorrectly gives his appointment as president of the Chancellery (*Na-yen*), a post actually bestowed on Shih Wu-tz'u on the same day.
65 See *CTS* 92, p. 2971; *HTS* 109, pp. 4101–2.
66 See *HTS* 61, p. 1654.
67 See *THY* 63, p. 1094; *TFYK* 556, p. 16b; *Yü-hai* 48, pp. 3b–4a; *Chün-chai tu-shu chih* (*Yüan-pen*) 2A, p. 126 (*Ch'ü-pen* 6, p. 1b). *HTS* 58, p. 1471, adds the name of Wei Ch'eng-ch'ing. It also says that it was subjected to abridgment and correction (*Shan-cheng*) by Liu Chih-chi and Wu-Ching. See discussion in entry IVC.
68 See *TFYK* 554, p. 17a.

been driven into exile by her nephew Wu San-ssu, who now dominated the court. There can be no doubt that Wu San-ssu, who we know exerted great pressure on the compilers, was anxious that they present a favorable picture of the empress's reign. The Veritable Record was very rapidly completed and presented to the throne on the ninth day of the fifth month of 706, a few days before the empress's interment, together with a collection of her writings in 120 chapters.[69] *T'ang hui yao* and *Ts'e-fu yüan-kuei* say that it comprised 20 chapters, but a quotation from the *Hüi yao* preserved in *Yü hai* says that the Veritable Record comprised 30 chapters, and the empress's literary collection 100 chapters. That this work in fact comprised 30 chapters is confirmed by a memorial from Chief Minister Yao Ch'ung presented in 716 after the completion of the revised *Tse-t'ien Shih-lu* (IVC) by Liu Chih-chi and Wu Ching.[70]

This same memorial also tells us that upon the presentation of the Veritable Record in 706 one of Wei Yüan-chung's sons was ennobled as baron of a county, and he himself was rewarded with a thousand pieces of silk, while Hsü Yen-po and the other compilers were each given a promotion of two degrees and five hundred lengths of silk, and the lesser officials involved were each promoted two degrees and rewarded with appropriate amounts of silk. All were honored with an imperial letter of commendation.

Among the compilers who actually did the work on this original draft were Liu Chih-chi and Wu Ching. Liu Chih-chi tells us in his *Shih t'ung* that "In 705 I, together with Hsü Chien and Wu Ching, recompiled the Veritable Record of Empress Tse-t'ien (*Tse-t'ien Shih-lu*) in thirty chapters [one variant text of *Shih t'ung* reads twenty chapters]. The corruption of the 'old history' was such that it was disordered as a tangled line, and its confusions difficult to unravel. Only after a full year were we finished. Although our words contain nothing worthy of notice, while the events are often matters to regret, perhaps they will provide a basis for future editing."[71] Liu Chih-chi's "old history" (*chiu-shih*) was presumably Tsung Ch'in-k'o's Veritable Record (IVA) or perhaps may refer to that work together with the Court Diaries for the reign. The "revision" must, in fact, have involved writing the history of the entire period from 690 to 705, with its many delicate political ramifications, ab initio.

Liu Chih-chi's work on the Veritable Record of Empress Wu Tse-t'ien presented in 706 is confirmed by his biography,[72] which says that for his achievement in compiling the Veritable Record he was ennobled as

---

69 See *THY* 63, p. 1094; *TFTK* 556, p. 15a–b.
70 See *THY* 63, pp. 1094–5.
71 See *Shih t'ung* 12, p. 374 (cf. Pulleyblank, "The *Tzyhjyh Tongjiann Kaoyih*," pp. 452–3).
72 See *CTS* 102, p. 3171.

viscount of Chü-ch'ao County. Wu Ching's biography also tells us that he compiled the *Tse-t'ien Shih-lu* together with Liu Tzu-hsüan (i.e., Liu Chih-chi), Ts'ui Jung, and Wei Ch'eng-ch'ing, and that after its completion he was promoted to court diarist.[73]

Wei Ch'eng-ch'ing (d. 709) is not mentioned as a collaborator by Liu Chih-chi. He had been briefly an ad hominem chief minister and director of the National History at the end of Empress Wu's reign. After her abdication, he was demoted because of his former involvement with the Chang brothers (Chang I-chih and Chang Ch'ang-tsung, the aged empress's corrupt favorites), and ordered to a distant provincial office. But before he had set out from the capital he was instead given a supernumerary post in the Imperial Library and made a concurrent compiler of the National History. As a reward for his work there on the *Tse-t'ien Shih-lu* he was ennobled as viscount of Fu-yang County and rewarded with five hundred lengths of silk.[74]

There were thus many persons both directly and indirectly involved in the compilation of the 706 *Tse-t'ien Shih-lu*. In addition to the frustrations arising from having such a large team working on the project, the unusually large number of high-ranking directors, and particularly the inclusion among them of Wu San-ssu (who was a nephew of the former empress) underline the extreme political pressures under which the work was completed. These factors made it all but impossible to produce a satisfactory historical record. That conditions in the Historiographical Office remained far from conducive to work even after Wu San-ssu's death in 707 is proved by the lengthy letter of resignation Liu Chih-chi addressed to Director Hsiao Chih-chung in 708.[75]

IVC. *Tse-t'ien Shih-lu*

Thirty chapters. Revised by Liu Chih-chi and Wu Ching.[76]

This revision of IVB was presented to the throne on the fourteenth day of the eleventh month of 716, together with the newly compiled Veritable Records for the reigns of Chung-tsung and Jui-tsung (see V and VIB). The three works were presented together shortly after

73 See *CTS* 102, p. 3182; *TFYK* 554, p. 17b.
74 See *CTS* 88, p. 2865.
75 See *Shih t'ung* 20, pp. 589–94; *THY* 64, pp. 1106–7; *TFYK* 559, pp. 5b–8b. This is translated, with copious annotation, in Hung, "A T'ang Historiographer's Letter of Resignation," pp. 5–52.
76 See *HTS* 58, p. 1471; *Yü hai* 48, pp. 3b–4a; *THY* 63, p. 1094; *TFYK* 556, p. 16b; *WHTK* 194, p. 1641b–c; *Ch'ung-wen tsung-mu* 3, p. 10b; *Chung-hsing Kuan-ko shu-mu chi-k'ao* 2, p. 13a; *Chün-chai tu-shu chih (Yüan-pen)* 2A, p. 12b (*Ch'ü-pen* 6, p. 1b); *Chih-chai shu-lu chieh-t'i* 4, pp. 37b–38a. Note that this gives only the name of Wu Ching as author.

the death of the retired emperor Jui-tsung in the sixth month, which marked the final stage in Hsüan-tsung's rise to undisputed power as sovereign. There is considerable confusion about its length. Both *T'ang hui yao* and *Ts'e-fu yüan-kuei* 556 give it as thirty chapters. Elsewhere in *Ts'e-fu yüan-kuei*, however, it is given as forty chapters.[77] The bibliographical monograph of *Hsin T'ang shu* lists it as in twenty chapters, as do *Ch'ung-wen tsung-mu*,[78] *Chün-chai tu-shu chih*,[79] *Chih-chai shu-lu chieh-t'i*,[80] and *Wen-hsien t'ung-k'ao*.[81] Pulleyblank accepts as a possible explanation for this confusion Ch'ao Kung-wu's surmise that an original thirty-chapter version was reduced to twenty in the revision.[82]

A further curious fact is that although this Veritable Record was formally presented to the throne and accepted, it seems not to have been placed in the Imperial Library, because it does not appear in the bibliographical chapter of *Chiu T'ang shu* which represents the contents of the Imperial Library in 721, only four years later. The Veritable Records for Jui-tsung presented with it in 716 are also missing from that list although those for Chung-tsung, also presented to the throne at the same time, are included.

This revised version is almost certainly the one cited in Ssu-ma Kuang's *Tzu-chih t'ung-chien k'ao-i*. According to *Wen-hsien t'ung-k'ao*[83] it covered the period from 684 to 705.[84]

V. *Chung-tsung huang-ti Shih-lu*

Twenty chapters. Compiled by Wu Ching.[85]

Presented to the throne on the fourteenth day of the eleventh month of 716 by Liu Chih-chi and Wu Ching. After Chief Minister Yao Ch'ung reported to the emperor their completion of this work, together with the Veritable Records for Jui-tsung and the revised Veritable Records for Empress Wu Tse-t'ien, they were each rewarded with five hundred

---

77 *TFYK* 554, p. 32b.
78 *Ch'ung-wen tsung-mu* 3, p. 10b.
79 See *Chün-chai tu-shu chih (Yüan-pen)* 2A, p. 12b (*Ch'ü-pen* 6, p. 1b).
80 See *Chih-chai shu-lu chieh-t'i* 4, p. 37b.
81 See *WHTK* 194, p. 1641b–c.
82 See Pulleyblank, "The *Tzyhjyh Tongjiann Kaoyih*," p. 452, n. 4.
83 See *WHTK* 194, p. 1541c.
84 For some general but incomplete remarks on the various Veritable Records of Empress Wu, see Guisso, *Wu Tse-t'ien and the Politics of Legitimation in T'ang China*, pp. 8–10.
85 See *CTS* 46, p. 1998; *HTS* 58, p. 1471; *TFYK* 556, p. 17b; *Yü hai* 48, p. 4a–b; *WHTK* 194, p. 1641c; *Ch'ung-wen tsung-mu* 3, p. 10b; *Chung-hsing Kuan-ko shu-mu chi-k'ao* 2, p. 13a–b; *Chün-chai tu-shu chih (Yüan-pen), hou-chih* 1, p. 15a (*Ch'ü-pen* 6, p. 2a); *Chih-chai shu-lu chieh-t'i* 4, p. 38a.

lengths of silk at Yao's suggestion.[86] According to the *Chung-hsing Kuan-ko shu-mu* as cited in *Yü hai*, the work covered the period from Chung-tsung's restoration to the throne in 705 to the succession of Jui-tsung in the eighth month of 710.[87]

VIA. *T'ai-shang-huang Shih-lu*

Ten chapters. Compiled by Liu Chih-chi.[88]

From the title, this recension of the Veritable Record for Jui-tsung must have been compiled after his abdication in favor of Hsüan-tsung on the fifteenth of the eighth month of 712, when Jui-tsung received the title "retired emperor" (*T'ai-shang huang-ti*), and before his death on the twentieth of the sixth month of 716. He was given the temple name Jui-tsung and the posthumous title *Ta-sheng chen huang-ti* on the twenty-fifth of the seventh month of 716. The exact date of its compilation is unknown. *Chung-hsing Kuan-ko shu-mu*, as cited by *Yü hai*, says that it began with Jui-tsung's birth and ended in the seventh month of 713, the date when the future Hsüan-tsung led the coup against Princess T'ai-p'ing, which finally ended her brother Jui-tsung's participation in government and led to his abdication.[89] This Veritable Record was thus compiled some time between the seventh month of 713 and the sixth month of 716. The 716 version (see the next section), presented shortly after Jui-tsung's death, was presumably an expanded version of this work.

VIB. *Jui-tsung Shih-lu*

Twenty chapters. Compiled by Liu Chih-chi and Wu Ching.[90]

Presented to the throne on the fourteenth day of the eleventh month

86 See *THY* 63, p. 1094; *TFYK* 556, p. 16b.
87 See *Yü hai* 48, p. 4b.
88 See *HTS* 58, p. 1471; *Yü hai* 48, p. 4a–b; *WHTK* 194, p. 1641c; *Ch'ung-wen tsung-mu* 3, p. 10b; *Chung-hsing Kuan-ko shu-mu chi-k'ao* 2, p. 13b (gives title as *Jui-tsung Shih-lu*); *Chih-chai shu-lu chien-t'i* 4, p. 38b.
89 Jui-tsung in fact abdicated twice, or rather in two stages. On his first abdication in 712, although Hsüan-tsung formally ascended the throne, Jui-tsung continued to hold court every fifth day, and retained authority to make all high-ranking appointments. See *CTS*. pp. 168–70; *TCTC* 210, pp. 6673–4. After the coup against the T'ai-p'ing princess, Jui-tsung formally divested himself of all his remaining powers on the fourth day of the seventh month of 713. See *CTS* 8, pp. 169–70. On this series of events, see Twitchett, *Cambridge History of China*, vol. 3, pp. 343–5.
90 See *THY* 63, p. 1094; *TFYK* 556, p. 16b; *Yü hai* 48, p. 4a–b; *Chün-chai tu-shu chih* (*Yüan-pen*), *hou-chih* 1, p. 15a (*Ch'ü-pen* 6, p. 2a [this gives its length as ten chapters, but clearly states that it was a continuation and expansion of the *T'ai-shang-huang Shih-lu*]); *WHTK* 194, p. 1641c.

of 716 by Liu Chih-chi and Wu Ching, together with the *Tse-t'ien Shih-lu* in its revised form and the *Chung-tsung Shih-lu*. This version is not listed in *Chiu T'ang shu* 46 among the books in the Imperial Library in 721, nor is it listed in *Hsin T'ang shu* 58, which only includes items VIA and VIC.

Wu Ching's *Hsin T'ang shu* biography provides an interesting piece of information concerning the Veritable Record for Jui-tsung. When the former emperor died in the palace in Ch'ang-an[91] on the twentieth of the fifth month of 716, the Veritable Record for his reign was in store in the eastern capital, Loyang, and Wu Ching was sent by express courier service to retrieve it so that it might be placed in the emperor's coffin.[92] The revised Veritable Record had not yet been formally presented to the throne, and it would hardly have been buried with the former emperor without this having been done. But there was already another Veritable Record for Jui-tsung's reign in existence, the shorter *T'ai-shang-huang Shih-lu* in ten chapters by Liu Chih-chi, and it may have been necessary to send Wu Ching posthaste to Loyang to fetch this for the interment because the longer version was not yet completed. But what was it doing in Loyang? The court had been in Ch'ang-an since 706, although we know that Liu Chih-chi and perhaps some other historians stayed for some time after this in Loyang, working in the Historiographical Office's branch bureau. But because the *T'ai-shang-huang Shih-lu* must from its title have been written after 712 and probably after 713, it surely must have been compiled in Ch'ang-an.

Clearly the Veritable Record cannot have been buried with every emperor, because it was normally not completed until years after the emperor's interment. It can only have been feasible to do so for a sovereign who had abdicated the throne. But in one other instance it does seem that it was possible. In the case of Empress Wu, the Veritable Record that had been rushed to completion immediately after her death was presented to the throne on the ninth day of the fifth month of 706, just nine days before her interment in Kao-tsung's mausoleum, the Ch'ien-ling.[93] It may well have been hurriedly completed to be in time for interment with her. In this case, because the Ch'ien-ling remains intact, it may still survive in her tomb.

---

91 See *THY* 1, p. 5. *CTS* 8, p. 176, gives the date as the nineteenth day of the sixth month.
92 See *HTS* 132, p. 4528. This account raises a problem. The Veritable Record of his reign by Wu Ching and Liu Chih-chi was formally presented to the throne on the fourteenth of the eleventh month (see *THY* 63, p. 1094), more than two weeks after Jui-tsung's burial in the Chiao-ling mausoleum on the twenty-eighth of the tenth month (see *CTS* 8, p. 176).
93 See *TCTC* 208, p. 6603.

VIC. *Jui-tsung Shih-lu*

Five chapters. Compiled by Wu Ching.[94]

The date of compilation is unknown. It was probably an abridgment of the version presented to the throne in 716. According to the *Chung-hsing Kuan-ko shu-mu* as cited in *Yü hai* 48, p. 4b, it gave an account beginning with Jui-tsung's period as prince of Hsiang (after 705) and ended in 716 (with his death). It is said to have been much more summary an account than the ten-chapter version (VIA).

VIIA. *Chin-shang Shih-lu*

Twenty chapters. Compiled by Chang Yüeh and T'ang Ying.[95]

The circumstances surrounding the compilation of this Veritable Record are obscure. Neither its commissioning nor its completion and presentation to the throne are recorded. Moreover, although the bibliographical chapter of *Hsin T'ang shu* only gives the information on length and compilers, with the note that it dealt with events at the beginning of the K'ai-yüan period, *Yü hai* quotes a fragment of the lost record of the Chi-hsien Academy, the *Chi-hsien chu-chi* of Wei Shu, which tells a somewhat different and more detailed story.[96] According to this source, after T'ang Ying had presented a historical work called the *Chi-tien*[97] to the throne, Chang Yüeh requested that T'ang be retained as a compiler in the Historiographical Office, and given a concurrent appointment as "scholar at the emperor's disposal" (*T'ai-shih*) in the Chi-hsien Academy. This was presumably after 725, when Chang Yüeh, who had been working as an official historian at least since 719,[98] was placed in charge of the newly renamed Chi-hsien Academy. T'ang Ying then, according to the *Chi-hsien chu-chi*, compiled a Veritable Record of the Reigning Sovereign (*Chin-shang Shih-lu*) in thirteen chapters. Later, when Wei Shu was

---

94 See *HTS* 58, p. 1471; *Yü hai* 48, p. 4a–b; *WHTK* 194, p. 1641c; *Ch'ung-wen tsung-mu* 3, p. 10b; *Chung-hsing Kuan-ko shu-mu chi-k'ao* 2, p. 13b.

95 See *HTS* 58, pp. 1471–2; *Yü hai* 48, pp. 4b–5b.

96 Wei Shu, author of the *Chi-hsien chu-chi*, should have known the facts here; not only was he a professional historian who served for the next three decades in the Historiographical Office; he was a protégé of Chang Yüeh, thanks to whose recommendation he was a member of the Chi-hsien Academy at the time.

97 This is listed, in 130 chapters, in *HTS* 58, p. 1467, among the "miscellaneous historical works" (*tsa-shih*).

98 See *CTS* 97, p, 3052, which explains that he was appointed a concurrent compiler when in 819 he was made governor-general of Ping-chou (T'ai-yüan) and commander of the T'ien-ping army. He was especially given a copy of the history so that he could work upon the compilation while he was with his command. In 721 he was given the title of an ad hominem chief minister, remaining a compiler. See *CTS* 97, p. 3053.

himself in charge of the Historiographical Office's business, he was ordered by the emperor to have a copy made of a *Chin-shang Shih-lu* in twenty chapters compiled by Chang Yüeh, and to have this stored in the library of the Chi-hsien Academy. This would suggest either that there were two works with this title, one by T'ang Ying and another later version by Chang Yüeh that have been conflated into one by the compilers of *Hsin T'ang shu*, or that T'ang Ying wrote a first version that was subsequently rewritten and enlarged by Chang Yüeh. Just what the relationship was between the two books, or two recensions, is impossible to establish.

The decision to undertake the compilation of a Veritable Record during the reign of the emperor was undoubtedly connected with the completion of the Feng and Shan sacrifices on T'ai-shan at the end of 725. These ceremonies celebrated both the overall prestige and power attained by the dynasty, and also the personal achievements of Hsüan-tsung. This would thus have been an appropriate time to record formally the events of his reign. Chang Yüeh had himself been largely responsible for the emperor's carrying out the enormously complex and costly ceremonies.[99]

It seems most probable that Chang Yüeh completed his version of the Veritable Records sometime after the second month of 727, when, after impeachment by his enemies, he was forced to retire from office and was ordered to "continue to compile the history" in his home.[100]

VIIB. *K'ai-yüan Shih-lu*

Forty-seven chapters. Compiler unknown.[101]

Even less is known about this work, which presumably covered the events of Hsüan-tsung's reign down to the adoption of the new reign title T'ien-pao in 742 and must have overlapped with VIIA for the first years of the reigns. It was certainly compiled during the later part of Hsüan-tsung's reign. During this period Li Lin-fu was the director of the National History, as he had been since the eleventh month of 736,[102] and the work may perhaps have been produced under his direction. The work is said to have been destroyed when the Historiographical Office was burned in 756.[103]

---

99 See *CTS* 97, pp. 3054–5.
100 See *CTS* 97, pp. 3054–5; *TCTC* 213. p, 6777. His memorial accepting this order is in Chang Yüeh, *Chang Yen-kung chi* (Shanghai, 1937) 10, p. 116; *WYYH* 592, p. 4a–b.
101 See *HTS* 58, p. 1472.
102 *CTS* 106, p. 3237.
103 See *THY* 63, p. 1095; *TFYK* 556, p. 19a; *CTS* 149, p. 4008.

VIIC. *Hsüan-tsung Shih-lu*

One hundred chapters. Compiled by Ling-hu Huan under the Direction of Yüan Tsai.[104]

This was the only Veritable Record for Hsüan-tsung that covered his whole reign. It was compiled under great difficulties by Ling-hu Huan, a great-great-grandson of Ling-hu Te-fen's (see IIIA) who had been recruited into the Historiographical Office by Yang Wan in 763, and was presented to the throne in 768.[105]

At the time of Ling-hu Huan's compilation, the earlier Veritable Record of the K'ai-yüan period, probably together with the Veritable Record of the Reigning Sovereign by Chang Yüeh, had been destroyed, as had the Court Diaries of Hsüan-tsung's reign. As his biographies explain the situation, "Although Huan's writing was diligent, in the aftermath of the great disorders [i.e., the An Lu-shan and subsequent rebellions] the Court Diaries were completely lost, and when he came to compile his account of the events of the K'ai-yüan and T'ien-pao periods, even though he obtained the collected works of all the authors and arranged the edicts and essays contained in them, the biographical accounts of famous statesmen lacked three or four out of every ten men. Later people, because of its great number of omissions, did not regard it as a good history."[106]

This Veritable Record, with all its imperfections, remained the standard account of the reign and survived into the Sung period. It was used by Ssu-ma Kuang and is cited in the *Tzu-chih t'ung-chien k'ao-i* and was also quoted by the compilers of *T'ai-p'ing kuang-chi*,[107] although they did not include it in their list of books cited.[108]

---

104 See *HTS* 58, p. 1472; *Yü hai* 48, p. 5a–b; *Ch'ung-wen tsung-mu* 3, p. 10b (which gives its title as *Ming-huang Shih-lu*); *Chung-hsing Kuan-ko shu-mu chi-k'ao* 2, pp. 13b–14a; *Chün-chai tu-shu chih (Yüan-pen)*, *hou-chih* 1, p. 15b (*Ch'ü-pen* 6, p. 2a); *Chih-chai shu-lu chieh-ti* 4, p. 38b; *WHTK* 194, p. 1641c.

105 Its completion about this date is confirmed by a passage in Yen Chen-ch'ing's spirit-path tablet (*shen-tao pei*) for Sung Ching, which was set up two years later, in 770. See *Yen Lu-kung wen-chi* (*SPTK* edition) 10, p. 6a. Ling-hu Huan had once served under Yen Chen-ch'ing, and eventually composed his spirit-path tablet. See *Yen Lu-kung wen chi* 14, p. 13a–b. I owe this reference to David McMullen.

106 See *CTS* 149, p. 4011; *THY* 63, p. 1095; *TFYK* 556, p. 19b; *HTS* 102, p. 3986. See also the derogatory remarks in Ling-hu Huan's biography in *Shun-tsung Shih-lu* 3, p. 4 (trans. Solomon, *Veritable Record*, pp. 29–31): "Though he expended great effort on them, there were many omissions and they were not considered good histories."

107 See *TPKC* 186, pp. 1382–3.

108 The note on this in Pulleyblank, "The *Tzhjyh Tongjiann Kaoyih*," p. 458, n. 1, is somewhat ambiguous – the connection of this quotation with Chang Yüeh (which is as he says impossible) is a conjecture by the compilers of the Harvard Yenching Index to *TPKC*, not by the original compilers of the book itself.

VIII. *Su-tsung Shih-lu*

Thirty chapters. Compiled under the direction of Yüan Tsai.[109]

The names of the compilers are unknown, as is the date of its completion and presentation to the throne. It does not seem to have been a very admirable work; in 812 Hsien-tsung read it, found its biographies of great officials were "all empty words and baseless praise," and ordered his own historians to stick to the true facts and avoid such empty literary embellishment.[110]

IX. *Tai-tsungShih-lu*

Forty chapters. Compiled by Ling-hu Huan.[111]

According to the *Chung-hsing Kuan-ko shu-mu* as cited in *Yü hai* it began with the first year of the Pao-ying period (762) and ended with the fourteenth year of the Ta-li period (779).

This work was completed and presented to the throne long after its initial compilation. Ling-hu Huan worked as a compiler in the Historiographical Office throughout Tai-tsung's reign, while holding successive offices as omissioner, court diarist, and then as undersecretary of the Board of Justice. After the accession of Te-tsung in 779 he became vice-president of the Board of Rites. Earlier, however, he had been involved in the bitter personal feud between Liu Yen, whom he had supported, and Yang Yen. In 779, Yang Yen became chief minister, and shortly after had him demoted to a distant prefecture in Hunan. Later, when Li Mi became chief minister (from the sixth month of 787 to the third month of 789) Huan was recalled to the capital, was appointed president of the heir apparent's Right Secretariat, and once again became a compiler in the Historiographical Office. However, he quarreled incessantly with his colleagues, especially K'ung Shu-jui, and after the death of his patron Li Mi in the third month of 789 the new chief minister, Tou Shen, who detested Huan, appointed him to a post in Chi-chou, in distant Chiang-hsi. He remained in various prefectural posts in the

---

109 See *HTS* 58, p. 1472; *Yü hai* 48, p. 5b; *Ch'ung-wen tsung-mu* 3, p. 11a; *Chung-hsing Kuan-ko shu-mu chi-k'ao* 2, p. 14a; *Chün-chai tu-shu chih (Yüan-pen), hou chih* 1, p. 15b (*Ch'ü-pen* 6, p. 2a–b); *Chih-chai shu-lu chieh-t'i* 4, pp. 38b–39a; *WHTK* 194, p. 1641c.
110 See *THY* 64, p. 1109.
111 See *HTS* 58, p. 1472; *Yü hai* 48, pp. 5b–6a; *CTS* 149, p. 4011; *CTS* 14, p. 421; *Ch'ung-wen tsung-mu* 3, p. 11a; *Chung-hsing Kuan-ko shu-mu chi-k'ao* 2, p. 14a; *Chün-chai tu-shu chih (Yüan-pen)* 2A, pp. 12b–13a (*Ch'ü-pen* 6, p. 2b); *Chih-chai shu-lu chieh-t'i* 4, p. 39a; *WHTK* 194, pp. 1641c–1642a.

south until his death in 805.[112] When he was banished, the director of the National History requested that he should be allowed to complete his work on the Veritable Record for Tai-tsung in his place of banishment.

In 808, three years after his death in 805, his son Ling-hu P'ei presented to the throne the *Tai-tsung Shih-lu* in forty chapters that his father had completed during his banishment.[113] Hsien-tsung ordered that the Veritable Record be sent to the Historiographical Office and granted Ling-hu Huan a posthumous promotion. Although Ling-hu Huan's *Chiu T'ang shu* biography suggests that the work had been begun after 787,[114] a note in *Yü hai* gives the impression that he had been commissioned to write the Veritable Record immediately after Te-tsung's accession in 779, before his first banishment.[115]

This Veritable Record, like Ling-hu Huan's earlier *Hsüan-tsung Shih-lu*, came in for severe criticism. "The arrangement of events, and what was included and omitted were completely inappropriate, and a great deal was omitted. Famous officials such as Fang Kuan were not provided with biographies, while outspoken criticisms like those of Yen Chen-ch'ing were omitted and not recorded."[116]

XA. *Chien-chung Shih-lu*

Ten chapters. Compiled by Shen Chi-chi.[117]

The bibliographical chapter of *Hsin T'ang shu* and the notice of Shen Chi-chi in the *Chiu T'ang shu* biography of his son, Shen Ch'uan-shih, give the length of the work as ten chapters. However, the *Chung-hsing Kuan-ko shu-mu* as cited by *Yü hai* says that it was in fifteen chapters and was compiled by Omissioner of the Left Shen Chi-chi. According to *Ch'ung-wen tsung-mu* and *Chung-hsing Kuan-ko shu-mu*, it covered not the

---

112 In his earlier banishment to Hunan, Ling-hu Huan had tried clumsily and unsuccessfully to impeach Provincial Governor Chao Ching. The latter served as chief minister from 792 until his death in 796, and kept him in distant posts in the south. See *CTS* 138, pp. 3778–9.

113 This event is dated 808 in his biography, *CTS* 149, p. 4014; on the eighth of the seventh month of 807 by the *THY* as cited in *Yü hai* and by *CTS* 14, p. 421; and in the seventh month of 807, without the day, in *THY* 63, p. 1097, and *TFYK* 556, p. 20a.

114 See *CTS* 149, pp. 4013–14; see also *HTS* 102, p. 3988.

115 See *Yü hai* 48, p. 6a.

116. *TFYK* 562, p. 4a. See also the note on the Veritable Records compiled by Ling-hu Huan included in his biography in the *Shun-tsung Shih-lu* 3, p. 4 (trans. Solomon, *Veritable Record*, pp. 29–31).

117 See *HTS* 58, p. 1472; *Yü hai* 48, p. 6a–b; *CTS* 149, p. 4037; *TFYK* 556, p. 20a; *Ch'ung-wen tsung-mu* 3, p. 11a; *Chung-hsing Kuan-ko shu-mu chi-k'ao* 2, p. 14a; *Chih-chai shu-lu chieh-t'i* 4, p. 39a; *WHTK* 194, p. 1642a.

entire Chien-chung period (780–3) but only the period from Te-tsung's accession in 779 to the tenth month of 781.[118] Shen Chi-chi was appointed omissioner and concurrently compiler in the Historiographical Office in late 779 or early in 780 on the recommendation of Yang Yen. When the latter fell from power in the seventh month of 781, Shen was demoted to a minor post in the south. If this Veritable Record was indeed written while Shen Chi-chi held the post of omissioner of the left, it can hardly have been a normal Veritable Record, because it dealt with events that were still in progress. It is said to have been praised in its time.[119]

Shen Chi-chi is otherwise notable as the first T'ang historiographer to have seriously questioned the status of Empress Wu as a legitimate monarch deserving of having basic annals devoted to her reign included in the National History.[120] He was also, as we have seen, the first historian to write a full treatment of the examination system.

XB. *Te-tsung Shih-lu*

Fifty chapters. Compiled by Chiang I, Fan Shen, Lin Pao, Wei Ch'u-hou, and Tu-ku Yü under the direction of P'ei Chi.[121]

The compilation of this Veritable Record was ordered in the second month of 807[122] and the finished work was presented to the throne in the tenth month of 810.[123] *Ts'e-fu yüan-kuei* preserves the text of P'ei Chi's memorial presenting the manuscript to the throne, and the emperor's edict in response to this.[124] P'ei Chi's memorial stated that the work had actually been completed late in the preceding year. The copy presented comprised fifty chapters of text plus one chapter of contents. The work had the reputation of being a reliable history.[125]

P'ei Chi became chief minister in the ninth month of 808 but was not appointed director of the National History and scholar of the Chi-hsien

---

118 See *Yü hai* 48, p. 6b; *Ch'ung-wen tsung-mu* 3, p. 11a; *Chung-hsing Kuan-ko shu-mu chi-k'ao* 2, p. 14a; *WHTK* 194, p. 1642a.

119 *CTS* 149, p. 4037; *HTS* 132, p. 4540.

120 See *CTS* 149, pp. 4034–6; *THY* 63, pp. 1095–7; *TFYK* 559, pp. 9b–11b.

121 See *HTS* 58, p. 1472; *Yü hai* 48, p. 6a–b; *THY* 63, p. 1097; *TFYK* 556, pp. 20a–21b; *Ch'ung-wen tsung-mu* 3, p. 11a; *Chung-hsing Kuan-ko shu-mu chi-k'ao* 2, p. 14b; *Chün-chai tu-shu chih (Yüan-pen), hou-chih* 1, p. 15b (*Ch'ü-pen* 6, p. 2b); *Chih-chai shu-lu chieh-t'i* 4, p. 39a–b; *WHTK* 194, p. 1642a.

122 According to the *Hui yao* as quoted by *Yü hai*; and *CTS* 149, p. 4028.

123 *CTS* 14, p. 432, gives the date as the thirteenth day of the tenth month of 810.

124 See *TFYK* 556, pp. 20a–21b.

125 See *CTS* 159, p. 4183.

Academy until 809.[126] The compilation of this Veritable Record was thus begun under his predecessor as director, Li Chi-fu.[127]

Compiler Chiang I (747–821) was a highly experienced historian[128] who had been a compiler in the Historiographical Office since 792. Early in Hsien-tsung's reign he was made vice-director of the Imperial Library and reappointed to the Historiographical Office.[129] Tu-ku Yü (?–814)[130] cannot have played a large role in the actual compilation of the Veritable Record, because he was made a compiler of the National History only in 810, shortly after which he also became a Han-lin scholar and court diarist. He was, however, also at that time placed in charge of the business of the Historiographical Office (*p'an kuan shih*), and it is perhaps in that capacity that he appears among the list of compilers.[131] Wei Ch'u-hou (773–828) was a collator in the Imperial Library, and was appointed an assistant in the Historiographical Office at the recommendation of P'ei Chi.[132] He certainly took a major part in the compilation.[133] Fan Shen is otherwise unknown. Lin Pao is known to have served as an erudit scholar in the Court of Imperial Sacrifices during Hsien-tsung's reign and was the author of the genealogical compendium *Yüan-ho hsing-tsuan*.

---

126 See *CTS* 14, p. 426; *CTS* 148, p. 3990.
127 This explains an incident early in 811. P'ei Chi was a sick man and ceased to act as chief minister shortly after the Veritable Record was presented, at the end of 810. Li Chi-fu was then reappointed chief minister and director of the National History. As soon as he returned from Yang-chou to take up his post, he removed Fan Shen, Wei Ch'u-hou, and Lin Pao from their duties as compilers, in anger because they were protégés of P'ei Chi, who he believed had not been entitled to present the Veritable Record to the throne. See *THY* 64, pp. 1108–9, which entitles the Veritable Record *Chen-yüan shih-lu*.
128 *TFYK* 556, p. 21a–b, and *CTS* 14, p. 432. His name is given in some sources as Chiang Wu. He changed his personal name to I after the compilation of this Veritable Record.
129 He was a member of a noted scholarly family and the founder of a dynasty of historians. His maternal great-uncle was the historian Wu Ching. His grandfather Chiang Kuei was a scholar in the Hung-wen Academy, his father Chiang Chiang-ming a member of the Chi-hsien Academy. No fewer than three of his sons, Chiang Hsi, Chiang Shen, and Chiang Chieh, served as compilers in the Historiographical Office, and a grandson, Chiang Shu, was a court diarist on the eve of Huang Ch'ao's rebellion, eventually becoming a Taoist priest. See *CTS* 149, pp. 4028–9; *HTS* 132, pp. 4534–5.
130 See *CTS* 149, p. 4028; *HTS* 132, pp. 4533–4.
131 See *CTS* 168, p. 4381.
132 On P'ei Chi, see *CTS* 148, pp. 3989–92; *HTS* 169, pp. 5147–50. He was chief minister from the ninth month of 808 until the eleventh month of 810, when he fell seriously ill. He was appointed chief scholar of the Chi-hsien Academy and director of the National History in 809 (see *CTS* 148, p. 3990) and was replaced in both positions by Li Chi-fu when the latter became chief minister in the first month of 811.
133 See *CTS* 159, pp. 4182–3; *HTS* 142, pp. 4674–6.

XIA. *Shun-tsung Shih-lu*

Three chapters. Compiled by Wei Ch'u-hou.[134]

The dates when this work was commissioned and completed are unknown. It was completed before 813, when Han Yü was ordered to revise it.

XIB. *Shun-tsung Shih-lu*

Five chapters. Compiled by Han Yü with Shen Ch'uan-shih and Yü-wen Chi, under the direction of Li Chi-fu.[135]

This compilation was ordered as a replacement for Wei Ch'u-hou's earlier Veritable Record. There were in fact two versions of this work. The first was presented in the summer (the precise month is not clear) of 815 and was referred back to Han Yü for revision, having been found unsatisfactory. The revisions must have been relatively trivial, because they took less than one month to complete. The bibliographical monograph of *Hsin T'ang shu* lists the work as having been compiled under the direction of Li Chi-fu (758–814). He, however, had died in 814,[136] the year before its completion, and no new director seems to have been appointed immediately to replace him. Perhaps this explains why Han Yü, rather than the director of the National History, wrote the memorial presenting it to the throne. At the time Han Yü and Shen Ch'uan-shih were both compilers in the Historiographical Office, while Yü-wen Chi was an assistant.[137] The first draft was presumably suppressed when the text was finally accepted in 815.

XIC. *Shun-tsung Shih-lu*

Five chapters. Compiled by Han Yü and others and revised by Lu Sui.[138]

In the 820s, successive emperors had ordered that Han Yü's version should be revised and corrected, largely owing to complaints from the eunuchs, now holding unprecedented political power, that his accounts of events involving them were untrue. Nothing had been done, however, all attempts at revision having been blocked by Chiang Hsi and Li Han,

134 See Han Yü, "Chin *Shun-tsung Huang-ti Shih-lu* piao chuang," in *Han Ch'ang-li chi* (Shanghai, 1937) 38, pp. 25–6.
135 See *HTS* 48, p. 1472; *Yü hai* 48, pp. 6b–7a; *Han Ch'ang-li chi* 38, pp. 25–6 (see entry XIA); *Ch'ung-wen tsung-mu* 3, p. 11b; *Chün-chai tu-shu chih* (*Yüan-pen*) 2A, p. 13a–b (*Ch'ü-pen* 6, p. 3a); *Chih-chai shu-lu chieh-t'i* 4, p. 39b; *WHTK* 194, p. 1642a.
136 He died on the first day of the tenth month. See *CTS* 15, p. 450.
137 *CTS* 160, p. 4209.
138 See *CTS* 159, p. 4192; *THY* 64, pp. 1111–12; *TFYK* 556, pp. 23b–25a.

both compilers in the Historiographical Office and both sons-in-law of Han Yü.[139]

Wen-tsung finally ordered Lu Sui to undertake a revision in 831 after the *Hsien-tsung Shih-lu* had been completed and presented to the throne.[140] Lu Sui's memorial to the throne accepting the command to revise Han Yü's Veritable Record makes it clear that there was a great deal of opposition to such a revision. He mentions by name[141] four persons who had presented detailed memorials opposing the idea, and adds that "very many among the ranks of officials at court were of the same opinion." He also makes it clear that he and his fellow chief ministers, Li Tsung-min and Niu Seng-ju, were opposed to any changes beyond the correction of a small number of errors of fact that the emperor was to specify in detail.[142] Lu Sui also refused to exclude Chiang Hsi and Li Han from working on the revision, as apparently had been suggested, saying that their relationship with Han Yü need not affect their objectivity as historians.

It is clear from the edict that followed Lu Sui's memorial that the revisions eventually ordered were very limited. They were specifically confined to the accounts of a number of affairs within the palace, the record of which had been based on erroneous reports and were untrustworthy. The rest was not to be altered.[143]

Wen-tsung was still not satisfied with the revision that had been made under Lu Sui's direction. In the second month of 837, during a discussion with his chief ministers Li Shih, Li Ku-yen, and Cheng T'an, he grumbled that the "Veritable Record for Shun-tsung's reign is still not really accurate" and suggested that this was perhaps due to Han Yü's personal resentment toward Shun-tsung, during whose reign he had been in disgrace.[144] He made no further attempt to have the Veritable Record revised, however.

---

139 See *CTS* 160, p. 4204.
140 See *CTS* 159, p. 4192; *THY* 64, p. 1112; *TFYK* 556, pp. 24b–25a; *TFYK* 562, pp. 10b–11a.
141 The persons named were Chou Chü-Ch'ao, president of the Court of Imperial Insignia; Wang Yen-wei, a grand counselor who subsequently was one of the compilers of the Veritable Record for Mu-tsung's reign, completed in 833; Li Ku-yen, chief secretary of the Chancellery and later chief minister from the fourth month of 836 until the tenth month of 837; and Su Ching-yin, a historiographer who worked on the Veritable Records for Hsien-tsung and Mu-tsung.
142 For the text of his memorial, see *CTS* 159, pp. 4192–3; *THY* 64, pp. 1111–12; *TFYK* 556, pp. 23b–24b; *TFYK* 562, pp. 9b–10b; *TPYL* 604, pp. 2b–3b.
143 See *CTS* 159, p. 4193; *HTS* 142, pp. 4677–8; *THY* 64, p. 1112; *TFYK* 556, pp. 24b–25a; *TFYK* 562, pp. 9b–10b; *TPYL* 604, pp. 3a–b.
144 See *TFYK* 562, p. 11a; *TPYL* 604, p. 3b. Wen-tsung compared Han Yü's treatment of Shun-tsung with Ssu-ma Ch'ien's hostile treatment of Han Wu-ti, the ruler under whom he had suffered the punishment of castration.

XID. [*Shun-tsung Shih-lu*]

Three chapters. Revised by Wei Ch'u-hou.[145]

In addition to the authentic revision carried out under Lu Sui in 831, there is a "ghost" revision reported in Han Yü's *Chiu T'ang shu* biography, which states that following the success of Chiang Hsi and Li Han in blocking attempts to have Han Yü's version of 815 rewritten, eventually Wei Ch'u-hou compiled a separate Veritable Record in three chapters.[146] This account presumably derives from a confusion between the revision actually made under Lu Sui in 830 or 831, and Wei Ch'u-hou's original three-chapter version, which had been completed before 813.[147]

XIE. *Shun-tsung Shih-lu*

Five chapters. Compiled by Han Yü. Extant, and included in the supplement to his collected works, *Han Ch'ang-li chi*, "wai-chi" chapters 6 to 10.

---

145 See *CTS* 160, p. 4204.
146 See *CTS* 160, p. 4204.
147 There is, however, a very remote possibility that such a later revision by Wei Ch'u-hou could have been carried out. Wei (773–828) had served as a compiler in the Historiographical Office from the ninth month of 808 until the eighth month of 816, during which term his original Veritable Record had been completed. Under Mu-tsung (probably in 823) he was again appointed a compiler, together with Lu Sui, so that they could undertake the Veritable Record of Hsien-tsung's reign. On the accession of Wen-tsung in the twelfth month of 826, Wei Ch'u-hou became chief minister and director of the National History (see *CTS* 159, pp. 4183, 4192). There is thus no compelling reason why Wei could not have both written the first Veritable Record, some time before 813, and then, after Han Yü had rewritten the new Veritable Record in five chapters to replace his work, himself have undertaken further revisions, either in 815–16, or more likely between 823 and his death in 828, during which period he was constantly employed in the Historiographical Office.

Pulleyblank has pointed out that a biography of Han Yü had already been prepared "for the National History" – that is, for inclusion in the Veritable Record of Ching-tsung's reign – before his son-in-law Li Han wrote the preface for the first version of his collected works in 827–30. This would undoubtedly have been the original from which his present *CTS* biography was derived. He suggests, however, that the passage about Wei Ch'u-hou's "new" compilation, because it comes in a postscript to the main biography summarizing Han Yü's literary and scholarly achievements, was probably a later addition, possibly added when the *CTS* was compiled in the tenth century. See E. G. Pulleyblank, "The *Shun-tsung Shih-lu*," *BSOAS* 19 (1957): 336–44. This may be probable but is by no means certain. It is worth remembering that this biography in its original form was almost certainly processed in the Historiographical Office while Wei Ch'u-hou himself was either a compiler or the director.

The length of his phantom revision, however, is given as three chapters, the same as the pre-813 original version, and this seems to me almost conclusive evidence that the *CTS* compilers have simply made an error and concluded that his version followed, rather than antedated Han Yü's version.

This is by no means the end of the confusion about the Veritable Records for Shun-tsung. A work with this title, in five chapters, actually survives intact, and has been included in the supplement (*wai-chi*) to the collected works of Han Yü since the eleventh century.[148] Some thirty years ago an integral translation was published by Bernard S. Solomon.[149] It is the only surviving Veritable Record from the T'ang and is invaluable in that it enables us to gain a clear picture of what the Veritable Records were like.

But although it has been attached to Han Yü's collected works at least since the early eleventh century, and although we know that Han Yü was in fact responsible for one recension of Shun-tsung's Veritable Record, there has been considerable controversy over which recension this surviving text represents. In the latter half of the eleventh century, when Ssu-ma Kuang was compiling the critical notes (*k'ao-i*) for his *Tzu-chih t'ung-chien*, there were available to him in the imperial libraries two quite different recensions of the *Shun-tsung Shih-lu* both in five chapters and both attributed to Han Yü. One is described by Ssu-ma Kuang as the "detailed version" (*hsiang-pen*), of which there were two copies, the other as the "abbreviated version" (*lüeh-pen*), of which there were five.[150]

It is clear from a comparison with the various quotations from these two different versions preserved in the *Tzu-chih t'ung-chien k'ao-i* that the present text is not the "detailed version," and it is reasonable therefore to have been rearranged into the present five-chapter format. Wei's unsatisfactory original draft was in any case probably discarded in 815 after Han Yü's version was completed, and all the complaints and controversy about the Veritable Records for Shun-tsung's reign in the 820s were specifically related to the Han Yü version. Nevertheless, this conjecture too cannot be ruled out, and all of these suggestions are worthy of consideration.

The vexed question remains of the relations between the "abbreviated version" represented by the present text and the various recensions through which the *Shun-tsung Shih-lu* is known to have passed. There are various possibilities, none of which can be proved beyond doubt. First, it may be exactly what it claims to be, the *Shun-tsung Shih-lu* presented to the throne by Han Yü in 815, presumably in its second, slightly revised

148 *Han Ch'ang-li chi*, "wai-chi" chapters 6–10. Li Han's preface says that the *Shih-lu* was deliberately excluded from the original collected works. On its later inclusion, see Pulleyblank, "The *Shun-tsung Shih-lu*," pp. 343–44.
149 Solomon, *The Veritable Record of the T'ang Emperor Shun-tsung*.
150 See *TCTC* 236, p. 7608 (*k'ao-i*); *Yü hai* 48, p. 7a.

state. Jack Dull has come to this conclusion, largely on stylistic grounds and on the basis of what we otherwise know about Han Yü's views on history.[151] Second, it may be either the 831 revision made under Lu Sui or, more likely, an authorized abridgment of this revised version, according to Solomon.[152] Third, E. G. Pulleyblank concluded that it has, in fact, nothing to do with Han Yü at all but may well be the original version written by Wei Ch'u-hou before 813.[153] This seems less likely because Wei's version was in only three chapters, so that the text would have to have been rearranged into the present five-chapter format. Wei's unsatisfactory original draft was in any case probably discarded in 815 after Han Yü's version was completed, and all the complaints and controversy about the Veritable Records for Shun-tsung's reign in the 820s were specifically related to the Han Yü version. Nevertheless, this conjecture too cannot be ruled out, and all of these suggestions are worthy of consideration.

Another possibility however, has not, to my knowledge, been suggested. Dull has carefully analyzed the text and shown that it is a very deliberately composed piece, organized didactically. Although I feel that he greatly overstates his case, and the six-month period covered by the Veritable Record is so short that it has an inevitable unity dictated by the pattern of events, his argument is to some degree persuasive.[154] He also makes the telling point that, to make the best of its didactic argument, the material is not arranged strictly chronologically, and suggests that the text we have was not a "normal" *Shih-lu*. Of course, because we have no "normal *Shih-lu*" with which to compare it, this suggestion is purely speculative. Nevertheless, it does suggest a possible solution. Han Yü may well have done what various of his predecessors in the Historiographical Office had done before him when frustrated by the constraints of writing official history and used the raw material of the official Veritable Record he had been commissioned to write to produce a better-organized private account in which he could give a free rein to his own ideas and interpretation of events. Wu Ching, Wei Shu, and Liu Fang, for example, had all done this in the previous century, compiling their own private chronological histories while working on the National History in their official capacities. Admittedly none of them had entitled

---

151 See Jack L. Dull, "Han Yü: A Problem in T'ang Dynasty Historiography," in *Proceedings of the Second Conference of Historians of Asia* (Taipei, 1964), pp. 71–99.
152 See Solomon, *The Veritable Record of the T'ang Emperor Shun-tsung*, pp. xvi–xxiii.
153 See Pulleyblank, "The *Shun-tsung Shih-lu*."
154 A similar impression is given in Charles Hartman, *Han Yü and the T'ang Search for Unity* (Princeton, 1986), p. 78.

his history a *Shih-lu*, but this title had been used for other private historical works in T'ang times,[155] and clearly in the T'ang period the title *Shih-lu* still had not the exclusively official connotation it was to develop in later centuries. Moreover, as Dull has shown, Han Yü had used this term to refer to private writings of his own as early as 807.[156] Certainly there is ample evidence that Han Yü had, even before he was appointed to the Historiographical Office, a strong ideal conception of a moralistic style of historical writing that would have been hard to reconcile with the constraints of compiling an official record, particularly a record of such a recent and controversial train of events.

Perhaps then the two versions existing in the eleventh century were *both* exactly what they claimed to be: versions of Han Yü's *Shun-tsung Shih-lu*. The "detailed version" may have been the official version produced for the Historiographical Office, probably in the form as subsequently revised under Lu Sui in 831. The other "abbreviated version," the extant text, may have been a private version in which Han Yü omitted some routine detail and tautened the organization of his material in order to express more forcibly the didactic purpose with which he certainly approached the task of writing history. This interpretation would also explain why, when Liu Yeh (968–1029) compiled the supplement to Han Yü's collected writings, including the *Shun-tsung Shih-lu*, in the early eleventh century, he chose what was clearly the inferior of the two then extant versions viewed as a historical source, but what was perhaps the superior version stylistically and as a vehicle for Han Yü's ideas on political history.[157]

All these theories are speculative. Whatever the precise origin of the current text, it remains the only surviving example of its genre, and an

155 For example, the still-extant *Chien-k'ang Shih-lu* in twenty chapters of Hsü Sung. See *HTS* 58, p. 1466; *Ch'ung-wen tsung-mu* 3, p. 16a (where it is listed among the miscellaneous historical works, *tsa-shih*); *Chün-chai tu-shu chih (Yüan-pen)* 2A, p. 13b; *(Ch'ü-pen* 6, p. 4b). Hsü Sung, a shadowy figure about whom almost nothing is known, seems to have written this work during the reign of Su-tsung. See *Ssu-k'u ch'üan-shu tsung-mu ti-yao* 50, pp. 1091–2; and the preface by Meng Chao-yin, Sun Shu-ch'i, and Wu I to their edition of *Chien-k'ang shih-lu* (Shanghai, 1987). It is attributed not to Hsü Sung, but to Ma Tsung (d. 823) in *Nihon koku genzai sho mokuroku* 7, p. 105 (Kariya Ekisai's edition). It is not, however, listed among Ma Tsung's writings in his biographies. See *CTS* 157, pp. 4151–2; *HTS* 163, pp. 5033–4. Another example is the *Wu-shu Shih-lu* in three chapters included in *Ch'ung-wen tsung mu* 3, p. 16a (with a note that it was missing in 1144).
156 See Dull, "Han Yü," pp. 80–2.
157 There is no doubt that Liu Yeh, who had served as an assistant scholar in the Lung-t'u ko Imperial Library shortly before the *Ch'ung-wen tsung-mu* was compiled (1034–41), must have seen both the detailed and the abbreviated texts. His choice of the shorter version was therefore certainly a deliberate one. See Pulleyblank, "The *Shun-tsung Shih-lu*," pp. 343–44.

invaluable, though perplexingly incomplete piece of evidence on a singularly obscure set of political events. It is worth remembering, when we look at the complex series of revisions to which the record of these few months was subjected, that the revisions dealt with crucial political events that not only were traumatic in themselves but were also the origins of tense political strains – the rivalry between eunuchs and officials, ideological differences, and the formation of embittered partisan alignments that subsisted for decades. Such partisan politics involved every official at court and poisoned the atmosphere of political life until the 840s. Han Yü himself had narrowly escaped personal involvement in the events[158] of Shun-tsung's reign. No one in his time could have written a purely objective *Shun-tsung Shih-lu*, and certainly not a record that would have satisfied all the parties with an interest in the events and their aftermath.

XIIA. *Hsien-tsung Shih-lu*

Forty chapters. Compiled, under the direction of Tu Yüan-ying, Wei Ch'u-hou, and Lu Sui, by Shen Ch'uan-shih, Cheng Han, Ch'en I-hsing, Li Han, Chiang Hsi, Yü-wen Chi, and Su Ching-yin (also written Su Ching-i).[159]

According to the *Chung-hsing Kuan-ko shu-mu* as cited in *Yu hai*, it began with Hsien-tsung's appointment to his princely fief and ended with the first month of 820 (the date of his death).

---

158 Han Yü served briefly in the Censorate in 803 as an examining censor, together with Liu Tsung-yüan and Liu Yü-hsi, both of whom were members of the party supporting Wang Shu-wen, which came to power when Wang's patron, the heir apparent, became emperor (posthumous title: Shun-tsung) in 805. All three were recommended for service in the Censorate by Li Wen (d. 804), who had been its vice-president since 798 and seems to have played an important role in the formation of Wang Shu-wen's party. It seems clear that Liu Yü-hsi and Liu Tsung-yüan attempted to recruit Han Yü to their cause when he joined the Censorate but that he rebuffed them. This is the most likely interpretation of his poem, "T'i Tan-ku chiu ssu-t'ang," *Han Ch'ang-li chi* 5, pp. 46–47. He was sent to a provincial post shortly after and held them to have been responsible for his "banishment" from the capital. Even though he had refused to become their ally, after the end of Shun-tsung's short reign, the fall of Wang Shu-wen's party, and the accession of Hsien-tsung, Han Yü still found it expedient to write poems violently attacking Wang Shu-wen and his allies to proclaim his opposition, such was the atmosphere of suspicion and political vendetta of the time. See Dull, "Han Yü," pp. 80–2; Hartman, *Han Yü and the T'ang Search for Unity*, pp. 52–6. See also Lo Lien-t'ien, *Han Yü yen-chiu* (Taipei, 1977), pp. 63–9; Chiang Fan, "Han Yü yü Wang Shu-wen chi-t'uan ti Yung-chen kai-ke," *Fu-tan hsüeh-pao* 4 (1980): 67–74.

159 See *HTS* 58, p. 1472; *Yü hai* 48, pp. 7b–8a; *CTS* 149, pp. 4028, 4037; *Ch'ung-wen tsung-mu* 3, p. 11b; *Chung-hsing Kuan-ko shu-mu chi-k'ao* 2, pp. 14b–15a; *Chün-chai tu-shu chih* (*Yüan-pen*), hou-chih 1, p. 16a (*Ch'ü-pen* 6, p. 3a–b); *Chih-chai shu-lu chieh-t'i* 4, pp. 39b–40a.

The compilation took place over a long period, and the three directors mentioned were successively in charge of the work. Tu Yüan-ying (d. 832) rose meteorically from the rank of Han-lin scholar and omissioner to become chief minister within a year at the beginning of Mu-tsung's reign. He was appointed chief minister in the second month of 821 and remained in office until the tenth month of 823 when he was sent to Szechwan as military governor of Chien-nan Hsi-ch'uan. He was presumably concurrently director of the National History (although his biographies do not mention this appointment) while chief minister. Wei Ch'u-hou and Lu Sui, who later became directors in turn, were both appointed concurrent compilers in the Historiographical Office and assigned to work on these Veritable Records on the eighteenth of the tenth month of 822.[160] In 823 Tu Yüan-ying, Shen Ch'uan-shih, Cheng Han, Yü-wen Chi, and Wei Piao-wei[161] were ordered to join Lu Sui and Wei Ch'u-hou, and to divide up the years of the reign between them. However, the work was never completed.[162] In the sixth month of 823, Shen Ch'uan-shih was appointed governor of Hu-nan and, at Tu Yüan-ying's specific request, was ordered to take with him his draft copy of the Veritable Record and to complete it there.[163] At the beginning of Ching-tsung's reign in 824, Niu Seng-ju became briefly director of the National History.[164] At the beginning of Wen-tsung's reign in 827, Shen Ch'uan-shih was recalled to the capital but died shortly after.[165] An edict was now promulgated ordering Su Ching-yin, Li Han, Ch'en I-hsing,[166] and Chiang Hsi to resume compiling the work. At this time Wei Ch'u-hou was director of the National History. When he died in 828, Lu Sui succeeded him, and it was he who finally presented the completed work to the throne on the twenty-third of the third month of 830.

On its completion Lu Sui and the five other compilers were rewarded with gifts of brocade and silver vessels.[167] Another source reports that the work was presented to the throne in 833, together with the Veritable Records for Mu-tsung's reign, but this is incorrect. [168]

---

160 *THY* 63, p. 1097; *CTS* 159, p. 4183.
161 See *CTS* 160, p. 4209.
162 See *THY* 63, pp. 1099–1100; *CTS* 160, p. 4209; *HTS* 132, p. 4541.
163 See *THY* 63, pp. 1099–1100; *CTS* 16, pp. 502–3; *CTS* 149, p. 4037; *HTS* 132, p. 4541.
164 See *CTS* 172, p. 4470.
165 See *CTS* 149, p. 4037; *HTS* 132, p. 4541.
166 According to Ch'en I-hsing's biography, he was appointed a diarist and compiler in the Historiographical Office only in 829, when he participated in compiling the Veritable Record for Hsien-tsung. See *CTS* 173, p. 4495. *HTS* 181, p. 5345, records the appointment without any date.
167 See *CTS* 17B, p. 536; *CTS* 149, p. 4028.
168 See *CTS* 159, p. 4193.

It originally consisted of forty chapters plus a single-chapter table of contents. This chapter was subsequently lost.[169]

XIIB. *Chung-hsiu Hsien-tsung Shih-lu*

Forth chapters. Revised under the direction of Li Shen, by Cheng Ya and others. [170]

In the fourth month of 841, almost immediately after Wen-tsung's death, an edict ordered: "Since the old version of Hsien-tsung's Veritable Record is still imperfect, the historians should revise it and present it to the palace. The old edition should not be destroyed but, after the new compilation is finished, should be presented along with it." This revision seems to have been ordered by the new chief minister, Li Te-yü, who resented the hostile way in which the Veritable Record, completed while his enemies the Niu Seng-ju faction were in power, had recorded the activities of his father, Li Chi-fu, during Hsien-tsung's reign.[171] Its recompilation was thus an episode in the prolonged Li-Niu factional strife that had by now continued through five reigns.

The new version was completed and presented to the throne in the tenth month of 843 by Li Shen, chief minister and director of the National History,[172] who was a staunch partisan of Li Te-yü, and by Cheng Ya, compiler in charge of the affairs of the Historiographical Office. Gifts of silk and silver vessels were apportioned to the compilers.[173]

In the eleventh month of 848, after the death of Wu-tsung, and the fall from power of Li Te-yü the revised version of 843 was suppressed and the earlier version again put into circulation. Special orders were issued to the local prefectural authorities to search out any copies of the revised version and to send them to the Historiographical Office at the capital. It was forbidden for anyone to keep them secretly.[174]

This episode conclusively proves the political motivation behind the revision of 841–3. It also gives clear proof that the Veritable Records, far from being confidential records as in later dynasties, were circulated widely during late T'ang times, not only among high court officials but

169 *TFYK* 554, p. 35a–b.
170 See *CTS* 18A, pp. 586–7 and 598; *THY* 63, p. 1098; *TFYK* 556, p. 25a–b; *Yü hai* 48, pp. 7b–8a.
171 See *CTS* 171, p. 4454, which tells how Li Han earned the bitter hatred of Li Te-yü for his part in compiling the *Hsien-tsung Shih-lu*.
172 Li Shen was appointed director in 841. See *CTS* 173, p. 4500. He was a long-time colleague and supporter of Li Te-yü. They had served together as Han-lin scholars in the early 820s. See *HTS* 181, p. 5348; *CTS* 173, p. 4497.
173 See *CTS* 18A, p. 598; *THY* 63, p. 1098; *TFYK* 554, p. 35b; *TFYK* 556, p. 25a–b.
174 See *THY* 63, p. 1098; *CTS* 18B, p. 621; *TFYK* 556, p. 25b; *TFYK* 562, p. 11a–b.

also in the provinces. This, of course, greatly amplified their political significance.

XIII. *Mu-tsung Shih-lu*

Twenty chapters. Compiled under the direction of Lu Sui by Su Ching-i, Wang Yen-wei, Yang Han-kung, Su T'iao, and P'ei Hsiu.[175]

The *Chung-hsing Kuan-ko shu-mu* as cited in *Yü hai* says that the work began with the first month of the fifteenth year of the Yüan-ho period (820) and ended with the eleventh month of the fourth year of the Ch'ang-ch'ing period (824).

It was completed and presented to the throne by Lu Sui in 833.[176] Lu Sui's *Chiu T'ang shu* biography says that it was presented together with the *Hsien-tsung Shih-lu* (XIIA) but this is clearly erroneous.[177] The biographies of Wang Yen-wei,[178] Yang Han-Kung,[179] and P'ei Hsiu[180] confirm that they were serving as compilers at the relevant dates but do not mention their work on this or any other specific Veritable Records.

XIV. *Ching-tsung Shih-lu*

Ten chapters. Compiled under the direction of Li Jang-i by Ch'en Shang and Cheng Ya.[181]

According to *Chung-hsing Kuan-ko shu-mu* as cited by *Yü hai*, this work began with the fourth year of the Ch'ang-ch'ing period (824) and ended with the second year of the Pao-li period (826). It was completed and presented to the throne in 845. Li Jang-i was chief minister from the seventh month of 842 until the seventh month of 846. He had served as court diarist under Wen-tsung after 836 and had risen quickly to the rank of chief minister as a supporter of Li Te-yü. He was presumably concurrently director of the National History in his capacity as chief minister, although his biographies[182] do not mention this appointment. Neither Ch'en Shang nor Cheng Ya has a biography. In the second

---

175 See *HTS* 58, p. 1472; *Yü hai* 48, p. 8a; *Ch'ung-wen tsung-mu* 3, p. 11b; *Chung-hsing Kuan-ko shu-mu chi-k'ao* 2, p. 15a; *Chün-chai tu-shu chih (Yüan-pen), hou-chih* 1, p. 16a (*Ch'ü-pen* 6, p. 3b); *Chih-chai shu-lu chieh-t'i* 4, p. 40a; *WHTK* 194, p. 1642b.
176 See *CTS* 159, p. 4193.
177 See *Yü hai* 48, p. 8a, note.
178 *CTS* 157, p. 4154; *HTS* 164, p. 5057.
179 *CTS* 176, p. 4564; *HTS* 175, p. 5249.
180 *CTS* 177, p. 4593.
181 See *HTS* 58, p. 1472; *Yü hai* 48, p. 8a–b; *Ch'ung-wen tsung-mu* 3, p. 11b; *Chung-hsing Kuan-ko shu-mu chi-k'ao* 2, p. 15a; *Chün-chai tu-shu chih (Yüan-pen)* 2A, p. 13b (*Ch'ü-pen* 6, pp. 3b–4a); *Chih-chai shu-lu chieh-t'i* 4, p. 40a; *WHTK* 194, p. 1642b.
182 See *CTS* 176, p. 4566; *HTS* 181, pp. 5350–1.

month of 845 Ch'en Shang was provisionally in charge of the examinations as counselor (*Chien-i tai-fu*)[183] and he later became director of
the Imperial Library.[184]

Ching-tsung was the elder half brother of Wu-tsung, under whom
these Veritable Records were compiled. His mother, Grand Dowager
Empress I-an, died in the first month of 845. Wu-tsung had treated her
with the utmost respect and on her death accorded her unusually lavish
mourning rites.[185] Because the events of her son Ching-tsung's reign
made an unsavory and generally deplorable story, it seems possible that
the presentation of the Veritable Records for his reign was deliberately
delayed until after her death.

XV. *Wen-tsung Shih-lu*

Forty chapters.[186] Compiled under the direction of Wei Mu by Lu T'an,
Chiang Chieh, Wang Feng, Lu Kao, and Niu Ts'ung.[187]

According to the *Chung-hsing Kuan-ko shu-mu* and the *Ch'ung-wen
tsung-mu* as cited by *Yü hai*, this compilation began with the second year
of the Pao-li period (826) and ended with the fifth year of the K'ai-
ch'eng period (840). It was presented to the throne in the third month
of 854.[188] Wei Mu (793–858) was chief minister from the tenth month
of 851 until the second month of 857, when he became military governor
of Chien-nan Hsi-ch'uan. At the time of the work's completion he was
thus chief minister[189] and concurrently director of the National History
and was also vice-president of the Board of Rites.[190]

Of the compilers listed by the *T'ang hui yao*, Lu T'an was chief
secretary of the Chancellery, Chiang Chieh[191] was vice-president of the
Count of Imperial Sacrifices, Wang Feng was undersecretary of the

183 See *CTS* 18A, p. 604.
184 See *HTS* 58, p. 1472.
185 See *CTS* 18A, p. 603. On Dowager Empress I-an, also known as the Kung-hsi
    Empress, see *CTS* 52, pp. 2199–2200; *HTS* 77, p. 3506. She was the daughter of
    Wang Shao-ch'ing, county magistrate of Chin-hua in Chekiang. She should not be
    confused with the I-an (different characters), empress of Hsien-tsung, a grand-
    daughter of the great general, Kuo Tzu-i.
186 Or in forty-two chapters according to *THY* 63, p. 1098.
187 See *HTS* 58, p. 1472; *Yü hai* 48, p. 8b; *THY* 63, p. 1098; *CTS* 18B, p. 632; *CTS* 176,
    p. 4570; *Ch'ung-wen tsung-mu* 3, p. 11b; *Chung-hsing Kuan-ko shu-mu chi-k'ao* 2, p. 15a;
    Chün-chai tu-shu chih (Yüan-pen), hou-chih 1, p. 16b (*Ch'ü-pen* 6, p. 4a); *Chih-chai shu-lu
    chieh-t'i* 4, p. 40b; *WHTK* 194, p. 1642.
188 See *THY* 63, p. 1098; *TFYK* 554, p. 35b; *CTS* 18B, p. 632.
189 See *THY* 63, p. 1098; *HTS* 63, pp. 1731–3.
190 See his biographies in *CTS* 176, p. 4570; *HTS* 97, p. 3884.
191 Chiang Chieh was a son of Chiang I; see XB. For brief biographical notices, see *CTS*
    149, p. 4029; *HTS* 132, p. 4535.

Department of Honorific Ranks, Lu Kao was omissioner of the right. Niu Ts'ung,[192] a son of Niu Seng-ju, is also included in the list of compilers given in *Chiu T'ang shu's* biographies of Wei Mu[193] and of Chiang Chieh.[194] On the completion of the Veritable Record the compilers were all rewarded with silk fabrics and silver vessels and given promotions in rank. Wei Mu was promoted to be president of the Chancellery and concurrent president of the Board of Finance.

XVI. *Wu-tsung Shih-lu*

Thirty chapters. Compiled under the direction of Wei Pao-heng.[195]

Wei Pao-heng was chief minister from the fourth month of 870 to the ninth month of 874.[196] It seems likely that the Veritable Records for Wu-tsung were completed during this period in office, but no precise date is given in our sources. *Yü hai* elsewhere states that the historians Chiang Chieh and Huang-fu Yü compiled Veritable Records both for Wu-tsung and for his successor Hsiuan-tsung during the Hsien-t'ung period (860–74) under Wei Pao-heng's direction,[197] but the compilation of Veritable Records for Hsiuan-tsung is uncorroborated by other evidence.

Yü hai also notes that by the Five Dynasties period only one chapter of this Veritable Record survived: The work was listed by the *Ch'ung-wen tsung-mu* as being in a single chapter. This surviving chapter covered only the first and second months of 841.[198] *Yü hai* also quotes the *Chunghsing Kuan-Ko shu-mu* as saying that the work began with the first month of the fifth year of the K'ai-ch'eng period (840) and ended with the third month of the sixth year of the Hui-ch'ang period (846).

192 See *HTS* 174, p. 5234, and also *CTS* 172, p. 4476, where his personal name is written with the character ts'ung (稯). His brief biographies do not mention his work as a compiler.
193 See *CTS* 176, p. 4570.
194 See *CTS* 149, p. 4029.
195 See *HTS* 58, p. 1472; *Yü hai* 48, pp. 8b–9a; *Yü hai* 48, p. 9b; *Ch'ung-wen tsung-mu* 3, p. 11b; *Chung-hsing Kuan-ko shu-mu chi-k'ao* 2, p. 15a–b; *Chün-chai tu-shu chih (Yüan-pen), hou-chih* 1, p. 16b (*Ch'ü-pen* 6, p. 4a); *Chih-chai shu-lu chieh-t'i* 4, p. 40b; *WHTK* 194, p. 1642b.
196 For Wei Pao-heng's biographies, see *CTS* 177, p. 4602; *HTS* 184, p. 5398. These make no mention of his having been involved in compiling the Veritable Record or his being director of the National History. He had, however, served as a diarist and as a scholar both of the Han-lin and the Chi-hsien academies.
197 See *Yü hai* 48, p. 9b.
198 See *Chün-chai tu-shu chih (Yüan-pen), hou-chih* 1, p. 16b (*Ch'ü-pen* 6, p. 4a), and *WHTK* 194, p. 1642b, citing Ch'ao Kung-wu. However, this may be misleading: Ssu-ma Kuang in his *Tzu-chih t'ung-chien k'ao-i* cites the *Wu-tsung shih-lu* referring to events in the tenth month of 840 (*TCTC* 246, p. 7948) and also in 846 (*TCTC* 248, p. 8023). A more complete copy must have been available to him.

XVII. *The Late T'ang Veritable Records*

The compilation of Veritable Records seems to have come to an end with those for Wu-tsung's reign. During the late 880s, Tu Jang-neng,[199] who had been appointed a compiler in the Historiographical Office at Hsi-tsung's court in exile in Ch'eng-tu in 880 and later had become chief minister and director of the National History from 886 to 893, apparently undertook the compilation of the "Veritable Records for the Three Reigns" (presumably those of Hsiuan-tsung, I-tsung, and Hsi-tsung), but nothing was ever completed.[200] In 891, at his suggestion, the vice-president of the Board of Civil Office, Liu Pi, and other scholars[201] were ordered to compile Veritable Records for the reigns of Hsiuan-tsung, I-tsung, and Hsi-tsung. But the task proved impossible, as the necessary documents and records had been lost or destroyed during the rebellion of Huang Ch'ao and the civil wars and political confusion that followed. After a year, "not a single character had been written." One of the compilers, the Han-lin scholar P'ei T'ing-yü, put together a collection of reminiscences of Hsiuan-tsung's court, entitled *Tung-Kuan tsou-chi*, in three chapters,[202] which seems to have been the sole result of this effort to produce an official record of the period.[203]

Another attempt to write a history for the last reigns of the T'ang in the last years of the dynasty was the *Yeh-shih* or *T'ai-ho yeh-shih* in ten chapters, completed in 889–90 by the retired scholar Kung-sha Chung-mu (or Sha Chung-mu), a history that dealt with the period from the T'ai-ho reign (827–3) to the Lung-chi reign (i.e. 827–89).[204]

199 See *CTS* 177, pp. 4612–15; *HTS* 96, pp. 3864–5; *TFYK* 562, p. 13a–b.
200 See *THY* 63, p. 1098; *Yü hai* 48, p. 10a; P'ei T'ing-yü, *Tung-kuan tsou-chi*, preface (*Ts'ung-shu chi-ch'eng* edition); also in *CTW* 841, pp. 3b–4a.
201 The persons appointed were Liu Pi, vice-president of the Board of Civil Office; P'ei T'ing-yü, omissioner of the right; Sun T'ai, omissioner of the left; Li Yün, under-secretary of the Department of Equipment in the Board of War; Cheng Kuang-t'ing, erudit of the Court of Imperial Sacrifices. None of these persons has an extant biography. See *THY* 63, p. 1098; *TFYK* 562, p. 13b.
202 The *Tung-kuan tsou-chi* still survives. I have used the edition included in *Ts'ung-shu chi-ch'eng*. See *HTS* 58, p. 1468; *Ch'ung-wen tsung-mu* 3, p. 19a; *Chün-chai tu-shu chih* (*Yüan-pen*), *hou-chih* 1, p. 16b (*Ch'ü-pen* 6, p. 14b); *Chih-chai shu-lu chieh-t'i* 5, p. 17a; *Ssu-k'u ch'üan-shu tsung-mu ti-yao* 51, p. 1131.
203 See *TFYK* 556, p. 26a; *TFYK* 562, p. 13a–b; *THY* 63, p. 1098.
204 See *THY* 63, p. 1098; *HTS* 58, p. 1469; *Yü hai* 47, p. 9b. *HTS* 58, p. 1469, lists this book as *Ta-ho yeh-shih* in ten chapters and gives the author's name as Kung-sha Chung-mu. It says that it began from the Ta-ho period (i.e., *T'ai-ho* period, 827–35) and ended with the Lung-chi period (889). *WHTK* 196, p. 1653b, lists a work with the same title in three chapters, and says that it had no author's name, but a preface by Yüan T'ao of Ch'en-chün dated 848. This said that it had originally been in a single chapter, describing events connected with seventeen persons beginning with Cheng Chu (this suggests that it began with the Sweet Dew incident), and that Yüan T'ao had divided it into three chapters.

After the fall of the T'ang, the Later T'ang Emperor Ming-tsung in 926 sent a Commissioner for seeking records (*Sou-fang t'u-chi shih*), to Szechwan, following up a report that all the T'ang Veritable Records were preserved in Ch'eng-tu, but this proved to be a red herring.[205] In 932 Ming-tsung, acting on a request from his historiographical officials, promulgated an edict ordering the collection of source material from which the Veritable Records for the reigns of Hsiuan-ısung, I-tsung, Hsi-tsung, and Chao-tsung might be compiled, but again nothing seems to have come of this order.[206] Under the Later Chin, when in 941 Chia Wei memorialized the throne suggesting the compilation of a T'ang history to continue and complete the National History (*Kuo shih*) of 759, he stated that the Veritable Records of the last reigns were entirely lacking, and that only one chapter of the Veritable Record for Wu-tsung's reign was extant. Chia Wei had himself earlier compiled a work to help fill this gap and to provide material on the late T'ang for future historians. This book was entitled *T'ang nien pu-i lu*[207] and comprised fifty-five (or, in another account, sixty-five) chapters, and seems to have covered the period from the accession of Wu-tsung to the fall of the dynasty.[208]

Another almost contemporary account flatly contradicts the information in Chia Wei's memorial. Two months later, in the fourth month of 941, Chao Ying, the chief minister and director of the National History, who as a result of Chia Wei's suggestion had been entrusted with the compilation of the dynastic history of the T'ang that would become the present *Chiu T'ang shu*, presented a memorial[209] saying that the Veritable Records for Wu-tsung and Hsiuan-tsung had been compiled during the latter's reign by Wei Pao-heng, Chiang Shen,[210] and Huang-fu Yü and those for I-tsung and Hsi-tsung by P'ei Chih in the Kuang-hua period (898–901), but that all had been lost.[211] It is impos-

---

205 *CWTS* 37, p. 510; *WTHY* 24, p. 390.
206 See *TFYK* 557, p. 5b; *WTHY* 18, p. 303; *CWTS* 43, pp. 595–6. The edict orders that a search for relevant documents and for unofficial histories be made in the Liang-che, Fu-chien, and Hu-kuang provinces, and that copies should be made and sent to court for presentation. The lack of results is hardly surprising: None of these areas was part of Later T'ang territory; all were controlled by the independent states of Wu, Wu-Yüeh, Min, and Ch'u.
207 This title is sometimes given as *Tang ch'ao pu-i lu* (see *Yü hai* 48, p. 10a) or as *T'ang nien pu lu* (see *CWTS* 131, p. 1727; *Ch'ung-wen tsung-mu* 3, p. 12a [which lists it as missing in 1144]; *Chih-chai shu-lu chieh-t'i* 4, p. 22b; *WHTK* 193, p. 1623b). It is cited frequently in Ssu-ma Kuang's *Tzu-chih t'ung-chien k'ao-i* under the title *T'ang nien pu lu*, with reference to events from 841 to 903.
208 See *TFYK* 557, pp. 9b–10b; *CWTS* 131, p. 1727.
209 See *TFYK* 557, pp. 11a–15b.
210 Not Chang Chieh as in *Yü hai* 48, p. 9b.
211 P'ei Chih's work is otherwise only mentioned in a passage, unusually without a cited,

sible to decide which account is correct. It seems probable, however, that Chao Ying's memorial confirms the compilation of the Veritable Records for Wu-tsung under Wei Pao-heng, but there is some confusion about his also having undertaken the Veritable Record for Hsiuan-tsung. P'ei Chih's compilation of Veritable Records for I-tsung and Hsi-tsung may have been another stage in the abortive attempt to compile Veritable Records for the later reigns undertaken in 891, or simply a confused memory on Chao Ying's part.

It is also possible that some parts of the diaries or other historical compilations from the late T'ang were in fact recovered, because in 890 a local magistrate was rewarded and given honorary rank for having presented to the throne 360 *chüan* of books lost from the Historiographical Office.[212]

Veritable Records for the last five reigns of the T'ang were eventually compiled by the prolific Sung official historian Sung Min-ch'iu (1019–79), but by his time it can have been possible to do no more than make a very incomplete compilation based on secondary sources.[213]

specific source, in *Yü hai* 48, p. 9b. This may derive from Chao Ying's memorial, but it is followed by a note saying that by the Five Dynasties period all these Veritable Records compiled by Wei Pao-heng and by P'ei Chih were lost, apart from one chapter of Wu-tsung's Veritable Record. P'ei Chih has a very short biography in *HTS* 182, p. 5376. He was chief minister under Chao-tsung from the ninth month of 900 until the end of 903, and thus may have been concurrently director of the National History. However, by this time the "court" was powerless, and the emperor a mere puppet manipulated by the powerful warlord Chu Wen, and these appointments were meaningless.

212 See *THY* 64, p. 1114.
213 On Sung Min-ch'iu (style Tz'u-tao), see the sources listed in *SJCCTLSY*, pp. 776–7. From 1045 to 1060, he was one of the principal compilers of *Hsin T'ang shu* and he was also responsible for the *T'ang ta chao ling chi*, the *Ch'ang-an chih*, *Ho-nan chih*, *Ch'un-ming t'ui-ch'ao lu*, and many other works that have not survived, in addition to working as a compiler of the Sung National History and the *Hui yao*. His Veritable Records for the last reigns of the T'ang were presented to the throne in the ninth month of 1045 by Wang Yao-ch'en. In consequence, Sung Min-ch'iu was appointed a collator in the Imperial Library, *kuan-ko chiao-k'an*. See *Hsü Tzu-chih t'ung-chien ch'ang-pien* 157, p. 5a, and also *Yü hai* 48, pp. 9b–10b. His compilations are not, of course, included in the *Ch'ung-wen tsung-mu*, compiled several years before this date. The *Chih-chai shu-lu chieh-t'i* 4, pp. 40b–41a lists them as follows: (1) *Hsiuan-tsung Shih-lu* in 30 chapters, (2) *I-tsung Shih-lu* in 25 chapters, (3). *Hsi-tsung Shih-lu* in 30 chapters, (4) *Chao-tsung Shih-lu* in 30 chapters, and (5) *Ai-ti Shih-lu* in 8 chapters. It adds a note that these works were written by Sung Min-ch'iu long after the events and that when they were first compiled, according to the Monograph on Literature in the Sung National History, *Liang-ch'ao shih*, completed in 1082, they comprised only 100 chapters, subsequently being expanded to 148. See *Yü hai* 48, p. 10a; *WHTK* 194, p. 1642b–c. See also Chao Shih-wei, *Sung Kuo-shih i-wen-chih chi-wen* (Peking, 1933) A, pp. 12b–13a. There seems to have been some confusion about the length of these works. *Chih-chai shu-lu chieh-t'i* notes that the Veritable Record for I-tsung, which was listed as having 35 chapters, comprised only 25 in the thirteenth century.

11

The National History
(*Kuo shih*)

The National History was the final stage in the compilation of the historical record of the reigning dynasty. It involved nothing less than the writing of a full-scale Standard History, in the annal–biography form appropriate for a dynastic history, covering the current dynasty down to a given date. Like the Veritable Records, it was a T'ang innovation. But whereas the Veritable Records came to be composed as a matter of course once a reign was over, whatever the delay in their commissioning and completion might be, there was no established convention governing when it would be appropriate to revise and update the National History.

The National History also differed from the Veritable Records in that, because it always began with the dynastic founding and therefore included the period that had been covered in its predecessors, its growth tended to be incremental, a process that continued until in 941–4 the last National History, which had been compiled in 759–60, was finally incorporated into the *Chiu T'ang shu*. The writing of a new National History, although it might edit or correct the account of earlier events in its forerunner, and perhaps introduce subtle changes to make the account of past events more acceptable in its own time, was essentially the continuation and updating of the record, using the Veritable Records as the main source of information on the period to be covered for the first time.

As in the case of the Veritable Records, the compilation of a new National History was a significant political act and was not undertaken out of purely academic motives. Each of the National Histories of the T'ang was commissioned for a clear political purpose, at a time when a summary of the dynasty's past achievements would provide appropriate justification for some new regime, and as an overt evidence of legitimacy. This will become clear as we look at each of the T'ang National Histories in turn.

One very intriguing question is why no attempt was made to write a

National History after 760, in spite of the fact that there were a number of occasions when it might have seemed appropriate – at the beginning of Te-tsung's reign, for example, or under Hsien-tsung. In the first years of Hsiuan-tsung's reign (847–59), when a whole series of measures designed to reestablish the dynasty's prestige and institutional stability, including a new legal codification, were put into effect,[1] it is noteworthy that the emperor ordered not the updating of the National History but the writing of continuations for two private historical works, Liu Fang's chronicle history, the *T'ang li*, and Su Mien's encyclopedia of administrative affairs, the *Hui yao*, both of which were completed, as officially sponsored projects, by the Historiographical Office.[2] Perhaps this was the result of the all-pervading sense of the loss of central authority after the An Lu-shan rebellion, a feeling (amply justified by political facts) that the dynasty was but a shadow of its former self, living on borrowed time. For much the same reasons, after the rebellion the T'ang court ceased regularly to codify the laws, another act that had a deep symbolic meaning as a reaffirmation of the regime's authority. Although there was much discussion of state historiography and of the historical record in the late T'ang period, as we have seen, nobody ever to my knowledge raised the possibility that the time had come for an updated National History.

Another problem, for which I can suggest no obvious explanation, relates to the keeping of the National Histories. When these were completed, they were presumably presented to the throne, as were the Veritable Records, though we have clear evidence of this only in the case of the *Wu-te Chen-kuan liang-ch'ao shih* presented in 656, and indirect evidence in the case of the National History completed by Liu Fang in

1 On these measures, see Twitchett, *Cambridge History of China*, vol. 3, pp. 673–4.
2 On the *Hsü T'ang li*, see Chapter 7, n. 119. Completed in 851, this continued Liu Fang's original account down to the death of Hsien-tsung in 820. The *Hsü Hui yao* was completed in 853 by Yang Shao-fu and others. It continued the record down to 852. See n. 121 in Chapter 9. Similarly, Hsiuan-tsung's efforts to reinforce the authority of codified law also avoided a full-scale recodification of the Code, Statutes, Regulations, and ordinances, as would have been done before An Lu-shan's rebellion. What was promulgated in 851 was a "Categorized Collection of Edicts Subsequent to the Regulations," the *Ta-chung Hsing-fa tsung-yao Ko-hou ch'ih*, which summarized legislative changes promulgated as edicts from the twentieth day of the sixth month of 628 until the date of compilation. This was a huge compilation including 2,165 (or 3,165 according to *TFYK* 613, p. 7a) articles arranged under 646 categories, and extending to sixty chapters. See *CTS* 18B, p. 628 (where its title is wrongly given as the *Ta-chung Hsing-fa t'ung-lei*); *CTS* 50, p. 2156; *TFYK* 613, p. 7a. Three years later, Chang K'uei produced a second digest of law, the *Ta-chung Hsing-fa t'ung-lei* in twelve chapters, which assembled together related provisions from the various categories of codified law. This included 1,250 articles grouped in 121 sections. See *CTS* 18B, p. 631; *CTS* 50, p. 2156; *TFYK* 613, p. 7a. The latter wrongly gives its length as sixty-two chapters.

759 or 760. In the former case we are told that the work was received by
the emperor and stored in the *Nei-fu*, the precise meaning of which in
this context is difficult to establish. The term is often used to refer in a
vague, general way to the various depositories for books in the palace[3]
and also as a general term for the palace storehouses or the emperor's
personal treasuries. However, it was also the name of a specific office,
the Inner Palace Treasury, the *Nei-fu chü*, a subordinate section of the
eunuch-staffed Inner Palace Intendancy (*Nei-shih sheng*).[4] The main
duties of this office were the preparation and provision of precious
objects for presentation to foreign envoys or to officials whom the
emperor wished to honor. Among its nonranking clerical staff, all of
whom were eunuchs, there were, according to one source, four "intendants of histories" (*tien-shih*), which might suggest that the office may
have been a depository for some histories.[5] The duties of the office were
such that historical precedents were clearly of great importance, and
the existence of such special officers seems not illogical.

However, it seems more probable that here the term *nei-fu* is used
in a vague general sense for one of the Inner Palace libraries. There is
evidence of many other important works of a nonhistorical nature being
deposited in the *Nei-fu*. For example, the great catalog of the Imperial
Libraries, the *Ch'ün-shu ssu-pu lu*, was placed in the *Nei-fu* after being
presented to the throne in 721.[6] Another interesting case is that of a
work that was deliberately suppressed, Yüan Hsing-ch'ung's subcommentary to the *Tz'u Li chi* (also entitled *Lei li*), Wei Cheng's controversial commentary on a classified rearrangement of the canonical

---

3 The *Pi-shu sheng* had its main book depository *shu-ko* not in the palace but in its premises
in the administrative city (the *Pi-shu wai-sheng*) to the east of the business office of the
director (*Chien-yüan*). See *Ch'ang-an chih* 7, p. 4a. It must also have had another library
within the palace, but its location remains unidentified. There was yet another library
building *shu-ko* in the Eastern Palace of the heir apparent. See *Liang-ching hsin-chi*
(*Chi-pen*) 1, p. 3a.
4 See *HTS* 47, p. 1224 (Rotours, *Fonctionnaires*, vol. 1, pp. 253–4); *CTS* 44, p. 1872; *TLT*
12, pp. 42a–43a; *TT* 27, p. 159c.
5 These officers are mentioned only in *HTS* 47, p. 1224. They are not included in *TLT* 12,
pp. 7b–8a or 43a, which gives a detailed list of the subaltern employees of the office.
Neither do they appear in the list of subaltern officials "outside the current" in *TT* 40,
pp. 229c–230b, which reproduces the Statutes on Official Ranks (*Kuan-p'in ling*) of 737.
Rotours, *Fonctionnaires*, vol. 1, p. 254, n. 4, suggests that the term *tien-shih*, "intendants of
histories," is merely an error. The term appears nowhere else in any of the descriptions
of the T'ang bureaucratic apparatus. Both *tien*, "intendant," and *shih*, "clerk," occur
frequently in lists cf minor office employees as separate categories, so that a textual
error is quite possible. However, in the *HTS* list, the two characters appear to belong
together, and the combined term is otherwise unknown. I find it hard to believe,
however, that politically important historical works such as these would be placed in the
keeping of lowly eunuch clerks.
6 See *CTS* 8, p. 182; *CTS* 36, p. 658.

Record of Rites (*Li chi*)[7]. Yüan Hsing-chung's subcommentary was presented to the throne in 726 and was adversely criticized by, among others, the influential Chang Yüeh, as a result of whose objections it was deemed unfit for general circulation[8] and was stored in the Inner Palace (*Nei-fu*).[9] This would suggest that the *Nei-fu* depositories were sometimes used for works to which access was restricted.

It is impossible to reach a certain conclusion about which palace depository received the National History. But I feel fairly confident in rejecting the possibility that it was stored in the Inner Palace Treasury, and prefer to understand *Nei-fu* in this instance in the general sense of the "palace collections."[10]

Whatever the precise location of the *Nei-fu* may have been, it is certain that the *Wu-te Chen-kuan liang-ch'ao shih*, even though it had been accepted by the emperor, was not placed in the main palace library, because it is not listed in the catalog dated 721 incorporated in the bibliographical monograph of the *Chiu T'ang shu*. Nor was any other National History included in that catalog, although we know that copies were kept in the Historiographical Office.[11] Why this was the case, in spite of the fact that the National Histories were of such obvious importance – clearly outweighing the Veritable Records of individual reigns, which *were* included in the Palace Library – is a mystery to which I can offer no solution.

The T'ang National Histories

I. [*Title unknown*]

Thirty chapters. Compiled by Yao Ssu-lien.[12]

According to Liu Chih-chi's *Shih t'ung*, Yao Ssu-lien (d. 637) compiled a history in annal–biography form at the beginning of the T'ai-tsung's

---

7 My attention was drawn to this case by David McMullen. Details about Yüan Hsing-ch'ung's subcommentary are given in R. P. Kramers, "Conservatism and the Transmission of the Confucian Canon: A T'ang Scholar's Complaint," *Journal of Oriental Studies* 2, no. 1 (1955): 122.

8 See *HTS* 200, p. 5691.

9 See *CTS* 102, p. 3178; *THY* 77, p. 1410.

10 For discussion of this point I am much indebted to a number of scholars; to my friend Professor Wang Yuquan of the Academy of Social Sciences in Peking, and to his two colleagues Chang Tse-hsien and Ch'ü Lin-tung, who were kind enough to write me their detailed opinions, and also to my old friend and former colleague David McMullen, who drew my attention to a number of other instances of major works being deposited in the *Nei-fu* after presentation to the throne.

11 See Wei Shu's *Chi-hsien chi-chu* as cited in *Yü hai* 46, p. 42a.

12 See *Shih t'ung* 12, p. 373 (trans. Pulleyblank, "The *Tzyjyh Tongjiann Kaoyih*," p. 450).

reign (627), and this was used as a foundation for the compilation of the later and fully documented National History completed in 656. It seems not to have been a polished work; Liu Chih-chi describes it as having been "roughly completed in thirty chapters." The work is not mentioned in either of Yao Ssu-lien's biographies or in any other source.

Yao Ssu-lien was a member of a family of learned historians from the south. While T'ai-tsung was still prince of Ch'in, Yao served as one of the retinue of scholars T'ai-tsung maintained in the Wen-hsüeh kuan. After T'ai-tsung usurped his father's throne in 626, Yao was appointed a secretary in the Office for Literary Composition, and a scholar of the Hung-wen Academy. His history was probably written between this date and 629 when he was appointed to compile the histories of the Liang and Ch'en dynasties.[13]

If Yao Ssu-lien did in fact write a history of the T'ang in annal–biography form, as Liu Chih-chi asserts, it must have been written to record only dynastic founding and the reign of Kao-tsu. In view of Yao's close association with T'ai-tsung both before and after his accession, it is most likely that it would have portrayed T'ai-tsung's role in the dynastic founding in a favorable light.

IIA. *Wu-te Chen-kuan liang-ch'ao shih*

(Or *Wu-te Chen-kuan erh-ch'ao shih*.) Eighty (or eighty-one). Compiled by Chang-sun Wu-chi, Yü Chih-ning, Ts'ui Tun-li, Ling-hu Te-fen, Li I-fu, Liu Yin-chih, Ku Yin, Yang Jen-ch'ing, Li Yen-shou, and Chang Wen-kung.[14]

This history in annal–biography form[15] documented the reigns of Kao-tsu and T'ai-tsung. It was presented to the throne on the third day of the seventh month of 656. Kao-tsung accepted it and ordered it to be stored in the Palace Treasury (*Nei-fu*).[16] Chang-sun Wu-chi and the other compilers were richly rewarded, and noble titles were granted either to themselves or to their sons.[17]

According to Liu Chih-chi the team of historians who undertook the work were Chang-sun Wu-chi, his fellow chief minister Yü Chih-ning,

---

13 See *CTS* 73, p. 2593; *THY* 63, p. 1091. Liu Chih-chi says that he began this work in 627 (see *Shih t'ung* 12, pp. 356–7). Yao Ssu-lien came from a family with a strong tradition of historical studies. Both the Liang and Ch'en histories had been begun by his father Yao Ch'a but left unfinished.
14 See *Shih t'ung* 12, p. 373 (trans. Pulleyblank, "The *Tzyjyh Tongjiann Kaoyih*," pp. 450–1); *THY* 63, p. 1093; *TFYK* 556, p. 14a–b; *HTS* 58, p. 1458; *Yü hai* 46, p. 40a–b.
15 See *TFYK* 556, p. 14b.
16 See *THY* 63, p. 1093; *TFYK* 656, p. 14b.
17 See *TFYK* 556, p. 14a–b; *THY* 63, p. 1093.

Filiation of the various T´ang National Histories

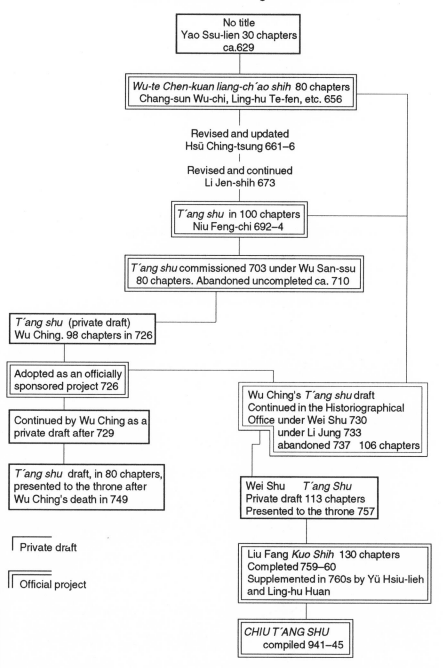

No title
Yao Ssu-lien 30 chapters
ca.629

Wu-te Chen-kuan liang-ch´ao shih 80 chapters
Chang-sun Wu-chi, Ling-hu Te-fen, etc. 656

Revised and updated
Hsü Ching-tsung 661–6

Revised and continued
Li Jen-shih 673

T´ang shu in 100 chapters
Niu Feng-chi 692–4

T´ang shu commissioned 703 under Wu San-ssu
80 chapters. Abandoned uncompleted ca. 710

T´ang shu (private draft)
Wu Ching. 98 chapters in 726

Adopted as an officially
sponsored project 726

Continued by Wu Ching as a
private draft after 729

T´ang shu draft, in 80 chapters,
presented to the throne after
Wu Ching's death in 749

Wu Ching's *T´ang shu* draft
Continued in the Historiographical
Office under Wei Shu 730
under Li Jung 733
abandoned 737   106 chapters

Wei Shu   *T´ang Shu*
Private draft 113 chapters
Presented to the throne 757

Liu Fang *Kuo Shih* 130 chapters
Completed 759–60
Supplemented in 760s by Yü Hsiu-lieh
and Ling-hu Huan

CHIU T´ANG SHU
compiled 941–45

Private draft

Official project

Ling-hu Te-fen, rector of the imperial university and scholar of the Ch'ung-wen Academy, the two secretaries of the Office for Literary Composition, Liu Yin-chih[18] and Yang Jen-ch'ing, and the diarist Ku Yin.[19] They took over what Yao Ssu-lien had written and added fifty chapters more dealing with later events (presumably those of T'ai-tsung's reign). Liu Chih-chi's judgment of their work is grudging: "Although it could be called overdetailed and confused, sometimes it has passages worthy of notice."[20]

Although Chang-sun Wu-chi, as the senior statesman at court and director of the National History, actually presented the work to the throne, the historian chiefly responsible for its compilation was Ling-hu Te-fen, who is given as its author by the eighth-century historian Wei Shu.[21]

IIB. [*Kuo shih*]

(Precise title unknown.) One hundred chapters. Compiled by Hsü Ching-tsung.[22]

According to Liu Chih-chi's account, in the Lung-shuo period (661–3) Hsü Ching-tsung, who was in general charge of historical duties, further expanded the *Wu-te Chen-kuan liang-ch'ao shih,* making all together one hundred chapters. This work was ordered by the emperor in 659.[23] Hsü Ching-tsung is said to have added the basic annals for the first years of Kao-tsung's reign, biographies of the famous officials of the Yung-hui (650–6) period, and the accounts of foreign peoples.[24]

18 Liu Yin-chih's name is written Liu Yün-chih in *THY* 63 and Liu I-chih in *TFYK* 556. These variants were replacements for the character Yin, tabooed under the Sung. Liu Yin-chih was a great-uncle of the great historian Liu Chih-chi.
19 *THY* 63, p. 1093, and *TFYK* 556, p. 14a, give a fuller list of compilers. They add Ts'ui Tun-li, who like Chang-sun Wu-chi and Yü Chih-ning was a chief minister and thus only nominally involved, the diarist Li Yen-shou, and a secretary in the Imperial Library named Chang Wen-kung. Li Yen-shou was an experienced historian who had taken part in the writing of the *Chin shu* and the Monographs for the Five Dynasties. In the 670s he also wrote a book on T'ai-tsung's reign entitled *T'ai-tsung cheng-tien* in thirty chapters, which was presented to the throne posthumously on the first day of the second month of 680. It was much admired by Kao-tsung and a special copy was made for the heir apparent (see *THY* 36, p. 657). He is of course best known for his general histories of the Northern and Southern Dynasties, the *Pei shih* and *Nan shih,* private compilations that later were accorded the status of Standard Histories. (See his biographies, *CTS* 73, pp. 2600–1; *HTS* 102, pp. 3985–6.)
20 See *Shih t'ung* 12, p. 373. The passage is translated in Pulleyblank, "The *Tzyjyh Tongjiann Kaoyih,*" pp. 450–1.
21 See the quotation from Wei Shu's *Chi-hsien chu-chi* preserved in *Yü hai* 46, p. 42a.
22 See *Shih t'ung* 12, p. 373 (trans. Pulleyblank, "The *Tzyjyh Tongjiann Kaoyih,*" p. 451).
23 See *THY* 63, p. 1093.
24 Hsü Ching-tsung had recently completed and presented to the throne in 658 a very large work on foreign peoples, the *Hsi-yü t'u-chih* in sixty chapters. This had been based

IIC. [*Kuo shih*]

(Precise title unknown.) Compiled by Li Jen-shih.[25]

Again according to Liu Chih-chi's account, this was later continued by the diarist of the left, Li Jen-shih, who added the biographies of Hsü Ching-tsung, Li I-fu, Yü Chih-ning, and others. His work must have been carried out after 672, the year of Hsü Ching-tsung's death (Yü Chih-ning had died in 665, Li I-fu in 666), and was almost certainly connected with the attempt to rectify the errors and distortions introduced into the historical record by Hsü Ching-tsung that led in 673 to the attempt to revise the Veritable Record for Kao-tsung's reign mentioned earlier. Li Jen-shih was also the historian designated by the chief ministers to undertake that revision. He died shortly after, with the revision of the Veritable Records and National History uncompleted. Liu Chih-chi praises his honesty in recording events, and regrets that he did not live long enough to complete his work on the National History.

All these works were cumulative. The National History (*Kuo shih*) of Ling-hu Te-fen referred to by Wei Shu in the next century as being preserved in the Historiographical Office[26] was almost certainly not the *Wu-te Chen-kuan liang-ch'ao shih* as originally completed, but the work as it was subsequently supplemented by Hsü Ching-tsung and Li Jen-shih.

III. *T'ang shu*

One hundred chapters. Compiled by Niu Feng-chi.[27]

According to Liu Chih-chi this was compiled during the Ch'ang-shou period (692–4) by Niu Feng-chi, vice-president of the Board of Rites

---

on the reports of envoys sent by Kao-tsung to Samarkand, Tokharistan, etc., to investigate the customs and products of these western states, and to report their findings together with pictures. See *HTS* 58, p. 1506.

25 See *Shih t'ung* 12, p. 373 (trans. Pulleyblank, "The *Tzyjyh Tongjiann Kaoyih*," p. 451).

26 Pulleyblank, "The *Tzyjyh Tongjiann Kaoyih*," pp. 454–5, reads the quotation from Wei Shu's *Chi-hsien chu-chi* preserved in *Yü hai* 46, p. 42a, as meaning: "In the Historiographical Office there were formerly the National History (*Kuo-shih*) and the T'ang History (*T'ang shu*) composed by Ling-hu Te-fen. Both were in the form of annals and biographies." He takes this passage to mean that Wei Shu says that Ling-hu Te-fen wrote both a *Kuo shih* and a *T'ang shu*. I believe, however, that the passage should read: "There were formerly in the Historiographical Office the National History compiled by Ling-hu Te-fen, and the *T'ang shu*," that is, the *T'ang shu* of Niu Feng-chi. I also do not agree that the Ling-hu Te-fen National History had necessarily been *destroyed* by Niu Feng-chi as he suggests (p. 455). Liu Chih-chi only says that it had been taken out of circulation.

27 See *Shih t'ung* 12, p. 373 (trans. Pulleyblank, "The *Tzyjyh Tongjiann Kaoyih*," pp. 451–2); Wei Shu's *Chi-hsien chu-chi* as cited in *Yü hai* 46, p. 42a.

(*Ch'un-kuan shih-lang*).[28] It is said to have covered the history of the dynasty from the accession of Kao-tsu until the end of Kao-tsung's reign in 683. Liu Chih-chi was extremely critical of this work and of its author's ability as a historian. Much of it is said to have depended on privately written *hsing-chuang*, the "Accounts of Conduct" of deceased persons prepared by colleagues, relatives, or friends as draft material for the eventual writing of their official biographies.

After its completion, Niu Feng-chi had copies of the earlier National Histories of Yao Ssu-lien and of Hsü Ching-tsung (i.e., of the revised and updated version of Ling-hu Te-fen's National History) collected, so that only his own version would remain in circulation. Because of this, according to Liu Chih-chi, "the records of the early acts of our royal house were almost completely lost."[29]

The date of this work and, indeed, its title – it was the first history to be entitled "History of the T'ang" (*T'ang shu*) – show that it was written at the beginning of Empress Wu's newly established "Chou Dynasty," which had been inaugurated in 690, as a dynastic history of the T'ang, which was now formally a defunct dynasty. These circumstances would imply that it must have attempted to justify the empress's usurpation of the throne and replacement of the T'ang royal house. Its compilation was thus carried out in a context similar to that of Tsung Ch'in-k'o's Veritable Record of her regime between 683 and 690, which already

28 Niu Feng-chi has no extant biography. He was a distant ancestor of Niu Seng-ju, the ninth-century chief minister, whose funerary inscriptions mention Niu Feng-chi's name and rank, and also his having been director of the National History, a post that Niu Seng-ju too was to hold briefly under Ching-tsung (see *CTS* 172, p. 4470). See Tu Mu, *Fan-ch'uan wen-chi* (Shanghai, 1978) 7, p. 114; *WYYH* 938, p. 1a; *CTW* 755, pp. 3a–9a, "Ch'eng-hsiang T'ai-tzu shao-pao Ch'i-chang chün k'ai-kuo kung tseng T'ai-wei Niu Kung mu-chih-ming." This says that Niu Feng-chi became vice-president of the Chancellery and Secretariat, and director of the National History, but gives no dates. See also Li Chüeh's "Ku Ch'eng-hsiang T'ai-tzu shao-shih tseng T'ai-wei Niu Kung shen-tao-pei-ming," in *CTW* 720, pp. 3a–8b; *WYYH* 888, pp. 5a–10, which gives his office as vice-president of the Board of Rites. Li Chüeh gives his name as Niu Feng, omitting the last character. Both inscriptions say that he was Niu Seng-ju's great-great-grandfather. The genealogical tables of chief ministers in *HTS* 75A, pp. 3365–6, show him as a member of the same lineage but not as a direct ancestor, and are thus probably in error. Li Chüeh also says that he was *Ch'un-kuan shih-lang* not under Empress Wu but under Chung-tsung. The title *Ch'un-kuan shih-lang* was used in place of *Li-pu shih-lang* only from 684 to 705, when Empress Wu wielded supreme power. Li Chüeh's statement does not, however, imply that Niu Feng-chi served at a different time. It simply means that Li Chüeh was denying Empress Wu status as a legitimate sovereign, and considered Chung-tsung to have remained the legitimate ruler throughout her period in power, a position later to be taken by some Sung historians.

29 See *Shih t'ung* 12, p. 373 (trans. Pulleyblank, "The *Tzyjyh Tongjiann Kaoyih*," p. 452). In spite of what Liu Chih-chi asserts, the National History of Ling-hu Te-fen and Hsü Ching-tsung certainly survived into the next century. See *Yü hai* 46, p. 42a.

has been described. This fact, as much as Niu Feng-chi's personal shortcomings as a historian, may partly explain Liu Chih-chi's palpable hostility to this work. It probably also explains why a new National History was ordered little more than a decade later, in the last years of Empress Wu when the political situation had entirely changed and the eventual reversion of the throne to the T'ang imperial house was once again assured.

IV. *T'ang shu*

(Or *T'ang shih*.) Eighty chapters, but never completed. Compiled by Wu Ching, Liu Chih-chi, Hsü Chien, Li Ch'iao, Ts'ui Jung, Chu Ching-tse, Hsü Yen-po, and Wei Chih-ku under the direction of Wu San-ssu, and others.[30]

The edict ordering the compilation of this history (entitled *T'ang shu* by Liu Chih-chi, and *T'ang shih* by the other sources) is dated the fifth day of the first month of 703.[31] The group of compilers appointed to the task was a large and talented one. Wu San-ssu, the unprincipled nephew of Empress Wu, was the dominant figure among the directors and made life impossible for the compilers by his constant interference in their work. Chu Ching-tse and Li Ch'iao, both of them his fellow chief ministers, were well-known scholars. Chu was already a compiler in the Historiographical Office and retained that post after his resignation as chief minister in the second month of 704.[32] Li Ch'iao was one of the foremost prose writers of his time and a notable scholar. Wei Chih-ku was a protégé of Chu Ching-tse, and remained in the Historiographical Office until Jui-tsung's reign. Liu Chih-chi and Wu Ching, who had also been recommended by Chu Ching-tse,[33] were both extremely influential

---

30 See *THY* 63, p. 1094; *TFYK* 554, p. 17a; *TFYK* 556, pp. 15b–16a; *Shih t'ung* 12, p. 374 (trans. Pulleyblank, "The Tyhjyh Tongjiann Kaoyih," p. 452).

31 See *THY* 63, p. 1094. The two passages in *TFYK* give the date of the edict as the first month. This cannot, however, be correct, since the edict mentions Li Ch'iao with the title president of the Chancellery (*Na-yen*). Li was appointed to this office only on the ninth day of the fourth month (see *CTS* 6, p. 131) or the nineteenth of the intercalary fourth month (according to *TCTC* 207, p. 6562; *HTS* 61, p. 1666) of the same year. William Hung therefore suggests that the "first month" (*cheng-yüeh*) was a scribal error for the "fifth month" (*wu-yüeh*). See "The T'ang Bureau of Historiography," p. 106, n. 33. This would accord with the title held by Chu Ching-tse, which is given as grand counselor (*Cheng-chien tai-fu*), a post he held until the thirteenth day of the seventh month, when he became an ad hominem chief minister. (See *HTS* 61, p. 1667; this promotion is dated in the ninth month by *CTS* 6, p. 131.)

32 See *HTS* 61, p. 1667. On Chu Ching-tse as a historian, see Hsü Ling-yün and Wang Hung-chün, "Chu Ching-tse te shih-hsüeh ssu-hsiang," *Shih-hsüeh shih yen-chiu*, 1987, no. 4: 47–52.

33 See *CTS* 102, p. 3182; *TFYK* 554, p. 17b.

historians and remained mainstays of the Historiographical Office until well into Hsüan-tsung's reign.[34] Liu Chih-chi was to write the *Shih t'ung*, the most important single book on the craft of the historian in Chinese; Wu Ching, the *Chen-kuan cheng yao*, which would remain the most influential book on early T'ang governance and eventually be translated into Khitan, Jurchen, Tangut, Mongol, and Manchu, and be widely read in Japan and Korea. Between them they were responsible for the final versions of the Veritable Records of four reigns, and both wrote numerous other historical works that have not survived. Hsü Chien was also a notable scholar, involved in many major works.

The project was almost certainly undertaken, as E. G. Pulleyblank suggested thirty years ago, in connection with the political situation in the final years of Empress Wu's reign.[35] In 698 the empress had finally abandoned her plans to keep the succession in her own family after her death and had appointed the dethroned Chung-tsung as the imperial heir. This had meant a tacit admission that her Chou dynasty would not survive her and that the T'ang house would be restored. In 701 she had left Loyang, her "Holy Capital," and transferred the court to Ch'ang-an, the primary locus of T'ang dynastic power, for the first time since 683. There was clearly a dynastic upheaval in progress.[36] It was therefore appropriate that Niu Feng-chi's *T'ang shu*, which had been written in the context of the temporary fall of the T'ang, should be rewritten in the light of subsequent events.

The new history was not rewritten *ab initio*. According to Hsü Chien's biography, the empress ordered him and his colleagues to "cut and alter" the *T'ang shih*, that is, Niu Feng-chi's history. The edict ordering the compilation says that the compilers were to "collect the opinions from the four quarters and subsume them into a single work, thus to hand down forever a standard and to bequeath admonitions to the future."

Whatever the aims of the directors, the work seems never to have

---

34 Liu Chih-chi remained in the office until 721, when he was appointed to a provincial post as a result of his trying to intercede in a case involving his eldest son, who had been sentenced to banishment. He died shortly after reaching his post in the provinces. Wu Ching served in the office, apart from short periods in mourning, until 729. Together in 716 they produced the definitive Veritable Records for the reigns of Empress Wu, Chung-tsung, and Jui-tsung.

35 See Pulleyblank, "The *Tzyjyh Tongjiann Kaoyih*," p. 452, n. 3. Subsequently Hung challenged this view (see "The T'ang Bureau of Historiography," p. 106, n. 38), but I remain convinced that Pulleyblank's suggestion fits the historical context of 703 more accurately.

36 On these events, see the accounts in Twitchett, *Cambridge History of China*, vol. 3, pp. 317–20, and in Guisso, *Wu Tse-t'ien and the Politics of Legitimation in T'ang China*, pp. 143–52.

been completed. The historiographers had great difficulty in gaining access to documents and information they required. The directors were inept and indecisive and were unable to produce a coherent plan or to allocate work among the compilers. The compilers felt intimidated by political pressures because it proved impossible to preserve confidentiality about what they were writing. As a result they resorted to procrastination and go-slow tactics. As Liu Chih-chi says, "They vied with one another in acquiring the habit of irresponsibility and in practicing the tactics of evasion. They will simply sit down and discuss the changing weather and will let the time pass with, of course, nothing accomplished."[37] Work on it was probably suspended when the empress was forced to abdicate in 705.[38] In the months following Chung-tsung's accession and the empress's death most of the compilers were transferred to work on the Veritable Records for her reign, and although it seems that work was resumed on the National History after the Veritable Records were completed, it gradually dragged to a halt during Chung-tsung's reign, under a succession of politically motivated, corrupt, and incompetent directors.[39] Now that the dynastic crisis had been resolved and the T'ang royal house safely restored, the Veritable Records, which established Empress Wu's place within the context of the history of the T'ang house, had become politically the more important project.

V. *T'ang shu*

Compiled by Wu Ching. There were several works with this title.

Wu Ching had, as we have seen, been one of the team of compilers appointed to participate in the abortive project to compile a National History begun in 703. Because of the frustrations he suffered under a succession of interfering political directors of the National History[40] he

---

37 See Liu Chih-chi, *Shih t'ung*, 20, pp. 591–2 (trans. Hung, "A T'ang Historiographer's Letter," pp. 6–9).

38 See *CTS* 102, p. 3175.

39 See the memorial presented by Wu Ching in 726 on his return to office after mourning for his father, preserved in *THY* 63, pp. 1098–9; *TFYK* 556, p. 17a–b; "Formerly in the years between the Ch'ang-an and Ching-lung periods (701–10), while holding office as Diarist and Omissioner of the Left I was also concurrently a Compiler of the National History. At that time there were Wu San-ssu, Chang I-chih, Chang Ch'ang-tsung, Chi Ch'u-na, Tsung Ch'u-k'o, and Wei Wen who succeeded one another in directing these duties. Wu San-ssu and the others were by nature evil: They failed to follow the emperor's directions, wrongly indulged in ornate phraseology, and failed to make a faithful record."

40 See the memorial presented by Wu Ching in 726, cited in *THY* 63, pp. 1098–9; *TFYK* 556, p. 17a–b. *HTS* 132, pp. 4528–9, gives a résumé of this same memorial.

began to write not one but two private histories of the T'ang. The first of these was a T'ang history (*T'ang shu*) in annal–biography form. The other was a history entitled *T'ang Ch'un-ch'iu*, written in the chronicle[41] (*pien-nien*) form much favored by eighth-century historians. Both works were begun in the first decade of the eighth century, but neither was ever completed.[42] At this time Wu Ching's official duties involved him not only in the continuing work on the National History but also in the compilation of the Veritable Records for Empress Wu, Chung-tsung, and Jui-tsung. He also took part in compiling the great empire-wide genealogical compilation *Hsing-tsu hsi lu*, completed in two hundred chapters in 713 under the direction of Liu Chung.[43] All this work in his official capacity can have taken up only a part of his energies, for at the same time he was also writing the work for which he is best remembered, and the only one of his many histories to survive, the *Chen-kuan cheng yao*.[44] However, pressure of work was not the only reason for the two T'ang histories remaining incomplete. Wu Ching was a compulsive perfectionist, unable to leave any of his work alone, constantly revising, improving, and above all condensing his writings. He had a passion for brevity and conciseness, which was carried in his later years to such an extreme that it seriously reduced the value of his writings.[45]

While holding a succession of court posts, he served concurrently in the Historiographical Office more or less continuously, with brief

41 During the T'ang the chronicle form of history was widely considered to be the equal, if not the superior of the composite annal–biography form. We know for example that in pre-T'ang and early T'ang times Hsün Yüeh's *Han chi* was considered as important a history of the Han period as Pan Ku's *Han shu*. (See Ch'en Ch'i-yün, "The Textual Problems of Hsün Yüeh's Writing: The *Han Chi* and the *Shen-chien*," *Monumenta Serica* 27 [1968]: 208–32, esp. 209.) There are some interesting remarks about the two rival forms in Liu Chih-chi's *Shih t'ung*, especially in chapter 2, "Erh t'i." (*Shih t'ung* 2, pp. 27–33.) This preference for the chronicle form is certainly connected with the great emphasis placed during this period upon studies of the Spring and Autumn Annals and the *Tso chuan* commentary. These were held to be exemplars of the chronicle (*pien-nien*) tradition.

In addition to Wu Ching, Wei Shu also wrote a *T'ang Ch'un-ch'iu* in thirty chapters. Later in the eighth century Liu Fang wrote a chronicle of the T'ang entitled *T'ang li* in forty chapters, and Lu Ch'ang-yüan (d. 798, a scholar manqué who ended his career by being murdered, cooked, and eaten by the mutinous troops of Hsüan-wu province, to which he had been appointed military governor) wrote a *T'ang Ch'un-ch'iu* in sixty chapters (see *HTS* 58, p. 1461). For other examples of histories in the chronicle style written by T'ang authors, see the titles listed in *HTS* 58, pp. 1460–1.

42 See *HTS* 132, pp. 4526–8.

43 See *CTS* 189B, pp. 4971–2; *THY* 36, p. 665; *TFYK* 554, p. 33b; *TFYK* 560, pp. 20a–21b.

44 On this work see Harada Taneshige, *Jōgan seiyō no kenkyū* (Tokyo, 1968). See also the unpublished master's thesis submitted to the University of Hong Kong in 1962, Winston George Lewis, "The Cheng-kuan Cheng-yao: A Source for the Study of Early T'ang Government," which includes a complete English translation.

45 See *CTS* 102, p. 3182; *HTS* 132, p. 4529.

absences for mourning his parents, until 729.[46] Besides his historical writing, he was also involved in a number of other state scholarly projects, including the great catalog of the Imperial Library, the *Ch'ün-shu ssu-pu lu*, completed in 721.[47]

In 726, having recently completed the period of mourning for his father, Wu Ching submitted a memorial to the throne drawing attention to his two private histories, which he admitted were incomplete and "still being pruned and polished," and requesting the aid of copyists and other assistance so that he could complete them and offer them for preservation in the Historiograhical Office. At the time his *T'ang Ch'un-ch'iu* comprised thirty chapters, and the *T'ang shu* ninety-eight chapters. The latter covered the history of the entire dynasty from 617 until the third month of 726.[48]

Wu Ching's memorial was presented at a singularly propitious moment. Hsüan-tsung had just completed the Feng and Shan sacrifices on Mount T'ai, marking symbolically a new peak in the dynasty's power and prestige, and there was already under way a variety of major scholarly projects designed to reaffirm the dynasty's achievements and enhance its prestige. The compilation of a Veritable Record for Hsüan-tsung's early reign was begun; work on the codification of law and administrative practice had been in progress since the beginning of the reign; work was about to begin on a major new ritual code, the *K'ai-yüan li*; and a number of large-scale literary projects were being undertaken under imperial sponsorship. A new National History fitted naturally into this pattern of activities.

Wu Ching's offer was accepted. He was given assistance and began work on his magnum opus, this time under official auspices. At first he worked in the newly renamed Chi-hsien Academy of which he had been appointed a scholar and then, after a new chief minister objected to his having documents he required for his work taken out of the Historiographical Office, his work was transferred there. But the history was never finished. Wu Ching, always the perfectionist, was constantly reediting, condensing, and cutting what he had written.[49]

46 See *CTS* 102, p. 3182; *HTS* 132, pp. 4526–8. He retired in mourning for his mother from 713 or 714 to 715, and for his father from 723 or 724 to 725 or 726.
47 See *CTS* 102, p. 3183. This information is given not in Wu Ching's own biography but in that of his younger colleague, Wei Shu, who was also involved in writing this catalog.
48 See *HTS* 132, pp. 4528–9: The full text of the memorial is preserved in *THY* 63, pp. 1098–9; *TFYK* 556, p. 17a–b.
49 At some time during these years he also produced a work in ten chapters entitled *T'ang shu pei-chüeh chi*, which provided materials to supplement gaps in the record of political events during the reigns of Kao-tsung, Empress Wu, Chung-tsung, and Jui-tsung, and the first years of Hsüan-tsung. See *HTS* 58, p. 1467; *Yü hai* 46, p. 42b; *Chung-hsing Kuan-ko shu-mu* cited in *Yü hai* 46, p. 42b.

In 729 the emperor banished him to a provincial post,[50] perhaps, as his *Hsin T'ang shu* biography tells us, because he had offended by writing something that was incorrect,[51] perhaps because his superiors despaired of his ever completing his work. Wu Ching, who was already more than sixty years old, was given special permission to take his draft history and continue work on it in his provincial post.[52] The newly appointed chief minister, Hsiao Sung, later memorialized the throne asking permission to send a messenger to retrieve from Wu Ching a copy of the National History on which he had been working.[53] The copy that was obtained, however, was now much shorter than before, its length being given in different sources either as "more than fifty," "more than sixty," or as sixty-five chapters,[54] and we are told that "its record of events was very much abbreviated so that it was not fit to be put into circulation."[55] I shall return later to its subsequent history in the Historiographical Office.

Wu Ching served in a series of important provincial posts[56] until 743, when he was recalled to Ch'ang-an and appointed to a high-ranking sinecure in the household of one of the imperial princes.[57] Though old and stooped, he sought reappointment to concurrent duties in the Historiographical Office, but the chief minister, Li Lin-fu, perhaps wisely, refused his request. Nevertheless, he continued with his private

---

50 See *CTS* 102, p. 3182; *HTS* 132, p. 4529.

51 See *HTS* 132, p. 4529. His offense must have been relatively trivial, because his provincial post, as senior administrator (*Ssu-ma*) of the government-general of Ching-chou was hardly a serious demotion. It carried the lower fourth rank, lower division, only two degrees below his previous rank as president of the Left Secretariat of the heir Apparent which carried the upper fourth rank, lower division. However, for an elderly scholar-official whose entire career had been spent in scholarly offices at court, such a provincial posting constituted a serious sort of banishment.

52 See *CTS* 102, p. 3182; *HTS* 132, p. 4529; *THY* 63, p. 1099; *TFYK* 562, p. 3b.

53 *CTS* 103, p. 3182; *HTS* 132, p. 4529. *THY* 63, p. 1099 and *TFYK* 562, p. 3b, say that Hsüan-tsung sent a eunuch messenger to get the copy.

54 Sixty-five chapters according to *CTS* 102; more than sixty chapters according to *HTS* 132; more than fifty according to *THY* 63, *TFYK* 559, *TFYK* 562.

55 See *TFYK* 556, p. 17b; *TFYK* 562, p. 3b.

56 See *CTS* 102, p. 3182. He was successively prefect of T'ai-chou in Chekiang, of Hung-chou and Jao-chou in Kiangsi, and, after being found guilty of another offense, of the less important Ch'i-chou in what is now north-central Anhwei. (There is a discrepancy in the sources here. *HTS* 132, p. 4529, says that he was found guilty of another offense while prefect of Hung-chou and demoted to be prefect of Shu-chou, a prefecture of inferior status.) He was finally posted as chief administrator of Hsiang-chou in southern Hopei. At some point he was ennobled as viscount of Hsiang-yüan County and given the nominal lower third rank.

57 He was made master (*Fu*) in the household of Li Chen, prince of Heng, Hsüan-tsung's twenty-seventh son, an ardent Taoist who always dressed in Taoist robes. This post carried the coveted third rank.

historical writings.[58] When he died in 749, his son presented to the throne yet another, and still incomplete, draft *T'ang shu*, this time in eighty chapters. It was said to be markedly inferior to the works of his prime.[59]

VI. *T'ang shu*

One hundred thirteen chapters. Compiled by Wei Shu.

The T'ang history of Wei Shu has a story almost as complicated as that of the various histories in which Wu Ching was involved.

In 729, after Wu Ching had been banished to the provinces, Chief Minister Hsiao Sung put the still incomplete draft that had been recovered from him into the hands of a much younger scholar-historian, Wei Shu, a protégé of Chang Yüeh's from the Chi-hsien Academy.[60] Wei Shu had worked together with Wu Ching not only in the Chi-hsien Academy after 726 but also earlier, when both men had participated in the compilation of the *Ch'ün-shu ssu-pu lu*, the definitive catalog of the Imperial Library produced between 715 and 721.[61] Wei Shu was

58 Wu Ching was a prolific author. In addition to the various National Histories, the *T'ang shu pei-chüeh chi*, the *T'ang Ch'un-ch'iu*, and the *Chen-kuan cheng yao* mentioned previously, he wrote short histories of the five pre-T'ang dynasties, a *Ch'i shih* in ten chapters, a *Liang shih* in ten chapters, a *Ch'en shih* in five chapters, a *Chou shih* in ten chapters, and a *Sui shih* in twenty chapters (see *CTS* 102, p. 3182; *HTS* 58, p. 1458). He was also the author of a work on Yüeh-fu poetry, the *Yüeh-fu ku-t'i yao chieh* in a single chapter (*HTS* 57, p. 1436), a history of military writings, the *Ping-chia cheng-shih* in nine chapters (see *HTS* 59, p. 1551), a medical compilation on diagnosis entitled *Wu-tsang-lun ying-hsiang* in a single chapter (*HTS* 59, p. 1571), and a collection of memorials by prominent T'ang statesmen in ten chapters entitled *T'ang ming-ch'en tsou* (*HTS* 60, p. 1624).

59 See *CTS* 102, p. 3182.

60 On Wei Shu, see Niu Chih-kung, "Yu kung yü T'ang-tai shih-hsüeh te Wei Shu," *Shih-hsüeh shih yen-chiu*, 1986, no. 2: 51–3.

61 This massive work in 200 chapters was produced under the direction first of Ma Huai-su (659–718) and, after his death, of Yüan Hsing-ch'ung (653–729). It was presented to the throne by the latter on the thirteenth of the eleventh month of 721 and stored in the palace depository (*Nei-fu*). It listed 2,655 works totaling 48,169 chapters. Wei Shu was responsible for the historical section "Shih-k'u" together with Yü Ch'in, and also wrote the preface and rules of compilation. See *CTS* 8, p. 182; *THY* 36, p. 658; *CTS* 46, p. 1962; *TCTC* 212, p. 6747; *TFYK* 604, pp. 11b–12a; *TFYK* 608, pp. 16b–17b. The last of these sources also gives the emperor's edict of acceptance. *TCTC* 212, p. 6747, *K'ao-i*, cites Wei Shu's *Chi-hsien chu-chi* as saying it was presented in the spring of 721, not in the eleventh month. *Yü hai* 52, p. 26a, cites this same passage. Wu Ching is listed among the compilers recommended by Ma Huai-su in *TFYK* 608, p. 17b. The *Ch'ün-shu ssu-pu lu* was subsequently abridged in the *Ku-chin shu-lu* of 40 chapters by Wu Chiung (his name is mistakenly given as Wu Chao in *THY* 36, p. 658). The books included totaled 51,852 chapters (see *CTS* 48, p. 1962; *Feng-shih wen-chien chi* 2, p. 10). This abridgment was used as the basis for the "Monograph on Literature" of the National History and subsequently of *CTS* 46–47. See McMullen, *State and Scholars in T'ang China*, pp. 221–2.

appointed a compiler in the Historiographical Office in 730, and placed in charge of the office's business. We have, at second hand, Wei Shu's own account of what followed. He and his colleagues took the seventh-century National History compiled by Ling-hu Te-fen, the T'ang history by Niu Feng-chi,[62] and the T'ang history of Wu Ching[63] and wove them together, adding supplementary material for the period after 685, so as to produce a new history in annal–biography form. The material they had to work with was in considerable disarray. Wei Shu finally brought some degree of order to the National History, writing a separate chapter setting out his principles for compilation.[64] Hsiao Sung, who wanted to have the history finished as quickly as possible, appointed three other scholars, a diarist named Chia Teng, an assistant secretary of the Office for Literary Composition, Li Jui,[65] and an erudit scholar of the Court of Imperial Sacrifices, Chu Ssu-kuang, to help in the compilation, and later memorialized the throne asking permission to add two more persons, Lu Shan-ching and Liang Ling-tsan, to the team.[66] Nevertheless, after a year or more had elapsed they were still not done. This was probably due to the competing claims of other projects involving much the same group of scholars, the *K'ai-yuan li* ritual code, completed in 732, and the *T'ang liu-tien*, eventually completed in 737.

Hsiao Sung fell from power in 733 and was replaced by a new group of chief ministers, one of whom, P'ei Yao-ch'ing, was Wei Shu's uncle. The other chief minister, Chang Chiu-ling, a famous writer and also a former associate of Chang Yüeh, selected a diarist, Li Jung, to take over responsibility for the compilation of the National History.[67] When the Taoist scholar Yin Yin was appointed to control the affairs of the

---

62 The *T'ang shu* mentioned here is taken by Pulleyblank to be another work by Ling-hu Te-fen. It refers in fact to Niu Feng-chi's T'ang history. See n. 27.

63 It would appear from his own account that Wei Shu did not use the 65-chapter *T'ang shu* that had been recovered from Wu Ching by Hsiao Sung, or his original *T'ang shu* in 98 chapters, but a larger version in 110 chapters, possibly the abandoned official history compiled in the early years of the century, or perhaps a longer version produced by Wu Ching in the Historiographical Office in the late 720s.

64 See *CTS* 102, p. 3184; *HTS* 132, p. 4530; *TFYK* 556, p. 19a.

65 See also *HTS* 132, p. 4530, which mentions only Chia Teng and Li Jui.

66 See Wei Shu's *Chi-hsien chu-chi*, quoted in *Yü hai* 46, p. 42a.

67 See *Yü hai* 46, p. 42a. Under the previous ministry Li Jung had been involved in a grandiose but abortive project, suggested to the emperor by Chief Minister P'ei Kuang-t'ing, to compose a "Continuation of the Spring and Autumn Annals" covering all history from the Warring States era to the end of the Sui. The "classic" itself was to be an imperial composition, to which P'ei himself planned to write a commentary in the style of the *Tso chuan*. Hsüan-tsung enthusiastically took up this suggestion, and Li Jung was deputed to write the work. It was never completed. See *CTS* 84, p. 2807; *Yü hai* 47, pp. 26b–27a. When P'ei Kuang-t'ing fell from power later in 733, many of his former subordinates and associates were sent into banishment. Li Jung was presumably saved from sharing their fate by Chang Chiu-ling.

Historiographical Office in 737[68] there was still no sign of the National History's completion, and work on it was stopped.[69]

Official work on the draft National History was abandoned at this point, according to Wei Shu's own account. He himself was suspended from his responsibility for the National History in 739, when he became vice-rector of the State University. He was, however, shortly reinstated both to the Historiographical Office and to the Chi-hsien Academy.[70] In 742, he became president of the heir apparent's Right Secretariat and was given the nominal third rank. Later, in 750, he became vice-president of the Board of Works and was ennobled as marquis of Fang-ch'eng County. All these posts were sinecure appointments. His substantive duties continued to be scholarly and historical ones. His biography attributes to him the completion of a *T'ang shih* in 113 chapters, accompanied by a separate chapter on "historical principles" (*Shih-li*)[71] This seems to have been a private draft, completed after the offical project was abandoned. Events had followed the same course as with Wu Ching; the official project was abandoned, but Wei Shu continued to work on his own private draft history in annal–biography form. Moreover, as Wu Ching had done, he simultaneously wrote a shorter work in chronological form entitled *T'ang Ch'un-ch'iu*.[72]

---

68 See *THY* 63, p. 1101; *HTS* 200, p. 5702.

69 See Wei Shu, *Chi-hsien chu-chi* as quoted in *Yü hai* 46, p. 42a–b.

70 Wei Shu was the author of many works. In addition to his *T'ang shih* and *T'ang Ch'un-ch'iu*, he compiled a new Veritable Record for Kao-tsung's reign (see *CTS* 102, p. 3185). He also completed in 722 a historical account of the two capital cities, the *Liang-ching hsin-chi* in five chapters, which was later used by Sung Min-ch'iu as the basis for his own much fuller monographs, the *Ch'ang-an chih* and *Ho-nan chih*. (A single chapter of this work survives in the Sonkeikaku Bunko, in an early Kamakura period manuscript. See Hiraoka Takeo, *Chōan to Rakuyō*, vol. 1, pp. 15–40.) He also wrote two works on specific government offices, the *Chi-hsien chu-chi* in a single chapter dealing with the Chi-hsien Academy, and the *Yü-shih-t'ai chi* in ten chapters dealing with the Censorate. A notable expert on genealogy, he produced the *K'ai-yüan p'u* in twenty chapters, a detailed supplement to Liu Ch'ung's *Hsing-tsu hsi lu*, the huge genealogical compendium on the prominent lineages of the empire that had been completed in 713. He was also a famous bibliophile, with a personal library said to have included 20,000 *chüan*. He was one of the chief compilers of the imperial catalog of 721, the *Ch'ün-shu ssu-pu lu*, and wrote a catalog of the Chi-hsien Academy's library, the *Chi-hsien shu-mu* in a single chapter. He wrote a work on calligraphy entitled *Shu-fa chi*, which is cited in *TPYL* 748, p. 5b. He was also the author of a large compendium on official behavior, the *T'ang Chih-i* in thirty chapters (see *CTS* 102, p. 3185), and took part in the compilation of the digest of administrative law, the *T'ang liu-tien*, and of the literary encyclopedia *Ch'u-hsüeh chi*.

71 *Ch'ung-wen tsung-mu* 3, p. 5b, gives its length as 112 chapters. The discrepancy is presumably due to his biography having counted the chapter of "historical principles" as an integral part of the book, or of having counted the table of contents as an additional chapter.

72 See *HTS* 58, p. 1461, which gives its length as thirty chapters.

At the end of Hsüan-tsung's reign there were in existence two entirely different T'ang histories by Wei Shu, both based on the previous work of Wu Ching. One was his official draft, further edited by other hands and later abandoned incomplete. This was destroyed in the burning of the Historiographical Office in 756, and is said to have comprised 106 chapters. The other was his own personal draft history, in 113 chapters, which survived the conflagration. This version was to play a major part in the next stage of compiling the "National History."

VII. *Kuo shih*

One hundred thirty chapters. Compiled by Liu Fang, with some sections added later by Yü Hsiu-lieh and Ling-hu Huan.[73]

During the occupation of the capital by An Lu-shan's army from the sixth month of 756 until the end of 757, Wei Shu, like many other T'ang officials, accepted office under the rebel "emperor." When the two capitals were recovered by the T'ang armies in 757, these unhappy officials were put on trial. Wei Shu was found guilty of collaborating with the rebels and sentenced to exile in Yü-chou (modern Chungking in Szechwan), where the local prefect so humiliated him that he starved himself to death. Some years later, in 763, his nephew Hsiao Chih, who was then serving on the staff of the successful general Li Kuang-pi, came to court and requested that Wei Shu's name be posthumously cleared, owing to the service he had rendered to the dynasty by preserving the National History during the chaos of the rebellion. As a result Wei Shu was posthumously reinstated and given a promotion in rank.[74]

The events that lay behind this posthumous rehabilitation were as follows. On the twenty-seventh day of the eleventh month of 757, Yü Hsiu-lieh (692–772), who had joined Su-tsung's court shortly after his seizure of power in 756 and had been appointed a compiler of the National History (a post he continued to hold until the reign of Tai-tsung),[75] presented a memorial drawing the emperor's attention to the

73 See *Ch'ung-wen tsung-mu* 3, pp. 5b–6a; *WHTK* 192, p. 1627b–c; *HTS* 58, p. 1458; *CTS* 149, p. 4030.
74 See *CTS* 102, p. 3184; *HTS* 132, p. 4530.
75 For biographies of Yü Hsiu-lieh, see *CTS* 149, pp. 4007–9; *HTS* 104, pp. 4007–8. He was a great-great-grandson of Yü Chih-ning, who had been one of the chief ministers responsible for the first T'ang National History. He had taken the *chin-shih* degree, and under Hsüan-tsung had an exemplary career as a "pure official," serving as a collator in the Imperial Library, an omissioner, a diarist, and a scholar of the Chi-hsien Academy. In 752, when Yang Kuo-chung became chief minister and got rid of those courtiers who were not his own adherents, Yü was sent out to be prefect of Fang-chou,

urgent need to try to replace the historical materials that had been destroyed when the Historiographical Office was deliberately burned down during the rebel occupation of Ch'ang-an. He suggested that the censors and local officials should trace former officials of the office and offer a reward to anyone who could send the authorities any surviving portions of the National History or Veritable Records. If the historians themselves had taken the books from the office, they would be given amnesty for their offense. Anyone who could present a complete work would receive a promotion in rank, and for every chapter recovered a reward of ten lengths of silk was offered.[76] This elicited little response, however, and after a few months only one or two chapters had been retrieved.[77]

At this point Wei Shu sent to the authorities[78] his own draft National History in 113 chapters, presumably in the hope that this would mitigate his treason. When Hsüan-tsung fled from Ch'ang-an before the arrival of the rebel armies in 756, Wei Shu had taken his draft for safekeeping to his country residence in Nan-shan south of the capital and concealed it there. It thus survived both the destruction of the Historiographical Office, in which the official draft of the National History, the Veritable Records for Hsüan-tsung's reign, the Court Diaries, and many other documents had perished, and also the destruction of Wei Shu's own city mansion together with his very large and famous personal library and his priceless collections of art and antiquities.[79] Wei Shu's presentation of his draft history failed, however, to save him. Although the emperor issued orders that he and his friend[80] and colleague Liu Fang[81] should complete and update his National History, by the time the order was put into effect Wei Shu had already died in exile.

Liu Fang was considerably younger than Wei Shu. He had passed the

to the north of Ch'ang-an. When after An Lu-shan's victory at T'ung-kuan in 756 the emperor fled to Szechwan, and the heir apparent usurped the throne and set himself up as sovereign in the northwest, Yü Hsiu-lieh joined the new emperor Su-tsung and was given a number of posts, chief secretary of the Chancellery, vice-president of the Court of Imperial Sacrifices with special responsibility for ritual observances, and compiler of the National History.

76 See *CTS* 149, p. 4008; *THY* 63, p. 1095.
77 See *CTS* 149, p. 4008; *THY* 63, p. 1095.
78 See *CTS* 149, p. 4008; *THY* 63, p. 1095. According to *HTS* 132, p. 4530, he sent his manuscript to Yü Hsiu-lieh. *HTS* 104, p. 4008, however, says it was presented to the throne.
79 See *CTS* 102, p. 3184.
80 *T'ang kuo shih pu* A, p. 20 and Li Fang, *T'ai-p'ing kuang-chi* (Peking, 1959) 235, p. 1803, attest to their close friendship. These same sources also tell us that after Wei Shu's death Liu Fang completed many of his writings.
81 For brief biographies of Liu Fang, see *CTS* 149, p. 4030; *HTS* 132, p. 4536.

chin-shih examination after several unsuccessful attempts in 735[82] and had later been recommended for promotion by Wei Shu[83] and had become an assistant in the Historiographical Office sometime in the 740s.[84] Like Wei Shu he had accepted office under the rebels, and when Loyang was recaptured by the T'ang armies in 757 he too was found guilty of collaboration and sentenced to eternal exile on the frontier and the loss of all rank.[85]

Liu Fang, however, was more fortunate than Wei Shu. He was almost immediately pardoned and reinstated, probably owing to the inter-cession of Chief Minister Ts'ui Yüan (705–68).[86] Ts'ui had on the eve of the rebellion been Yang Kuo-chung's deputy as military governor of Chien-nan (Szechwan) and had received Hsüan-tsung and his much depleted entourage when they reached Ch'eng-tu. Hsüan-tsung ap-pointed him vice-president of the Secretariat and a chief minister. In the eighth month of 756, he was sent, together with his fellow chief ministers, Wei Chien-su, Fang Kuan, and Ts'ui Huan, to Su-tsung's temporary court at Ling-chou, bearing Hsüan-tsung's formal abdication and the state seal. All four were confirmed as chief ministers under Su-tsung and remained influential for some time. The others were removed from their chief ministerships one after another during 757, as Su-tsung steadily deprived of any real power[87] all of his ministers who had been closely associated with his father. Alone among them, Ts'ui

---

82 See *Teng-k'o chi k'ao* 8, p. 12a–b. Among his fellow graduates were Chia Chih, Li Hua, and Hsiao Ying-shih.

83 According to a quotation from the *Ting-ming lu* preserved in *TPKC* 222, p. 1706, he had failed the examination in successive years before this. The same source tells us that sometime later Wei Shu recommended him as an erudit scholar in the Court of Imperial Sacrifices.

84 See *HTS* 149, p. 4536.

85 See Yao Ju-meng, *An Lu-shan shih-chi* 3, p. 2a (*Hsüeh-hai lei-pien* edition Shanghai, 1920; trans. Rotours, *Histoire de Ngan Lou-chan*, p. 230). This text does not list Wei Shu among the collaborators tried and punished at the time. Rotours (ibid., p. 230, n. 5) raises the possibility that the Liu Fang condemned in 757 was actually a different person. There are no grounds, however, for such an interpretation.

86 I owe this idea to David McMullen (personal communication 3 March 1987). Ts'ui Yüan's biographies are in *CTS* 108, pp. 3279–80, and *HTS* 140, pp. 4641–2. See also Li Hua's two memorial inscriptions, Ts'ui Yüan's own *pei* (*WYYH* 869, pp. 6a–8a) and the *shen-tao pei* for his father (*WYYH* 900, pp. 7a–10b).

87 Wei Chien-su, the last remaining pre-rebellion chief minister, appointed in 754, lost his chief ministership in the third month; Fang Kuan, with whom the emperor had lost patience after his naive attempts to conduct strategy according to classical precedent led to a military disaster involving more than 40,000 casualties late in 756 (see *TCTC* 219, pp. 7003–4) after which he ceased to attend court (*TCTC* 219, p. 7024), followed in the fifth month; and Ts'ui Huan in the seventh month. See *CTS* 10, p. 246. Ts'ui Yüan was thus the only one of Hsüan-tsung's chief ministers in Szechwan who was still in power in the twelfth month of 757 when the former emperor was brought back to Ch'ang-an.

Yüan remained in power until the fifth month of 758,[88] from the end of 757 holding the highest ministerial rank as president of the Secretariat. He was also concurrently senior scholar of the Chi-hsien Academy and director of the National History.[89] He held these posts when Loyang was recaptured in the tenth month of 757, and we know that at this time he successfully intervened to help a number of other officials who had collaborated with the rebel regime, ensuring that they were leniently treated and banished to "good places."[90] Ts'ui had entered his official career in 735,[91] the same year that Liu Fang took the *chin-shih* degree, and is known to have been closely associated with two of Liu Fang's fellow graduates, Hsiao Ying-shih and Li Hua.[92] He thus must also have known Liu Fang (and Wei Shu), and probably arranged for them to be pardoned to work on the history under his direction.

Liu Fang was ordered to collaborate with Wei Shu in updating the National History,[93] but by the time this order was issued Wei Shu had already been sent into his distant exile, where he died before he could be recalled. Liu Fang was therefore left to undertake the completion of the National History alone, on the basis of Wei Shu's draft. He continued the work according to the plan laid out by Wei Shu, and eventually completed a National History in 130 chapters, beginning with Kao-tsu's reign and continuing until the Ch'ien-yüan period (758–9). It is not clear exactly when it was completed and presented to the throne.

At some unknown date during the Shang-yüan period (760–2), Liu Fang was again found guilty of some unspecified offense and was banished to Ch'ien-chung, the then wild frontier province roughly equivalent to modern Kweichow. On the road he met the aged eunuch Kao Li-shih, Hsüan-tsung's lifelong intimate servant and adviser, who had been banished at the end of the seventh month of 760 as a result of the machinations of Su-tsung's favorite eunuch, Li Fu-kuo. He was one of a group of court officials banished and degraded at this time, because Li Fu-kuo and Su-tsung feared that an attempt might be made to reinstate the aged Hsüan-tsung on the throne.[94] Kao Li-shih was able to explain

88 See *CTS* 10, p. 252; *CTS* 108, p. 3279; *TCTC* 220, p. 7054.
89 See *WYYH* 900, p. 9b.
90 Among those he rescued from jail was the poet-painter Wang Wei, who was moved to Ts'ui's mansion and set to decorating the walls with his paintings. See *TPKC* 179, p. 1332.
91 See *T'eng-k'o chi k'ao* 8, p. 13a.
92 Li Hua was also tried as a collaborator, and rescued thanks to the intervention of Liu Chih, who was a close associate of Fang Kuan. See Pulleyblank, "Neo-Confucianism and Neo-Legalism," p. 85.
93 See *CTS* 149, p. 4030. This says that they were ordered to update the National History compiled by Wu Ching.
94 See *TCTC* 221, pp. 7093–5.

various dubious points about the palace affairs of Hsüan-tsung's reign to Liu Fang, who subsequently incorporated this information into his private history of the dynasty, the *T'ang li*, because his National History had already been presented to the throne. Liu Fang's work had thus already been completed by 760.[95]

Liu Fang subsequently returned from his banishment to work in the Historiographical Office under Tai-tsung.[96] But he was employed on other works,[97] and the National History he had completed in 759–60 was further supplemented by other hands. At some point, after Su-tsung's death in 762, Yü Hsiu-lieh added the Basic Annals for his reign.[98] In addition Ling-hu Huan, the compiler whose work on the reconstruction of the Veritable Record for Hsüan-tsung's reign has been mentioned, made some additions to the ends of various chapters, presumably to update them to include recent events, to add the details of the careers of notable sons to their fathers' biographies, and so on. The date of these additions is not known and they may very well have been made piecemeal over a period of several years, but they must have been made

95 This assumes that their meeting was on the road to their respective places of banish-ment and thus that Liu Fang too was banished in 760. This seems likely because he too may have been suspect as sympathetic to Hsüan-tsung. But Kao Li-shih's place of banishment was Wu-chou, also in Ch'ien-chung, and their meeting may have taken place later during their period of banishment. Liu Fang's National History must have been presented before his banishment, but we do not know the precise date of his conviction. Kao Li-shih was amnestied in 762 after Su-tsung's death but died at Lang-chou on the road back to the capital, from shock and distress on hearing of the recent death of his old master, Hsüan-tsung. See *CTS* 184, p. 4759.

96 As an assistant according to *CTS* 148, p. 4030; as a compiler according to *HTS* 132, p. 4536.

97 Notably in the compilation of the official genealogy of the imperial clan, the *Huang-shih Yung-t'ai p'u* or *Yung-t'ai Hsin-p'u* in twenty chapters, which was presented to the throne in 766 by Li Ch'i, prince of Wu, the president of the Court of Imperial Clan Affairs. When in 839 a continuation of this genealogy was commissioned, the work was entrusted to one of Liu Fang's grandsons, the Han-lin scholar Liu Ching. See *CTS* 149, p. 4033. Surviving evidence of Liu Fang's genealogical learning is his "Essay on Surnames and Lineages," "Hsing-hsi lun," preserved in abbreviated form as an appen-dix to Liu Ch'ung's biography in *HTS* 199, pp. 5676–80. Another of his genealogical works was the *Ta-T'ang tsai-hsiang piao* in three chapters (see *HTS* 58, p. 1478), which may have been the basis for the genealogical tables of chief ministers in *HTS*.

The study of genealogy was a preoccupation of many mid T'ang historians. Both Liu Chih-chi and Wei Shu were notable genealogists. *HTS* 199, p. 5676, appears to assume a family relationship (although this is unspecified) between Liu Fang and Liu Ch'ung (d. 717), who had been the principal compiler of the great genealogical compilation *Hsing-tsu hsi lu* in two hundred chapters, presented in 713. See *CTS* 189B, pp. 4971–7. Liu Fang was also an acknowledged expert on ritual, a field of expertise in which his son Liu Mien later became well known.

98 See *Ch'ung-wen ts'ung-mu* 2, p. 5b. The biographies of Yü Hsiu-lieh make no mention of his work on the Basic Annals for Su-tsung's reign, or on the National History.

after 763, when Ling-hu Huan was first recruited into the Historio-graphical Office.[99]

In 1950, E. G. Pulleyblank, in a meticulously documented study, identified as far as is possible Liu Fang's additions to the National History of Wei Shu, with the completion of which he had been entrusted.[100] These comprised the basic annals for Hsüan-tsung's reign, the biographies of people who had died between 713 and 758, some parts of the monographs, and additions to the records of foreign peoples.

There remain, however, some insoluble questions. What were the terminal dates of Wei Shu's National History and of Wu Ching's National History, on which Wei Shu's was based? When did Liu Fang's new contribution begin? According to a memorial of Wu Ching, submitted in 726, his private history then extended to the third month of that same year. But there is evidence from Wei Shu's own hand that the version of the National History he took over from Wu Ching was a different one. We cannot be sure either of its terminal date or that of Wei Shu's subsequent version. Pulleyblank assumes that Wei Shu's history ended with the beginning of Hsüan-tsung's reign, but there is no firm evidence for this. The evidence might equally well mean that it ended with the end of the K'ai-yüan reign-period in 741.[101] Nor do we know for certain whether Liu Fang made any considerable changes to Wei Shu's account of the period before Hsüan-tsung's accession.

We can never give a definite answer to these questions, although there is evidence from his other writings that supports Liu Fang's authorship of some sections of the history and gives us a clear idea of his attitudes toward the political struggles of Hsüan-tsung's reign.

The circumstances under which this National History was composed are worth remembering. It was compiled at the direct orders of Su-tsung, who had recently usurped his father's throne and urgently needed moral justification for having done so. The sketchy yet hostile account of the regimes of Li Lin-fu and Yang Kuo-chung and of the last years of Hsüan-tsung's reign given in the National History would certainly have suited Su-tsung's political needs. When it was written, moreover, the civil war that followed An Lu-shan's rebellion was still in progress – it would not be resolved until 763 – and An Lu-shan's successors, An

---

99 See *CTS* 149, p. 4011; *HTS* 102, p. 3986.
100 Pulleyblank, "The *Tzyjyh Tongjiann Kaoyih*," p. 466.
101 McMullen, "The Death of Chou Li-chen: Imperially Ordered Suicide, or Natural Causes?" p. 47, n. 92, adduces some suggestive evidence that Wei Shu wrote a history extending at least to 733, and concludes that Wei Shu's history came down to the end of the K'ai-yüan period and included both basic annals and biographies.

Ch'ing-hsü and Shih Ssu-ming, still controlled large areas of eastern China and in turn claimed the title of emperor of the rival dynasty of Yen. In addition the political situation in the capital was unstable. Although Su-tsung had systematically removed from high office all those who had been closely associated with his father's regime, the deposed emperor Hsüan-tsung was still alive, living in the Hsing-ch'ing Palace in Ch'ang-an, and enjoying considerable public popularity. So much so that in 760 Su-tsung forced him to live in seclusion in the old Western Palace to prevent his becoming the focus of opposition.[102]

It has been suggested[103] that even among the official historiographers of Su-tsung's court there were two rival[104] political groups, the one comprising Yü Hsiu-lieh and Yang Wan, both of whom were among the first scholar-officials to rally to Su-tsung after his usurpation, the other comprising Liu Fang and, in intention, Wei Shu, who were closely associated with Fang Kuan and Ts'ui Yüan, Hsüan-tsung's ministers in exile, and who were thus suspect as "Hsüan-tsung loyalists."[105] According to this hypothesis, Liu Fang's original National History was considered too favorable to Hsüan-tsung,[106] and was later edited by Yü

---

102 See *TCTC* 221, pp. 7093–5. See also Liu Ch'eng, *Ch'ang-shih yen chih* (*T'ang-tai ts'ung-shu* edition), p. 1a–b, a work written by Liu Fang's grandson.
103 See McMullen, *State and Scholars in T'ang China*, pp. 188–9, n. 141.
104 Yang Wan's appointment as a compiler of the National History after his arrival at Su-tsung's court is noted in his biography, *CTS* 119, p. 3430, but the date of his appointment is not clear. It came after several promotions and probably only at the end of Su-tsung's reign. He had earlier served Su-tsung as a court diarist and as a drafter of edicts. We know that he was a compiler in 763.
105 Another close associate of Fang Kuan was the well-known historian Liu Chih, best known for his "legalist" views on statecraft and as the author of the *Cheng-tien*. There are some resonances of similar ideas in Liu Fang's remaining writings. Liu Chih was a chief secretary in the Chancellery at this time, but did not hold a position in the Historiographical Office.
106 The idea that Liu Fang's views were favorable to Hsüan-tsung was earlier put forward in Howard S. Levy, *Biography of An Lu-shan* (Berkeley and Los Angeles, 1960), pp. 11–14. The author suggests that Liu Fang favored Hsüan-tsung both in the National History and in his *T'ang li*. Because the latter work was partly derived from the reminiscences of Kao Li-shih, Hsüan-tsung's lifelong eunuch confidant, this seems very likely. Levy also cites a passage from Liu Ch'eng's *Ch'ang-shih yen-chih*, which is clearly partial toward Hsüan-tsung. This short work in a single chapter, which survives in a truncated version in *Shuo-fu* (Wan-wei shan t'ang edition, *chüan* 49) and in *T'ang-tai ts'ung shu*, 1st series, is listed in *HTS* 59, p. 1542. *WHTK* 215, pp. 1757c–1758a, citing *Chün-chai tu-shu chih*, explains that it recorded what the author's uncle Liu Fang had written. In their entry on Liu Ch'eng's other known work, the *Liu-shih chia-hsüeh yao-lu* in two chapters (see *HTS* 59, p. 1541), a collection of notes on politics and institutions by various members of his family, Liu Ch'eng is stated to have been the son of Liu Mien, and hence Liu Fang's grandson. See *WHTK* 215, p. 1757c, citing *Chün-chai tu-shu chih* (*Yüan-pen*) 2A, p. 19b.

Hsiu-lieh and his protégé Ling-hu Huan,[107] to incorporate a more favorable judgment on Su-tsung. I am not entirely convinced by this suggestion, but it is an attractive hypothesis. The possibility that Liu Fang was perceived as a partisan of Hsüan-tsung might well explain his banishment soon after the completion of the National History, which coincided with a purge of many other court officials in the summer of 760, apparently motivated by fear of an attempt to restore Hsüan-tsung to the throne, and with the sequestration of the former emperor in the old Western Palace. It is also possibly relevant that a new chief minister, Hsiao Hua, who was appointed at the end of 760, was concurrently appointed director of the National History and chief scholar of the Chi-hsien Academy. This appointment may indicate that Su-tsung and his entourage felt that changes needed to be made to the Liu Fang history and in the scholarly establishment generally.[108] The hypothesis would also explain why, after his reinstatement under Tai-tsung, Liu Fang, though by far the most experienced member of the Historiographical Office, was never again himself employed on the National History or on the Su-tsung Veritable Records.

When he undertook his National History, Liu Fang was in an insecure position. Many of the prominent people who figured in the events Liu Fang had to describe were still active, powerful, and dangerous. He himself had been reprieved from a charge of treasonable collaboration

---

107 Ling-hu Huan was living in seclusion in his mountain estate during the early days of the rebellion, and Yang Wan, who was fleeing the rebels, stayed for a while in his home, and formed a very favorable impression of him. Later, in 763, when Yang Wan was vice-president of the Board of Rites and a compiler in the Historiographical Office, he recruited Ling-hu Huan as a historian. See *CTS* 149, p. 4011; *Shun-tsung shih-lu* 3, p. 4 (trans. Solomon, *Veritable Record*, p. 29); *HTS* 102, p. 3986. This appointment must have been during Yang Wan's term as vice-president of the Board of Rites from 763–5, for which see Yen Keng-wang, *T'ang P'u Shang Ch'eng lang piao* (Taipei, 1956), vol. 1, p. 136. It was presumably Ling-hu Huan who added to the National History the various memorials by Yü Hsiu-lieh that are quoted at sometimes tedious length; see for example *CTS* 28, p. 1052; *CTS* 24, pp. 914 and 916; *CTS* 196A, pp. 5232–3. That is, if we assume that Yü Hsiu-lieh did not do so himself to ensure a posthumous reputation.

108 Hsiao Hua was the son of Hsüan-tsung's chief minister Hsiao Sung who had been director of the National History from 729–33. He too had accepted office under the rebels, but had secretly assisted the T'ang cause. His double-dealing was discovered, but luckily he was saved from a rebel prison by the T'ang armies and treated as a loyal hero. He became director of the National History when he was made ad hominem chief minister and chief scholar of the Chi-hsien Academy late in 760. See *CTS* 99, p. 3096. He soon fell foul of Li Fu-kuo and was replaced by Yüan Tsai in the third month of 762, shortly before Su-tsung's death. There is no record of his having been active in his direction of the state historians.

with the rebels and thus he could hardly have written anything that did not suit the needs of his political masters. In addition, the documentation he would have needed to write a more thorough account had largely been destroyed. Only ten years later, Ling-hu Huan attempted to compile Veritable Records for Hsüan-tsung's reign and, as we have seen, found himself totally frustrated by the lack of the necessary source material.

In the circumstances nobody could have written a National History that would have met the highest standards, or have maintained detached and dispassionate judgment on what were after all very recent events indeed. Not surprisingly, Liu Fang's National History was not well received; according to the *Hsin T'ang shu*, "the Historiographers all found fault with it because, in narrating the events from the T'ien-pao period (742–55) on, there was no principle in what he rejected and what he accepted."[109] The *Chiu T'ang shu* is only slightly less grudging: "In narrating the events from the T'ien-pao period on, he was completely lacking in principle and form, and without skill in selecting or rejecting [materials], so that it was not praised by the historians. Yet Liu Fang was diligent in his recording of events, untiring in his attention to minute detail. Coming as he did in the period of division and disorder of the An [Lu-shan] and Shih [Ssu-ming] rebellions when the National History had been scattered and lost, he compiled together what he was able to find. But there was a great deal that was missing or defective."[110]

Similar hostility was aroused in the 770s and 780s by the *T'ang li*, Liu Fang's private history of the T'ang in which he incorporated the information on Hsüan-tsung's reign given him by Kao Li-shih after the National History had been completed. In this case we are told that the objectors were the "Confucian scholars" who disagreed violently with his "apportionment of praise and blame" – that is, with his moral judgments on men and events.[111]

Whatever its faults, his was the only T'ang National History that survived. It was still in the Imperial Library in Sung times, when it is listed in the *Ch'ung-wen tsung-mu*.[112] But the compilers of that catalog attribute it to Wei Shu and give Liu Fang no credit for his part in its compilation, although the subsequent work of Yü Hsiu-lieh and Ling-hu

109 See *HTS* 132, p. 4536.
110 See *CTS* 149, p. 4030.
111 See *HTS* 132, p. 4536.
112 *Ch'ung-wen tsung-mu* 3, pp. 5b–6a; *WHTK* 192, p. 16276–c. Because the work was not listed as missing in the short version of *Ch'ung-wen tsung-mu* completed in 1144, we can assume that it survived into the Southern Sung period.

Huan is duly noted.[113] By Sung times, however, it was largely irrelevant, since it had been incorporated, almost in its entirety, into the *Chiu T'ang shu* compiled in the 940s.

Ssu-ma Kuang seems never to have cited it in the *Tzu-chih t'ung-chien k'ao-i*, although this very frequently cites Liu Fang's *T'ang li*. The only plausible reason for this is that the still surviving *Kuo shih* and the corresponding sections of the *Chiu T'ang shu* were virtually identical.

---

113 The entry is translated in Pulleyblank, "The *Tzyjyh Tongjiann Kaoyih*," pp. 449–50, as follows: "Composed by Wei Shu of the T'ang dynasty. Originally Wu Ching composed a history of the T'ang from the foundation of the dynasty to the period K'ai-yüan (713–741) 110 chapters in all. Wei Shu took over Wu Ching's old work, abridged it and added to it, removed the chapter on cruel officials (k'u-li chuan) and made 112 chapters of Basic annals, monographs and biographies. After the periods Chih-te and Ch'ien-yüan (756–759) the historiographer Yü Hsiu-lieh also added basic annals of Su-tsung is two chapters, and the Historiographer Ling-hu Huan and others made additions at the ends of basic annals, monographs and biographies without increasing the number of chapters. The present work contains 130 chapters. We cannot discover the name of the author of the remaining 16 chapters."

The missing author was, as we have seen, Liu Fang.

Part III
The *Chiu T'ang shu*

12

The compilation of the
Chiu T'ang shu

The writing of history was not high among the priorities of the military regimes that inherited power in northern China after the final disintegration of the T'ang empire in the late ninth and early tenth centuries.[1] Under the Later T'ang (923–37), however, the situation was gradually stabilized, and some measure of orderly bureaucratic government was restored. In 924, the Historiographical Office was reorganized, and the routine that had been established in the early T'ang for transferring documentation needed for the compilation of the historical record to the office from various ministries was revived.[2] Work was begun in 929 on the Veritable Records for Chuang-tsung. These covered not only his own reign (923–7) but also the preceding Liang dynasty (907–23), to which the Later T'ang denied legitimate status. In 933, serious work commenced on the Biographies of Meritorious Officials (*T'ang kung-ch'en lieh-chuan*) for the same period.[3] For the remainder of the Five Dynasties period down to 960, the Court Diaries, Records of Administrative Affairs, the Daily Calendar, and Veritable Records were regularly compiled in spite of the chronic instability of the successive administrations.

There was also renewed interest in the history of the T'ang. In 926 the new emperor, Ming-tsung (reigned 926–33), appointed Yü Ch'üan-mei as commissioner for seeking records in the three provinces of Szechuan (*San-ch'uan sou-fang t'u-chi shih*).[4] Yü Chüan-mei had originally been an official in the Ch'ien Shu kingdom under its ruler Wang Yen

---

1 See *WTHY* 18, pp. 293–4.
2 See *TFYK* 557, p. 5b; *CWTS* 43, pp. 595–6; *WTHY* 18, p. 303.
3 On historiographical activities under the Five Dynasties, see Wang Gungwu, "*Chiu Wu-tai shih*," pp. 1–22; Chin Yü-fu, "T'ang-Sung shih-tai she kuan hsiu-shih chih-tu k'ao," pp. 6–18.
4 San-ch'uan is written san-chou in the original text of *CWTS*, which is emended in the Chung-hua shu-chü edition after *WTHY* 24.

(reigned 918–25) and was from a Ch'eng-tu family. He claimed, as a plan to visit his home, that in Ch'eng-tu were preserved all the Veritable Records of the T'ang house. This claim must have seemed plausible because the T'ang court had spent four years, from 881 to the beginning of 885, in exile in Ch'eng-tu. When Yü Ch'üan-mei returned from his mission, however, all he had been able to collect were the Veritable Records of nine reigns and fragments of various other books.[5]

In 932 a memorial was submitted by the Historiographical Office[6] to Ming-tsung requesting that Veritable Records for the last four reigns of the T'ang should be compiled. Nothing, however, came of this request.[7] The Later T'ang considered themselves the continuation of the T'ang dynasty proper, and it was probably for this reason that they contemplated the completion of the T'ang Veritable Records, rather than the compilation of a Standard History, which would have implied that the legitimate succession had passed to the Liang in 907.

Under the Chin dynasty, which replaced the Later T'ang in 936, this objection no longer applied, and a more ambitious project was proposed: In the second month of 941 Emperor Kao-tsu (reigned 936–42) ordered the compilation of a full-scale dynastic history of the T'ang.[8] The compilers named by the edict to undertake the task[9] were the vice-president of the Board of Finance, Chang Chao-yüan (895–972);[10] the diarist Chia Wei (d. 952);[11] the vice-president of the Imperial Library,

5 *CWTS* 37, p. 510; *WTHY* 24, p. 390.
6 The director of the National History at this time was Li Yü, who had been appointed some three months earlier: see *CWTS* 43, p. 594.
7 See *TFYK* 557, p. 5b; *WTHY* 18, p. 303; *CWTS* 43, pp. 595–6.
8 See *TFYK* 557, pp. 10b–11a; *CWTS* 79, p. 1045. See Fujita Junko, "*Kyū Tō sho* no seiritsu ni tsuite," *Shisō* 27 (1969): 50–59, and "Tōdai no shigaku–zendaishi shūsen to Kokushi hensan no aida," *Shisō* 33 (1975): 65–71. Also see Fukui Shigemasa, "*Kyū Tō sho*: sono sohon no kenkyū josetsu," in Waseda daigaku bungakubu Tōyō kenkyūshi·su, eds., *Chūgoku seishi no kisoteki kenkyū* (Tokyo, 1984), pp. 241–65.
9 See *TFYK* 554, p. 21b; *WTHY* 18, p. 294; *CWTS* 79, p. 1045.
10 See *TFYK* 554, p. 21b; *Sung shih* 263, pp. 9085–91, where his name is given as Chang Chao. His name at this time was, however, correctly Chang Chao-yüan. He dropped the last character of his name to avoid the taboo on the personal name of the emperor Kao-tsu of the Han (whose original personal name was Liu Chih-yüan) in 947. Chang Chao-yüan was a scholar of broad interests, an important professional historian, and an expert on ritual. His is a good example of the continuity of many officials' careers through the political vicissitudes of the Five Dynasties. He had been previously involved in the compilation of the Veritable Records of the Later T'ang emperors Chuang-tsung (completed 929) and Ming-tsung (completed 935–6) and later compiled those for Min-ti (completed 957) and Fei-ti (957), as well as those of Han Yin-ti (also completed 957) and Chou T'ai-tsu (completed 957–8).
11 See *CWTS* 131, pp. 1727–9; *HWTS* 57, pp. 657–8. Chia Wei was a somewhat controversial professional historian who was later involved in writing the Veritable Records for Emperors Kao-tsu and Shao-ti of the Chin (in 950–1) and those for Kao-tsu of the Han (in 949). He was said to have had a strong will and equally intransi-

Chao Hsi;[12] the chief secretary of the Board of Civil Office, Cheng Shou-i;[13] and the under secretary of the Left Bureau of the Department of State Affairs, Li Wei-kuang.[14] A separate institute, the *Shih-yüan* was established to undertake the work,[15] with Chang Chao-yüan in charge (*chien-p'an yuan shih*). Chief Minister Chao Ying[16] was appointed the director of the project.

Almost immediately Chia Wei, who was an experienced historian and, after Chang Chao-yüan, the most important member of the team, was forced to retire to observe the mourning period for his mother, probably late in the second month of 941. He then addressed a memorial to the throne offering to make available to "the responsible officials" – that is, to his fellow compilers – his *T'ang nien pu-i lu* in sixty-five chapters, a large selection of material dealing with the last reigns of the T'ang that he had previously compiled both from a wide variety of written sources and from the reminiscences of survivors from the period.[17] The emperor accepted it, rewarded Chia Wei with the customary gifts of silver vessels and silks, and had the book deposited in the Historiographical Office.[18] After Chia's resignation, in the fourth month of 941, Director Chao Ying asked that the vice-president of the Board of Justice, Lü Ch'i (d. 943),[19] and the serving censor, Yin Cho (891–971), also an experienced historian who had previously been associated with Chang Chao-yüan,[20] be

gent opinions and prejudices, which he expressed freely in his historical writings. He was nicknamed "Chia the Iron-mouthed" by his colleagues. He repeatedly fell out with his political masters. In 951 he was in trouble for the last time for defaming previous chief ministers in the Daily Calendar (*Jih-li*) and was removed from his post. See *CWTS* 131, p. 1728; *TFYK* 562, pp. 11b–12a; Wang Gung-wu, "*Chiu Wu-tai shih*," p. 8, also pp. 14–15.

12 See *CWTS* 93, p. 1235. Chao Hsi had served as a compiler in the Imperial Library and as a diarist under the Later T'ang.
13 See *CWTS* 96, p. 1279.
14 He has no biography in either of the standard histories of the Five Dynasties period. *WTHY* 18, p. 294, gives his name as Li Wei-hsien.
15 See *Sung shih* 263, p. 9090.
16 See *CWTS* 89, pp. 1169–71; *HWYS* 56, p. 641. His *CWTS* biography suggests that he was the real moving force behind the project, not simply a nominal "director" of the National History.
17 See *Ch'ung-wen tsung-mu* 3, p. 12a; *Chih-chai shu-lu chieh-t'i* 4, p. 22b; *WHTK* 193, p. 1623b; *Yü hai* 48, p. 10a; *CWTS* 131, p. 1727.
18 See *CWTS* 79, p. 1046.
19 See *CWTS* 92, pp. 1215–16; *HWYS* 56, pp. 644–6. *CWTS* says that his work on the T'ang history and also his work as an examiner won praise.
20 See *Sung shih* 431, pp. 12817–18. Yin Cho had passed the special examinations on the "Three Histories" in 919. He served as an assistant in the Historiographical Office under the Later T'ang from 933 (see *CWTS* 44, p. 605) until 934, at the time when the plan to write Veritable Records for the last T'ang reigns was still in the air. At that time he had been associated with Chang Chao-yüan (see *TFYK* 554, p. 21a–b). He later served at the Chin court as an omissioner and since 939 had been a serving

added to the team of compilers.[21] He also asked that an edict be issued seeking and offering to purchase copies of those T'ang Veritable Records that the Historiographical Office lacked.[22]

Chao Ying presented another memorial to the throne in the same fourth month of 941, in which he outlined his plan for the history. It was to comprise Basic Annals, ten monographs (only nine of which he actually named), and biographies.[23] Some changes seem to have been made to the original plan as work proceeded: The history as completed has not ten but eleven monographs, the names of several of which differ from those in the memorial, and their order is quite different. Either the Monograph on State Finance or, more probably, that on Dress and Equipages was apparently added as an afterthought during the course of compilation.

Work was begun at once, and steady progress was made in spite of the rapidly deteriorating political situation of the Chin court. Kao-tsu died in 942. His successor, Shao-ti (reigned 942–7), was dominated by his generals, who demanded the opening of hostilities with the Khitan, the people with whose backing the Chin regime had gained power. The result was a disastrous war, which ended in 947 with the fall of the dynasty. The outbreak of hostilities caused a very unstable political situation at court: Under the circumstances, the writing of the T'ang history must have been an activity of minor consequence; it is very easy to understand why the compilers were willing to take over, lock, stock, and barrel, the already completed material in Liu Fang's National History and to rely so heavily on other already completed works such as the *Hui yao* and *Hsü Hui yao* in writing the monographs.

The political instability of the time had its effects on the compilers. Chao Ying fell from power and ceased to be director of the National

censor. Subsequently, under the Chou, he became rector of the State University and controller of the Court of Ritual in the Court of Imperial Sacrifices and helped compile the Veritable Records of the Later T'ang emperors Min-ti and Fei-ti (compiled in 957). He also played a part in compiling Veritable Records for Han Yin-ti and Chou T'ai-tsu (compiled in 957–98). In all these projects he worked in collaboration with Chang Chao-yüan.

21 See *CWTS* 79, p. 1046; *WTHY* 18, p. 295; *Sung shih* 431, p. 12817. Elsewhere the name of Ts'ui Cho is also mentioned together with Lü Ch'i as working on the T'ang history (*Sung shih* 263, p. 9090). Ts'ui Cho (ca. 876–943; *chin-shih* 917) was at this time a Han-lin scholar and a principal secretary in the Central Bureau of the Department of State Affairs. He was known as a prolific writer of memorial inscriptions and in 943 resigned his post as a Han-lin scholar after a difference of opinion with Sang Wei-han. For his biographies, see *CWTS* 93, pp. 1231–2; *HWYS* 55, pp. 635–7. Neither mentions his being connected with the T'ang history project.

22 *CWTS* 79, p. 1046.

23 See *TFYK* 557, pp. 11b–15b; *WTHY* 18, pp. 294–8.

History in the third month of 943, when he was replaced by Sang Wei-han (898–947).[24] The latter seems to have had a particularly unhappy relationship with the historians. He forced the resignation of Ts'ui Cho and quarreled bitterly with Chia Wei. In the fifth month, Chang Chao-yüan was made vice-president of the Board of Civil Office,[25] and later, in the tenth month, concurrently appointed a compiler in the Historiographical Office in charge of the office's affairs (*p'an kuan shih*).[26] It seems possible that the special office established earlier under his control (the *shih-yüan*) was now merged into the Historiographical Office.[27] Before the completion of the T'ang history itself, probably in 942 or 943,[28] Chang Chao-yüan completed and presented to the throne a long set of essays on the relations between rulers and their ministers during the T'ang period, entitled *T'ang-ch'ao chün-ch'en cheng-lun* in twenty-five chapters.[29] Sometime in the same year, 943, Lü Ch'i died.[30] Chia Wei was reappointed a diarist and concurrently a compiler in the Historiography Office after the completion of his period of mourning in 944[31] and resumed his work on the history, although he too almost immediately quarreled with the director, Sang Wei-han, who treated him disrespectfully.[32] The work was completed and presented to the new emperor, Shao-ti, in the sixth month of 945[33] by the chief minister and

24 See *CWTS* 81, p. 1075.
25 See *CWTS* 81, p. 1077.
26 See *CWTS* 82, p. 1083.
27 However, it is also possible that the *shih-yüan* established in 941 was responsible only for the compilation of the T'ang history, whereas the Historiographical Office continued to conduct the routine business of assembling material for the Veritable Records, etc., and that Chang Chao-yüan now became controller of both offices. This arrangement would have been somewhat similar to that under T'ang T'ai-tsung when special arrangements were made for the compiling of the histories of previous dynasties.
28 See *Sung shih* 263, p. 9090.
29 This work was in the early Sung Imperial Library. See *Ch'ung-wen tsung-mu* 5, p. 4b, where its title is given as *Ch'ien-ch'ao chün-ch'en cheng-lun* and it is classified under "Confucian writers."
30 See *HWYS* 56, p. 646. He was alive in the fifth month when he was appointed vice-president of the Board of War. See *CWTS* 81, p. 1077.
31 See *CWTS* 131, p. 1728. In the tenth month of 944, he was promoted to principal secretary of the Board of Finance with responsibility for drafting edicts. See *CWTS* 83, p. 1096.
32 Later under the Han (947–51) Chia Wei was the historian responsible for writing Sang's biography, in which he defamed his memory by implying that he had improperly accumulated a vast personal fortune. This led to protests from one of his fellow historians, and eventually to his dismissal from the Historiographical Office. See *CWTS* 131, p. 1728; *TFYK* 562, pp. 11b–12a.
33 See *CWTS* 84, p. 1108; *WTHY* 18, p. 298; *Chung-hsing Kuan-ko shu-mu* as cited in *Yü hai* 46, p. 43b.

director of the National History, Liu Hsü (888–947),[34] who is traditionally named as its author. But although Liu Hsü wrote the memorial
that accompanied the completed work when it was presented to the
throne, he can have played no very significant part in its compilation, for
he had become chief minister and director of the National History in
succession to Sang Wei-han only in the seventh month of 944[35] and so
had been involved as the nominal director of the project for less than a
year. Among the actual compilers who were rewarded by the emperor
with the customary gifts of silk textiles and silver vessels after their
work was accepted, only the compiler Chang Chao-yüan, who had been
given charge of the Historiographical Office's business (*p'an kuan shih*) in
the tenth month of 943,[36] and the assistant Wang Shen[37] are specifically
named together with Liu Hsü, and they and Chia Wei were probably its
principal compilers.[38] No evidence survives that would suggest which
compilers were responsible for what parts of the work.

The history presented in 945, which is entitled *T'ang shu* by the *Chiu
Wu-tai shih* and is referred to as the *Ch'ien-ch'ao Li-shih shu* ("The History
of the Li Imperial House of the Former Dynasty") by *Wu-tai hui yao*, was
the *Chiu T'ang shu* that survives today, although some small portions
may have been subsequently lost.[39] The extant work has 200 chapters,
but reports of its presentation to the throne in 945 in various sources
give us different accounts of its size. According to the *Chiu Wu-tai shih* it
had "203 chapters of basic annals, monographs, and biographies, together with a table of contents."[40] According to *Wu-tai hui yao*, however,

34 See *CWTS* 89, pp. 1171–3; *HWTS* 55, pp. 625–6. Liu Hsü had had some previous
   experience in directing historical compilation, having briefly been chief minister and
   director of the National History in 934. *CWTS* 46, p. 636; *CWTS* 89, p. 1172. See the
   note by Wang Ming-sheng, *Shih Ch'i shih shang-chüeh* 69, p. 727, which claims that Chao
   Ying was the real compiler (that is to say, director) of *CTS*, not Liu Hsü.
35 See *TCTC* 284, p. 9274; *CWTS* 89, p. 1173; *CWTS* 83, p. 1094.
36 See *CWTS* 82, p. 1083.
37 His name is incorrectly written Wang Chung in *TFYK* 554, p. 37a. Wang Shen was
   later involved together with Chia Wei in compiling the Veritable Records of the Chin
   emperors Kao-tsu and Shao-ti (compiled 950–1) and of Han Kao-tsu (completed 949).
   See *Chih-chai shu-lu chieh-t'i* 4, p. 42a. See Wang Gungwu,"Chiu Wu-tai shih," p. 8.
38 See *WTHY* 18, p. 298; *TFYK* 554, p. 37a.
39 A systematic attempt to assemble "lost portions" of CTS was made in the early nineteenth century by Ts'en Chien-kung in his *Chiu T'ang-shu i-wen*, first published in 1848.
   This work, largely compiled from quotations entitled *T'ang shu* or *T'ang shih* included in
   T'ai-p'ing yü-lan, unfortunately collects together many quotations that never formed
   part of *CTS*, but originated from the National History (probably from more than one
   recension) and from various Veritable Records.
40 See *CWTS* 84, p. 1108. Robert des Rotours suggested that the figure 203 given in
   CWTS represents the two hundred chapters of the work as it exists today, plus a table
   of contents divided into 3 chapters, but this contradicts the information that the table
   of contents formed 1 chapter given in *WTHY* and *TFYK*. See his *Traité des examens*,
   pp. 66–67.

it had "220 chapters of basic annals, monographs, and biographies, together with a single chapter table of contents."[41] According to a passage included as commentary to the edict ordering its compilation in *Ts'e-fu yüan-kuei*, the history comprised "213 chapters together with a single-chapter table of contents."[42] According to the *Chung-hsing Kuan-ko shu-mu* catalog of 1178 as cited by *Yü hai*,[43] it "comprised 20 chapters of basic annals, 50 chapters of monographs, and 150 chapters of biographies, in all 200 [*sic*] chapters. It was presented to the throne in the sixth month of the second year of the K'ai-yün period (945), the whole filling 20 cases [*chih*]." The figure of 50 chapters of monographs given here is probably a simple graphic corruption of 30, the number in the existing *Chiu T'ang shu*.[44] But it is not possible to account with any confidence for all these variant figures. All are probably the result of corruptions in copying.

Almost all the surviving Sung period catalogs list the work as having 200 chapters,[45] and the earliest extant printed edition, dating from the twelfth century, was in 200 chapters.[46]

41 See *WTHY* 18, p. 298. However, the *K'ao-i* note to the Chung-hua shu-chü edition of *CWTS* 84, p. 1108, cites *WTHY* as giving its length as 202 chapters plus a table of contents in a single chapter.
42 See *TFYK* 557, p. 11a.
43 See *Yü hai* 46, p. 43b. *WHTK* 192, p. 1627c, cites Ch'ao (i.e., *Chün-chai tu-shu chih*) as saying that it had "added and subtracted from Wei Shu's Old History (i.e., his National History), to make 20 chapters of basic annals and 150 chapters of biographies." The number of chapters of monographs is not specified.
44 However, its figures give a total of 220 chapters, suggesting a possible source of the error in the total given by *WTHY* 18.
45 See, for example, *Ch'ung-wen tsung-mu* 3, p. 6a; *Chün-chai tu-shu chih* (*Yüan pen*) 2A, p. 10b; *Chih-chai shu-lu chieh-t'i* 4, p. 10b. See also *Yü hai* 46, pp. 43b–44b; *WHTK* 192, p. 1627c. The only exception is *Chung-hsing Kuan-ko shu-mu*, as was mentioned.
46 On the Sung and Yüan printings of *CTS*, see Ozaki Yasu, "Sō Gen kan ryō *Tō-sho* oyobi *Godai-shiki* ni tsuite," *Shidō Bunko ronshū* 21 (1985): 121–50. The Po-na edition of *CTS* published in 1936 in part reproduces an early Southern Sung print made in Yüeh-chou, Chekiang, during Shao-hsing's reign (1131–62). The missing chapters are supplied from the Ming edition of Wen-jen Ch'üan, published in 1539.

13

The *Chiu T'ang shu* and its sources: the Basic Annals

This chapter and the following chapter present a detailed analysis of the process of compilation through which various sections of the *Chiu T'ang shu* came into being and show how this process affects its use as a historical source and how it circumscribes our understanding of the events of T'ang history. But as a preliminary to this, a number of general points need to be stated.

During all the stages of compilation, editing, and recompilation of the national record, it seems that there was comparatively little actual new writing ab initio. The process was more one of constant and repeated condensation, summarization, and elimination of surplus verbiage and unwanted material than one of active composition. Apart from the sections dealing with the last few reigns, almost the only completely new materials written and added by the *Chiu T'ang shu*'s compilers were the historians' "comments" and "judgments" that conclude most chapters,[1] and there is evidence that, in some cases at least, even these were taken over, either (in the case of the earlier chapters) from the National History or (in some later instances) from the Veritable Records.[2]

---

1 The monographs (*chih*) have neither a historian's comment nor a judgment (*tsan*). The collective biographies (*CTS* 51–52, 183–93) have only a judgment, no historian's comment.

2 The evidence for this is that in some chapters the "historian's comment" actually gives the name of the historian concerned. These historians had lived in T'ang times and had been dead for a century or more before *CTS* was compiled. See, for example, *CTS* 14, p. 410 – "The Historiographer Han Yü says..." (*Shih-ch'en Han Yü yueh...*) (Annals of Shun-tsung) – and *CTS* 15, p. 472 – "The Historiographer Chiang Hsi says..." (*Shih-ch'en Chiang Hsi yüeh...*) (Annals of Hsien-tsung). The presence of Han Yü can easily be explained, because he was the compiler of one version of the Veritable Record for the reign. He was not, however, connected with the final version compiled some years after his death by Lu Sui in 831. Chiang Hsi was one of the compilers of the Veritable Record for Hsien-tsung's reign under Director Wei Ch'u-hou. The "Historiographer Wei Shu" is also cited twice in the text, *CTS* 84, p. 2797, and *CTS* 85, p. 2907. These passages, which refer to events in the late seventh century, probably survive from one or another of the National Histories.

Perhaps the most remarkable feature of all the T'ang historical sources is their extraordinary textual integrity. This is true not only of the different parts of the *Chiu T'ang shu* but also of the collections of documents contained in such encyclopedic works as the *T'ung tien, T'ang hui yao, Ts'e-fu yüan-kuei* and *T'ang ta chao ling chi* – all of which derived their material ultimately from the same officially compiled records. Not only do they form a coherent body of texts, but when the full original versions of documents have survived independently of the historio-graphical process – for example, through their inclusion in their writer's collected works or in a literary anthology, or by their chance survival either among the documents recovered from Tun-huang or Turfan or in an epigraphic source – and these can be compared with the versions included in the official histories or in the encyclopedic collections of documents, it is generally clear that the process of condensation and editing to which they have been subjected has been both thoughtful and skillful. The official history has normally preserved in summary form the author's original words in such a way as seldom to distort their original meaning. Those subjects that the historians decided were worthy of inclusion in their account of the past were thus usually described fairly and accurately.

This does not mean that the record was impersonal, impartial, objec-tive, or free of historical judgments. That would have gone diametrically contrary to all traditional beliefs about the purposes of history, which was always conceived of as a judgmental activity. Even if the historians' views are rarely expressed explicitly, except in the "judgments" at the end of chapters, they could nevertheless be expressed by the compilers in various subtle ways.

The whole process of compilation as described in the earlier chapters, however, inevitably resulted in what seems to us a curiously unbalanced record of events. It placed overwhelming emphasis on central govern-ment and on decision making at the highest levels of the regular bureaucracy, and automatically excluded or disregarded most events in the provinces and much of the routine functioning of government. This is not a result of active editorial intervention or of conscious decisions made by the compilers; it is, rather, a direct reflection of the methods by which the court records were compiled. It is also important to remember that, even if this top-heavy or one-sided account of government leaves twentieth-century historians feeling frustrated, it met exactly the basic aim of official historiography, which was the writing of a record of the exercise of dynastic power.

The crucial subjective element in the editing process was the selection of what was to be included, and to what degree of detail; perhaps even more crucial were those decisions on the total exclusion of matters from the record. For example, editorial bias against whole groups of people felt to be inimical to the interests of the scholar-bureaucrat elite whose own members wrote the record – such groups as eunuchs, generals, and specialist financial officials – could be effectively expressed by the simple omission of all mention of them except in negative contexts. Equally important was the fact that entire episodes that might have thrown a bad light on an emperor or his ministers could be omitted from the record, or could be mentioned only obliquely or in the barest outline in the Basic Annals while further detail was given separately in the biography of one of the participants in the events so as to dissociate the throne from any suggestion of blame.

There is no question, too, that in some cases the historians deliberately distorted the account of events, and it is clear from contemporary criticisms that some historians (Hsü Ching-tsung was a notorious example) were well known for the distortions they perpetrated. Some of the abiding mysteries of T'ang history are mysterious precisely because the record is twisted beyond straightening and no independent evidence survives to resolve them. In some cases newly discovered memorial inscriptions provide evidence that the records of Ch'ung-tsung's and Hsüan-tsung's early reigns were deliberately falsified.[3] And the record of some extended periods has been whittled away until only a bare skeleton remains. The political record of the period of Wu-hou's dominance is a case in point.

There is, unfortunately, no way in which we can follow the editorial process in detail, since for any given incident we rarely have more than one or, at most, two stages of the process of compilation surviving. When we consider that Ssu-ma Kuang, when he compiled his *Tzu-chih t'ung-chien k'ao-i*, had the *Shih-lu* at his disposal, yet apparently found relatively little in them to supplement the *Chiu T'ang shu*'s account, it suggests that this drastic editing began during the early stages of the compilation of the record. The modern historian, nevertheless, needs to be constantly aware of the process through which his sources came into their present form, to know who had a hand in the compilation, to be aware that many matters were simply passed over in silence, to be conscious of possible sources of bias and silent judgment, to be watchful for evidence of falsification, and to remember, above all, that the historiographical process was far from constant throughout the T'ang.

There can be no doubt that for the historians who wrote the National

---

3 For an interesting discussion of one such case, see McMullen, "The Death of Chou Li-chen: Imperially Ordered Suicide or Natural Causes?" pp. 23–82.

Histories, and for the compilers of the *Chiu T'ang shu*, the Basic Annals (*pen-chi*) constituted the section to which they attached the gravest importance. I have already mentioned the analogy traditional historians drew between the Basic Annals and the most prestigious of all histories, the canonical Spring and Autumn Annals, while the biographies were compared with the lesser Three Commentaries. The annals incorporated the major events affecting the emperor and his court; and that, for the traditional historian, was the basic core of history. Modern historians are likely to find them the least revealing section of a Standard History, a bare string of events, official appointments, and court happenings, useful in the main for establishing a chronology, because they provide precise dates, but with neither a clear narrative thread nor any causal insights. For the traditional Chinese historian, however, they were of vital importance. The entire machinery of state historiography was geared to their compilation; the Court Diaries, Records of Administration, Daily Calendars, and Veritable Records were all preliminary stages in the eventual compilation of the Basic Annals for their period.

In some histories, the *Hsin T'ang shu* being a notorious example, the Basic Annals are reduced to such a skeletal form that they are of little use to a modern historian. Those of the *Chiu T'ang shu*, on the other hand, are still comparatively full and retain considerable importance, preserving much information not to be found elsewhere. It is essential, therefore, that we understand as fully as possible how they came into being.

The Appendix to the present volume tabulates in detail the known stages of compilation through which the material in each chapter of the Basic Annals of the *Chiu T'ang shu* had passed before reaching its present form. The information presented in the Appendix can be summarized as follows:

1. The record down to 756 was taken in its entirety from the National History of Liu Fang, completed in 758–9, and that for the period from 756 to Su-tsung's death in 762 from the same National History as it was subsequently supplemented by Yü Hsiu-lieh and Ling-hu Huan under Tai-tsung in the 760s.
2. The record of the period from 762–847,[4] by contrast, derived from the successive Veritable Records that had been separately compiled for each reign.
3. The entire record incorporated in the Basic Annals until 847 ultimately derived from a variety of official records contemporaneous with the events.

4 The terminal date of this section may have been 841, if the bulk of the Wu-tsung Veritable Records was indeed already lost by the 940s.

4. The record for the later years of the dynasty (from 847 to 907) was assembled at the time of *Chiu T'ang shu*'s compilation in 941–5, from such Daily Calendars and Court Diaries as survived and from a variety of less authoritative private sources, some of which had been compiled long after the events they describe under great difficulties due to the loss of essential documentation.

These differences in the sources for the Basic Annals covering these successive periods of the T'ang are closely parallelled in the other surviving historical literature from the period. The huge array of historical documents collected in the *T'ung tien*, the *T'ang hui yao*, and especially in the *Ts'e-fu yüan-kuei* and *T'ang ta chao ling chi* is too vast and varied for a systematic and detailed analysis. However, in broad terms it presents a similar pattern. Far the greater part of the material relating to the early and mid T'ang, down to 758, in all these encyclopedic works can be associated directly with what was included in the National History of 759–60 and is still extant in *Chiu T'ang shu*. This seems somewhat surprising in view of the fact that the main Veritable Records for the reigns before 760, which must have included much material omitted from the National History, seem to have remained in existence at least until the late Southern Sung and thus could have been available to the compilers of all of these collections.[5]

On the period from 760 to 847, for which the Veritable Records were clearly their main source, the *T'ang hui yao* and *Ts'e-fu yüan-kuei* contain much richer documentation. On the late T'ang, after 847, the encyclopedic works, just like the *Chiu T'ang shu*, contain only scrappy information.

It is clear from the foregoing analysis that we are much better informed about some periods of the T'ang than about others. An impressionistic statistical picture of the relative density and level of information available for each reign can be derived from the Basic Annals of the *Chiu T'ang shu*, which have of all our sources the most direct and immediate connection with the process of official historiography. The nearby table sets out the relative coverage the Basic Annals give per year for each reign, and correlates this both with the known size of the Veritable Record for the period and also with the space devoted to the reign in *Tzu-chih t'ung-chien*, the most consistent and carefully compiled general account of the whole T'ang period, which drew

5 Perhaps the most interesting cases are those of Tu Yu when compiling the original *T'ung tien*, and Su Mien when producing his *Hui yao* around A.D. 800. Both were writing as private individuals far removed from the capital, and yet clearly they had access to copious documentation, quite possibly including copies of the Veritable Records.

Coverage of reigns in the Basic Annals of Chiu T'ang shu

Reign	Years	Veritable Records		Basic Annals CTS		Tzu-chih t'ung-chien	
		Chapters	Chapters/Year	Pages	Pages/Year	Pages	Pages/Year
Kao-tsu	8	20	2.5	19	2.4	246	31
T'ai-tsung	23	40	1.7	40	1.7	251	10.9
Kao-tsung	34	100	3.0	49	1.4	207	6.1
Wu Tse-t'ien	21	20	1.0	18	0.9	161	7.7
Chung-tsung	5	20	4.0	116	3.2	61	12.2
Jui-tsung	2	20	10.0	12	6.0	31	15.5
Hsüan-tsung	44	100	2.3	69	1.5	312	7.1
Su-tsung	6	30	5.0	25	4.1	142	32.7
Tai-tsung	17	40	2.3	49	2.6	132	7.8
Te-tsung	25	50	2.0	77	3.1	351	14.0
Shun-tsung	0.6	5	8.6	6	10.0	19	32.6
Hsien-tsung	15	40	2.7	59	3.9	151	10.1
Mu-tsung	4	20	5.0	29	7.3	54	13.5
Ching-tsung	3	10	3.3	15	5.0	21	7.0
Wen-tsung	13	40	3.1	57	4.4	91	7.0
Wu-tsung	6	30	5.0	28	4.7	79	13.2
Hsiuan-tsung	13	—	—	33	2.5	53	4.1
I-tsung	14	—	—	36	2.6	91	6.5
Hsi-tsung	15	—	—	41	2.7	209	13.9
Chao-tsung	16	—	—	48	3.0	260	16.3
Ai-ti	3	—	—	27	9.0	34	11.3

Note: The reigns with abnormally full coverage in *TCTC* are those during which there were complex military campaigns that are described in great detail. These particular figures thus do not approximately reflect the density of the political record.

Sources: Shih-lu: The number of chapters given is that included in the version most likely to have remained authoritative. Basic Annals *CTS:* The number of pages devoted to each reign in the Chung-hua shu-chü edition. *Tzu-chih t'ung-chien:* The number of pages devoted to the reign of each emperor in the Ku-chi ch'u-pan she edition 1956. This is *not* the sum of the chapters entitled "The reign of Emperor X," but of the actual text from the accession to the death, dethronement, or abdication of each monarch.

upon all the sources extant in the second half of the eleventh century. This tabulation shows how strikingly uneven is the density of the record preserved for different reigns and how variable is the level of our information about different periods of the T'ang. There is a marked increase in the volume of information following the accession of Su-tsung. For the next ninety years, for which the compilers of *Chiu T'ang shu* certainly had Veritable Records available as well as the National History, the coverage in the Basic Annals is almost exactly proportional to the size of the Veritable Records. After 847, when the Veritable Records were no longer compiled, the density of coverage decreases markedly, and the quality and coherence of the record also rapidly deteriorate.

When we bear in mind the almost total absence of material on the years after 852 in the monographs of *Chiu T'ang shu*, the comparatively small number of biographies of individuals flourishing during the latter half of the ninth century in the *lieh-chuan* of the history, and the shortage of documentation from that period in the *T'ang hui yao*, *Ts'e-fu yüan-kuei* and *T'ang ta chao ling chi*, these very unsatisfactory basic annals for the later reigns of the T'ang become far more important in the general pattern of historiography than are the basic annals for the earlier, better-documented periods. Largely as a result of the breakdown of the processes of official historiography we will always remain comparatively ill-informed about this period, which was clearly of great importance in political, social and economic development.

This disproportion in coverage between the various subperiods of the T'ang is further exaggerated by the fact that, by coincidence, those periods for which the official historical records are comparatively rich are also the periods from which we possess the greatest number of surviving literary collections of individual authors.[6] Moreover, in contrast with the early T'ang collections that survive, most of which are comparatively small, only a few of them exceeding ten *chüan* in length, many of those from the late eighth and ninth centuries are very large indeed.

Although it is impossible to quantify precisely the literary writings surviving from each period, we can get a rough but nevertheless striking impression from the contents of the *Ch'üan T'ang-wen*, the sizable collection of T'ang prose commissioned in 1808 by the Chia-ch'ing emperor and completed in 1814. This devotes roughly 200 *chüan* (an average of 1.4 chapters per year) to the work of authors writing before 758,

---

6 See the list of surviving literary collections in Hiraoka Takeo, Ichihara Kōkichi, and Imai Kiyoshi, *Tōdai no sanbun sakuhin* (Kyoto, *Tōdai kenkyū no shiori*, vol. 10, 1960), introduction, pp. 4–9.

compared with some 450 *chüan* (5 chapters per year) to authors from the period 758–848, and only about 60 *chüan* (1 chapter per year) to writings from the period 848–907.[7] This distribution coincides very closely with the relative richness of historical material from different periods described earlier.

The uneven level of information available about different periods of the T'ang dynasty has a number of very important and serious implications, which have generally been overlooked by even the most critical of modern historians. Obviously it means that any attempt at statistical analysis and comparison covering the entire dynasty needs to be made with the greatest possible caution: An uneven distribution of occurrences across long periods of time may simply reflect some historiographical anomaly, or the unequal level of information surviving from different periods, rather than any real secular change.[8]

Moreover, the crucial role that changes and developments during the "post–An Lu-shan period" of the late eighth and early ninth centuries play in accounts of almost every aspect of T'ang social, economic, and institutional history may simply be a reflection of the disproportionately greater amount and variety of information we have at our disposal for this period, compared with those preceding and following it, rather than a true representation of events.

---

7 These figures can be only rough approximations, because many authors' lives overlapped these arbitrary dates. The first 130 chapters of *CTW* are taken up by writings of emperors, empresses, and royal princes, both from the T'ang and from the period of the Five Dynasties and the Ten Kingdoms. Likewise, a good deal of space is devoted to the writings of Five Dynasties authors. The last 40 chapters are comprised of anonymous works and writings by foreigners. All these sections are excluded from the calculations given here.

8 An example of the dangers inherent in such a process is the study of T'ang literati by Hans Frankel, "T'ang Literati: A Composite Biography," in Wright and Twitchett, *Confucian Personalities*, pp. 65–83. Here the author, in the course of an otherwise most perceptive study of the biographies devoted to men of literary talent, and some of the stereotypes they embody, points out the apparent anomaly that of the 101 biographies in the three chapters of biographies devoted to literary figures (*CTS* 190A–C), only 17 of the subjects came from the period after 756. Of course there is a very simple explanation for this: The 84 biographies of men active before 756 were taken from the National History of 758–59, the remaining 17 are those added somewhat casually by the compilers of *CTS* in 941–45.

14

The *Chiu T'ang shu* and its sources: the monographs

The various monographs included in the *Chiu T'ang shu* have been the subject of a large body of scholarship. I propose here to concentrate on the most important questions: How and when were the extant monographs written? Did the compilers inherit monographs from Liu Fang's National History or even from one of the earlier National Histories and update them by adding material on the period after 758–60, or were they written completely ab initio in the 940s?

This is more than a purely academic question. The monographs approach perhaps more nearly than any other section of the traditional Standard Histories our modern conception of "problem-focused" historical writing, and attempt more than other parts of the dynastic histories to follow problems from beginning to end and to establish a causal nexus between events. Their importance for the modern historian is reflected in the number of western translations based on them.[1] Because each of them has a preface that sets out to present a brief but coherent interpretation of the area of institutional history covered by the monograph, it is important to discover whether these interpretations view developments from the standpoint of the time when Liu Fang hastily compiled his National History, during the still unresolved wartime crisis of the An Lu-shan rebellion in the late 750s, or from a period

---

1 See for example the translations by E. Balázs of the Monographs on Law and on Finance from *SS*: Etienne Balázs, *Le traité juridique du Souei chou* (Leiden, 1954); *Le traité économique du Souei chou* (Leiden, 1953); translations from the Financial Monograph of *HTS* occupy much of Stefan Balázs, "Beiträge zur Wirtschaftsgeschichte der T'ang-Zeit (618–906)," *Mitteilungen des Seminars für Orientalische Sprachen zu Berlin* 34 (1931): 1–92; 35 (1932): 1–73; 36 (1933): 1–62. See also the translations of the Monographs on Law from both *CTS* and *HTS* in Karl Bünger, *Quellen zur Rechtsgeschichte der T'ang-Zeit* (Peking, 1946), and, above all, the masterly translations by Robert des Rotours of the monographs on the examinations, the bureaucracy, and the military from *HTS*; Rotours, *Traité des examens* and *Traité des fonctionnaires et traité de l'armeé*.

nearly two centuries later, in 941–5, when the T'ang had finally fallen, the empire had been fragmented, and the historians needed above all to address the reasons for the dynasty's final collapse.

We are somewhat hampered in such an inquiry because, first, we do not know for certain which monographs had been included in the *Kuo shih* of Liu Fang and, second, as we have seen, there also seems to have been some confusion, or possibly even a change of plan during the compilation of the *Chiu T'ang shu*, about which monographs it was to include.[2] The only way to answer these questions is by word-by-word textual analysis of all these chapters and close critical comparison of the material they contain with all the other surviving documents. Such a detailed critical analysis would, however, involve years of extremely tedious work and would range far beyond the scope of this general study. The following remarks are based on a relatively superficial examination of the monographs, without subjecting each of them to the careful word-by-word scrutiny that would be ideal. Even on that basis, however, in most cases there is clear evidence showing the provenance of the text.

The Monograph on Ritual Observances (*Li-i chih*)

Following the model of the *Shih chi*,[3] the monograph section of *Chiu T'ang shu* begins with the monographs on ritual and on music. That on ritual observances (*Li-i chih*)[4] is by far the longest and most detailed of all the monographs, quoting extensively from important writings on the subject, a clear indication of the paramount importance still placed on ritual and ceremonial matters by T'ang scholars. It occupies seven chapters, 21 to 27.

Chapter 21, after a brief general introduction,[5] is devoted to the sacrifices to Heaven conducted each year at the winter solstice at the southern suburban altar.[6] The bulk of this chapter deals with events and discussions of the ritual and ceremonial details down to the reign of Hsüan-tsung,[7] culminating in the definitive code of ritual embodied in

---

2 See *TFYK* 557, pp. 11b–15b; *WTHY* 18, pp. 294–8.
3 There were two standard models for the "precedence" of the monographs in the Standard Histories. The one, dating to *Shih chi*, placed the Monographs on Ritual and Music first. The other, which began with *Han shu*, placed the Monograph on the Calendar in first place. Balázs's account of this in his *Chinese Civilization and Bureaucracy* (1964), pp. 136–7, has this matter somewhat confused.
4 The title used by CTS (*Li-i chih*) first appears in the monograph now included in *Hou Han shu*, (*chih*, chapters·4–6), which was originally part of the *Hsü Han shu* of Ssu-ma Piao (240–306).
5 See *CTS* 21, pp. 815–19.
6 See *CTS* 21, pp. 819–45.
7 Ending with p. 836.

the *K'ai-yüan li* promulgated in 732.[8] This material most probably was taken directly from the National History as completed in 759–60 by Liu Fang. A good deal of space is then given to the early years of Tai-tsung's reign,[9] much of it taken up by a single lengthy memorial presented by Li Han in 763,[10] and another by Tu-ku Chi written after Tai-tsung's accession in the same year.[11] This section was probably added when the National History was updated early in Tai-tsung's reign by Yü Hsiu-lieh and Ling-hu Huan. Subsequent events are very summarily dealt with; the last event mentioned dates from shortly after Mu-tsung's accession to the throne in 820.[12] This short section must have been added by the *Chiu T'ang shu* compilers in the 940s. In line with other monographs, they may have taken their material from the neatly categorized information available in the *Hui yao* and *Hsü Hui yao*, but unfortunately the relevant chapters of *T'ang hui yao* have been lost, those in modern editions having been put together from other historical sources (including this monograph) during the early Ch'ing period, so that we cannot examine this possibility.[13]

Chapter 22 is entirely devoted to the interminable discussions and controversies about the construction and design of a *Ming t'ang* (hall of illumination). This was a major issue during the early T'ang. The account ends with 737,[14] the latest date mentioned in the chapter, which was probably taken over more or less integrally from Liu Fang's or even from Wei Shu's National History. There was no need to supplement its account later; after An Lu-shan's rebellion there was no longer a *Ming t'ang*, and the whole matter was a dead issue.[15]

Chapter 23 also deals with a single issue, the Feng and Shan sacrifices. These were the most solemn and awesome of all the sacrifices to Heaven, performed on one of the Holy Peaks, usually on T'ai-shan in Shantung. The material in this extremely detailed account ends effectively with Hsüan-tsung's performance of the sacrifices in 725,[16] although there is a brief mention of an aborted attempt to perform the rites on Hua-shan in 750.[17] Like the preceding chapter, this probably was taken directly from the National History of Liu Fang. The perform-

---

8 See *CTS* 21, pp. 833–6.   9 See *CTS* 21, pp. 836–43.   10 See *CTS* 21, pp. 836–42.
11 See *CTS* 21, pp. 842–3.   12 See *CTS* 21, pp. 843–5.
13 See previous discussion in Chapter 9, especially n. 139.   14 See *CTS* 22, p. 876.
15 Cf. the material collected in *THY* 11, pp. 271–81, which ends with the same date, though a commentary mentions 739. Cf. also *HTS* 13, pp. 337–8, which also ends with 737.
16 See *CTS* 23, pp. 891–904.   17 *CTS* 23, p. 904.

ance of the Feng and Shan sacrifices was never again discussed under the T'ang. They were considered to mark a peak of dynastic achievement, and it would clearly have been an act of hubris to have suggested their performance after the dynastic collapse and military disasters following An Lu-shan's rebellion.

Chapter 24 is far more complex. It deals in turn with the various recurrent festivals and observances of the court. This section ends in 766, and with a mention of Yü Hsiu-lieh, who was one of the historians responsible for updating and revising the National History of Liu Fang.[18] There follows a substantial section on the *Shih-tien* ceremony in honor of Confucius, again ending with 766;[19] a description of Empress Wu's observances in connection with the magic stone recovered from the Lo River in 688;[20] the various observances honoring Lao Tzu and Taoism instituted by Hsüan-tsung from 741 on;[21] the observances to the Lord of the Earth (*Hou-t'u*) under Hsüan-tsung, between 722 and 732;[22] the cult of the deities of the nine cardinal directions (*Chiu-kung kuei-shen*), the only section of this chapter in which the information extends beyond 766, including memorials submitted in 842;[23] and observances to the Yellow Emperor,[24] to various Holy Mountains and Rivers,[25] the cult of Ch'i T'ai-kung,[26] and various points of ceremonial.[27] None of these later sections mentions events after 762. It therefore seems almost certain that chapter 24 was originally written for Liu Fang's National History and updated in the early years of Tai-tsung's reign, whereas the *Chiu T'ang shu* compilers merely inserted the later material on the cult of the deities of the nine cardinal directions incorporating memorials submitted in 828 and 842.[28]

Chapters 25 and 26 are devoted to the ritual observances in the imperial ancestral temple (*T'ai-miao*). Most of chapter 25 deals with the always complex and emotive problem of which ancestors should be included in the ancestral cult, and which empresses should be associated with these observances. This material is presented in chronological order and extends down to the last years of the dynasty, the latest entry being dated 890.[29] The first part of this account,[30] down to the abolition of the separate ancestral temple for Jui-tsung's two empresses (the *I-k'un miao*) in 733, probably derives from the National History. The

---

18 See *CTS* 24, pp. 909–16. 19 See *CTS* 24, pp. 916–24. 20 See *CTS* 24, p. 925.
21 See *CTS* 24, pp. 925–8. 22 See *CTS* 24, pp. 928–9. 23 See *CTS* 24, pp. 929–34.
24 See *CTS* 24, p. 934. 25 See *CTS* 24, pp. 934–5. 26 See *CTS* 24, p. 935.
27 See *CTS* 24, pp. 935–6. 28 See *CTS* 24, pp. 929–34.
29 See *CTS* 25, p. 964. 30 *CTS* 25, pp. 941–54.

rest[31] must have been added by the *Chiu T'ang shu* compilers in the 940s. The chapter concludes with two separate sections, the first dealing with a dispute dated 734 over the detailed arrangements for the provision of sacrifices in the ancestral temples, in which the compiler of the draft National History Wei Shu was a principal participant,[32] and the second dealing with visits by the emperor to the imperial mausoleums and with the observances such visits entailed.[33] This ends with an entry dated 754. These last sections also may well have formed part of the original chapter in the National History.

Chapter 26 begins with a long section[34] dealing with the discussions that took place from 780 onward about the second ancestral temple maintained in Loyang. It ends with the accession of Hsiuan-tsung in 846.[35] This section was clearly added by the *Chiu T'ang shu* compilers in the 940s; all the material was ready to hand, in the *Hui yao* and *Hsü hui yao*.[36] The next section deals with the *Ti* and *Hsia* sacrifices[37] that were held in the imperial temple at infrequent intervals. This section again covers the whole period down to 846, the bulk of its material dealing with events after 781. It is likely that the first part of the section was included in the National History and has subsequently been supplemented by the *Chiu T'ang shu* compilers using material from the *Hui yao* and *Hsü hui yao*.[38] The final section[39] deals with the associated offerings to notable ministers made in the ancestral temples of emperors down to

31 See *CTS* 25, pp. 954–69. One piece of evidence about the relations between *CTS* and the various National Histories emerges from this section. In 887, when the unfortunate Emperor Hsi-tsung finally returned to his devastated capital after Huang Ch'ao's rebellion, a ritual problem arose. He should immediately have gone to pay his respects at the imperial ancestral temple, but this was impossible, because the temple had been destroyed by fire and the spirit-tablets of his ancestors had been lost and destroyed. In the counsel offered to him by the Court of Ritual (*Li-yüan*) not only is canonical authority cited from the *Tso chuan*, but T'ang precedents are cited from the National History (see *CTS* 25, pp. 962–3).

Two instances are cited. The first, dated 717, is however not identical either with the text of the monograph dealing with the event (see *CTS* 25, p. 952) or with the appropriate entry in the *CTS* Basic Annals (see *CTS* 8, p. 177). The second item cited, dealing with Su-tsung's return to the capital in 762, is not mentioned at all in the monograph, and the pertinent section of the Basic Annals for the last months of 761 and the first months of 762 is missing.

I cannot offer a solution to this problem, but it is quite clear that the relationship between the present *CTS* and the National History that was available to courtiers in 887 (in a period of extreme confusion) is not straightforward. The most plausible explanation might be that the writers of the memorial were using "National History" in the broad sense of the "National Record" including the Veritable Records. Such a usage was not uncommon.

32 See *CTS* 25, pp. 969–72.   33 See *CTS* 25, pp. 972–3.   34 *CTS* 26, pp. 979–95.
35 *CTS* 26, p. 995.   36 See *THY* 15, pp. 327–33, 16, pp. 336–48.
37 See *CTS* 26, pp. 996–1010.   38 See *THY* 13–14, pp. 303–17.
39 See *CTS* 26, p. 1011.

Jui-tsung, and with the temples to various heirs apparent. The latest date mentioned in this section is 752, apart from the last sentence, which mentions a temple to Su-tsung's son Li Shao who died in 760.[40] This section probably derives from the National History, with the last sentence added by Yü Hsiu-lieh or Ling-hu Huan during the 760s.

Chapter 27 is devoted to problems concerning mourning and mourning observances. It is entirely concerned with events and memorials dated before the end of Hsüan-tsung's reign; all but a single-line item dated 747 comes from before the end of the K'ai-yüan period.[41] It probably derives in its entirety from the National History of Liu Fang, who may well have adopted it from the draft history of Wei Shu.

It is thus clear that the *Chiu T'ang shu* compilers based the Monograph on Ritual Observances (*Li-i chih*) on an existing monograph in the National History. Three of the chapters, 22, 23, and 27, were probably taken over unchanged. The other chapters were supplemented by the addition of material related to later events, in some cases at least clearly derived from the *Hui yao* and *Hsü Hui yao*.

At least two separate works in the form of a Monograph on Ritual were written during the period after An Lu-shan's rebellion. In 762, Yuan Tsai suggested to the new emperor, Tai-tsung, that the scholars of the Chi-hsien Academy should produce a work entitled the *T'ung chih* ("Comprehensive Monographs"). Because the same project is elsewhere given the title *Li-tai shu-chih*, it was clearly intended to be a set of "universal" monographs, not confined to the T'ang. We know that its Monograph on Ritual Observances (*Li-i chih*) was the responsibility of Kuei Ch'ung-ching, a noted expert on ceremonial.[42] Because, at that time, work was still being done on the updating and revision of Liu Fang's National History, it is possible that some of the material in the *Chiu T'ang shu* monograph dealing with events during Su-tsung's reign and the early years of Tai-tsung may have been connected in some way with Kuei Ch'ung-ching's work on the *T'ung chih*, which seems never to have been completed.

In the ninth century, Ting Kung-chu (769–832), a scholar of the Chi-hsien Academy and after 828 a Han-lin academician expositor in waiting, wrote an extensive Monograph on Ritual (*Li chih*) in ten chapters which is listed as a separate book by the bibliography of *Hsin T'ang shu*.[43]

---

40 See *CTS* 116, p. 3388.   41 See *CTS* 27, p. 1036.
42 See *CTS* 149, p. 4016; *TFYK* 556, p. 19b; *TFYK* 607, p. 13b. See discussion in Chapter 9.
43 See *CTS* 188, p. 4937; *HTS* 57, p. 1434.

The Monograph on Music (*Yin-yüeh chih*)[44]

The Monograph on Music occupies four lengthy chapters, numbered 28 to 31. The first chapter begins with a short general introduction outlining developments in court music under earlier dynasties. It then continues with a chronological account of court music (*Ya-yüeh*) under the T'ang, divided into two sections, the first devoted to the music performed in the ancestral temple (*Miao-yüeh*),[45] the second to the music performed on festive occasions (*Yen-yüeh*).[46] The first of these sections is very detailed down to the K'ai-yüan period (713–41) of Hsüan-tsung's reign. Subsequent developments are hastily summarized in five lines of text covering the period from the T'ien-pao reign period (742–56) to the observances for Wu-tsung,[47] the material for which may well have been added by the *Chiu T'ang shu* compilers to an original account in the National History.

The second section, on music for festive occasions, is also extremely detailed down to the end of the K'ai-yüan period and very scrappy thereafter. It is curious that all the material relating to the early phase of Su-tsung's reign after the outbreak of the An Lu-shan rebellion (756–8),[48] material that might also have derived from the National History, relates to Yü Hsiu-lieh, the official historian who worked on the National History after its initial completion by Liu Fang, and wrote the Basic Annals for Su-tsung's reign after the emperor's death in 762.[49] The rest of the dynasty gets very short shrift. The only substantial item dated after 758 is a lengthy memorial from the Court of Ritual (*Li-yüan*) of the Court of Imperial Sacrifices relating to changes in the performance of triumphal music (*K'ai-yüeh*) and dated 829.[50] The latest date mentioned in this section is 838.[51] All the material relating to the period after 760 is included in the *T'ang hui yao*[52] and was thus readily available to the *Chiu T'ang shu* compilers in the *Hui yao* and *Hsü Hui yao*. Once again it seems likely that the first part of this section was derived directly from the National History, the section dealing with 756–8 from Yü Hsiu-lieh's expansion of the National History under Tai-tsung, and the rest added by *Chiu T'ang shu's* compilers in the 940s.

Chapter 29 begins with a detailed account of the repertories of various types of court music; the pieces performed by the "Standing

---

44 A version of this chapter has previously appeared in Denis C. Twitchett, "A Note on the 'Monograph on Music,'" in *Chiu T'ang shu*," *Asia Major*, 3d ser., 3, no. 1 (1990): 51–62.

45 See *CTS* 28, pp. 1040–5. 46 See *CTS* 28, pp. 1045–54.

47 See *CTS* 28, p. 1045, lines 3–7. 48 See *CTS* 28, p. 1052, lines 5–13.

49 See *Ch'ung-wen tsung-mu* 2, p. 5b. 50 See *CTS* 28, pp. 1053–4.

51 See *CTS* 28, p. 1053, line 5. 52 See *THY* 33, p. 599, pp. 607–8.

Orchestra" (*Li-pu chi*),[53] and the "Seated Orchestra" (*Tso-pu chi*),[54] the repertory of southern "Pure Music" (*Ch'ing-yüeh*),[55] the various categories of foreign music,[56] and the different types of "Variety Music" (*San-yüeh*).[57] Apart from a two-line item mentioning the Burmese orchestra presented at court in 802,[58] there is nothing in this section dealing with any event subsequent to Hsüan-tsung's reign.

The second part of chapter 29 is a description of various musical instruments.[59] This contains very few dates, but all except one of the dates mentioned refer to Hsüan-tsung's reign or earlier. The sole exception[60] refers to 765.

The third section of this chapter gives specifications for the instrumental layout for various types of court performance,[61] similar to those we know were included in the Statutes on Music.[62] The latest date mentioned in this section relates to the reign of Empress Wu (690–705).[63] The section may well derive from the Statutes in force at the time when the National History was compiled. It is impossible to guess which of the several series of Statutes it came from. If it was inserted by Wei Shu, they were probably the Statutes of 719; if by Liu Fang, they would rather have been taken from the then current Statutes of 737.[64]

The chapter ends with what is clearly a later postscript, a section dealing with the loss of the tradition of court music in the aftermath of Huang Ch'ao's rebellion, which is mostly taken up with a long memorial presented by Chief Minister Chang Chün to Chao-tsung some time between 888 and 891.[65]

Apart from this last section, which was certainly added by the compilers of *Chiu T'ang shu* in the 940s,[66] the whole of this chapter was certainly taken over from the existing National History, amended only by the addition of a few short items of information. Besides the evidence of its contents, there is further specific internal evidence to help us pinpoint the date, to which I shall return.

The third and fourth chapters of the monograph, chapters 30 and 31, are devoted to the texts of the various hymns and dances performed at

53 See *CTS* 29, pp. 1059–61.   54 See *CTS* 29, pp. 1061–2.
55 See *CTS* 29, pp. 1062–8.   56 See *CTS* 29, pp. 1068–72.
57 See *CTS* 29, pp. 1072–4.   58 See *CTS* 29, p. 1070.
59 See *CTS* 29, pp. 1074–9.   60 See *CTS* 29, p. 1077, line 13.
61 See *CTS* 29, pp. 1079–81.   62 See Niida Noboru, *Tōryō shūi*, pp. 525–41.
63 See *CTS* 29, p. 1081, line 6.
64 It was probably taken not directly from the Statutes, but from section 17 of Liu K'uang's *T'ai-yüeh ling pi-chi*, entitled "The Formalities for Presentation."
65 See *CTS* 29, pp. 1081–3.
66 This section is virtually identical with *THY* 33, pp. 599–600. In this case, however, the *CTS* compiler cannot have taken this passage from the *Hsü Hui yao*, because this ended in 852–3. Here the *THY* compilers in 960 must have copied the passage from *CTS*.

great state ceremonies. These are quite specifically stated to have been "appended to the monograph according to the old precedent of the former history."[67] I take it that the "former history" (*ch'ien shih*) here, as elsewhere in *Chiu T'ang shu*,[68] refers to the National History. Certainly the contents of these chapters would confirm the impression that they were simply taken over from the National History of 759–60, and that they had been in large part actually composed still earlier, during the reign of Hsüan-tsung.

The texts are arranged under the ceremonies at which they were performed. With two exceptions they contain no item dated after 729.[69] The exceptions are both sets of additional items added to the list of hymns appropriate for specific rites, introduced in each case by "In addition there were..." The first of these additional sets[70] gives hymns to be used in the shrines to later emperors in the imperial ancestral temple (T'ai-miao). The original text gave the list compiled in 729 by Chang Yüeh, which covered the observances for the imperial ancestors down to Jui-tsung.[71] The additions give an additional fourteen pieces for use in worship in the ancestral temple in respect of the emperors from Hsüan-tsung down to Hsien-tsung. No hymns are included for the observances for later emperors from Mu-tsung onward although these were duly established and are listed in the *T'ang hui yao*.[72] The second addition[73] is to the section dealing with the music to be used in the I-k'un miao, the special ancestral temple established by Hsüan-tsung in what had once been his father Jui-tsung's mansion in the capital in honor of Jui-tsung's two empresses, Su-ming and Chao-ch'eng.[74] The rites for Empress Chao-ch'eng (Hsüan-tsung's mother) were transferred to the imperial ancestral temple after Jui-tsung's death in 716. Those for Empress Su-ming were also transferred to the imperial ancestral

---

67 See *CTS* 30, p. 1090.
68 See, for example, *CTS* 32, pp. 1152–3.
69 See *CTS* 31, p. 1136. The date in the text has been corrupted to 719 by omission of *shih* and should be corrected (see the collation notes to the Chung-hua shu chü edition of *CTS*, p. 1149).
70 See *CTS* 31, pp. 1138–40.
71 See *CTS* 31, p. 1138. This list was finalized in 737 in a five-chapter collection of texts compiled by Wei T'ao. See *CTS* 31, p. 1080.
72 See *THY* 33, pp. 603–4. See also *HTS* 21, p. 467.
73 See *CTS* 31, p. 1142.
74 The title Chao-ch'eng empress used in this section for Jui-tsung's consort née Tou (the mother of Hsüan-tsung) was formally changed in 749 to Chao-ch'eng Shun-sheng Huang-hou. The monograph is usually careful to use the full posthumous titles of emperors. The use of the earlier posthumous title Chao-ch'eng Huang-hou may indicate that this section was written between 711 and 749, although the shorter title was commonly used in later T'ang times.

temple in 733, after which the I-k'un miao was transformed into a Taoist nunnery, at first called the Su-ming Kuan, and renamed the Ta-chen Kuan after the death of Hsüan-tsung in 762.[75] Thus there was, strictly speaking, no I-k'un miao after 733. However, the monograph continues first with two additional or alternative hymns to be used there, and then with a set of nine hymns to be used in the shrine established for Te-tsung's Empress Chao-te, who died in 786.[76]

In both cases it is clear that these additional song texts were later interpolations into an original text dating from Hsüan-tsung's reign, and very probably from before 733. This general dating is confirmed by the last sections, which give the hymns to be sung in the temples established for "Emperor Hsiao-ching" (Li Hung, the fifth son of Kao-tsung, who died, probably having been murdered, in 675), the "concealed heir apparent" (Li Chieng-ch'eng, Kao-tsu's oldest son, murdered 626), the Chang-huai heir apparent (Li Hsien, Kao-tsung's sixth son, banished and forced to commit suicide in 684), the "I-te heir apparent" (Li Ch'ung-jun, Chung-tsung's eldest son, murdered in 701), and the Chieh-min heir apparent (Li Ch'ung-chün, Chung tsung's third son, who died during a rebellion in 707 and was rehabilitated in 710).[77] All these posthumous titles were those in use during the early reign of Hsüan-tsung. The cults mentioned here were, moreover, all abolished by an edict promulgated in 747, which gathered them together in a single ancestral temple for the seven heirs apparent, the Ch'i T'ai-tzu miao.[78] The section ends with the hymns sung in the Ch'ung-hsien miao, the ancestral temple set up by Empress Wu for the worship of her own ancestors, and in the Pao-te miao, a similar ancestral temple established by Chung-tsung's consort, Empress Wei.[79]

All this evidence suggests that, as with chapters 28 and 29, the *Chiu T'ang shu* compilers took over what are now chapters 30 and 31 more or less verbatim from the National History, making only a small number of almost random interpolations referring to changes made after the An Lu-shan rebellion.

But the question remains, from what source did Liu Fang take his material for the monograph? Did he compile it himself? Did he take it ready-made from Wei Shu's draft history? Or did he or Wei Shu take it from some other source, and, if so, what sources were available to them?

One source that is a distinct possibility for chapters 28 and 29 is the wall inscription for the director of the Imperial Music Office (*T'ai-yüeh*

75 See *T'ang liang-ching ch'eng-fang k'ao* 3, p. 10a.
76 See *CTS* 12, p. 355; *TFKY* 569, p. 10a.   77 See *CTS* 31, pp. 1143–8.
78 See *CTS* 26, p. 1011; *THY* 19, p. 383.   79 See *CTS* 31, pp. 1148–9.

ling pi-chi), a work in three chapters by Liu K'uang.[80] This work is no longer extant, but it was still in existence in the eleventh, twelfth, and thirteenth centuries. It was included in the *Ch'ung-wen ts'ung-mu* catalog of 1042. It is also listed in the bibliography of *Sung shih*,[81] which would confirm its existence at some date before the 1170s.[82] The *Yü hai* of Wang Ying-lin (1223–96) cites several extracts from it, including a detailed table of its contents and its lengthy preface.[83] The table of contents for its second and third chapters corresponds almost exactly with the sections of the first and second chapters of the monograph.[84] Only the contents of its first chapter, entitled "The Origins of Music," and the very last section of the third chapter, "Rise and Decay," have no clear parallel in the monograph.

Ten or so sections of the *T'ai-yüeh ling pi-chi* are quoted in *Yü hai*.[85] With the exception of the preface, all have close textual parallels with

---

80 The relationship between Liu K'uang's work and the *CTS* monograph and also the relationship between the *T'ai-yüeh ling pi-chi* and the chapters on music in the *TT* were recognized by Kishibe Shigeo in his *Tōdai ongaku no rekishiteki kenkyū*, 2 vols. (Tokyo, 1960–1); see, for example, vol. 2, pp. 327–8, 345, 358–9. Kishibe does not, however, appreciate the complications raised by the process of compilation through the National History.

81 See *Sung shih* 202, p. 5053b.

82 The *Chung-hsing Kuan-ko shu-mu* of 1178 cited in *Yü hai* 105, p. 21a–b.

83 See *Yü hai* 105, p. 21a–23a.

84 See *Yü hai* 105, p. 21a–b, cited as from the *Shu-mu* (i.e., *Chung-hsing Kuan-ko shu-mu*). The table of contents of the three *chüan* as cited by *Yü hai* 105, p. 21a, is as follows:

Chüan shang ("The Origins of Music"): 1. Song; 2. Poetry; 3. Dance; 4. Clapping; 5. The Pitch-pipes.

Chüan chung ("Standard Music," *Cheng yüeh*): 6. "Refined Music"; 7. The Standing Orchestra; 8. The Seated Orchestra; 9. "Pure Music"; 10. The Music of Hsi-liang.

Chüan hsia ("Foreign Musics"): 11. The Eastern I; 12. The Southern Man; 13. The Western Jung; 14. The Northern Ti; 15. Variety Music; 16. The Measurement of Music; 17. Formalities for Presentation; 18. Rise and Decline.

85 The following passages from the *T'ai-yüeh ling pi-chi* are quoted in *Yü hai*:

Yü hai (ch. and pp.)	Section Heading
104:13a	Han Chiao miao yüeh ch'i
105:7a–b	T'ang hsüan-kung yüeh
105:11b–12a	T'ang chiu pu yüeh
105:15a	T'ang Wu-fang shih-tzu yüeh
105:21a–23a	T'ang T'ai-yüeh ling pi chi

[This section gives table of contents, p. 21b, and full text of preface, pp. 21b–23a.]

107:20b–21a	T'ang Chih-k'ang K'ai-an wu
107:24b–25a	T'ang san ta wu
107:27b	T'ang Ching-yün ch'eng-t'ien yüeh wu
107:28a–29a	T'ang pa wu
109:11b	Chou chin tsou
109:39a	T'ang yü ch'ing

the Monograph on Music, parallels so close that the two texts must be intimately related.[86]

But perhaps the clinching evidence is a passage in the section devoted to southern "Pure Music" where the compilers of the National History have inadvertently left in the text an item relating to Liu K'uang himself, in a context that makes it quite clear that the passage was written in the early K'ai-yüan period, not in the late 750s for the National History, and most certainly not in the 940s for the *Chiu T'ang shu*:[87]

From the Ch'ang-an period [701–5] onward the court did not value these ancient pieces, the musicians' tradition of their performance was broken off, and only the eight pieces *Ming chün, Yang pan, Hsiao-hu, Ch'un-ko, Ch'iu-ko, Pai-hsüeh, T'ang-t'ang,* and *Ch'un-chiang hua-yüeh* could still be performed with wind and stringed accompaniment.

The ancient hymn texts for these pieces were in many cases several hundred words in length, but by Empress Wu's time that for *Ming chün* only stretched to some forty words, while what is now transmitted is only twenty-six words, some of which are corrupt, and they have been greatly changed from the original form in the music of Wu.

Liu K'uang considered that musicians should be obtained from Wu, who should be made to transmit these pieces and train musicians in their performance. He asked the singer [*ko-kung*] Li Lang-tzu about this. Li Lang-tzu was a northerner, and he said that the true melodies were already lost, and claimed to have studied them with Yü Ts'ai-sheng, who was a man from Chiang-tu. But now Li Lang-tzu has absconded, and the songs of the "Pure Music" repertory have been lost with him.[88]

It is most probable that here Liu K'uang was recording his own experience. It seems almost certain, then, that the Monograph on Music in the National History was closely modeled on Liu K'uang's book.

Liu K'uang was a remarkable scholar, skilled not only in classical studies but in astronomy, calendrical science, mathematics, and medicine, as well as in music.[89] He was the eldest son of the great historian Liu Chih-chi, one of six exceptionally gifted brothers, all of whom were noted scholars and achieved high official ranks. He was probably born in

---

86 For example, *Yü hai* 107, p. 24b (lines 8–9) is nearly identical with *CTS* 29, p. 1062, line 7; *Yü hai* 107, p. 27b (lines 2–8) is nearly identical with *CTS* 29, p. 1061, line 4 – p. 1062, line 7; *Yü hai* 107, p. 27b (line 10) to p. 29a (line 1) is almost identical with *CTS* 29, p. 1059, line 1 – p. 1061, lines 3–4.

87 There is a close parallel in *THY* 33, pp. 610–11.

88 The parallel text in *THY* 33, pp. 610–11, omits all mention of Liu K'uang, and ends "After Li Lang-tzu's death [or disappearance – the word used is ambiguous] they have only sung a single piece of 'Pure Music,' its words are formal, and its music refined."

89 See *CTS* 102, p. 3174.

the mid or early 680s,[90] but his exact dates are unknown. He held office as remembrancer of the left (*Tso Shih-i*) in 713,[91] at some point was promoted to chief musician (*Hsieh-lü lang*),[92] and by 721 was director of the Office of Imperial Music.[93] It was probably at this time that he wrote the *T'ai-yüeh ling pi-chi*. In 721 some offense committed in his official capacity, the nature of which is unknown, led to his banishment and also to the fall from office of his father, who had protested against his sentence. His father died in exile, but Liu K'uang was recalled to court some time in the early 720s[94] and appointed a court diarist (*Ch'i-chu lang*) and a compiler of the National History.[95]

Two of his brothers were also historians. Liu Su was a scholar in the Chi-hsien Academy, where much historical research was centered during the 720s, and later, like Liu K'uang, became a compiler in the Historiographical Office. This was during the T'ien-pao period (742–56).[96] Liu Chih, Liu Chih-chi's fourth son, was the author of the *Cheng tien*, the first great institutional encyclopedia, which we have discussed already.[97]

Given these facts, it is not surprising that the *T'ai-yüeh ling pi-chi* and the monograph in the National History are so closely interrelated. Because Liu K'uang's service as a compiler in the Historiographical Office was most probably in the 720s or 730s, he and his brother Liu Su were almost certainly participants in the compilation of the National History, first under Wu Ching and later under Wei Shu, and given his reputation as a musical scholar, Liu K'uang may well have been responsible for writing its Monograph on Music. The fact that the material in our existing monograph so rarely deals with events after the K'ai-yüan period (713–41) would add some weight to this conjecture, making it unlikely that Wei Shu did much work on the monograph in his draft history after he ceased to be director, or that Liu Fang gave this monograph much attention when he prepared the National History in 758–60.

The ultimate source of chapters 30 and 31 is also fairly clear. Wei Shu

---

90 Liu K'uang's father lived from 661 to 721, and his own second son, Liu Tz'u, who became a chief minister under Te-tsung, lived from 729 to 794. Hence, Liu K'uang probably was born in the 680s.

91 See *CTS* 136, p. 3751.

92 See *WHTK* 186, p. 1589c, citing *Ch'ung-wen tsung-mu*.

93 See *CTS* 102, p. 3173; *HTS* 132, p. 4522.

94 According to *HTS* 132, p. 4522, after Liu Chih-chi's death Hsüan-tsung issued an edict to seek his descendants, and consequently Liu K'uang was appointed a diarist.

95 See *CTS* 102, p. 3174; *CTS* 136, p. 3751; *HTS* 132, p. 4522.

96 See *CTS* 102, p. 3174; *HTS* 132, p. 4523.

97 See *CTS* 102, p. 3174; *HTS* 132, p. 4524.

and Liu Fang both had available to them two official repertories of song texts, which they must have used as an authoritative source. The song texts, *Yüeh-chang*, had been composed in 627 by a group of T'ai-tsung's favorite scholars led by Tsu Hsiao-sun, and including Wei Cheng, Yü Shih-nan, and Ch'u Liang. They were completed in 631 and revised later in T'ai-tsung's reign.[98] Subsequently the texts in current use were extensively changed, especially under Empress Wu. In 725 Hsüan-tsung ordered Chang Yüeh to revise them. The work, which coincided with preparation for a new ritual code,[99] was done in the newly established Chi-hsien Academy, to which the musicians of the Court of Imperial Sacrifices were summoned to be instructed and practice new song texts.[100] However, the new texts were used indiscriminately with those written in T'ai-tsung's time, and in 737 the president of the court of Imperial Sacrifices (*T'ai-ch'ang ch'ing*), Wei T'ao, and a group of experts in music and ritual produced an authoritative repertory of song texts in five scrolls, which were sent to the music departments, and their musicians were ordered to practice them.[101] It was almost certainly this collection that Wei Shu used as the source for his National History. The collation and composition of the texts were done in the Chi-hsien Academy, of which he was a member from 730 on and in which a great deal of historical compilation was also carried out.

The Monograph on the Calendar (*Li chih*)

The Monograph on the Calendar comprises chapters 32 to 34 of the *Chiu T'ang shu*. Its preface deals in very general terms with the history of the various calendars prepared under the T'ang down to and including the *Kuan-hsiang li* of Hsü Ang prepared in 807 under Hsien-tsung.[102] The bulk of the monograph comprises detailed descriptions of the three major T'ang calendars, those of Fu Jen-chün, Li Ch'un-feng, and I-hsing, each of which occupies a separate chapter. The end of the preface gives us a clear indication of the monograph's earlier history.

The former history (*ch'ien shih*) took the calendars compiled by the four scholars Fu Jen-chün, Li Ch'un-feng, Nan-kung Yüeh and I-hsing to make a Monograph

---

98 *CTS* 30, p. 1089; *Yü hai* 106, p. 206. *THY* 33, pp. 589–91.
99 See McMullen, *State and Scholars in Tang China*, pp. 134–6.
100 *THY* 33, p. 595; *CTS* 30, p. 1089, gives the date *at the beginning* of the Kai-yuan period (i.e., 713) but this is in error. *Yü hai* 106, p. 20b, quotes *CTS* 30, but with the date 725 as in *THY*.
101 *CTS* 30, p. 1089; *Yü hai* 106, p. 20b.
102 *CTS* 32, pp. 1151–3.

on the Calendar in four chapters. The experts on calculation of recent times all agree that the methods of Li Ch'un-feng and I-hsing are without error, even when traced through the ages. Later men changed their calendars, simply making a point of introducing some novelty, but have not gone beyond their level of precision. The Ching-lung calendar was never put into practice and the world considered it false. Hence we omit it and do not record it here. We have taken only the three calendars Wu-yin [of Fu Jen-chün], Lin-te [of Li Ch'un-feng], and Ta-yen [of I-hsing] to prepare this monograph and present them to [future] officials concerned with computation.[103]

This strongly suggests that the *Chiu T'ang-shu* monograph simply reproduced that in the "former history," that is the National History completed by Liu Fang in 759–60, omitting the chapter that had dealt with the Ching-lung calendar (the calendar of Nan-kung Yüeh), which presumably had been the third of the four chapters forming the National History's monograph.

This monograph in the "former history" had thus ended with the account of I-hsing's *Ta-yen calendar*, which was prepared between 721 and 727 and officially promulgated in 728. It is as a result impossible to decide whether this "former monograph" was newly compiled under Liu Fang in 758–60 or whether it was simply taken over by him from the earlier draft National History by Wei Shu. When Wei Shu was in charge of the compilation of the National History during the 730s, the I-hsing calendar had already been officially adopted, so it is quite possible that the monograph of the "former history" had already been composed under his direction.

The compilers of *Chiu T'ang shu* in 941–5 merely added a new or revised preface to the original monograph of the National History and cut out the chapter that had described the Ching-lung calendar.

The preface poses a curious historiographical problem. Revision of the calendar was rather frequent under the T'ang and in fact continued until the very end of the dynasty. The monograph mentions the *Chih-te li* calendar of Han Ying,[104] the *Wu-chi li* calendar of Kuo Hsien-chih compiled in 762,[105] the *Cheng-yüan* calendar of Hsü Ch'eng-ssu completed in 783,[106] and the *Kuan-hsiang li* calendar of Hsü Ang, completed in

---

103 See *CTS* 32, pp. 1152–3.
104 See also *THY* 42, p. 751. This calendar was soon found inaccurate and replaced in 762. See *HTS* 29, p. 695. For details, see also *Yü hai* 10, pp. 16b–17a. This calendar was never included in the list of "Eight T'ang Calendars." See, for example, Hiraoka Takeo, *Tōdai no Koyomi* (Kyoto, 1954), introduction, p. 6.
105 See *HTS* 29, pp. 695–716; *THY* 42, p. 752.
106 See *HTS* 29, pp. 716–36. *THY* 42, p. 752, calls this the Chen-yüan calendar.

807.[107] It stops at this point.[108] The Hsü Ang calendar, however, proved unsatisfactory, and was replaced after only fourteen years by a new calendar, the *Hsüan-ming li*, promulgated in 822.[109] This was, in turn, replaced in 892 by the *Ch'ung-hsüan li* of Pien Kang, Hu Hsiu-lin, and Wang Ch'ih.[110] This last calendar was still in use under the Five Dynasties until 939.[111]

One can easily understand why, if the compilers of *Chiu T'ang shu* considered the various calendars compiled after the An Lu-shan rebellion to have been inferior to those of the early T'ang, as they suggest in their preface, they should have dismissed them with a few words. But even so it is very difficult to understand why their account stops short as it does with Hsien-tsung's reign. Why were the calendars of 822 and 893, both of them far more important and long-lasting than that of 807, not mentioned? More curious still, why did they end the monograph with an account of a calendar, that of Hsü Ang, which was soon found unsatisfactory and replaced within a few years, and which had already been consigned to oblivion by the eleventh century?[112]

This, however, is not the end of the mystery. The section dealing with the calendar in *T'ang hui yao* also comes to an abrupt and inexplicable end at exactly the same date.[113] This suggests that in this case, as in others of the monographs, the compilers of *Chiu T'ang shu* found it more convenient to adapt for their own purposes the material already conveniently brought together, classified, and arranged in the *Hui yao* and *Hsü Hui yao*, rather than compile it afresh from the Veritable Records.[114]

---

107 See *HTS* 30A, pp. 739–44. This notes that the Kuan-hsiang calendar was no longer preserved, presumably at the time of the compilation of *HTS* in the mid eleventh century.

108 See *CTS* 32, p. 1152.   109 See *HTS* 30A, pp. 744–69; *TCTC* 242, p. 7823.

110 See *HTS* 30B, p. 771.   111 See *HTS* 25, p. 534; *WTHY* 10, p. 166.

112 See *HTS* 30A, p. 745, which says, "The present officials [of the Astronomical Service] have not had it transmitted to them."

113 See *THY* 42, p. 752. Yet when *WTHY* was completed three years later, its compilers, some of whom had worked on *THY*, list the Kuan-hsiang, Hsüan-ming, Cheng-yüan, and Ch'ung-hsüan calendars, and also a calendar *Pao-ying li*, which must date from 762 and is clearly another name for Kuo Hsien-chih's *Wu-chi li*. See *WTHY* 10, p. 166.

114 The Basic Annals of *CTS* also make no mention of the introduction of the *Hsüan-ming li* in its entry covering the relevant year of 822 or of the new *Ch'ung-hsüan li* in its entry for 893. See *CTS* 16, pp. 493–502; *CTS* 20, pp. 748–51. The introduction of a new calendar was an event of great symbolic and ritual importance, as well as having serious practical consequences, and it is strange that the Basic Annals for 822, which were, of course, derived from the Veritable Records of Mu-tsung's reign, omit all mention of this important event. On the symbolic and ritual importance of a new calendar, see Howard J. Wechsler, *Offerings of Jade and Silk: Ritual and Symbol in the Legitimation of the T'ang Dynasty* (New Haven, 1985), pp. 212–23. On the introduction of the new calendar, see *HTS* 30A, pp. 744–69; *TCTC* 242, p. 7823 and note. No compiler's name is given for this new calendar in either source.

There is, of course, a remote possibility that the present text of this last section of the *Chiu T'ang shu* monograph may be derived from a revision and continuation of the monograph from the National History of Liu Fang made at some date after 807 and before 822. But there is not a scrap of evidence to confirm that any such revision or supplementation of the National History was carried out at that time, or indeed at any other time after Ling-hu Huan and Yü Hsiu-lieh completed their work early in the reign of Tai-tsung, although there was a good deal of scholarly work written later on the subjects of various of the monographs, particularly under Te-tsung and Hsien-tsung. Moreover, such an explanation would not explain the identical anomaly in the *T'ang hui yao*.

It seems far more likely that in this case the compilers of the *Chiu T'ang shu* monograph took their information on events after 760 from the *Hui yao* and from its continuation the *Hsü Hui yao*, compiled in 852. The official compilers of *Hsü Hui yao*, in the same way as the historians writing the Basic Annals of the *Chiu T'ang shu*, certainly extracted most of their information from the Veritable Records. It seems quite likely then that the Veritable Record of Mu-tsung's reign, for reasons that remain inexplicable, omitted all mention of the *Hsüan-ming li*. As a result, both the Basic Annals of the reign and the *Hsü Hui yao* fail to mention the 822 calendar. This pattern of compilation would also explain why the monograph also makes no mention of the *Ch'ung-hsüan li* calendar of 893, which of course appeared long after the completion of *Hsü Hui yao*, and in a period when the regular historiographical processes were in total confusion.[115]

The Monograph on Astronomy (*T'ien-wen chih*)

The Monograph on Astronomy occupies chapters 35 and 36. The first part, including all of chapter 35 and the beginning of chapter 36,[116] was certainly derived from Liu Fang's National History. It includes no material relating to the period after 760, apart from a few terse notices of eclipses, the latest dated 846, that have been subsequently inserted.[117] The fact that this first part was taken from Liu Fang's history substantially unchanged is underlined by the subtitle of the following section, "A Chronology of Heavenly Portents After the Chih-te period

---

115 This calendar, too, is not mentioned in the relevant section of *CTS* Basic Annals; *CTS* 20A, p. 748–51. However, the record for the last two decades of the T'ang, when no Veritable Record was compiled and the court was in constant turmoil, is so poor in general that no significance can be read into this fact.

116 The section ends with *CTS* 36, p. 1324.

117 See *CTS* 35, pp. 1318–19.

(756–8)."[118] The latest entry in this chronology is dated 845, the date when the Veritable Records ceased to be compiled. A final section of the monograph deals with the reorganization of the old Astronomical Service (the *T'ai-shih chü*) as the Imperial Observatory (the *Ssu-t'ien t'ai*), an event that took place in 758.[119] The last entry in this section is dated 840.

It is thus clear that the compilers of *Chiu T'ang shu* took the monograph from the earlier National History and supplemented it with later material from a source that ended around 846. It is almost certain that this source, as in the other monographs, was either the Veritable Records themselves or, much more likely, the material extracted from them and rearranged in the *Hui yao* and its continuation the *Hsü Hui yao*.

The Monograph on Portents (*Wu-hsing chih*)

The Monograph on Portents occupies chapter 37. It is by no means clear when this extremely disordered and unsatisfactory monograph was put together. The introduction[120] contains no clue to its date of composition. The rest of the monograph consists of some fifteen short sections, each listing the occurrence of portents of a specific sort. The latest date mentioned in the monograph is that of an earthquake in 849. Some of the sections mention no events *before* 760; other sections include nothing after that date. It is possible that the monograph was based on a short monograph in the National History, which was copiously supplemented from the *Hui yao* and *Hsü Hui yao*. It is equally possible that the monograph was written ab initio in 941–5. Whatever its origin, it is noticeable that the great majority of the many portents listed both in the *T'ang Hui yao* and also in the Basic Annals for various reigns in *Chiu T'ang shu* itself were not included in this monograph. Its compilation was carelessly done.

The following is a list of the various sections with a note on the dates of the material in each. (1) Earthquakes.[121] Less than half the material deals with the period before 760. The latest date mentioned is 849. (2) Landslides, Strange Rocks, Meteorites.[122] Most of the material is dated before 760. The latest date mentioned is 783. (3) Excessive rain:[123] Most of the material comes from the period before 760, but a large proportion of this consists of a lengthy quotation from a single memorial.[124] The

---

118 See *CTS* 36, pp. 1324–4.   119 See *CTS* 36, pp. 1335–6.
120 See *CTS* 37, pp. 1345–7.   121 See *CTS* 37, pp. 1347–9.
122 See *CTS* 37, pp. 1349–51.   123 See *CTS* 37, pp. 1351–63.
124 See *CTS* 37, pp. 1351–8, deal with the pre–760 period, pp. 1359–63, with the years following 760. But pp. 1353–6 are entirely given over to a long memorial from Sung Wu-kuang.

latest date mentioned is 836. (4) Rain connected with government affairs:[125] Only one item is from later than 760. This dates from 806. (5) Locusts and Drought:[126] Roughly half the material relates to the period after 760. The latest date mentioned is 840. (6) Fire:[127] More than half deals with the period after 760. The latest date given is 843, apart from a single item dated 891. (7) Birds:[128] More than half the material comes from after 760. The latest date mentioned is 837. (8) Animal prodigies:[129] Almost all material comes from after 760. The latest date mentioned is 835. (9) Dragons, serpents, insects:[130] Roughly half of the material dates from later than 760. (10) Magic fungi, trees.[131] (11) Springs, rivers flowing unnaturally clear or in strange colors.[132] Almost all the material comes from after 760. The latest occurrence is from 825. (12) Buildings:[133] This begins with 712 and ends with the 820s. (13) Men:[134] This material all comes from after 760. (14) Folksongs:[135] Only one item in this section dates from after 685. (15) Dress:[136] All this material is dated before 710.

This evidence gives no clear indication of the date when this monograph was compiled or whether there was ever a Monograph on Portents in Liu Fang's National History. Some sections may come from the National History, whereas others were certainly added in 941–45. Clearly, in this instance, the *Chiu T'ang shu* compilers were neither particularly concerned about the subject nor conscientious in their work, because they not only failed to collect for inclusion in the monograph much information that they had already extracted from the Veritable Records for their own Basic Annals, but also did not even bother to avail themselves of the relatively rich materials conveniently available to them in the *Hui yao* and *Hsü Hui yao*.

The Monograph on Administrative Geography
(*Ti-li chih*)

The Monograph on Administrative Geography occupies chapters 38 to 41. It comprises a preface[137] followed by a detailed administrative gazetteer of the T'ang empire as of 752.[138] Arranged under the ten circuits (*tao*) of early T'ang times, first established in 637,[139] the monograph lists

125 See *CTS* 37, p. 1363.　　126 See *CTS* 37, pp. 1363–5.
127 See *CTS* 37, pp. 1366–7.　　128 See *CTS* 37, pp. 1368–9.
129 See *CTS* 37, pp. 1369–71.　　130 See *CTS* 37, pp. 1371–2.
131 See *CTS* 37, pp. 1372–3.　　132 See *CTS* 37, p. 1373.　　133 See *CTS* 37, p. 1374.
134 See *CTS* 37, pp. 1374–5.　　135 See *CTS* 37, pp. 1375–6.
136 See *CTS* 37, pp. 1376–7.　　137 *CTS* 38, pp. 1383–93.
138 For this date, see *CTS* 38, p. 1393. In the body of the monograph, however, place names and administrative readjustments are systematically updated to 758.
139 *CTS* 38, p. 1384; *THY* 70, pp. 1231–2.

each prefectural-level administrative unit (*chou, tu-tu fu, tu-hu fu*), gives its status, identifies it with its equivalent in Sui times, and gives a very detailed history of all administrative changes in its name, boundaries, and affiliation. This is done systematically for all prefectures down to 758 when the prefectures (*chou*) resumed their old names after having been known as commanderies (*chün*) with different names since 742. Each entry then gives the prefecture's number of constituent counties, registered households, and registered individuals in two censuses. The first of these, referred to only as the "old" (*chiu*) figures, dates from the late 630s or early 640s, probably from 639.[140] The second of these censuses, identical with that preserved in *Hsin T'ang shu*, dates from 742. The entry on each prefecture ends with its distance from Ch'ang-an and from Lo-yang, the two capital cities. After this, each subordinate county (*hsien*) is listed in turn with details of its status and name under the Sui and subsequent administrative changes.

The monograph confines itself to administrative matters. It provides none of the rich material on local products, local military forces, and special local government establishments given in the parallel monograph in *Hsin T'ang shu*, but its detail on administrative changes during the first half of the dynasty is much fuller.

The preface falls into several sections. The first section[141] begins with a survey of the changing size and population of the empire under successive dynasties, down to the division of the T'ang empire into fifteen circuits (*tao*) in 733. Then the second section gives[142] a detailed account of the frontier commands established under provincial governors (*chieh-tu shih*) in Hsüan-tsung's reign and the military organization in each of these frontier commands.[143] This material is similar to a section in *T'ung tien*[144] and probably refers to the later years of the

---

140 There is considerable disagreement about this census, which shows a dramatic decline in registered population from the Sui census of 609, especially in northeastern China. Views expressed about the figures range from the belief that the figures are not a census but a list of tax figures, as proposed in Hans Bielenstein, "The Census of China during the Period A.D. 2–742," *BMFEA* 19 (1947): 125–63, to the theory that the figures for southern China come not from the T'ang but from a census compiled under the Ch'en in the sixth century, propounded in E. G. Pulleyblank, "Registration of Population in China in the Sui and T'ang Periods," *JESHO* 4 (1961): 289–301. I agree with Hino Kaisaburō, who, in his "Tō Jōgan jūsan nen no kokō-tōkei no chiiki-teki kōsatsu," *Tōyō shigaku* 24 (1961): 1–24, dates these figures to 639, and I believe their manifest deficiencies are an index of the ineffectual local administration of T'ai-tsung's time.

141 *CTS* 38, pp. 1382–5, line 7.

142 *CTS* 38, p. 1385, line 7 – p. 1389, line 6.

143 *CTS* 38, pp. 1385–9.

144 *TT* 172, pp. 911a–912a, where the figures are attributed to 733.

K'ai-yüan period (713–41). Up to this point, the material in the preface probably comes directly from Liu Fang's National History.

There follows a third section[145] a brief mention of the establishment of provincial governors throughout China "after the Chih-te period (756–58)," and lists of each of the new *chieh-tu shih* established during the An Lu-shan rebellion, giving the administrative seat and subordinate prefectures of each new province.[146] This list cannot be precisely dated, but it may have been added by Yü Hsiu-lieh or Ling-hu Huan in the 760s. One of the entries mentions events late in the reign of Hsien-tsung (after 817),[147] but this may well be a later interpolation.

A short fourth section[148] then mentions the loss of the northwestern provinces of Lung-yu and Ho-hsi to the Tibetans in 763, and their recovery in the Ta-chung (847–60) and Hsien-t'ung (861–74) periods; clearly this section must have been added when *Chiu T'ang shu* was compiled. The fifth and last section[149] of the preface compares the territory and population in 752 with that of the Han, giving total figures for the empire's prefectures, counties, registered households and individuals, and land due to be distributed under the *chün-t'ien* system as of 740. This section reads as though it might perhaps originally have followed immediately after the first section. Finally a brief note describes the lack of reliable data from the later part of the T'ang.

It seems probable that the preface came into its present shape in several stages. The first stage, perhaps in Wei Shu's National History, comprised the first and fifth sections.

This was supplemented in Liu Fang's National History by the addition of the second section, and possibly further supplemented with the third section, by Ling-hu Huan and Yü Hsiu-lieh, around 765. The remainder, only a few sentences in all, was added in 941–5.

The body of the monograph certainly came directly from Liu Fang's National History. A few minor additions referring to changes subsequent to 758 were inserted, but they are quite haphazard and incomplete. Some of these additions may have been made by Yü Hsiu-lieh or Ling-hu Huan during Tai-tsung's reign. Others may be the work of K'ung Shu-jui (730–800),[150] who served twice as a compiler in the Historiographical Office and is said to have been famous for his geo-

---

145 *CTS* 38, p. 1389, line 7 – p. 1392, line 11.   146 *CTS* 38, pp. 1389–92.
147 *CTS* 38, p. 1391.   148 *CTS* 38, p. 1392, line 12 – p. 1393, line 2.
149 *CTS* 38, p. 1393, line 3.
150 This case was kindly drawn to my attention by David McMullen.

graphical knowledge and to have "revised a *Ti-li chih* that was praised highly for its attention to detail."[151] There are questions, first, about what book this was a revision of[152] and, second, about its date.[153] The present *Chiu T'ang shu* monograph certainly does not incorporate any such systematic revisions made during Te-tsung's reign. Probably K'ung Shu-jui's work circulated as a separate book and was subsequently lost. Most of the almost casual additions of material related to events after 758 in the present monograph were almost certainly made by the compilers of *Chiu T'ang shu* in 941–5.

It is possible that the bulk of this monograph was originally derived by the compilers of the earlier National History from one or another of the geographical works compiled during the early T'ang. The most obvious such source was the *Kua-ti chih*, the large-scale geography of the empire (in no less than 550 chapters) compiled by the prince of Wei, Li T'ai, and several collaborators[154] over a five-year period between 638 and 642. One reason for believing the monograph to have at least some connection with the *Kua-ti chih* is that we know that the latter used as one of

---

151 See *CTS* 192, pp. 5130–1; *HTS* 196, p. 5610. See also *TFYK* 560, p. 32b, which wrongly dates his service to Hsien-tsung's reign.

152 The title of this revised work is given in different forms: *HTS* calls it *Ti-li chih* with the same characters as the monograph in the present *CTS*, while *CTS* calls it *Ti-li chih* with a different third character: 誌. Because the latter is the more reliable source, it may refer to a separate book. If so, however, there is no trace of it in the bibliographical monograph of *HTS* or elsewhere.

153 K'ung Shu-jui was a scholar of great learning who lived in seclusion on Sung-shan. Early in Tai-tsung's reign he was recommended to the emperor by the financial commissioner Liu Yen and appointed to a succession of posts, including compiler in the Historiographical Office. At first sight, it appears that he might well have participated in the final editing of the National History at that time. However, his biographies tell us that each time Tai-tsung appointed him to a post he would briefly come to court to express his gratitude, and after a few days resign on the grounds of sickness and retire again into seclusion.

Under Te-tsung he was specially summoned to court, treated with extraordinary ceremony, and lavished with gifts, and at last persuaded to accept office, as vice-president of the Imperial Library and once again concurrently as compiler in the Historiographical Office. The exact date of this appointment is unknown, but it was probably in the mid 780s, because Ling-hu Huan was appointed a compiler, as his junior, on the recommendation of Li Mi in 787. We are told that Ling-hu Huan constantly tried to provoke him into a quarrel until he was sent out to a provincial post in 789. K'ung Shu-jui remained in office as compiler until his retirement in 793. See *THY* 67, p. 1174. The revision of the Monograph on Administrative Geography might have been completed during his tenure as a compiler from about 785 to 793, assuming that it was undertaken as an official project. *HTS* 196, p. 5610, clearly dates the revision to this second tenure.

154 *CTS* 76, p. 2653; *TFYK* 560, p. 28b; *HTS* 58, p. 1506, list Hsiao Te-yen, Ku Yin, Chiang Ya-ch'ing, Hsieh Yen, and Su Hsü.

227

its basic sources a census dated 639,[155] which date fits exactly with the probable date of the "old" census figures cited in the monograph. It would also explain why the monograph has such profuse detail on the first two decades of the T'ang. It is of course possible that this material came originally from a monograph included in the very first National History, the *Wu-te Chen-kuan liang-ch'ao shih*, completed in 656. If this work had a geographical monograph the *Kua-ti chih* would have been its obvious source.[156]

If this was so, it had certainly been much modified and expanded by the time of Liu Fang. By his time there had been many further changes in local administration, and there were other fairly large-scale geographical works available. The imperial library in 721 contained two "Maps of the Ten Circuits" (*Shih-tao t'u*), one in thirteen chapters dated 704 and the other in ten chapters dated 715.[157] In Chung-tsung's short reign (705–10), Liang Tsai-yen also compiled a "Monograph on the Ten Circuits and Four Barbarian Regions" (*Shih-tao ssu-fan chih*) in sixteen chapters.[158] But no work approaching the *Kua-ti chih* in scale was compiled until the end of the eighth century or the early ninth century.[159] In Hsüan-tsung's reign and the decades that followed, the *Kua-ti chih* remained the single most authoritative geography of the empire.[160] The updating of the monograph's information on local administrative changes, which seems to have been done fully and carefully down to 758, may have used some of these later compilations but must also have checked them against detailed information from elsewhere.

The tenth-century compilers of *Chiu T'ang shu* made no such efforts to update the material in the monograph included in the National

---

155 See the reconstructed edition of fragments of the *Kua-ti chih*, Ho Tzu-chün, *Kua-ti chih chi-chiao* (Peking, 1980), introduction, p. 1; summary of the original preface, p. 2 (this is preserved in *Ch'u hsüeh chi* [Peking, 1962] 8, pp. 165–6). Strangely, the *Kua-ti chih* itself does not appear in the *CTS* Monograph on Literature, only the five-chapter *Kua-ti chih hsü-lüeh*, the "abbreviated preface" to the work being included. See *CTS* 46, p. 2015.

156 The last years of T'ai-tsung's reign and the early years of Kao-tsung also saw the completion of other works on historical geography. In the 630s Fang Hsüan-ling and Chu Sui-liang had completed the Geographical Monograph for the *Sui shu*. See *TFYK* 560, pp. 28b–29a. In 658 Hsü Ching-tsung presented a sixty-chapter work on the Western Regions, the *Hsi-yü t'u-chih*; see *HTS* 58, p. 1506; *THY* 36, p. 656; *TFYK* 560, p. 29a.

157 See *CTS* 46, p. 2016; *HTS* 58, p. 1506.

158 See Aoyama Sadao, *Tō Sō jidai no kōtsū to chishi, chizu no kenkyū* (Tokyo, 1963), pp. 447–9. This article originally appeared in *Tōyō gakuhō* 28, nos. 1–2 (1941).

159 See Aoyama, *Tō sō jidai no kōtsū*, pp. 449–50.

160 The *Kua-ti chih* was for example used as the basis for the geographical identifications of ancient place names in Chang Shou-chieh's commentary to *Shih chi*, the *Shih chi cheng-i*, completed in 736 or 737.

History, although sweeping changes had altered the local administration of the empire after 755. They ignored K'ung Shu-jui's revised monograph entirely, and took no account of a series of detailed geographies produced in the early ninth century from which the needed information could easily have been extracted. Most important of these works were the *Ku-chin Chün kuo hsien tao ssu-i shu* completed in forty chapters by the famous geographer and chief minister Chia T'an in 801,[161] and the *Yüan-ho chün-hsien t'u-chih* in forty chapters and accompanied by a large set of maps completed by the then chief minister and director of National History, Li Chi-fu, in 813, the greater part of which still survives.[162] Li Chi-fu had earlier completed, in 807, a statistical abstract of the empire in ten chapters entitled *Yüan-ho kuo-chi pu*. This dealt in detail with the population, taxes, and military dispositions of the empire.[163] All these works were available to the official historians who compiled *Chiu T'ang shu*, but they made no use of them.

The Monograph on Officials (*Chih-kuan chih*)

The Monograph on Officials, which occupies chapters 42 to 44, provides a detailed description of the structure of the T'ang bureaucracy. There can be no doubt that this is essentially the monograph that was included in Liu Fang's National History, with a small number of minor additions relating to changes made after 759.

Chapter 42 comprises, first, an introductory section dealing with various changes made in the official establishment between 617 and the twelfth month of 758[164] and, second, a detailed table of precedence listing the various civil and military, substantive and nominal offices under each rank.[165] The introductory section is clearly taken from Liu

161 See *HTS* 58, p. 1506; *CTS* 13, p. 345; *CTS* 138, pp. 3784–6, which quotes Chia T'an's preface in full. See also *Yü hai* 15, pp. 23a–25a, and Naitō Torajirō, "Ko Gi-kō nen fu," in *Ogawa Hakase Kanreki kinen shigaku chirigaku ronsō* (Tokyo, 1930), pp. 941–60, reprinted in his collected works, *Naitō Konan zenshū* (Tokyo, 1970), vol. 7, pp. 599–614.
162 See the edition edited by Ho Tz'u-chün: *Yüan-ho chün-hsien t'u-chih*, 2 vols. (Peking, 1983). *CTS* 148, p. 3997; and *HTS* 58, p. 1506, give its length as fifty-four chapters and lists a supplementary collection of maps in ten chapters entitled *Shih-tao t'u*. Although the original work included maps, these were lost by the time *Chung-hsing kuan-ko shu-mu* was compiled in 1178. By that time editions were organized in forty chapters with a two-chapter table of contents. See *Yü hai*: 15, p. 28a–b. Later the table of contents and five of the chapters were also lost.
163 See *CTS* 148, p. 3997; *THY* 36, p. 660; *CTS* 14, p. 424; *THY* 84, pp. 1552–3; *TCTC* 237, pp. 7647–8. The commentary to the last passage shows that the work was still extant in the eleventh century and known to Sung Pai (936–1012). The quotations most probably come from his *Hsü T'ung tien* of 1001.
164 See *CTS* 42, pp. 1783–90.
165 See *CTS* 42, pp. 1791–1803.

Fang's history. Many other institutional changes were made after 758, some of them major reforms, the importance of which any tenth-century historian would have recognized immediately because they deeply affected the government structure of the Five Dynasties. Hardly any of these changes are even mentioned in the monograph. The only plausible reason why this introductory section should have ended with 758 is that it was written immediately thereafter.

The table of offices in order of precedence that follows was certainly taken from the first chapter of the Statutes, the *Kuan p'in ling*, as promulgated in 737.[166] The section is closely paralleled by a similar but somewhat more extensive[167] list incorporated in the *T'ung tien*, which almost certainly also took this material from the Statutes of 737, possibly via Liu Chih's *Cheng tien*, which was probably written in the late 730s or early 740s.[168] This section of the monograph goes farther than simply reproducing the Statutes of 737, however, because it adds a commentary detailing differences between the ranks attributed to various offices in the Statutes of 737 and those in the earlier *Wu-te* Statutes of 624, the *Chen-kuan* Statutes of 637, the *Ch'ui-kung* Statutes of 685, the former *K'ai-yüan* Statutes of 715 and the *K'ai-yüan* Statutes of 719. It also mentions many specific changes in rank introduced at other times, down to the 750s.

Chapters 43 and 44 list in detail all the established posts in each organ of government, together in each case with a formal description of the incumbent's responsibilities. This material is taken from the relevant sections of the six chapters of the Statutes (*Chih-yüan ling*) of 737 that prescribed the duties of each of the offices of central and local government.[169]

There are clear indications again that the material in this section of the monograph was compiled in 759–60, although a few short sections such as that dealing with the Shen-ts'e Armies[170] must have been added at the time of *Chiu T'ang shu*'s compilation. A crucial piece of evidence

166 See Niida Noboru, *Tōryō shūi*, pp. 101–23.
167 *TT* lists not only regular offices "within the current" (*liu-nei kuan*) but also subaltern posts "outside the current" (*liu-wai kuan*), which are omitted by *CTS*.
168 See also the list given in the Tun-huang manuscript P. 2504, under the title *Kuan p'in ling*, which internal evidence dates from the T'ien-pao (742–56) period.
169 Chapter 43 derives from chapter 2 of the Statutes of 737, and chapter 44 from chapters 3 to 7 as these were reconstructed by Niida Noboru, *Tōryō shūi*, pp. 124–58. The distribution of these materials over the various chapters of the Statutes in Niida's reconstruction published in 1933 does not agree, however, with the manuscript copies of passages from these Statutes preserved at Tun-huang that have more recently been reassembled and published. But it remains clear that *CTS* 43 and 44 derive from chapters 2 to 7 of the Statutes, the *Chih-yüan ling*.
170 See *CTS* 44, pp. 1904–5.

in this respect is the section dealing with the military provincial governors[171] (*Chieh-tu shih*), which comes down only to 758, ignoring the many important developments of the following decades. Another piece of evidence comes from the description of the Imperial Observatory (*T'ai-shih chü*). The reorganization of this office as the *Ssu-t'ien t'ai* in 756 is duly recorded, and after giving its old location the description continues: "The office is now in the southeastern corner of the Yung-ning ward."[172] This move took place in 758.[173]

The Monograph on Carriages and Dress (*Yü-fu chih*)

The Monograph on Carriages and Dress occupies chapter 45. It certainly derives almost unchanged from the monograph in Liu Fang's National History. It contains nothing whatever relating to changes subsequent to 758. The latest entry relates to a change in one form of conveyance used by frontier generals attending court, which became effective in 758.[174] The only points reflecting later editing are the use of their temple names to refer to Hsüan-tsung and Su-tsung. These temple names were confered in the third month of 763.

The Monograph on Literature (*Ching-chi chih*)

The Monograph on Literature occupies chapters 46 and 47. It was certainly taken over by the compilers of the *Chiu T'ang shu* from Liu Fang's National History and probably already formed part of Wei Shu's National History. We can, however, be still more precise about its origin. It is an abstract of the imperial library catalog *Ku-chin shu-lu* in forty chapters compiled by Wu Chiung, listing the titles of works in the imperial collections in 721. This was a condensed and updated version of his catalog *Ch'ün-shu ssu-pu lu* in two hundred chapters, completed under the direction of Yüan Hsing-ch'ung, which was presented to the throne earlier.[175] Wei Shu had been one of its main compilers.[176]

---

171 See *CTS* 44, p. 1922.
172 See *CTS* 44, p. 1855.
173 See *Ch'ang-an chih* 8, p. 6b. The new premises were placed in the former mansion of Chang Shou-kuei and the Yung-ning park, which had been given to An Lu-shan as the site for his mansion in the capital.
174 See *CTS* 45, p. 1957.
175 See McMullen, *State and Scholars in T'ang China*, pp. 221–2, and sources cited there. The date of the completion and presentation of the work is variously given as 719 (in *Chi-hsien chu-chi* cited in *Yü hai* 52, p. 24a), or the first month of 720 (in *THY* 64, p. 1118) or the eleventh month of 721 (*CTS* 46, p. 1962).
176 See *THY* 36, p. 658; *CTS* 102, p. 3181; *CTS* 46, p. 1962.

The preface to the monograph alone[177] seems to have been written or rewritten in the 940s by the compilers of *Chiu T'ang shu*. They probably took the existing preface from Liu Fang's National History, inserting some additional material giving the history of the imperial collections after An Lu-shan's rebellion,[178] together with a note explaining how they had extracted the titles, numbers of chapters, and authors from the *Ku-chin shu-lu* so as to give a picture of the Imperial Library collection during the K'ai-yüan period, at the peak of the T'ang's cultural glory, and had deliberately refrained from adding works written subsequently.[179] Details of such later works were to be appended to the biographies of their authors.[180] Unfortunately, when the monograph was first written, it was decided to omit the supplement to the *Ku-chin shu-lu*, entitled *Shih-Tao lu-mu*, that listed the Buddhist and Taoist works in the Imperial Library, totaling more than twenty-five hundred titles.

The postscript to chapter 47, which gives a brief history of the imperial collections,[181] comes down only to the early K'ai-yüan period and, therefore, like the main contents of these chapters, may have been either taken from the *Ku-chin shu-lu* itself or written specially for the résumé of this prepared for the National History. Internal evidence proves that this postscript was written under the T'ang, not in the 940s.[182]

The Monograph on State Finance (*Shih-huo chih*)

The Monograph on State Finance occupies chapters 48 and 49. I published a detailed analysis of the text some thirty years ago.[183] At that time, I concluded that the bulk of the monograph was taken from the *Hui yao* and *Hsü Hui yao* and that the monograph did not derive from the National History but was compiled ab initio in 941–5. I have recently reexamined the problem, and although the evidence for large parts of

---

177 See *CTS* 46, pp. 1961–6.
178 See *CTS* 46, p. 1962, line 8 – p. 1963, line 1. This passage has many omissions, for example, making no mention of Ch'en Ching's catalog of the Imperial Library, *Chen-yuan Yü-fu ch'ün-shu hsin-lu*, completed around 792. See *Yü hai* 52, pp. 29b–30. For Ch'en Ching's Account of Conduct (*Hsing-chuang*), see Liu Tsung-yüan, *Liu Ho-tung chi* (Shanghai, 1958) 8, p. 125.
179 See *CTS* 46, p. 1966.
180 See *CTS* 46, p. 1966, lines 1–6.
181 See *CTS* 47, pp. 2081–2.
182 See *CTS* 47, p. 2082, line 4, which says, "When *our dynastic house (kuo-chia)* pacified Wang Shih-ch'ung, they took over his library collection."
183 See Twitchett, "The Derivation of the Text of the *Shih-huo chih* of the *Chiu T'ang-shu*," pp. 48–62. Another study of which I made use in that article is Suzuki Shun, "*Kyū Tō jo* shokkashi no shiryō-keitō ni tsuite," *Shien (Kyūshū)* 45 (1951): 77–84.

the monograph having been taken from *Hui yao* and *Hsü Hui yao* remains unassailable, I am now convinced that the compilers of *Chiu T'ang shu* did begin with an existing monograph from the National History of Liu Fang.

The main evidence for this is the preface. As I pointed out in my earlier article, the basic ideas of the preface, particularly its judgments on the changes in financial administration undertaken during the reign of Hsüan-tsung, closely parallel those expounded in an essay by Liu Fang that has been preserved elsewhere.[184] They are also remarkably similar to the "historian's judgments" appended to the *Chiu T'ang shu* biographies of the financial experts of Hsüan-tsung's reign – biographies that are almost certainly Liu Fang's work.[185] These common ideas and judgments suggest a common author but are not conclusive evidence.

What clinches the matter is that the preface, which sets out to make an overall judgment on the changes in T'ang financial policy, on closer examination proves to contain a startling historical discontinuity, the significance of which I missed in my earlier study. After dealing in some detail with the gradual shift of financial authority to new and irregular offices under Hsüan-tsung and with Hsüan-tsung's reliance on exploitative financial advisers, the preface mentions the An Lu-shan rebellion and Hsüan-tsung's flight to Szechwan, Su-tsung's assumption of the throne, and a number of minor emergency measures taken to raise revenue as a consequence of this crisis in 756–7.[186] It then jumps immediately to the consequences of the rebellions of the Ho-pei governors in the early 780s, making no mention either of the additional emergency tax measures and innovations in raising revenue undertaken by Su-tsung's ministers after 757 and during the early years of Tai-tsung's reign or of the far more fundamental changes undertaken during the same period that permanently reshaped the entire financial system, such as the beginning of the salt monopoly in 758, the reorganization of the grain transport system under Liu Yen in 763, the abandonment of the *Chün-tien* land allocation as the basis for tax liabilities, and the series of piecemeal tax reforms that led up to the institution by Yang Yen of the *Liang-shui* tax system in 780. These were by far the most important financial changes in T'ang times, and they are dealt with in some detail

---

184 See Liu Fang "Shih-huo lun," in *WYYH* 747, pp. 10b–12a; translated in Denis C. Twitchett and Howard L. Goodman, *A Handbook for T'ang History* (Princeton, 1986), vol. 1, pp. 94–102.
185 See my unpublished paper "Liu Fang, a Forgotten T'ang Historian," presented to the Yale Seminar on Chinese and Comparative Historiography in 1970. See also Twitchett and Goodman, *Handbook for T'ang History*, pp. 121–2.
186 This break occurs after p. 2087, line 6, in the Chung-hua shu-chü edition of *CTS* 48.

in the body of the monograph; yet there is no mention of them in the preface.

The facts that the break in the structure of the monograph comes *exactly* when Liu Fang began work on his National History and that the text to this point makes a generally sound assessment of developments up to this date that agrees with his judgments as expressed elsewhere lead one to the inevitable conclusion that the preface up to this point (with a few minor interpolations added in 941–5) is from his original National History, whereas the remainder was added, not very skillfully, in 941–5.

This explanation also suggests that the following section,[187] deriving ultimately from the T'ang Statutes (*ling*), which gives a summary of the early T'ang rules on land allocation, households, and taxation,[188] also came from the National History.[189] It would also explain the strange anomaly that the salt-taxation system is dealt with in two separate sections of the monograph. This may well have arisen because the beginning of the section in chapter 48 dealing with the salt pools of the northwest that refers to Hsüan-tsung's reign originally formed a part of the monograph in Liu Fang's National History, which was subsequently supplemented with details taken from the *Hui yao* on the inland salt-monopoly system later operated by the Public Revenue Commission (*Tu-chih shih*), whereas the extensive material in chapter 49 dealing with the coastal salt-monopoly system administered by the Salt and Iron Commission (*Yen-t'ieh shih*), which is undeniably derived from the *Hui yao* and *Hsü Hui yao*,[190] was added en bloc in 941–5. There can, of course, have been no section dealing with the Salt and Iron Commission's monopoly system in the National History, because the monopoly was initiated only as a local experiment in 756, the first commissioner was appointed only in 758, and the system did not achieve its full form until the 760s, some years after the completion of the National History.[191]

My earlier conclusions about the close relations between the material contained in the main part of the monograph and in the *Hui yao* and *Hsü*

---

187 From *CTS* 48, p. 2088, line 10 – p. 2090, line 1.
188 Niida Noboru, in his reconstruction of the fragments of the T'ang Statutes, *Tōryō shūi*, takes these passages as parts of the *Wu-te* Statutes of 624, as stated by *CTS* 48, p. 2088.
189 The additional materials appended to the text of the Statutes in this section are all dated before 750.
190 See Twitchett, "Derivation," pp. 52–5.
191 On these developments, see Denis C. Twitchett, *Financial Administration Under the T'ang Dynasty* (Cambridge, 1963), pp. 51–3, and the very detailed study by Hino Kaisaburō, "Government Monopoly on Salt in T'ang in the Period Before the Enforcement of the *Liang-shui fa*," *Memoirs of the Research Department of the Tōyō Bunko* 22 (1963): 1–55.

Hui yao nevertheless remain valid. Nothing whatever in the monograph relates to the period after the *Hsü Hui yao* was completed in 853. Almost everything relating to the period after 758 is paralleled in the present *T'ang hui yao* text but usually is found there in a fuller form, suggesting that the compilers of *Chiu T'ang shu* condensed the material they selected from the *Hui yao* and *Hsü Hui yao*. Some passages contain clear evidence that some individual sections of the monograph were written in 807, and others completed in 853, the dates of Su Mien's *Hui yao* and Yang Shao-fu's *Hsü Hui yao*, respectively.[192] The first part of chapter 49,[193] dealing with the salt-monopoly and transport systems, which is almost identical with a section in *T'ang hui yao*,[194] is an articulated account of events, not a series of résumés of edicts or memorials that could be explained by both the *Hui yao* and *Chiu T'ang shu* having taken their material from identical sources in the Veritable Records. It can be shown to be a composite account in which the join between the *Hui yao* and *Hsü Hui yao* remains plainly visible.[195] Finally, the imbalance between the material relating to the period ending in 803 and the much denser coverage of the next half century again reflects the more detailed material in *Hsü Hui yao*, which devoted the same number of chapters to this period as the *Hui yao* had to the period from 618–803.

These points show conclusively that the *Chiu T'ang shu* compilers took all their material for the period 758–853 from the *Hui yao* and *Hsü Hui yao*, running the material in the two books together just as Wang P'u and his collaborators were to do a few years later, when they compiled the *T'ang hui yao* in 961.

The material on the period before 758 is also largely paralleled in *T'ang hui yao*, although there are a few passages in which it is not. I formerly argued that this early material too was taken directly from the *Hui yao*, supplemented by material from the *T'ung tien*, which includes all the material not included also in the *T'ang hui yao*. But it is equally possible that the material on the period before 758 in the present *T'ang hui yao* was taken by Su Mien when he compiled his *Hui yao* in 804 from the monograph included in Liu Fang's existing National History. This would have made it natural and convenient for the compilers of *Chiu T'ang shu* in 941–5 simply to have incorporated into their new

---

192 See Twitchett, "Derivation," pp. 53–4.
193 *CTS* 49, pp. 2114–22. Only the short first part of this section (p. 2113) dealing with events down to 708 has no parallel in *THY*.
194 *THY* 87, pp. 1581–94. *THY* continues with material covering the period from 856 to the end of the dynasty. This must have been added by Wang P'u in 961. It is not parallelled by *CTS*. The *Hsü Hui yao* material must end with line 8, p. 1594.
195 *CTS* 49, p. 2120, line 1.

monograph the later material that had been added to this in the *Hui yao* and *Hsü Hui yao*.

The Monograph on Law (*Hsing-fa chih*)[196]

The Monograph on Law occupies chapter 50. It probably was based on an existing monograph in the National History that corresponded to the first and much more substantial part of the monograph[197] covering the period from 617–760. The events of the rest of the dynasty occupy only a few pages,[198] a large part of which is taken up by an integral quotation of Han Yü's famous essay "On Vengeance."[199] The last event mentioned is dated in the fifth month of 853, and it seems likely that the compilers of *Chiu T'ang shu* took the existing monograph from Liu Fang's National History and supplemented it with material dealing with the period from 760–853 culled from the *Hui yao* and *Hsü Hui yao*.

One problem relates to the passage in this monograph dealing with the trial and punishment of those who had collaborated with the An Lu-shan rebels. This passage[200] was probably one of the additions made by Yü Hsiu-lieh to Liu Fang's National History in the 760s. Liu Fang would hardly have described a legal process in which he himself had been among the accused – although his name is not mentioned in the monograph.

196 There is an integral translation of this monograph in Bünger, *Quellen*, pp. 73–140. The author also translates the relevant parallel sections of *THY*, on pp. 174–232.
197 *CTS* 50, pp. 2133–52 (Bünger, *Quellen*, pp. 73–128).
198 *CTS* 50, pp. 2152–6 (Bünger, *Quellen*, pp. 128–40).
199 See *CTS* 50, pp. 2153–4.
200 See *CTS* 50, pp. 2151–2 (trans. Bünger, *Quellen*, pp. 127–8).

236

Appendix

Appendix

Derivation of the Basic Annals chapters
of Chiu T´ang shu

Chapter 1.   Kao-tsu Basic Annals   pp. 1–19[a]

From

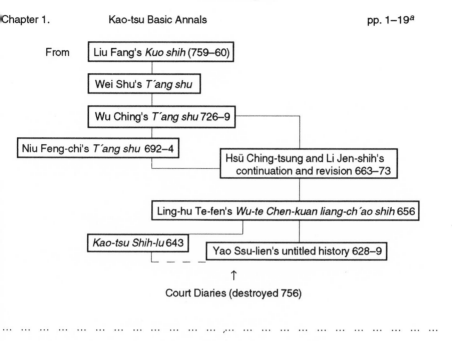

Court Diaries (destroyed 756)

··· ···

[a]Page numbers refer to Chung-hua Shu-chü edition of *Chiu T´ang-shu.*

Chapter 2. T´ai-tsung Basic Annals A (to A.D. 629) pp. 21–37

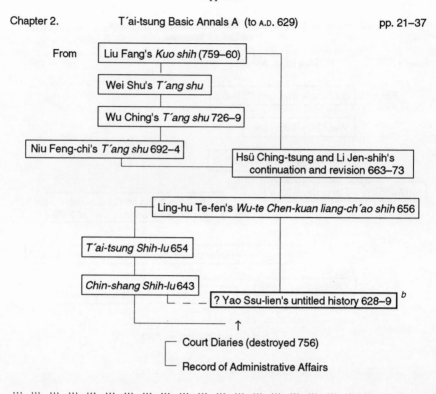

From Liu Fang's *Kuo shih* (759–60)

Wei Shu's *T´ang shu*

Wu Ching's *T´ang shu* 726–9

Niu Feng-chi's *T´ang shu* 692–4

Hsü Ching-tsung and Li Jen-shih's continuation and revision 663–73

Ling-hu Te-fen's *Wu-te Chen-kuan liang-ch´ao shih* 656

T´ai-tsung Shih-lu 654

Chin-shang Shih-lu 643

? Yao Ssu-lien's untitled history 628–9   *b*

Court Diaries (destroyed 756)

Record of Administrative Affairs

*b*The break in the Basic Annals of T´ai-tsung at 629 may possibly represent the date at which Yao Ssu-lien's history ended. The *Chin-shang Shih-lu* ended in 640, which would have been one natural breakpoint. Kao-tsu's death in 635 would have been another.

Chapter 3.   T´ai tsung Basic Annals B (630–49)   pp. 39–63

From

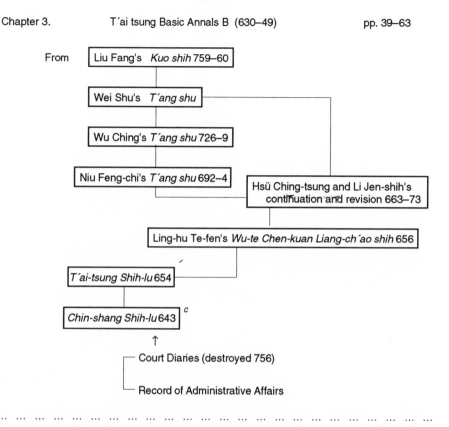

Liu Fang's *Kuo shih* 759–60

Wei Shu's *T´ang shu*

Wu Ching's *T´ang shu* 726–9

Niu Feng-chi's *T´ang shu* 692–4

Hsü Ching-tsung and Li Jen-shih's continuation and revision 663–73

Ling-hu Te-fen's *Wu-te Chen-kuan Liang-ch´ao shih* 656

T´ai-tsung Shih-lu 654

Chin-shang Shih-lu 643   c

↑

Court Diaries (destroyed 756)

Record of Administrative Affairs

---

[c] Coverage of the *Chin-shang Shih-lu* ended in 640. Section of Basic Annals down to p. 52 may derive ultimately from this.

Chapter 4. Kao-tsu Basic Annals A (649–65)[d] pp. 65–133

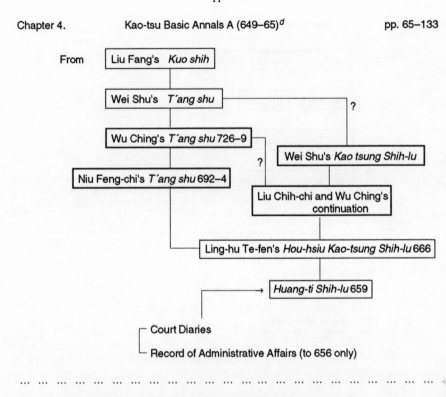

From Liu Fang's *Kuo shih*

Wei Shu's *T'ang shu* ?

Wu Ching's *T'ang shu* 726–9

Wei Shu's *Kao tsung Shih-lu*

?

Niu Feng-chi's *T'ang shu* 692–4

Liu Chih-chi and Wu Ching's continuation

Ling-hu Te-fen's *Hou-hsiu Kao-tsung Shih-lu* 666

Huang-ti Shih-lu 659

Court Diaries

Record of Administrative Affairs (to 656 only)

... ...

---

[d] This chapter covers that part of Kao-tsung's reign recorded in Ling-hu Te-fen's *Hou-hsiu Kao-tsung Shih-lu*. In this and the next chapter it is impossible to assess the role, if any, of the *Kao-tsung Shih-lu* recorded under the names of Empress Wu Tse-t'ien and of Wu Hsüan-chih.

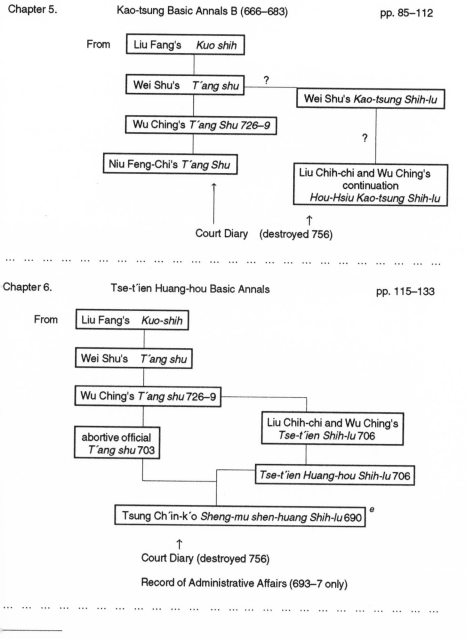

Chapter 5.   Kao-tsung Basic Annals B (666–683)   pp. 85–112

From   Liu Fang's *Kuo shih*

Wei Shu's *T'ang shu*   ?

Wei Shu's *Kao-tsung Shih-lu*

Wu Ching's *T'ang Shu 726–9*

?

Niu Feng-Chi's *T'ang Shu*

Liu Chih-chi and Wu Ching's continuation *Hou-Hsiu Kao-tsung Shih-lu*

Court Diary   (destroyed 756)

Chapter 6.   Tse-t'ien Huang-hou Basic Annals   pp. 115–133

From   Liu Fang's *Kuo-shih*

Wei Shu's *T'ang shu*

Wu Ching's *T'ang shu* 726–9

Liu Chih-chi and Wu Ching's *Tse-t'ien Shih-lu* 706

abortive official *T'ang shu* 703

Tse-t'ien Huang-hou Shih-lu 706

Tsung Ch'in-k'o *Sheng-mu shen-huang Shih-lu* 690 [e]

Court Diary (destroyed 756)

Record of Administrative Affairs (693–7 only)

---

[e]The material possibly derived ultimately from the *Sheng-mu shen-huang Shih-lu* ends at p. 120. Its coverage extended from 783 to 790.

243

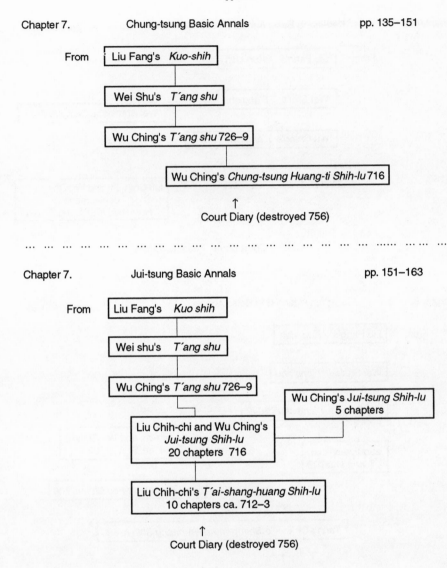

Chapter 7.   Chung-tsung Basic Annals   pp. 135–151

From   Liu Fang's *Kuo-shih*

Wei Shu's *T´ang shu*

Wu Ching's *T´ang shu* 726–9

Wu Ching's *Chung-tsung Huang-ti Shih-lu* 716

↑
Court Diary (destroyed 756)

… …… … … … …

Chapter 7.   Jui-tsung Basic Annals   pp. 151–163

From   Liu Fang's *Kuo shih*

Wei shu's *T´ang shu*

Wu Ching's *T´ang shu* 726–9

Wu Ching's J*ui-tsung Shih-lu*
5 chapters

Liu Chih-chi and Wu Ching's
Jui-tsung Shih-lu
20 chapters 716

Liu Chih-chi's *T´ai-shang-huang Shih-lu*
10 chapters ca. 712–3

↑
Court Diary (destroyed 756)

… … … … …… … … … … … … … … … …… … … … … … … … … …

Chapter 8.   Hsüan-tsung Basic Annals A (712–36)   pp. 165–204

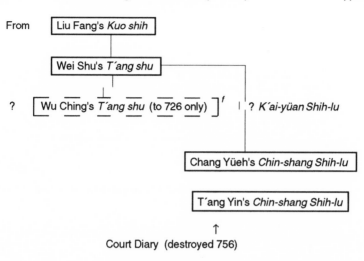

From   Liu Fang's *Kuo shih*

Wei Shu's *T´ang shu*

?   Wu Ching's *T´ang shu* (to 726 only)]^f | ? *K´ai-yüan Shih-lu*

Chang Yüeh's *Chin-shang Shih-lu*

T´ang Yin's *Chin-shang Shih-lu*

↑
Court Diary (destroyed 756)

… … … … … … … … … … … … … … … …… … … … … … … … … …… … … … …

^f It is uncertain whether Wu Ching's material on the period to 726 was incorporated in Wei Shu's draft *T´ang-shu*. Nor is the date and possible relationship of the *K´ai-yüan Shih-lu*, the author and date of which are unknown, with Liu Fang and Wei Shu's history ascertainable. Nor is it clear whether Chang Yüeh extended T´ang Yin's book . The date at which this chapter ends does not correspond with that of the *Chin-Shang Shih-lu* (about 728) or the *K´ai-yüan Shih-lu* (presumably 741). A possible explanation is that the date marks the end of Wei Shu's draft *T´ang shu* or that it is the date at which Yin Yin suspended work on Wei Shu's *T´ang Shu*. In either case, chapter 9 was presumably added in 759–60 by Liu Fang, whereas in chapter 8 he was still basing his account on Wei Shu's history.

… …

Chapter 9.   Hsüan-tsung Basic Annals B (737–56)   pp. 207–237

From   Liu Fang's *Kuo shih* 759–60

?
? Wei Shu's *T´ang shu* (to 741)

Court Diary (destroyed 756)

… …

Appendix

Chapter 10.   Su-tsung Basic Annals   pp. 239–64

From Yü Hsiu-lieh's supplement to Liu Fang's *Kuo Shih*
(written between 762–72)

Su-tsung Shih-lu (n.d.)[g]
↑
Court Diary

... ...

Chapter 11.   Tai- tsung Basic Annals   pp. 267–316

From   Ling-hu Huan's *Tai-tsung Shih-lu* (789–805)
↑
Court Diary

... ...

Chapter 12.   Te-tsung Basic Annals A (779–787)   pp. 319–58

From   ┌ *Chien-chung Shih-lu* (for 779–80 only)
       └ *Te-tsung Shih-lu* (810)
↑
Court Diary

... ...

Chapter 13.   Te-tsung Basic Annals B (788–805)   pp. 363–401

From *Te-tsung Shih-lu* (810)
↑
┌ Court Diary
└ Record of Administrative Affairs (796–803 only)

... ...

---

[g]It is unknown whether the *Su-tsung Shih-lu* was written before or after Yü Hsiu-lieh added these basic annals to the *Kuo-shih.*

246

Chapter 14.   Shun-tsung Basic Annals[h]   pp.. 405–10

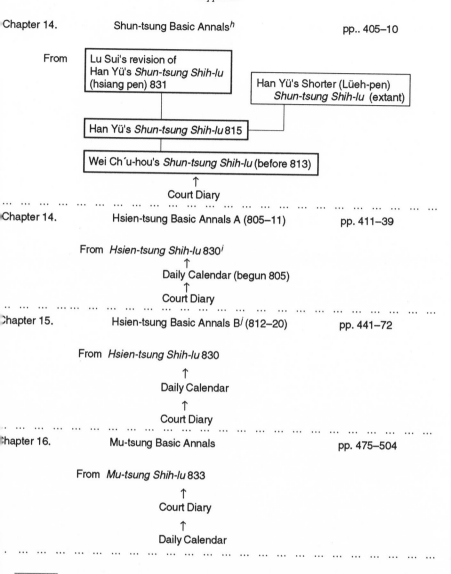

From   Lu Sui's revision of
            Han Yü's *Shun-tsung Shih-lu*
            (hsiang pen) 831

                                    Han Yü's Shorter (Lüeh-pen)
                                    Shun-tsung Shih-lu (extant)

            Han Yü's *Shun-tsung Shih-lu* 815

            Wei Ch´u-hou's *Shun-tsung Shih-lu* (before 813)
                                    ↑
                            Court Diary

… … … … … … … … … … … … … … … … … … … …

Chapter 14.   Hsien-tsung Basic Annals A (805–11)   pp. 411–39

            From *Hsien-tsung Shih-lu* 830[i]
                            ↑
                    Daily Calendar (begun 805)
                            ↑
                    Court Diary

… … … … … … … … … … … … … … … … … … …

Chapter 15.   Hsien-tsung Basic Annals B[j] (812–20)   pp. 441–72

            From *Hsien-tsung Shih-lu* 830
                            ↑
                    Daily Calendar
                            ↑
                    Court Diary

… … … … … … … … … … … … … … … … … …

Chapter 16.   Mu-tsung Basic Annals   pp. 475–504

            From *Mu-tsung Shih-lu* 833
                            ↑
                    Court Diary
                            ↑
                    Daily Calendar

· …

---

[h] Historian's note under the name of Han Yü.
[i] The 833 *Hsien-tsung Shih-lu* was replaced by the *Hou-hsiu Hsien-tsung Shih-lu* in 843,
but was restored as authoritative in 848.
[j] Historian's note under the name of Chiang Hsi.

Chapter 17A.   Ching-tsung Basic Annals   pp. 507–522

From *Ching tsung Shih-lu* 845
↑
Daily Calendar
↑
Court Diary

... ...

Chapter 17A.   Wen-tsung Basic Annals A (827–29)   pp. 522–534

From *Wen-tsung Shih-lu* 854
↑
Daily Calendar
↑
Court Diary

... ...

Chapter 17B.   Wen-tsung Basic Annals B (830–40)   pp. 535–80

From *Wu-tsung Shih-lu* 854
↑
Daily Calendar ←
↑
Court Diary

Record of Administrative Affairs (spasmodic)

... ...

Chapter 18A.   Wu-tsung Basic Annals   pp. 583–611

From *Wu-tsung Shih-lu* (870–4)[k]
↑
Daily Calendar ←
↑
Court Diary

Record of Administrative Affairs (after 843)

... ...

---

[k]Only the first chapter covering the first two months of 840 survived at the time *Chiu T'ang shu* was compiled.

Appendix

Chapter 18B.   Hsiuan-tsung Basic Annals   pp. 613–46

No Veritable Records

From   Daily Calendar ←┐
                     ↑   │
                Court Diary   │
                                │
                Record of Administrative Affairs (at least until 852)
... ...
Chapter 19A.   I-tsung Basic Annals   pp. 649–85

No Veritable Records

From   Daily Calendar (lost by 890)
                     ↑
                Court Diary   (lost by 890)
... ...
Chapter 19B.   Hsi-tsung Basic Annals   pp. 687–733

No Veritable Records

From   Daily Calendar (lost by 890)
                     ↑
                Court Diary   (lost by 890)
... ...
Chapter 20A.   Chao-tsung Basic Annals   pp. 735–83

No Veritable Records

From   ?Daily Calendar
                     ↑
                Court Diary
... ...
Chapter 20B.   Ai-ti Basic Annals   pp. 758–812

No Veritable Records

From   Daily Calendar*/*
                     ↑
                Court Diary
... ...

---

*/*Part survived until the twelfth century.

249

Bibliography

Original sources and works of pre–twentieth century scholarship

An Lu-shan shih-chi 安祿山事蹟. By Yao Ju-neng 姚汝能. *Hsüeh-hai lei-pien* 學海類編. Shanghai: Han-fen lou, 1920.

Chang Yen-kung chi 張燕公集. By Chang Yüeh 張説. Shanghai: Shang-wu yin-shu kuan, *Wan-yu wen-k'u*, 1937.

Ch'ang-an chih 長安志. By Sung Min-ch'iu 宋敏求. *Ching-hsün-t'ang ts'ung-shu* 經訓堂 叢書 (1784 edition). Reprint, Shanghai: T'ung-wen shu-chü, 1887. Reprint (*chüan* 6–10 only) in Hiraoka Takeo 平岡武夫 ed., *Chōan to Rakuyō* 長安と洛陽 (shiryō hen), vol. 6, pp. 89–121. Kyoto: Jimbun kagaku kenkyūsho, *Tōdai kenkyū no shiori*, vol. 6, 1956.

Ch'ang-shih yen-chih 常侍言旨. By Liu Ch'eng 柳珵. In *T'ang-tai ts'ung-shu* 唐代叢書, 1st ser. Pien-shan lou 弁山樓 edition, 1806. Reprint, Taipei: Hsin-hsing shu-chü, 1968.

Chen-kuan cheng yao 貞觀政要. By Wu Ching 吳兢. (1) Variorum edition of Harada Taneshige 原田種成, *Jōgan seiyō teihon* 貞觀政要定本. Tokyo: (mukyūkai) Tōyō bunka kenkyūjo kiyō 3, 1962. (2) Shanghai: Shanghai Ku-chi ch'u-pan she, 1978.

Ch'eng-chih hsüeh-shih yüan chi 承旨學士院記. By Yüan Chen 元稹. *Chih-pu-tsu chai ts'ung-shu*, ser. 13. Reprint, Taipei: Hsing-chung shu-chü, 1964.

Chien-k'ang shih-lu 建康實錄. By Hsü Sung 許嵩. Shanghai: Shanghai Ku-chi ch'u-pan she, *Nan-ching ta-hsüeh ku-tien wen-hsüeh yen-chiu so chuan-k'an*, 1987.

Chih-chai shu-lu chieh-t'i 直齋書錄解題. By Ch'en Chen-sun 陳振孫. Original work lost; reconstructed from *Yung-lo ta-tien* and edited in 1773–82 for inclusion in *Ssu-k'u ch'üan-shu*. Reprinted in *Ssu-k'u ch'üan-shu chen-pen*. *Pieh-chi*, vols. 150–5. Taipei: Shang-wu yin-shu kuan, 1975.

Chih-i chi 摭異記. By Li Chün 李濬. *T'ang-tai ts'ung-shu* 唐代叢書. Ser. 5. Pien-shan lou 弁山樓 edition, 1806. Reprint, Taipei: Hsin-hsing shu-chü, 1968.

Chih-kuan fen-chi 職官分紀. By Sun Feng-chi 孫逢吉. *Ying-yin Wen-yüan ko Ssu-k'u ch'üan shu*, vol. 923. Reprint, Taipei: Shang-wu yin-shu kuan, 1983.

Chin-shih ts'ui-pien 金石萃編. By Wang Ch'ang 王昶, comp. Ching-hsün t'ang 經訓堂 edition, 1805.

250

Chin shu 晉書. By Fang Hsüan-ling 房玄齡 et al., comps. Peking: Chung-hua shu-chü, 1974.

Chiu T'ang shu 舊唐書. By Liu Hsü 劉昫 et al., comps. Peking: Chung-hua shu-chü, 1975.

Chiu T'ang shu i-wen 舊唐書遺文. By Ts'en Chien-kung 岑建功. Appended to Ts'en Chien-kung and Lo Shih-lin 羅士琳, eds., *Chiu T'ang shu chiao-k'an chi* 舊唐書校勘記. Edition of Ting Yüan-fang 定遠方, 1872. Reprint, Taipei: Cheng-chung shu-chü, 1971.

Chiu Wu-tai shih 舊五代史. By Hsüeh Chü-cheng 薛居正 et al., comps. Peking: Chung-hua shu-chü, 1976.

Ch'u-hsüeh chi 初學記. By Hsü Chien 徐堅 et al., comps. 3 vols. Peking: Chung-hua shu-chü, 1962.

[*Ch'in-ting*] *Ch'üan T'ang wen* 欽定全唐文. By Tung Kao 董誥 et al., comps. Preface dated 1814. Reprint, 20 vols. Taipei: I-wen shu-chü, 1966. Reprint, Taipei: Hua-wen shu-chü, 1965.

Ch'üan Tsai-chih wen-chi 權載之文集. By Ch'üan Te-yü 權德輿. *Ssu-pu ts'ung-k'an*, 1st ser. Shanghai: Shang-wu yin-shu kuan, 1936.

Ch'un-ming t'ui-ch'ao lu 春明對朝錄. By Sung Min-ch'iu 宋敏求. *Ts'ung-shu chi-ch'eng*. Shanghai: Shang-wu yin-shu kuan, 1936.

Chün-chai tu-shu chih 郡齋讀書志: title refers to two separate books by Ch'ao Kung-wu 晁公武.

(1) *Yüan-pen* 袁本. Comprising Ch'ao Kung-wu's original *Tu-shu chih* in 4 chapters; Chao Hsi-pien 趙希弁, *Fu-chih* 附志 in 1 chapter (1249); and Chao Hsi-pien, *Hou-chih* 後志 in 2 chapters (1250). Original print published by the prefect of Yüan-chou 袁州 (Kiangsi) in 1249–50, reprinted in *Ssu-pu ts'ung-k'an*, 3rd ser., vols. 48–9. Shanghai: Shang-wu yin-shu kuan, 1936.

(2) *Ch'ü-pen* 衢本. An enlarged version by Ch'ao Kung-wu in twenty chapters. Edited by Yao Ying-chi 姚應績 and first printed in 1249 by the prefect of Ch'ü-chou 衢州 (Chekiang). Manuscript copy with postface by Yu Chün 淤鈞, dated 1249, reprinted in Juan Yüan 阮元, ed., *Wan-wei pieh-tsang* 宛委別藏. Vols. 54–5. Reprint, Taipei: Taiwan Shang-wu yin-shu kuan, 1981.

Ch'ung-hsiu Ch'eng-chih hsüeh-shih pi-chi 重修承旨學士壁記. By Ting Chü-hui 丁居晦. *Chih-pu-tsu chai ts'ung-shu*, ser. 13. Reprint, Taipei: Hsing-chung shu-chü, 1964.

Ch'ung-wen tsung-mu 崇文總目. By Wang Yao-ch'en 王堯臣. Edition in *Ssu-k'u ch'üan-shu chen-pen pieh chi*, vols. 148–9. Taipei: Shang-wu yin-shu kuan, 1975.

Fan-ch'uan wen-chi 樊川文集. By Tu Mu 杜牧. Shanghai: Shanghai ku-chi ch'u-pan she, 1978. Reprint, 1984.

Feng-shih wen-chien chi chiao-chu 封氏聞見記校注. By Feng Yen 封演. Edition of Chao Chen-hsin 趙貞信. Peking: Chung-hua shu-chü, 1958.

Haku-shi monshū 白氏文集. By Po Chü-i 白居易. Variorum edition. Hiraoka Takeo 平岡武夫 and Imai Kiyoshi 今井清. 3 vols. Kyoto: Kyoto Daigaku Jimbun kagaku kenkyūsho, 1971–3.

Han Ch'ang-li chi 韓昌黎集. By Han Yü 韓愈. Shanghai: Shang-wu yin-shu kuan, *Kuo-hsüeh chi-pen ts'ung-shu*, 1937.

Han-lin chih 翰林志. By Li Chao 李肇. *Chih-pu-tsu chai ts'ung-shu*, ser. 13. Reprint, Taipei: Hsing-chung shu-chü, 1964. See translation under Bischoff.

Han-lin hsüeh-shih chi 翰林學士記. By Wei Ch'u-hou 韋處厚. *Chih-pu-tsu chai ts'ung-shu*, ser. 13. Reprint, Taipei: Hsing-chung shu-chü, 1964.

Han-lin hsüeh-shih-yüan chiu-kuei 翰林學士院舊規. By Yang Chü 楊鉅. *Chih-pu-tsu chai ts'ung-shu*, ser. 13. Reprint, Taipei: Hsing-chung shu-chü, 1964.

Han-lin pi-chi 翰林壁記. By Ting Chü-hui 丁居晦. *Shuo-fu*. Wan-wei shan t'ang edition. *chüan* 51. *Shuo-fu san-ch'ung*, 10 vols. Vol. 5, pp. 2345–6. Shanghai: Shanghai ku-chi ch'u-pan she, 1986.

Han-lin yüan ku-shih 翰林院故事. By Wei Chih-i 韋執誼. *Chih-pu-tsu chai tsung shu*, ser. 13. Reprint, Taipei: Hsing-chung shu-chü, 1964.

Han shu 漢書. By Pan Ku 班固. Peking: Chung-hua shu-chü, 1962.

Han-shu i-wen chih 漢書藝文志. By Pan Ku 班固 with Yen Shih-ku 顏師古's commentary and index. Shanghai: Shang-wu yin-shu kuan, 1955.

Ho-nan chih 河南志. Anonymous Yüan author. Edited and reconstructed by Hsü Sung 徐松. 4 *chüan*. *Ou-hsiang ling-shih* 藕香零拾, 1908. Reprinted in Hiraoka Takeo, ed., *Chōan to Rakuyō* (shiryō hen), vol. 6, pp. 123–78. Kyoto: Jimbun kagaku kenkyūsho, *Tōdai kenkyū no shiori*, vol. 6, 1956.

Hou Han shu 後漢書. By Fan Yeh 范曄. Peking: Chung-hua shu chü, 1965.

Hsin T'ang shu 新唐書. By Ou-yang Hsiu 歐陽修, Sung Ch'i 宋祁, et al., comps. Peking: Chung-hua shu-chü, 1975.

Hsin Wu-tai shih 新五代史. By Ou-yang Hsiu 歐陽修. Peking: Chung-hua shu-chü, 1974.

Hsü Tzu-chih t'ung-chien ch'ang-pien 續資治通鑑長編. By Li T'ao 李濤. Peking: Chung-hua shu-chü, 1979.

I-wen lei-chü 藝文類聚. By Ou-yang Hsün 歐陽詢, comp. 2 vols. Peking: Chung-hua shu-chü, 1965.

Jih chih lu 日知錄. By Ku Yen-wu 顧炎武. Edition of Huang Ju-ch'eng 黃汝成, *Jih chih lu chi-shih* 日知錄集釋. Shanghai: Shang-wu yin-shu kuan, *Kuo-hsüeh chi-pen ts'ung-shu*, 1937. Reprinted, Taipei, 1956, 1968.

Kua-ti chih 括地志. By Li T'ai 李泰 et al., comp. Fragments edited and reconstructed by Ho Tz'u-chün 賀次君. *Kua-ti chih chi-chiao* 括地志輯校. Peking: Chung-hua shu-chü, *Chung-kuo ku-tai ti-li tsung-chih ts'ung-k'an*, 1980.

K'un-hsüeh chi-wen 困學紀聞. By Wang Ying-lin 王應麟. 3 vols. Peking: Shang-wu yin-shu kuan, 1935. Reprint, 1959.

Kuo-shih ching-chi chih 國史經籍志. By Chiao Hung 焦竑. 1590. Included in *Ming-shih i-wen chih, p'u-pien, fu-pien*, vol. 2, pp. 783–1194. Peking: Shang-wu yin-shu kuan, 1959.

Li T'ai-po chi 李太白集. By Li Po 李白. Shanghai: Shang-wu yin-shu kuan, *Kuo-hsüeh chi-pen ts'ung-shu*, 1938.

Li Wen-kung chi 李文公集. By Li Ao 李翺. *Ssu-pu ts'ung-k'an*, 1st ser. Shanghai: Shang-wu yin-shu kuan, 1936.

Liang-ching hsin-chi 兩京新記. By Wei Shu 韋述. (1) Original version: *chüan* 3 only (sole surviving section), Japanese (late Heian, or early Kamakura) manuscript preserved in Sonkeikaku Bunko, reprinted in Hiraoka Takeo, ed., *Chōan to Rakyuō* (shiryō hen), vol. 6, pp. 181–96, Kyoto: Jimbun kagaku kenkyūsho, *Tōdai kenkyū no shiori*, vol. 6, 1956. With detailed editorial note, pp. 15–34. (2) Reconstruction (*chi-pen* 輯本) of fragments preserved in quotation, edited by Ts'ao Yüan-chung 曹元忠 (preface 1895), reprinted in *Chōan to Rakuyō*, pp. 199–210.

Liang shu 梁書. By Yao Ssu-lien 姚思廉. Peking: Chung-hua shu-chü, 1973.

Liu Ho-tung chi 柳河東集. By Liu Tsung-yüan 柳宗元. Shanghai: Shang-wu yin-shu kuan, 1958.

Ming-shih i-wen chih, p'u-pien, fu-pien 明史藝文志補編附編. By Chang T'ing-yü 張廷玉 et al., comps. 2 vols. Peking: Shang-wu yin-shu kuan, 1959. Includes, in addition to the bibliographical monograph of *Ming-shih*: (1) the bibliographical chapters of Fu Wei-lin 傅維鱗. *Ming shu* 明書, based on Yang Shih-ch'i 楊士琦. *Wen-yüan ko shu-mu* 文淵閣書目, 1441; (2) the bibliographical section of Wang Ch'i 王圻. *Hsü Wen-hsien t'ung-k'ao* 續文獻通考, 1586; (3) the bibliographical section of the *Ch'in-ting Hsü Wen-hsien t'ung-k'ao* 欽定續文獻通考 compiled in 1747 as a replacement of this; (4) Ch'iao Hung 焦竑, *Kuo-shih ching-chi chih* 國史經籍志, 1590; (5) the supplement to this, Sung Ting-kuo 宋定國 and Hsieh Hsing-ch'an 謝星纏, *Kuo-shih ching-chi chih pu* 國史經籍志補, 1735.

Nan shih 南史. By Li Yen-shou 李延壽. Peking: Chung-hua shu-chü, 1975.

Nien-erh shih cha-chi 廿二史劄記. By Chao I 趙翼. Edited by Tu Wei-yün 杜維運. 2 vols. Taipei: Shih-hsüeh ch'u-pan she, 1974.

Nihon koku genzai sho mokuroku 日本國現在書目錄. By Fujiwara no Sukeyo 藤原佐世. (1) Kariya Ekisai 狩谷棭齋, ed. *Nihon genzai shomoku shōchū kō* 日本現在書目證注稿. *Nihon koten zenshū*. Tokyo: Nihon koten zenshū kankōkai, 1928; also (2) Kohase Keikichi 小長谷惠吉, ed. *Nihonkoku genzai sho mokuroku gaisetsu kō* 日本國現在書目錄解説稿. Tokyo: Komiyayama shoten, 1956. Reprint, 1976; (3) Yajima Genryō 矢島玄亮, ed., *Nihonkoku genzai sho mokuroku: Shūshō to kenkyū* 日本國現在書目錄：集証と研究. Tokyo: Kyūko shoin, 1984.

Nü Lun-yü 女論語. By Sung Jo-chao 宋若昭. Abridgment, 1 *chüan* (originally 10 *chüan*). *Shuo-fu* 説郛. Wan-wei shan t'ang 宛委山堂 edition. *Chüan* 70. In *Shuo-fu san chung* 説郛三種, 10 vols. Vol. 5, pp. 3291–4. Shanghai: Shanghai Ku-chi ch'u-pan she, 1986.

Ou-hsiang ling-shih 藕香零拾. By Miao Ch'üan-sun 繆荃孫. N.p., 1896.

Pei shih 北史. By Li Yen-shou 李延壽. Peking: Chung-hua shu-chü, 1974.

Pei-t'ang shu-ch'ao 北堂書鈔. Complied by Yü Shih-nan 虞世南 and others. Edition of K'ung Kuang-t'ao 孔廣陶, 1888. Photographic reprint, 2 vols. Taipei: Wen-hai ch'u-pan she, 1962.

Po Chü-i chi 白居易集. By Po Chü-i 白居易. 4 vols. Edited by Ku Hsüeh-chi 顧學頡. Peking: Chung-hua shu-chü, *Chung-kuo ku-tien wen-hsüeh chi-pen ts'ung shu*, 1979.

Po K'ung liu-t'ieh 白孔六帖. By Po Chü-i 白居易, comp., supplemented by K'ung Ch'uan 孔傳. Ming (Chia-ching) edition. Reprint, Taipei: Hsin-hsing shu-chü, 1969.

Po-shih liu-tieh shih-lei chi 白氏六帖事類集. By Po Chü-i 白居易, comp. Sung edition. Reprint, Taipei: Hsin-hsing shu-chü, 1969.

[*Shan-t'ang hsien-sheng*] *Ch'ün-shu k'ao-so* 山堂先生群書考索. By Chang Ju-yü 章如愚.

Shen-tu-chai 慎獨齋 edition, 1508. Photographic reprint, 8 vols. Taipei: Hsin-hsing shu-chü, 1969.

Shih-ch'i shih shang-chüeh 十七史商榷. By Wang Ming-sheng 王鳴盛. Shanghai: Shang-wu yin-shu kuan, 1937. Reprint, 1959.

Shih-lin yen-yü 石林燕語. By Yeh Meng-te 葉夢得. With critical notes by Yü-wen Shao-i 宇文紹奕. Peking: Chung-hua shu-chü, *T'ang Sung shih-liao pi-chi ts'ung-k'an*, 1984.

Shih t'ung 史通. By Liu Chih-chi 劉知幾. Cited from P'u Ch'i-lung 浦起龍 and P'u Hsi-ling 浦錫齡, comm. *Shih t'ung t'ung-shih* 史通通釋. Shanghai: Shanghai Ku-chi ch'u-pan she, 2 vols., 1978.

(Ch'in-ting) Ssu-k'u ch'üan-shu tsung-mu t'i-yao 欽定四庫全書總目提要. By Chi Yün 紀昀et al., comps. (1782). Shanghai: Shang-wu yin shu kuan, 1934.

Sui shu 隋書. Wei Cheng 魏徵, Ling-hu Te-fen 令狐德棻, et al., comps. Peking: Chung-hua shu-chü, 1973.

Sui shu ching-chi chih 隋書經籍志, with index. By Ch'ang-sun Wu-chi 長孫無忌 et al., comps. Shanghai: Shang-wu yin-shu kuan, 1955.

Sung-chuang tsa-chi 松窗雜記. By Tu Hsün-ho 杜荀鶴. Also entitled *Sung-chuang tsa-lu* 松窗雜錄. In *T'ang-tai ts'ung-shu* 唐代叢書, ser. 5. Pien-shan lou 弁山樓 edition, 1806. Reprint, Taipei: Hsin-hsing shu-chü, 1968.

Sung-ch'uang tsa-lu 松窗雜錄. By Li Chün 李濬. Peking: Chung-hua shu-chü, *Chung-kuo wen-hsüeh ts'an-k'ao tzu-liao ts'ung-shu*, 1958.

Sung shih 宋史. By T'o-t'o 脱脱 et al., comps. Peking: Chung-hua shu-chü, 1977.

Sung-shih i-wen-chih, pu, fu-pien 宋史藝文志, 補, 附編. By T'o-t'o 脱脱 et al., comps. Shanghai: Shang-wu yin-shu kuan, 1957. Includes, in addition to the bibliographic monograph of *Sung Shih*, (1) Huang Yü-chi 黃虞稷 and Ni Ts'an 倪燦. *Sung shih i-wen-chih pu* 宋史藝文志補, edited by Lu Wen-chao 盧文弨; (2) *Ssu-k'u ch'üeh-shu mu* 四庫闕書目, reconstructed from the *Yung-lo ta-tien* 永樂大典 by Hsü Sung 徐松, 1832; (3) *Pi-shu sheng hsü-pien-tao ssu-k'u ch'üeh-shu mu* 祕書省續編到四庫闕書目, of 1145, critical edition of Yeh Te-hui 葉德輝. Originally published 1903; (4) abbreviated versions of Chao Shih-wei's 趙士煒 reconstructions of fragments of the *Chung-hsing Kuan-ko shu-mu* 中興館閣書目 of 1178; of its continuation *Chung-hsing Kuan-ko hsü shu-mu* 中興館閣續書目 of 1220; and of the bibliographical monographs from the *Chung-hsing ssu-ch'ao kuo-shih* 中興四朝國史 of 1254. The original versions of these reconstructions are listed under Chao Shih-wei.

Ta-T'ang ch'uang-yeh ch'i-chü chu 大唐創業起居注. By Wen Ta-ya 温大雅. Edition in Miao Ch'üan-sun 繆荃孫. *Ou-hsiang ling-shih* 藕香零拾, 1905.

Ta T'ang hsin yü 大唐新語. By Liu Su 劉肅. Edited by Hsü Te-nan 許德楠 and Li Ting-hsia 李鼎霞. Peking: Chung-hua shu-chü, *T'ang Sung shih-liao pi-chi ts'ung-k'an*, 1984.

T'ai-p'ing kuang-chi 太平廣記. By Li Fang 李昉 et al., comps. 5 vols. Peking: Jen-min wen-hsüeh ch'u-pan she, 1959.

T'ai-p'ing yü-lan 太平御覽. By Li Fang 李昉 et al., comps. Reprinted from Sung editions, 4 vols. Peking: Chung-hua shu-chü, 1960.

T'ang hui yao 唐會要. By Wang P'u 王溥. Shanghai: Shang-wu yin-shu kuan, *Kuo-hsüeh chi-pen ts'ung-shu*, 1935. Reprint, Peking: Chung-hua shu-chü,

1955. With occasional reference to an early Ch'ing manuscript copy in Sonkeikaku Bunko.

T'ang kuo shih pu 唐國史. By Li Chao 李肇. Shanghai: Ku-tien wen-hsüeh ch'u-pan she, *Chung-kuo wen-hsüeh ts'an-k'ao tzu-liao ts'ung shu*, 1957.

T'ang liang ching ch'eng fang k'ao 唐兩京城坊攷. By Hsü Sung 徐松. *Lien-yün-i ts'ung-shu* 連筠簃叢書. Edition collated and supplemented by Chang Mu 張穆. 1848. Reprinted in Hiraoka Takeo, ed., *Chōan to Rakuyō* (shiryō hen), vol. 6, pp. 3–74. Kyoto: Jimbun kagaku kenkyūsho, *Tōdai kenkyū no shiori* vol. 6, 1956.

[*Ta*] *T'ang liu-tien* 大唐六典. By Li Lin-fu 李林甫 et al., comps. Edition of Konoe Iehiro 近衞家熙, 1724. Reprint, Taipei: Wen-hai ch'u-pan she, 1962. Reedited with introduction and notes by Hiroike Senkurō 廣池千九郎 and Uchida Tomoō 內田智雄 and published as *Dai Tō rikuten* 大唐六典. Tokyo: Hiroike Gakuen jigyōbu, 1973.

T'ang shu ching-chi i-wen ho chih 唐書經籍藝文合志. By Liu Hsü 劉昫 and Ou-yang Hsiu 歐陽修, comps. With index. Shanghai: Shang-wu yin-shu kuan, 1956.

T'ang ta chao ling chi 唐大詔令集. By Sung Min-ch'iu 宋敏求. Peking: Shang-wu yin-shu kuan, 1959.

T'ang-wen shih-i 唐文拾遺, *T'ang-wen hsü shih-i* 唐文續拾遺. By Lu Hsin-yüan 陸心源, comp. *Ch'ien-yüan Tsung-chi* 潛園總集 edition, with preface of Yü Yüeh 俞樾, 1888. Reprint, Taipei: Wen-hai ch'u-pan she, 1962.

T'ang wen ts'ui 唐文粹. By Yao Hsüan 姚鉉. 1011. With supplement by Kuo Lin 郭麐 *T'ang wen-ts'ui pu-i* 唐文粹補遺. Preface dated 1819. Shanghai: Shang-wu yin-shu kuan, *Wan-yu wen-k'u*, 1937.

T'ang yü lin 唐語林. By Wang Tang 王讜. Edition of Chou Hsün-ch'u 周勛初, *T'ang Yü-lin chiao-cheng* 唐語林校證. 2 vols. Peking: Chung-hua shu-chü, *T'ang Sung shih-liao pi-chi ts'ung-k'an*, 1987.

Teng-k'o chi k'ao 登科記考. By Hsü Sung 徐松. Edition of *Nan-ching Shu-yüan ts'ung-shu* 南菁書院叢書, 1888. Reprint, with supplement *pu-i* 補遺 by Lo Chi-tsu 羅繼祖 and index by Nasu Tomoko 那須和子. 3 vols. Taipei: Ching-sheng wen-wu kung-ying kung-ssu, 1972.

Ti-fan 帝範. By T'ai-tsung 太宗. (1) Edition in four *chüan* with extensive commentary, in *Ying-yin Wen-yüan ko Ssu-k'u ch'üan-shu*. Reprint, Taipei: Shang-wu yin-shu kuan, 1983. (2) Edition in two *chüan* with notes by Lo Chen-yü 羅振玉 in *Tung-fang hsüeh-hai ts'ung-shu* 東方學海叢書, 1924.

Ts'e-fu yüan-kuei 冊府元龜. By Wang Ch'in-jo 王欽若 et al., comps. (1) Edition with preface of Li Ssu-ching 李嗣京, 1642. Photographic reprint, 10 vols. Peking: Chung-hua shu-chü, 1960. (2) Fragmentary Sung editions, reprinted in *Sung-pen Ts'e-fu yüan-kuei* 宋本冊府元龜, 4 vols. Peking: Chung-hua shu-chü, 1989.

Tu Hsün-ho wen chi 杜荀鶴文集. By Tu Hsün-ho 杜荀鶴. Sung, Szechwan edition. Reprint, Shanghai: Shanghai Ku-chi ch'u-pan she, 1980.

Tung-kuan tsou-chi 東觀奏記. By P'ei T'ing-yü 裴廷裕. Shanghai: Shang-wu yin-shu kuan, *Ts'ung-shu chi-ch'eng*, 1937.

Tung tien 通典. By Tu Yu 杜佑. Cited in footnotes from *Shih T'ung* edition. Shanghai: Shang-wu yin-shu kuan, 1935. Reprint, Taipei: Hsin-hsing shu-chü,

1959. With occasional reference also to (1) facsimile reprint of Sung edition in the Kunaichō Shoryōbu, Tokyo, published with introduction by Nagasawa Kikūya 長澤規矩也 and Ozaki Yasu 尾崎康. 10 vols. Tokyo: Kyūko shoen, 1980–1. (2) Photolithographic reprint of an unidentified Ming large-character edition published by Ta-hua shu-chü 大化書局. 2 vols. Taipei, 1978.

Tzu-chih t'ung-chien 資治通鑑. By Ssu-ma Kuang 司馬光. Peking: Ku-chi ch'u-pan she, 1956.

Tzu-chih t'ung-chien k'ao-i 資治通鑑考異. By Ssu-ma Kuang 司馬光. Incorporated as commentary in *Tzu-chih t'ung-chien* Peking: Ku-chi ch'u-pan she, 1956.

Tz'u Liu-shih chiu wen 次柳氏舊聞. By Li Te-yü 李德裕. Also entitled *Ming-huang shih-ch'i shih* 明皇十七事. Edition of Yeh Te-hui 葉德輝 in *T'ang K'ai-yüan hsiao-shuo liu chung* 唐開元小説六種, 1911, and in *Hsi-yüan hsien-sheng ch'üan shu* 郋園先生全書, 1935.

Wei shu 魏書. By Wei Shou 魏收. Peking: Chung-hua shu-chü, 1974.

Wen-hsien t'ung k'ao 文獻通考. By Ma Tuan-lin 馬端臨. *Shih T'ung* 十通 edition. Shanghai: Shang-wu yin-shu kuan, 1935. Reprint, Taipei: Hsin-hsing shu-chü, 1959.

Wen-kuan tz'u-lin 文館辭林. By Hsü Ching-tsung 許敬宗, Liu Po-chuang 劉伯莊, et al., comps. Fragment, 4 *chüan* of an original 1,000, reprinted from Kamakura-period Japanese manuscript. In Hayashi Hitoshi 林衡, ed., *Isson Sōsho* 佚存叢書, ser. 2. Shanghai, 1924, photographic reprint of original edition, 1799–1810.

Wen-yüan ying-hua 文苑英華. By Li Fang 李昉 et al., comps. Ming edition, 1567. Reprint, 6 vols. Peking: Chung-hua shu-chü, 1966.

Wu-tai hui yao 五代會要. By Wang P'u 王溥. Shanghai: Shanghai Ku-chi ch'u-pan she, 1978.

Yeh-ko ts'ung-shu 野客叢書. By Wang Mao 王楙. Peking: Chung-hua shu-chü, *Hsüeh-shu pi-chi ts'ung-k'an*, 1987.

Yen Lu-kung wen chi 顏魯公文集. By Yen Chen-ch'ing 顏真卿. *Ssu-pu ts'ung-k'an*, 1st ser. Shanghai: Shang-wu yin-shu kuan, 1936.

Yü hai 玉海. By Wang Ying-lin 王應麟. Yüan edition, 1337–40. Photographic reprint, 8 vols. Taipei: Hua-wen shu-chü, 1964.

Yüan-ho chün-hsien t'u-chih 元和郡縣圖志. Edited by Li Chi-fu 李吉甫. Edition of Ho Tz'u-chün 賀次君, 2 vols. Peking: Chung-hua shu-chü, *Chung-kuo ku-tai ti-li tsung-chih ts'ung-k'an*, 1983.

Works of modern scholarship

Aoyama Sadao 青山定雄. "Zui Tō yori Sōdai ni itaru Sōshi oyobi Chihōshi ni tsuite 隋唐より宋代に至る總誌及び地方誌に就て." *Tōyō gakuhō* 28, no. 1 (1941): 36–86; 28, no. 2 (1941): 46–97.

Aoyama Sadao 青山定雄. *Tō Sō jidai no kōtsū to chishi, chizu no kenkyū* 唐宋時代の交通と地誌地圖の研究. Tokyo: Yoshikawa kōbunkan, 1963.

Balázs, Stefan (Etienne). "Beiträge zur Wirtschaftsgeschichte der T'ang-Zeit

(618–906)." *Mitteilungen des Seminars für Orientalische Sprachen zu Berlin* 34 (1931): 1–92; 35 (1932): 1–73; 36 (1933): 1–62.

Balázs, Etienne. *Le traité économique du Souei chou.* Leiden: E. J. Brill, 1953.

Balázs, Etienne. *Le traité juridique du Souei chou.* Leiden: E. J. Brill, 1954.

Balázs, Etienne. "L'histoire comme guide de la pratique bureaucratique (Les monographies, les encyclopédies, les receuils de statuts)." In W. G. Beasley and E. G. Pulleyblank, eds., *Historians of China and Japan,* pp. 78–91. London: Oxford University Press, 1961. Translated in Etienne Balázs, *Chinese Civilization and Bureaucracy, Variations on a Theme,* pp. 129–49. New Haven: Yale University Press, 1964.

Balázs, Etienne. *Chinese Civilization and Bureaucracy, Variations on a Theme.* New Haven: Yale University Press, 1964.

Beasley, W. G., and E. G. Pulleyblank, eds. *Historians of China and Japan.* London: Oxford University Press, 1961.

Bielenstein, Hans. "The Census of China during the Period A.D. 2–742." *Bulletin of the Museum of Far Eastern Antiquities* 19 (1947): 125–63.

Bielenstein, Hans. "The Restoration of the Han Dynasty: With Prolegomena on the Historiography of the *Hou Han Shu.*" *Bulletin of the Museum of Far Eastern Antiquities* 26 (1954): 1–210.

Bielenstein, Hans. *The Bureaucracy of Han Times.* Cambridge: Cambridge University Press, 1980.

Bingham, Woodbridge. "Wen Ta-ya: The First Recorder of T'ang History." *Journal of the American Oriental Society* 57 (1937): 368–74.

Biot, Edouard Constant. *Le Tcheou-li; ou, rites des Tcheou.* 3 vols. in 2. Paris: Imprimerie Nationale, 1851.

Bischoff, F. A. *La forêt des pinceaux: Etude sur l'Académie du Han-lin sous la dynastie des T'ang, et traduction du Han-lin tche.* Paris: Presses Universitaires de France, *Bibliothèque de l'Institut des Hautes Etudes Chinoises,* vol. 18, 1963.

Bünger, Karl. *Quellen zur Rechtsgeschichte der T'ang-Zeit.* Peking: The Catholic University, *Monumenta Serica Monograph,* vol. 9, 1946.

Chang Jung-fang 張容芳. *T'ang-tai ti Shih-kuan yü shih-kuan* 唐代的史館與史官. Taipei: Ssu-li Tung Wu ta-hsüeh Chung-kuo hsüeh-shu chu-tso chiang-chu wei-yüan hui 私立東吳大學, 中國學術著作, 1984.

Chang Shun-hui 張舜徽. *Shih-hsüeh san shu p'ing-i* 史學三書平議. Peking: Chung-hua shu-chü, 1983.

Ch'ang Pi-te 昌彼得, Ch'eng Yüan-min 程元敏, Hou Chün-te 侯俊德, and Wang Te-i 王德毅, comps. *Sung jen chuan-chi tzu-liao so-yin* 宋人傳記資料索引. 6 vols. Taipei: Ting-wen shu-chü, 1974–6.

Chao Shih-wei 趙士煒. "*Chung-hsing Kuo-shih* I-wen chih 中興國史藝文志." *Kuo-li P'ei-p'ing t'u-shu kuan kuan-k'an* 6 (1932): 413–36.

Chao Shih-wei 趙士煒, ed. fragments. *Chung-hsing Kuan-ko shu-mu chi-k'ao* 中興館閣書目輯考. Peking: P'ei-p'ing t'u-shu kuan, 1933.

Chao Shih-wei 趙士煒. *Sung Kuo-shih i-wen chih chi-wen* 宋國史藝文志輯文. Peking: Pei-p'ing t'u-shu kuan, *Ku i shu-lu ts'ung-chi* 古佚書錄叢輯, no. 5, 1933.

Chao Shih-wei 趙士煒. "Shih-lu k'ao 實錄考." *Fu-jen Hsüeh-chih* 5, nos. 1–2 (1936): 1–55.

Chavannes, Edouard, and Paul Pelliot. "Un traité Manichéen retrouvé en Chine." *Journal Asiatique*, ser. 10, 18 (1911): 499-617; ser. 11, 1 (1913): 100–99, 261–394.

Ch'en Ch'i-yün. "The Textual Problems of Hsün Yüeh's Writing: The *Han Chi* and the *Shen-chien*." *Monumenta Serica* 27 (1968): 208–32.

Ch'en Kuang-ch'ung 陳光崇. "T'ang shih-lu tsuan-hsiu k'ao 唐實錄纂修考." *Liao-ning Ta-hsüeh hsüeh-pao* 3 (1978): 45–59.

Ch'en Kuang-ch'ung 陳光崇. "Chi wan-T'ang shih-chia Yao K'ang ho Ch'en Yüeh 記晚唐史家姚康和陳岳." *Shih-hsüeh shih yen-chiu*, 1984, no. 2: 51–4.

Cheng Ho-sheng 鄭鶴聲. *Tu Yu nien-p'u* 杜佑年譜. Shanghai; Shang-wu yin-shu kuan, *Chung-kuo shih-hsüeh ts'ung-shu*, 1934.

Cheng Ming 鄭明. "*T'ang hui-yao* ch'u t'an 唐會要初探." Chung-kuo T'ang-shih hui, eds., *Chung-kuo T'ang-shih hui lun-wen chi* 中國唐史會論文集, vol. 3 pp. 167–82. Hsi-an: San-ch'in ch'u-pan she, 1969.

Chiang Fan 蔣凡. "Han Yü yü Wang Shu-wen chi-t'uan ti Yung-chen kai-ke 韓愈與王叔文集團的永貞改革." *Fu-tan hsüeh-pao* 4 (1980): 67–74.

Chin Yü-fu 金毓黻. "T'ang Sung shih-tai she kuan hsiu-shih chih-tu k'ao 唐宋時代設官修史制度考." *Kuo-shih-kuan kuan-k'an* 1, no. 2 (1948): 6–18.

Chin Yü-fu 金毓黻. *Chung-kuo shih-hsüeh shih* 中國史學史. Chungking, 1944. Revised edition, Peking: Chung-hua shu-chü, 1962.

Chou Shao-ch'uan 周少川. "*Hsin T'ang-shu* I-wen-chih tsai shih-chih mu-lu shang ti kung-hsien 新唐書藝文志在史志目錄上的貢獻." *Shih-hsüeh shih yen-chiu*, 1986, no. 2: 35–8.

Chu Hsi-tsu 朱希祖. "Han Shih-erh shih chu-chi k'ao 漢十二世著紀考." *Kuo-hsüeh chi-k'an* 2, no. 3 (1930): 397–409.

Chu Hsi-tsu 朱希祖. "Han, T'ang, Sung *Ch'i-chü chu* k'ao 漢唐宋起居注考." *Kuo-hsüeh chi-k'an* 2, no. 4 (1930): 629–40.

Chü Lin-tung 衢林東. *T'ang-tai shih-hsüeh lun kao* 唐代史學論稿. Peking: Pei-ching shih-fan ta hsüeh ch'u-pan she, 1989.

Couvreur, Seraphim. *Li Ki ou mémoires sur les bienséances et les cérémonies*. 2 vols. Ho-kien fu, 1913. Reprint, Paris: Cathasia, 1951.

Couvreur, Seraphim. *Tch'ouen-ts'iou et Tso tchouan*; *La chronique de la principauté de Lou*. 3 vols. Ho-kien-fou, 1914. Reprint, Paris: Cathasia, 1951.

Dull, Jack L. "Han Yü: A Problem in T'ang Dynasty Historiography." In *Proceedings of the Second Conference of Historians of Asia*, pp. 71–99. Taipei: International Association of Historians of Asia, 1964.

Edwards, E. D. *Chinese Prose Literature of the T'ang Period A.D. 618–906*. 2 vols. London: Arthur Probsthain, 1937–8.

Franke, Herbert. "Some Remarks on the Interpretation of Chinese Dynastic Histories." *Oriens* 3 (1950): 113–22.

Frankel, Hans. "T'ang Literati: A Composite Biography." In Arthur F. Wright and Denis C. Twitchett, eds., *Confucian Personalities*, pp. 65–83. Stanford: Stanford University Press, 1962.

Fu Chen-lun 傅振倫. *Liu Chih-chi nien-p'u* 劉知幾年譜. Shanghai: Shang-wu yin-shu kuan, 1935. Reprint, 1956.

Fu Hsüan-tsung 傅璇琮, Chang Ch'en-shih 張忱石, and Hsü I-min 許逸民 , eds.

T'ang Wu-tai jen-wu chuan-chi tzu-liao tsung-ho so-yin 唐五代人物傳記資料綜合索引. Peking: Chung-hua shu-chü, 1982.

Fujita Junko 藤田純子. "*Kyū Tō sho* no seiritsu ni tsuite 舊唐書の成立について." *Shisō* 27 (1969): 50–9.

Fujita Junko 藤田純子. "Tōdai no shigaku – zendaishi shūsen to Kokushi hensan no aida 唐代の史學 – 前代史修撰と國史編纂の間." *Shisō* 33 (1975): 65–71.

Fukui Shigemasa 福井重雅. "*Dai Tō sōgyō kikyochū* kō 大唐創業起居注考." *Shikan* 63 (1961): 82–94.

Fukui Shigemasa 福井重雅. "*Kyū Tō-sho*: sono sohon no kenkyū josetsu 舊唐書その祖本の研究序説." In Waseda daigaku bungakubu Tōyō kenkyūshitsu, eds., *Chūgoku seishi no kisoteki kenkyū* 中國正史の基礎的研究, pp. 241–65. Tokyo: Waseda Daigaku shuppanbu, 1984.

Funakoshi Taiji 船越大次. *Sō Haku Zoku Tsūten shūhon fu kaidai* 宋白續通典輯本附解題. Tokyo: Kyūko shoin, 1985.

Gardner, Charles S. *Chinese Traditional Historiography*. Cambridge, Mass.: Harvard University Press, 1938.

Giles, Lionel. *Descriptive Catalogue of the Chinese Manuscripts from Tun-huang in the British Museum*. London: British Museum, 1957.

Guisso, R. W. L. *Wu Tse-t'ien and the Politics of Legitimation in T'ang China*. Bellingham, Wash.: Western Washington University Press, 1978.

Haeger, John W. "The Significance of Confusion: The Origins of the *T'ai-p'ing yü-lan*." *Journal of the American Oriental Society* 88 (1968): 401–10.

Hanabusa Hideki 花房英樹. "*Bun'en eiga* no hensan 文苑英華の編纂." *Tōhō gakuhō* (*Kyoto*) 19 (1950): 116–35.

Hanabusa Hideki. "*Kai-yō* ni tsuite 會要について." *Shinagaku kenkyū*, special issue 11 (1954): 4–11.

Harada Taneshige 原田種成. *Jōgan seiyō no kenkyū* 貞觀政要の研究. Tokyo: Yoshikawa kōbunkan, 1968.

Hartman, Charles. *Han Yü and the T'ang Search for Unity*. Princeton: Princeton University Press, 1986.

Hino Kaisaburō 日野開三郎. "Tō Jōgan jūsan nen no kokō-tōkei no chiiki-teki kōsatsu 唐貞觀十三年の户口統計の地域的考察." *Tōyō shigaku* 24 (1961): 1–24.

Hino Kaisaburō. "Government Monopoly on Salt in T'ang in the Period before the Enforcement of the *Liang-shui fa*." *Memoirs of the Research Department of the Tōyō Bunko* 22 (1963): 1–55.

Hiraoka Takeo 平岡武夫, ed. *Chōan to Rakuyō* 長安と洛陽. Kyoto: Kyoto daigaku Jimbun kagaku kenkyūsho, *Tōdai kenkyū no shiori* 唐代研究のしおり, vols. 6–8, 1956.

Hiraoka Takeo 平岡武夫, Ichihara Kōkichi 市原亨吉, and Imai Kiyoshi 今井清. *Tōdai no sanbun sakuhin* 唐代の散文索引. Kyoto: Jimbun kagaku kenkyūsho, *Tōdai kenkyū no shiori*, vol. 10. 1960.

Hsü Ling-yün 許凌云 and Wang Hung-chün 王洪軍. "Chu Ching-tse ti shih-hsüeh ssu-hsiang 朱敬則的史學思想." *Shih-hsüeh shih yen-chiu*, 1987, no. 4: 47–52.

Hulsewé, A. F. P. "Notes on the Historiography of the Han Period." In W. G. Beasley and E. G. Pulleyblank, eds., *Historians of China and Japan*. London: Oxford University Press, 1961.

Hung, William (Hung Yeh 洪業). "The T'ang Bureau of Historiography before 708." *Harvard Journal of Asiatic Studies* 23 (1960–1): 93–107.

Hung, William. "A T'ang Historiographer's Letter of Resignation." *Harvard Journal of Asiatic Studies* 29 (1969): 5–52.

Ikeda On 池田温. "Sei Tō no Shūken'in 盛唐の集賢院." *Hokkaidō Daigaku Bungakubu kiyō* 19, no. 2 (1971): 47–98.

Inaba Ichirō 稻葉一郎. "*Junsō Jitsuroku* kō 順宗實錄考." *Ritsumeikan bungaku* 280 (1968): 1–42.

Kanai Yukitada 金井之忠. *Tōdai no shigaku shisō* 唐代の史學思想. Tokyo: Kōbundō, 1940.

Ke Chao-kuang 葛兆光. "Tu Yu yü chung-T'ang shih-hsüeh 杜佑與中唐史學." *Shih-hsüeh shih yen-chiu*, 1981, no. 1: 9–23.

Kishibe Shigeo 岸邊成雄. *Tōdai ongaku no rekishiteki kenkyū* 唐代音樂の歷史的研究. 2 vols. Tokyo: Tokyo Daigaku shuppankai, 1960–1.

Koga Noboru 古賀登. "*Shin Tō sho' shokkashi' naigai kan* 新唐書食貨志內外看." In Waseda daigaku bungakubu Tōyōshi kenkyūshitsu, eds., *Chūgoku seishi no kisoteki kenkyū* 中國正史の基礎の研究, pp. 267–86. Tokyo: Waseda Daigaku shuppanbu, 1984.

Kramers, R. P. "Conservatism and the Transmission of the Confucian Canon: A T'ang Scholar's Complaint." *Journal of Oriental Studies* 2, no. 1 (1955): 119–32.

Kuo Po-kung 郭伯恭. *Sung ssu ta shu k'ao* 宋四大書考. Shanghai: Shang-wu yin-shu kuan, 1937. Reprint, Taipei: Shang-wu yin-shu kuan, 1967.

Legge, James. *The Li Ki, Book of Rites*. Oxford: Oxford University Press, *The Sacred Books of the East*, vols. 27–28, 1885.

Legge, James. *The Chinese Classics*, Vol. 5, *The Ch'un-ts'ew with the Tso Chuen*. Hong Kong and London: Trübner, 1872. 2d. rev. ed., Oxford: Oxford University Press, 1893. Reprint, Hong Kong: Hong Kong University Press, 1960.

Levy, Howard S. *Biography of An Lu-shan*. Berkeley and Los Angeles: University of California, *Chinese Dynastic Histories Translation*, no. 8, 1960.

Lewis, Winston George. "The *Cheng-kuan Cheng-yao*: A Source for the Study of Early T'ang Government." Master's thesis, University of Hong Kong, 1962.

Li Chih-t'ing 李志庭. "Li Chi-fu yü *Yüan-ho chün-hsien chih* 李吉甫與元和郡縣志." *Shih-hsüeh shih yen-chiu*, 1984, no. 2: 24–31.

Li Tsung-tung 李宗侗. *Chung-kuo shih-hsüeh shih* 中國史學史. Taipei: Chung-kuo wen-hua hsüeh-yüan ch'u-pan pu, 1953. Reprint, 1979.

Li Tsung-tung. *Shih-hsüeh kai-yao* 史學概要. Taipei: Cheng-chung shu-chü, 1968.

Liu Chien-ming 劉健明. "Lun Pei-men hsüeh-shih 論北門學士." In Chung-kuo T'ang-shih-hsüeh hui, eds., *Chung-kuo T'ang-shih-hui lun-wen chi* 中國唐史會論文集, pp. 205–18. Hsi-an: San-chin ch'u-pan she, 1989.

Liu Nai-ho 劉乃和, ed. *Ts'e-fu yüan-kuei hsin-t'an* 冊府元龜新探. Cheng-chou: Chung-chou shu-hua she, *Chung-kuo ku-tai shih-hsüeh ming-chu yen-chiu*, vol. 1, 1983.

Liu Po-chi 劉伯驥. *T'ang-tai cheng-chiao shih* 唐代政教史. Taipei: Tai-wan Chung-hua shu-chü, 1954. Reprint, 1974.

Lo Hsiang-lin 羅香林. "T'ang shu yüan-liu k'ao 唐書源流考." *Kuo-li Chung-shan Ta-hsüeh Wen-shih hsüeh Yen-chiu so yüeh-k'an* 2, no. 5 (1934): 53–114.

Lo Hsiang-lin 羅香林. "*Ta T'ang ch'uang-yeh ch'i-chü chu* k'ao-cheng 大唐創業起居注考證." In *T'ang-tai wen-hua shih* 唐代文化史, pp. 1–28. Taipei: Shang-wu yin-shu kuan, 1955.

Lo Lien-t'ien 羅聯添. *Han Yü yen-chiu* 韓愈研究. Taipei: T'ai-wan Hsüeh-sheng shu-chü, 1977.

McMullen, David. *State and Scholars in T'ang China.* Cambridge: Cambridge University Press, 1988.

McMullen, David. "The Death of Chou Li-chen: Imperially Ordered Suicide, or Natural Causes?" *Asia Major*, 3d. ser., 2 (1989): 23–82.

Mao Han-kuang 毛漢光 and Lu Chien-jung 盧建榮, eds. *T'ang-tai mu-chih-ming hui-pien fu k'ao* 唐代墓誌銘彙編附考. Vol. 1, 1984 (ongoing series). Taipei: Chung-yang Yen-chiu so, 1984.

Naitō Kenkichi 內藤乾吉. "Tō rikuten no kōyō ni tsuite 唐六典の行用に就いて." *Tōhō gakuhō (Kyoto)* 7 (1938): 103–34. Reprinted in the author's *Chūgoku hōseishi kōshō* 中國法制考證, pp. 64–89. Tokyo: Yuhikaku, 1963.

Naitō Torajirō 內藤虎次郎. "Ko Gi-kō nen fu 賈魏公年譜." In *Ogawa Hakase kanreki kinen shigaku chirigaku ronsō* 小川博士還曆記念史學地理學論叢, pp. 941–60. Tokyo: Kōbundō, 1930. Reprinted in his collected works, *Naitō Konan zenshū*, vol. 7, pp. 599–614. Tokyo: Chikuma shobō, 1970.

Naitō Torajirō 內藤虎次郎. "Ni-ts'e i-tao 擬策一道." In *Kanō kyōju kanreki kinen Shinagaku ronsō* 狩野教授還曆記念支那學論叢, pp. 5–8. Tokyo: Kōbundō, 1930.

Naitō Torajirō. *Shina shigaku shi* 支那史學史. Tokyo: Kōbundō, 1948.

Needham, Joseph. *Clerks and Craftsmen in China and the West.* Cambridge: Cambridge University Press, 1970.

Niida Noboru 仁井田陞. *Tōryō shūi* 唐令拾遺. Tokyo: Tōhōbunka gakuin Tōkyo kenkyūjo, 1933. Reprint, Tokyo: Tōkyo Daigaku shuppankai, 1964.

Niu Chih-kung. "Kuan yü *Ta-T'ang ch'uang-yeh ch'i-chü chu* chung ti chi-ko wen-t'i 關于大唐創業起居注中的幾個問題." In Chung-kuo T'ang-shih yen-chiu hui, eds., *T'ang-shih yen-chiu hui lun-wen chi* 唐史研究會論文集. Hsi-an: Shan-hsi Jen-min ch'u-pan she, 1983.

Niu Chih-kung 牛致功. "Wen Ta-ya yü *Ta-T'ang ch'uang-yeh ch'i-chü chu* 溫大雅與大唐創業起居注." *Shih-hsüeh shih yen-chiu*, 1983, no. 1: 54–8.

Niu Chih-kung. "Yu kung yü T'ang-tai shih-hsüeh ti Wei Shu 有功于唐代史學的韋述." *Shih-hsüeh shih yen-chiu*, 1986, no. 2: 51–3.

Niu Chih-kung. "Liu Fang chi ch'i shih-hsüeh 柳芳及其史學." In Shih Nien-hai 史念海, ed., *T'ang shih lun-ts'ung* 唐史論叢, vol. 2, pp. 246–60. Hsi-an: Shan-hsi Jen-min ch'u-pan she, 1987.

Niu Chih-kung. *T'ang-tai ti shih-hsüeh yü "T'ung chien"* 唐代的史學與通鑑. Hsi-an: Shan-hsi shih-fan ta-hsüeh ch'u-pan she, 1989.

Olbricht, Peter. "Die Biographie in China." *Saeculum* 8 (1957): 224–35.

Ota Shōjirō. "Tōreki ni tsuite 唐曆について." In *Yamada Takao tsuioku Shigaku Gogaku ronshū*, pp. 99–128. Tokyo: 1963.

Ozaki Yasu 尾崎康. "Sō Gen kan ryō Tō-sho oyobi Godai-shiki ni tsuite 宋元刊兩唐書および五代史記について." *Shidō Bunko ronshū* 21 (1985): 121–50.

Pulleyblank, E. G. "The *Tzyjyh Tongjiann Kaoyih* and the Sources for the History of the Period 730–763." *Bulletin of the School of Oriental and African Studies* 13 (1950): 448–73.

Pulleyblank, E. G. "The *Shun-tsung Shih-lu.*" *Bulletin of the School of Oriental and African Studies* 19 (1957): 336–44.

Pulleyblank, E. G. "Neo-Confucianism and Neo-Legalism in T'ang Intellectual Life, 755–805." In Arthur F. Wright, ed., *The Confucian Persuasion*, pp. 77–114. Stanford: Stanford University Press, 1960.

Pulleyblank, E. G. "Chinese Historical Criticism: Liu Chih-chi and Ssu-ma Kuang." In W. G. Beasley and E. G. Pulleyblank, eds., *Historians of China and Japan*, pp. 135–66. London: Oxford University Press, 1961.

Pulleyblank, E. G. "Registration of Population in China in the Sui and T'ang Periods." *Journal of Economic and Social History of the Orient* 4 (1961): 289–301.

Rotours, Robert des. *Le traité des examens: Traduit de la nouvelle histoire des T'ang (Chaps. XLIV, XLV)*. Paris: Ernest Leroux, *Bibliothèque de l'Institut des Hautes Etudes Chinoises*, vol. 2. 1932.

Rotours, Robert des. *Traité des fonctionnaires et traité de l'armée: Traduits de la nouvelle histoire des T'ang (Chaps. XLVI–L)*. 2 vols. Leiden: E. J. Brill, *Bibliothèque de l'Institut des Hautes Etudes Chinoises*, vol. 6, 1947–8.

Rotours, Robert des. *Histoire de Ngan Lou-chan (Ngan Lou-chan Che Tsi)*. Paris: Presses Universitaires de France, *Bibliothèque de l'Institut des Hautes Etudes Chinoises*, vol. 18, 1962.

Rotours, Robert des. *Les inscriptions funeraires de Ts'ouei Mien (673–739), de sa femme née Wang (685–734) et de Ts'ouei Yeou-fou (721–780)*. Paris: Adrien-Maisonneuve, *Publications de l'Ecole Française d'Extrême-Orient*, vol. 49, 1975.

Rotours, Robert des. "Le T'ang Lieou tien décrit-il exactement les institutions en usage sous la dynastie des T'ang?" *Journal Asiatique* 263 (1975): 183–201.

Shimada Tadao. "Zai Taihoku Kokuritsu Chūō Toshokan Shōhon *Tōkaiyō* ni tsuite 在臺北國立中央圖書館抄本唐會要に就いて." In *Takigawa Masajirō Hakase Bei ju kinen ronshū; Ritsuryōsei no shomondai*. Tokyo: 1984.

Solomon, Bernard S. *The Veritable Record of the T'ang Emperor Shun-tsung (February 28, 805 – August 31, 805) Han Yü's Shun-tsung Shih Lu*. Translated with introduction and notes. Cambridge, Mass.: Harvard University Press, 1955.

Somers, Robert. "The Historiography of the T'ang Founding." Paper presented to the Yale Seminar on Chinese and Comparative Historiography, 1971.

Sun Kuo-t'ung 孫國棟. *T'ang-t'ai chung-yang chung-yao wen-kuan ch'ien-chuan tu-ching yen-chiu* 唐代中央重要文官遷轉途徑研究. Hong Kong: Lung-men shu-tien, 1978.

Sung Ta-ch'uan 宋大川. "*Ta T'ang ch'uang-yeh ch'i-chü chu* ch'eng yü ho shih 大唐創業起居注成于何時?" *Shih-hsüeh shih yen-chiu*, 1985, no. 4: 57–60.

Suzuki Shun 鈴木俊. "*Kyū Tō jo* shokkashi no shiryō-keitō ni tsuite 舊唐書食貨志の史料系統に就と." *Shien (Kyūshū)* 45 (1951): 77–84.

Tamai Zehaku 玉井是博. "*Dai Tō Rikuten* oyobi *Tsūten* no Sō kampon ni tsuite." *Shinagaku* 7, no. 2 (1934): 61–79; 7, no. 3 (1934): 83–103. Reprinted in the author's *Shina shakai keizai shi kenkyū* 支那社會經濟史研究, pp. 429–61. Tokyo: Iwanami shoten, 1943.

Tamai Zehaku. "Tō no Jitsuroku senshū ni kansuru ichi kōsatsu 唐の實錄撰修に關する一考察." *Keijō teidai shigakkai hō* 8 (1935). Reprinted in his *Shina shakai keizai shi kenkyū* 支那社會經濟史研究, pp. 415–28. Tokyo: Iwanami Shoten, 1943.

T'an Ying-hua 潭英華. "Lüeh lun *Hsin T'ang-shu* shih-huo chih ti pien-tsuan fang-fa ho shih-liao chieh-chih 略論新唐書食貨志的編纂方法和史料價值." *Shih-hsüeh shih yen-chiu*, 1983, no. 1: 59–68.

T'ang Chung 湯中. *Sung Hui-yao yen-chiu* 宋會要研究. Shanghai: Shang-wu yin-shu kuan, 1932.

Taniguchi Akio 谷口明夫. "*Kyū Tō sho* to *Shiji Tsugan kōi* hikareru *Tōreki* ni tsuite no ichi shitan 舊唐書と資治通鑑考異所引唐曆についての一試探." *Kagoshima joshi tanki daigaku kiyō* 15 (1980): 85–90.

Tjan Tjoe Som. *Po hu t'ung* 白虎通. 2 vols. Leiden: E. J. Brill, 1949, 1952.

Toyama Gunji 外山軍治. *Sokuten Bukō* 則天武后. Tokyo: Chūō kōronsha, *Chūkō shinsho* 中公新書, vol. 99, 1966.

Ts'en Chung-mien 岑仲勉. *Lang-kuan shih-chu t'i-ming hsin k'ao-ting* 郎官石柱題名新考訂. Shanghai: Shang-hai ku-chi ch'u-pan she, 1984.

Tseng I-fen 曾貽芬. "Lun *T'ung-tien* tzu chu 論通典自注." *Shih-hsüeh shih yen-chiu*, 1985, no. 3: 1–10.

Twitchett, Denis C. "The Derivation of the Text of the *Shih-huo Chih* of the *Chiu T'ang-shu*." *Journal of Oriental Studies* 3, no. 1 (1956): 48–62.

Twitchett, Denis C. "Chinese Biographical Writing." In W. G. Beasley and E. G. Pulleyblank, eds., *Historians of China and Japan*, pp. 95–114. London: Oxford University Press, 1961.

Twitchett, Denis C. "Problems of Chinese Biography." In Arthur F. Wright and Denis C. Twitchett, eds., *Confucian Personalities*, pp. 24–39. Stanford: Stanford University Press, 1962.

Twitchett, Denis C. *Financial Administration Under the T'ang Dynasty*. Cambridge: Cambridge University Press, 1963. 2nd rev. ed., 1970.

Twitchett, Denis C. "Chinese Social History from the Seventh to the Tenth Centuries: The Tunhuang Documents and Their Implications." *Past and Present* 35 (1966): 28–53.

Twitchett, Denis C. "Liu Fang, a Forgotten T'ang Historian." Paper presented to the Yale Seminar on Chinese and Comparative Historiography, 1970.

Twitchett, Denis C. "Some Notes on the Compilation of the T'ang Dynastic Record." Paper presented to the Yale Seminar on Chinese and Comparative Historiography, 1971.

Twitchett, Denis C. "The Composition of the T'ang Ruling Class: New Evidence from Tun-huang." In Arthur F. Wright and Denis C. Twitchett, eds., *Perspectives on the T'ang*, pp. 47–85. New Haven: Yale University Press, 1973.

Twitchett, Denis C., ed. *Cambridge History of China*, Vol. 3, *Sui and T'ang China, 589–906*, Part 1. Cambridge: Cambridge University Press, 1979.

Twitchett, Denis C. "The Inner Palace Diary (Nei ch'i-chü chu)." *T'ang Studies* 4 (1986): 1–9.

Twitchett, Denis C. "A Note on the 'Monograph on Music' in *Chiu T'ang shu*." *Asia Major*, 3rd ser., 3, no. 1 (1990): 51–62.

Twitchett, Denis C., and Howard L. Goodman. *A Handbook for T'ang History*. 2 vols. Princeton: Princeton Linguistics Project, 1986.

Uematsu Yasukazu 末松保和. *"Tōreki to Tōroku* 唐暦と唐録." In *Iwai Hakase koki kinen Denseki ronshū* 岩井博士古稀記念典籍論集, pp. 284–90. Tokyo: Daian, for Iwai Hakase koki kinen jigyōkai, 1961.

Van der Loon, Piet. *Taoist Books in the Libraries of the Sung Period*. London: Ithaca Press, *Oxford Oriental Institute Monographs*, vol. 7, 1984.

Waley, Arthur. *The Analects of Confucius*. London: Allen and Unwin, 1937.

Waley, Arthur. *The Book of Songs*. London: Allen and Unwin, 1938.

Wang Chung-lo 王仲犖. *Pei-Chou Liu-tien* 北周六典. 2 vols. Peking: Chung-hua shu-chü, 1979.

Wang Ch'ung-min 王重民. *Tun-huang ku-chi hsü-lu* 敦煌古籍敍録.
Peking: Shang-wu yin-shu kuan, 1958.

Wang Gungwu. "The *Chiu Wu-tai Shih* and History Writing during the Five Dynasties." *Asia Major*, n.s., 6, no. 1 (1957): 1–22.

Wang Yü-ch'üan. "An Outline of Central Government of the Former Han Dynasty." *Harvard Journal of Asiatic Studies* 12 (1949): 134–87.

Wang Yün-hai 王雲海. *Sung Hui-yao chi-kao k'ao-chiao* 宋會要輯稿考校. Shanghai: Shanghai Ku-chi ch'u-pan she, 1986.

Watson, Burton. *Ssu-ma Ch'ien, Grand Historian of China*. New York: Columbia University Press, 1958.

Wechsler, Howard J. *Mirror to the Son of Heaven: Wei Cheng at the Court of T'ang T'ai-tsung*. New Haven: Yale University Press, 1974.

Wechsler, Howard J. *Offerings of Jade and Silk: Ritual and Symbol in the Legitimation of the T'ang Dynasty*. New Haven: Yale University Press, 1985.

Wright, Arthur F., ed. *The Confucian Persuasion*. Stanford: Stanford University Press, 1960.

Wright, Arthur F., and Denis C. Twitchett, eds. *Confucian Personalities*. Stanford: Stanford University Press, 1962.

Wright, Arthur F., and Denis C. Twitchett, eds. *Perspectives on the T'ang*. New Haven: Yale University Press, 1973.

Yamamoto Tatsuro, Ikeda On, and Okano Makoto, eds. *Tun-huang and Turfan Documents Concerning Social and Economic History*, Vol. 1, *Legal Texts*. A. Introduction and Texts. B. Plates. Tokyo: The Tōyō bunko, 1980, 1978.

Yang, L. S. (Lien-sheng). "The Organization of Chinese Official Historiography: Principles and Methods of the Standard Histories from T'ang through the Ming Dynasty." In W. G. Beasley and E. G. Pulleyblank, eds., *Historians of China and Japan*, pp. 44–59. London: Oxford University Press, 1961.

Yeh Ch'ing-p'ing 葉慶炳. "Yu kuan *T'ai-p'ing kuang-chi* ti chi-ko wen-t'i 有關太平廣記的幾個問題." In K'o Ch'ing-ming 柯慶明 and Lin Ming-te 林明德, eds., *Chung-kuo ku-tien wen-hsüeh yen-chiu ts'ung-k'an: Hsiao-shuo chih pu* 中國古典文學研究叢刊：小說之部, pp. 11–44. Taipei: Ch'ü-liu t'u-shu kung-ssu, 1977.

Yen Keng-wang 嚴耕望. "Lüeh lun *T'ang Liu-tien* chih hsing-chih yü shih-hsing wen-t'i 略論唐六典之性質與施行問題." *Chung-yang yen-chiu yüan, Li-shih Yü-yen yen-chiu so chi-k'an* 24 (1953): 69–76.

Yen-Keng-wang 嚴耕望. *T'ang P'u Shang Ch'eng Lang piao* 唐僕尚丞郎表. 4 vols.

Taipei: Academia Sinica, *Chung-yang yen-chiu yüan, Li-shih Yü-yen yen-chiu so ch'uan-k'an*, vol. 36, 1956.

Lost works by Sui, T'ang, and Sung authors mentioned in the text and footnotes

Ai-ti Shih-lu 愛帝實錄. 8 *chüan* (1045). By Sung Min-ch'iu 宋敏求.

Ch'ang-shih yen-chih 常侍言旨. 1 *chüan*. By Liu Ch'eng 柳珵. Survives only in truncated form; see first section of bibliography.

Chao-tsung Shih-lu 昭宗實錄. 30 *chüan* (1045). By Sung Min-ch'iu 宋敏求.

Chen-kuan Shih-lu. 貞觀實錄. 40 *chüan* (654). By Chang-sun Wu-chi 長孫無忌, dir., and Ku Yin 顧胤, comp.

Chen-yüan Yü-fu Ch'ün-shu hsin lu 貞元御府群書新錄. By Ch'en Ching 陳京.

Ch'en shih 陳史. 5 *chüan*. By Wu Ching 吳兢.

Cheng tien 政典. 35 *chüan*. By Liu Chih 劉秩.

Cheng-yüan li 正元曆. Also entitled *Chen-yüan li* 貞元曆. Calendar. (783). By Hsü Ch'eng-ssu 徐承嗣.

Chi-hsien chu-chi 集賢注記. 3 *chüan*. By Wei Shu 韋述.

Chi-hsien shu-mu 集賢書目. 1 *chüan*. By Wei Shu 韋述.

Chi tien 稽典. 150 *chüan*. By T'ang Ying 唐穎.

Ch'i shih 齊史. 10 *chüan*. By Wu Ching 吳兢.

Chiang-shih jih-li 蔣氏日曆. 1 *chüan*. By Chiang I 蔣乂.

Chien-chung Shih-lu 建中實錄. 10 *chüan* (781). By Shen Chi-chi 沈既濟.

[Ch'ien-ling] Shu sheng chi 乾陵述聖記. 1 *chüan*. By Wu Tse-t'ien 武則天.

Chih-ko chi 止戈記. 7 *chüan*. By Liu Chih 劉秩.

Chih-tao chi 治道集. 10 *chüan*. Also entitled *Li-tao chi* 理道集. By Li Wen-po 李文博.

Chih-te hsin-i 至德新儀. 12 *chüan*. By Liu Chih 劉秩.

Chih-te li 至德曆. Calendar (758). By Han Ying 韓穎.

Chih-yao 指要. 3 *chüan*. By Liu Chih 劉秩.

Chin Ch'i-chü chu 晉起居注. 317 *chüan*. By Liu Tao-hui 劉道會.

Chin Ch'un-ch'iu lüeh 晉春秋略. 20 *chüan*. By Tu Yen-yeh 杜延業 (also written as Tu Kuang-yeh 杜光業).

Chin Kao-tsu Shih-lu 晉高祖實錄. 30 *chüan* (950–1). By Chia Wei 賈緯 et al., comps.

Chin-shang Shih-lu 今上實錄. 20 *chüan* (or 13 *chüan*). By T'ang Ying 唐穎, edited by Chang Yüeh 張説.

Chin-shang Shih-lu 今上實錄. 20 *chüan* (643). By Fang Hsüan-ling 房玄齡, dir., and Ching Po 敬播, comp.

Chin-shang wang-yeh chi 今上王業記. 6 *chüan*. By Wen Ta-ya 溫大雅.

Chin Shao-ti Shih-lu 晉少帝實錄. 20 *chüan* (950–1). By Chia Wei 賈緯 et al., comps.

Ch'in-fu shih-pa hsüeh-shih 秦府十八學士. By Chiang I 蔣乂.

Ching-lung li 景龍曆. Calendar (707–10). By Nan-kung Yüeh 南宮説.

Ching-tsung Shih-lu 敬宗實錄. 10 *chüan* (845). By Li Jang-i 李讓夷, dir., and Ch'en Shang 陳商 and Cheng Ya 鄭亞, comps.

Chou shih 周史. 10 *chüan*. By Wu Ching 吳兢.

Chou T'ai-tsu Shih-lu 周太祖實錄. 30 *chüan* (957–8). By Chang Chao 張昭, Yin Cho 尹拙, et al., comps.

Chu-chia k'o-mu chi 諸家科目記. 13 *chüan*. By Cheng Hao 鄭顥.

Chuang-tsung lieh-chuan 莊宗列傳. 30 *chüan* (934). Also entitled [*Hou*] *T'ang kung-ch'en lieh-chuan* 後唐功臣列傳. By Chang Chao-yüan 張昭遠 (Chang Chao 張昭).

Chuang-tsung Shih-lu 莊宗實錄. 30 *chüan* (929). By Chang Chao-yüan 張昭遠, et al., comps.

Chün-ch'en t'u-i 君臣圖翼. 25 *chüan*. By Lu Chih 陸質.

Ch'ün-shu ssu-pu lu 群書四部錄. 200 *chüan* (719). By Yüan Hsing-ch'ung 元行沖 et al., comps.

Chung-hsiu Hsien-tsung Shih-lu 重修憲宗實錄. 40 *chüan*. (843). By Li Shen 李伸, dir., and Cheng Ya 鄭亞 et al., comps.

Chung-t'ai chih 中台志. 10 *chüan*. By Li Ch'üan 李筌.

Chung-tsung huang-ti Shih-lu 中宗皇帝實錄. 20 *chüan*. By Wu Ching 吳兢.

Ch'ung-hsüan li 崇玄曆. Calendar (892). By Pien Kang 邊岡 et al.

Fang-lin yao-lan 芳林要覽. 300 *chüan*. By Hsü Ching-tsung 許敬宗 et al., comps.

Han Kao-tsu Shih-lu 漢高祖實錄. 20 *chüan* (949). By Chia Wei 賈緯 et al., comps.

Han-lin nei-chih 翰林內誌. 1 *chüan*. Anonymous author.

Han-lin sheng shih 翰林盛事. 1 *chüan*. By Chang Chu 張著 or Chang Ch'u-hui 張處晦.

Han Yin-ti Shih-lu 漢隱帝實錄. 15 *chüan* (957). By Chang Chao 張昭, Yin Cho 尹拙, et al., comps.

Ho-Lo hsing-nien chi 河洛行年記. 10 *chüan*. Also entitled *Liu-shih hsing-nien chi* 劉氏行年記. 20 *chüan*. By Liu Jen-kuei 劉仁軌.

Hou Wei Ch'i-chü chu 後魏起居注. 336 *chüan*. Anonymous author.

Hou Wei shu 後魏書. 50 *chüan*. By Ling-hu Te-fen 令狐德棻.

Hsi-tsung Shih-lu 僖宗實錄. By P'ei Chih 裴贄. Probably never existed.

Hsi-tsung Shih-lu 僖宗實錄. 30 *chüan* (1045). By Sung Min-ch'iu 宋敏求.

Hsi-yü t'u-chih 西域圖志. 50 *chüan* (658). By Hsü Ching-tsung 許敬宗, ed.

Hsieh hsüan 寫宣. 10 *chüan*. By Wang Ch'i 王起.

Hsien-tsung Shih-lu 憲宗實錄. 40 *chüan* (830). By Lu Sui 路隨 et al., dirs., and Shen Ch'uan-shih 沈傳師 et al., comps.

Hsin Shih fa 新謚法. 3 *chüan*. By Ho Ch'en 賀琛.

Hsing-tsu hsi-lu 姓族系錄. 200 *chüan* (713). By Liu Ch'ung 柳沖.

Hsiuan-tsung Shih-lu 宣宗實錄. By Wei Pao-heng 韋保衡, dir., and Chiang Chieh 蔣偕 and Huang-fu Yü 皇甫煥, comps. Probably never existed.

Hsiuan-tsung Shih-lu 宣宗實錄. 30 *chüan* (1045). By Sung Min-ch'iu 宋敏求.

Hsü Han shu 續漢書. By Ssu-ma Piao 司馬彪.

Hsü Hui yao 續會要. 40 *chüan* (853). By Yang Shao-fu 楊紹復, dir., and Hsüeh Feng 薛逢, Ts'ui Yüan 崔瑑, and Cheng Yen 鄭言, comps.

Hsü Niu-Yang jih-li 續牛羊日曆. By Huang-fu Sung 皇甫松.

Hsü T'ang li 續唐曆. 30 *chüan* (851). By Ts'ui Kuei-ts'ung 崔龜從, dir., and Wei Ao 韋澳, Li Hsün 李荀, Chiang Chieh 蔣偕, Chang Yen-yüan 張彥遠, and Ts'ui Yüan 崔瑑, comps.

Hsü T'ung tien 續通典. 200 *chüan* (1001). By Sung Pai 宋白 et al., comps. See second section of Bibliography for fragments reconstructed by Funakoshi Taiji 船越太次.

Hsüan-chü chih 選舉志. 10 *chüan*. By Shen Chi-chi 沈既濟.

Hsüan-ming li 宣明曆. Calendar (822). Anonymous author.

Hsüan-tsung Shih-lu 玄宗實錄. 100 *chüan*. Also entitled *Ming-huang Shih-lu* 明皇實錄. By Yüan Tsai 元載, dir., and Ling-hu Huan 令狐峘, comp.

Huang-shih Yung-t'ai p'u 皇氏永泰譜. 20 *chüan* (766). Also entitled *Yung-t'ai hsin-p'u* 永泰新譜. By Liu Fang 柳芳.

Huang-ti Shih-lu 皇帝實錄. Later renamed *Kao-tsung shih-lu* 高宗實錄. 30 *chüan* (659). By Hsü Ching-tsung 許敬宗 et al., comps.

Hui yao 會要. 40 *chüan* (804–5). By Su Mien 蘇冕 and Su Pien 蘇弁.

I-tsung Shih-lu 懿宗實錄. 25 *chüan* (1045). By Sung Min-ch'iu 宋敏求.

I-tsung Shih-lu 懿宗實錄. By P'ei Chih 裴贄. Probably never existed.

Jui-tsung Shih-lu 睿宗實錄. 5 *chüan*. By Wu Ching 吳兢.

Jui-tsung Shih-lu 睿宗實錄. 20 *chüan* (716). By Liu Chih-chi 劉知幾 and Wu Ching 吳兢.

K'ai-yüan Ch'i-chü chu 開元起居注. 3682 *chüan*. Anonymous author. Probably non-existent; title an error by *HTS* compiler.

K'ai-yüan p'u 開元譜. 20 *chüan*. By Wei Shu 韋述. Supplement to Liu Ch'ung 柳沖, *Hsing-tsu hsi-lu* 姓族系錄.

K'ai-yüan Shih-lu 開元實錄. 47 *chüan*. Anonymous author.

Kao-tsu Shih-lu 高祖實錄. Anonymous author.

Kao-tsu Shih-lu 高祖實錄. 20 *chüan* (643). By Fang Hsüan-ling 房玄齡 dir., and Hsü Ching-tsung 許敬宗 and Ching Po 敬播, comps.

Kao-tsung Hou-hsiu Shih-lu 高宗後修實錄. 30 *chüan* (666). By Ling-hu Te-fen 令狐德棻, later continued and completed by Liu Chih-chi 劉知幾 and Wu Ching 吳兢.

Kao-tsung Shih-lu 高宗實錄. 30 *chüan*. By Wei Shu 韋述.

Kao-tsung Shih-lu 高宗實錄 60 *chüan*. By Wu Hsüan-chih 武玄之. Also written Wu Yüan-chih 武元之.

K'o-ti lu 科第錄. 16 *chüan*. By Yao K'ang 姚康. Also written Yao K'ang-fu 姚康復.

Ku-chin chao chi 古今詔集. 100 *chüan*. By Li I-fu 李義府 and Hsü Ching-tsung 許敬宗.

Ku-chin chao chi 古今詔集. 30 *chüan*. By Wen Yen-po 溫彥博.

Ku-chin chün kuo hsien tao ssu-i shu 古今郡國縣道四夷述. 40 *chüan* (801). By Chia T'an 賈耽.

Ku-chin kuo-tien 古今國典. 100 *chüan*. By Su Mien 蘇冕.

Ku-chin Shu-lu 古今書錄. 40 *chüan* (721). By Wu Chiung 毋煚. Also written in error Wu Chao 毋照.

Ku-kung lun 股肱論. By Kao-tsung 高宗.

Kua-ti chih 括地志. 500 *chüan* (642). Only fragments survive; see first section of Bibliography. By Li T'ai (Prince of Wei) 魏王李泰 et al., comps.

Kuan-hsiang li 觀象曆. Calendar (807). By Hsü Ang 徐昂.

K'un-wai ch'un-ch'iu 閫外春秋. 10 *chüan*. By Li Ch'üan 李筌.

Kuo-ch'ao chiu shih 國朝舊事. 40 *chüan*. By Liu Su 劉餗 (?).

Kuo-ch'ao chuan-chi 國朝傳記. 3 *chüan*. By Liu Su 劉餗.

Kuo-ch'ao ku-shih 國朝故事. Anonymous author.

Kuo shih 國史 [precise title unclear]. 100 *chüan*. By Hsü Ching-tsung 許敬宗 et al.

Kuo shih 國史 [precise title unclear]. By Li Jen-shih 李仁實.

Kuo shih 國史. 130 *chüan* (759 or 760). By Liu Fang 柳芳.

Lei-li i-shu 類禮義疏. 50 *chüan* (726). By Yüan Hsing-ch'ung 元行沖.

Lei pi 累璧. 630 *chüan* (661). By Hsü Ching-tsung 許敬宗 et al., eds.

Li-cheng wen-yüan 麗正文苑. 20 *chüan*. By Hsü Ching-tsung 許敬宗 et al., comps.

Li chih 禮志. 10 *chüan*. By Ting Kung-chu 丁公著 (769–832).

"*Li-i chih* 禮儀志." By Kuei Ch'ung-ching 歸崇敬. Part of never completed *T'ung chih* 通志 of Yüan Tsai 元載.

Li-tao yao-chüeh 理道要訣. 10 *chüan*. By Tu Yu 杜佑.

Li tien 理典. 12 *chüan*. May be confused with the following. By P'ei Che'ng 裴澄.

Li tien 禮典. 12 *chüan* (795). By P'ei Ch'eng 裴澄.

Liang ching hsin-chi 兩京新記. 5 *chüan*. Also entitled *Liang ching chi* 兩京記. By Wei Shu 韋述. *Chüan* 3 alone survives in a Japanese manuscript copy. See first section of Bibliography.

Liang Huang-ti Shih lu 梁皇帝實錄. 3 *chüan* (or 2 *chüan*). By Chou Hsing-ssu 周興嗣.

Liang Huang-ti Shih-lu 梁皇帝實錄. 5 *chüan*. By Hsieh Wu 謝吳 (or Hsieh Hao 謝昊).

Liang lieh-chuan 梁列傳. 15 *chüan*. Also entitled *Liang kung-ch'en lieh-chuan*. 梁功臣列傳. Anonymous author.

Liang shih 梁史. 10 *chüan*. By Wu Ching 吳兢.

Liang T'ai-ching Shih-lu 梁太清實錄. 8 *chüan*. Also entitled *Liang T'ai-ch'ing lu* 梁太清錄. Anonymous author.

Lin-te li 麟德曆. Calendar (665). By Li Ch'un-feng 李淳風.

Ling-yen ko kung-ch'en 淩煙閣功臣. By Chiang I 蔣乂.

Liu-shih chia-hsüeh yao-lu 柳氏家學要錄. 2 *chüan*. By Liu Ch'eng 柳珵.

Ming-huang chih-chao lu 明皇制詔錄. 1 *chüan*. By Hsüan-tsung 玄宗.

Mu-tsung Shih-lu 穆宗實錄. 20 *chüan* (833). By Lu Sui 路隨, dir., and Su Ching-i 蘇景裔 et al., comps.

National History [exact title unknown]. By Yao Ssu-lien 姚思廉.

Ni-chuang chu chih 擬狀注制. 10 *chüan*. Anonymous author.

Niu-Yang jih-li 牛羊日曆. 1 *chüan*. By Liu K'o 劉軻.

Ping-chia cheng shih 兵家正史. 9 *chüan*. By Wu Ching 吳兢.

San-kuo tien lüeh 三國典略. 30 *chüan*. By Ch'iu Yüeh 丘悅.

Sheng-ch'ao chao chi 聖朝詔集. 30 *chüan*. By Hsüeh K'o-kou 薛克構.

Sheng-mu shen-huang Shih-lu 聖母神皇實錄. 18 *chüan* (690). By Tsung Ch'in-ko 宗秦客.

Sheng-yü yüeh-ling 乘輿月令. 12 *chüan* (795). By P'ei Ch'eng 裴澄.

Shih-ch'en chuan 史臣傳. By Chiang I 蔣乂.

Shih cheng chi 時政記. 40 *chüan*. By Yao Shou 姚璹.

Shih-fa 諡法. 2 *chüan*. By Chang Ching 張靖.

Shih-fa 諡法. 5 *chüan*. By Ho Ch'ang 賀瑒.

Shih-li 諡例. 10 *chüan*. Also entitled *Shih-fa* 諡法. 10 *chüan*. By Shen Yüeh 沈約.

Shih-Tao lu-mu 釋道錄目. Supplement to *Ku-chin shu-lu* 古今書錄 (721). By Wu Chiung 毋煛.

Shih-tao ssu-fan chih 十道四蕃志. 16 *chüan*. Also entitled *Shih-tao chih* 十道志. By Liang Tsai-yen 梁載言.

Shih-tao t'u 十道圖. 13 *chüan* (704). Anonymous author.

Shih-tao t'u 十道圖. 10 *chüan* (715). Anonymous author.

Shih tao t'u 十道圖. 10 *chüan* (813). By Li Chi-fu 李吉甫.

Shu-fa chi 書法記. By Wei Shu 韋述.

Shun-tsung Shih-lu 順宗實錄. 3 *chüan* (813 or before). By Wei Ch'u-hou 韋處厚.

Shun-tsung Shih-lu 順宗實錄. 5 *chüan* (815). By Han Yü 韓愈.

Shun-tsung Shih-lu 順宗實錄. 5 *chüan* (831). By Han Yü 韓愈, revised by Lu Sui 路隨.

Su-tsung Shih-lu 肅宗實錄. 30 *chüan*. By Yüan Tsai 元載, dir.

Sui-chi ko-ming chi 隋季革命記. 5 *chüan*. By Tu Ju-t'ung 杜儒童.

Sui hou lüeh 隋後略. 10 *chüan*. By Chang Ta-su 張大素.

Sui Shih 隋史. 20 *chüan*. By Wu Ching 吳兢.

Ta Ch'eng-hsiang T'ang-wang kuan-shu chi 大丞相唐王官屬記. 2 *chüan*. By Wen Ta-ya 溫大雅.

Ta-chung Hsing-fa ts'ung-yao ko-hou chih 大中刑法總要格後敕. 60 *chüan* (851). By Liu Yüan 劉瑑.

[*Ta-chung*] *Hsing-fa t'ung-le* 大中刑法統類. 12 *chüan* (853). By Chang K'uei 張戣.

Ta Liang pien-i lu 大梁編遺錄. 30 *chüan*. Also entitled *Chu Liang hsing-ch'uang i-pien* 朱梁興創遺編, 20 *chüan*, or *Liang T'ai-tsu pien-i lu* 梁太祖編遺錄. By Ching Hsiang 敬翔.

Ta-T'ang tsai-fu lu 大唐宰輔錄. 70 *chüan*. By Chiang I 蔣乂.

Ta-T'ang tsai-hsiang piao 大唐宰相表. 3 *chüan*. By Liu Fang 柳芳.

Ta-yeh lüeh-chi 大業略記. 3 *chüan*. By Chao I 趙毅.

Ta-yeh shih-i 大業拾遺. 10 *chüan*. Anonymous author. May be identical with Tu Pao 杜寶, *Ta-yeh tsa-chi* 大業雜記.

Ta-yeh shih-i lu 大業拾遺錄. 1 *chüan*. By Yen Shih-ku 顏師古.

Ta-yeh tsa-chi 大業雜記. 10 *chüan*. Also entitled *Ta-yeh shih-i* 大業拾遺. By Tu Pao 杜寶.

Ta-yen li 大衍曆. Calendar (728). By I-hsing 一行.

Tai-tsung Shih-lu 代宗實錄. 40 *chüan* (presented 807). By Ling-hu Huan 令狐峘, comp.

T'ai-p'ing nei chih 太平內制. 5 *chüan*. Anonymous author.

T'ai-shang-huang Shih-lu 太上皇實錄. 10 *chüan*. (713–16). By Liu Chih-chi 劉知幾.

T'ai-tsung hsün-shih 太宗勳史. 1 *chüan*. By Wu Ching 吳兢.

T'ai-tsung Shih-lu 太宗實錄. Anonymous author.

T'ai-tsung Shih-lu 太宗實錄. By Hsü Ching-tsung 許敬宗, ed.

T'ai-tsung Wen huang-ti Cheng tien 太宗文皇帝政典. 30 *chüan*. Also entitled *T'ai-tsung Cheng tien* 太宗政典, or *Cheng tien* 政典. By Li Yen Shou 李延壽.

T'ai-yüeh ling pi-chi 太樂令壁記. 3 *chüan*. By Liu K'uang 劉貺.

T'ang-ch'ao chün-ch'en cheng-lun 唐朝君臣正論. 25 *chüan* (943). Also entitled *Ch'ien-ch'ao chün-ch'en cheng-lun* 前朝君臣正論. By Chang Chao-yüan 張昭遠 (Chang Chao 張昭).

T'ang-ch'ao ku-shih 唐朝故事. 3 *chüan*. By Ts'ui Yin-ju 崔引儒.

T'ang-ch'ao nien-tai chi 唐朝年代記. 10 *chüan*. By Chai Lu 焦璐.

T'ang Chih-i 唐職儀. 30 *chüan*. By Wei Shu 韋述.

T'ang chiu-chih pien lu 唐舊制編錄. 6 *chüan*. By Mr. Fei 費氏 (personal name unknown).

T'ang Ch'un-ch'iu 唐春秋. 60 *chüan*. By Lu Ch'ang-yüan.

T'ang Ch'un-ch'iu 唐春秋. 30 *chüan*. By Wei Shu 韋述.

T'ang Ch'un-ch'iu 唐春秋. 30 *chüan*. By Wu Ching 吳兢.

T'ang Fei-ti Shih-lu 唐廢帝實錄. 17 *chüan*. (957). By Chang Chao 張昭, Yin Cho 尹拙, et al., comps.

T'ang Kung-ch'en lieh-chuan 唐功臣列傳. 30 *chüan*. Also entitled [*Hou T'ang*] *Kung-ch'en lieh-chuan* 後唐功臣列傳, or *Chuang-tsung lieh-chuan* 莊宗列傳. By Chang Chao 張昭 et al., comps.

T'ang li 唐曆. 40 *chüan* (779 or later). By Liu Fang 柳芳.

T'ang-li mu-lu 唐曆目錄. 1 *chüan*. Anonymous author.

T'ang-li nien tai chi 唐曆年代記. Anonymous author.

T'ang Min-ti shih-lu 唐閔帝實錄. 3 *chüan* (957). By Chang Chao-yüan 張昭遠 (Chang Chao 張昭), Yin Cho 尹拙, et al., comps.

T'ang ming-ch'en tsou 唐名臣奏. 10 *chüan*. By Wu Ching 吳兢.

T'ang Ming-tsung Shih-lu 唐明宗實錄. 30 *chüan*. (935–6). By Chang Chao-yüan 張昭遠 (Chang Chao 張昭) et al., comps.

T'ang nien pu-i lu 唐年補遺錄. 55 (or 65) *chüan*. Also entitled *T'ang nien pu lu* 唐年補錄, or *T'ang-ch'ao pu-i lu* 唐朝補遺錄. By Chia Wei 賈緯.

T'ang Shih-lu 唐實錄. 90 *chüan*. By Hsü Ching-tsung 許敬宗.

T'ang Shih-lu 唐實錄. 90 *chüan*. By Fang Hsüan-ling 房玄齡.

T'ang shu 唐書. 100 *chüan*. (692–4). By Niu Feng-chi 牛鳳及.

T'ang shu 唐書. 98 *chüan* (726): *T'ang shu*. 65 *chüan* (729): *T'ang shu*. 80 *chüan* (749). Official Draft. *T'ang shu*. 110 *chüan*. By Wu Ching 吳兢.

T'ang shu 唐書. 110 *chüan*. Official draft, 106 *chüan*. Personal draft, 113 *chüan* (755). By Wei Shu 韋述.

T'ang shu 唐書, or *T'ang shih* 唐史. Uncompleted. By Wu San-ssu 武三思 et al., dirs.

T'ang shu hui yao 唐書會要. May refer to *T'ang hui yao*. Anonymous author.

T'ang shu pei-ch'üeh chi 唐書備闕記. 10 *chüan*. By Wu Ching 吳兢.

T'ang te-yin lu 唐德音錄. 30 *chüan*. Anonymous author.

T'ang teng-ko chi 唐登科記. 2 *chüan*. By Li I 李弈.

T'ang t'ung-chi 唐統記. 100 *chüan*. By Ch'en Yüeh 陳嶽.

Te-tsung Shih-lu 德宗實錄. 50 *chüan*. Also entitled *Chen-yüan Shih-lu* 貞元實錄. (810). By P'ei Chi 裴垍, dir., and Chiang I 蔣艾 et al., comps.

"Ti-li chih" 地理志. By K'ung Shu-jui 孔述睿. Possibly part of never completed *T'ung chih* 通志 of Yüan Tsai 元載.

Ti-wang cheng-t'ung 帝王正統. 10 *chüan*. By Yao K'ang 姚康.

T'ien hsün 天訓. 4 *chüan* (657). By Kao-tsung 高宗 with commentary by Hsü Ching-tsung 許敬宗 et al.

T'ien-kuan chiu-shih 天官舊事. 1 *chüan*. By Liu K'uang 劉貺.

T'ien-yu jih-li 天佑日曆. 1 *chüan*. Anonymous author.

Ting ming lu 定命錄. 2 *chüan*. By Lü Tao-sheng 呂道生.

Tse-t'ien Huang-hou Shih-lu 則天皇后實錄. 30 *chüan* (706). By Wu San-ssu 武三思 et al., dirs.

Tse-t'ien Shih-lu 則天實錄. 30 *chüan* (716). By Liu Chih-chi 劉知幾 and Wu Ching 吳兢, comps.

[*Ts'ui-shih*] *T'ang Hsien-ch'ing teng-k'o chi* 崔氏唐顯慶登科記. 5 *chüan*. Edited by Chao Tan 趙儋

Tsung-chi shih-fa 總集謐法. 165 *chüan*. By Shen Yüeh 沈約.

Tun-huang Shih-lu 燉煌實錄. 20 *chüan*. By Liu Ping 劉昞 (Liu Yen-ming 劉延明).

Tun-huang Shih-lu 燉煌實錄. 10 *chüan*. By Liu Ching 劉景.

Tung chih 通志, or *Li-tai shu chih* 歷代書志. By Yüan Tsai 元載, dir. Never completed. See also under (1) Kuei Ch'ung-ching. *Li-i chih*; and (2) K'ung Shu-jui. *Ti-li chih*.

Tung feng chi 東封記. 1 *chüan*. By Wei Shu 韋述.

T'ung shih 通史. 300 *chüan* (851). By Yao K'ang 姚康.

Tz'u Li-chi 次禮記. Also entitled *Lei Li* 類禮. 20 *chüan* (640). By Wei Cheng 魏徵.

Wang-yen hui-tsui 王言會最. 5 *chüan*. By Ma Wen-min 馬文敏.

Wei chi 魏紀. 12 *chüan*. By Wei T'an 魏澹.

Wei shu 魏書. 100 *chüan*. By Chang Ta-su 張大素.

Wei shu 魏書. 107 *chüan*. By Wei T'an 魏澹.

Wei tien 魏典. 30 *chüan*. By Yüan Hsing-ch'ung 元行沖.

Wen-kuan tz'u-lin 文館辭林. 1000 *chüan* (658). By Hsü Ching-tsung 許敬宗, Liu Po-chuang 劉伯莊, et al., comps. Four *chüan* only have survived in Japan, and reprinted in Hayashi Hitoshi, ed., *Isson sōsho*.

Wen-tsung Shih-lu 文宗實錄. 40 *chüan* (854). By Wei Mu 魏謩, dir., and Lu T'an 盧耽 et al., comps.

Wu-chi li 五紀曆. Calender (762). Also entitled *Pao-ying li* 寶應曆. By Kuo Hsien-chih 郭獻之

Wu-shu Shih-lu 吳書實錄. 3 *chüan*. Anonymous author.

Wu-te Chen-kuan liang-ch'ao shih 武德貞觀兩朝史. 80 *chüan* (656). By Chang-sun Wu-chi 長孫無忌, dir., and Ling-hu Te-fen 令狐德棻 et al., comps.

Wu-tsang-lun ying-hsiang 五藏論應象. 1 *chüan*. By Wu Ching 吳兢.

Wu-tsung Shih-lu 武宗實錄. 30 *chüan* (870–4). By Wei Pao-heng 韋保衡, dir., and Chiang Chieh 蔣偕, and Huang-fu Yü 皇甫煥, comps.

Wu-yin li 戊寅曆. Calendar (619). By Fu Jen-chün 傅仁均.

Yao-shan yü-ts'ai 搖山玉彩. 500 *chüan* (663). By Hsü Ching-tsung 許敬宗 et al., comps.

Yeh shih 野史. 10 *chüan*. Also entitled *T'ai-ho Yeh shih* 太和野史. By Kung-sha Chung-mu 公沙仲穆 (or Sha Chung-mu 沙仲穆).

Yü-shih t'ai chi 御史臺記. 10 *chüan*. By Wei Shu 韋述.

Yü-shih t'ai chi 御史臺記. 12 *chüan*. By Han Wan 韓琬.

Yü-shih t'ai ku-shih 御史臺故事. 3 *chüan*. By Li Kou 李構.

Yü-shih t'ai tsa-chu 御史臺雜注. 5 *chüan*. By Tu I-chien 杜易簡.

Yüan-ho chih chi 元和制集. 10 *chüan*. By Hsien-tsung 憲宗.

Yüan-ho kuo-chi pu 元和國計簿. 10 *chüan* (807). By Li Chi-fu 李吉甫.

Yüan-shou ch'ien-hsing wei-ch'eng ku-kung chieh 元首前星維城股肱誡. By Kao-tsung 高宗.

Yüeh chang 樂章. (627). Revised edition (631). By Tsu Hsiao-sun 祖孝孫, Wei Cheng 魏徵, Ch'u Liang 褚亮, Yü Shih-han 虞世南 et al., comps. Also entitled *Chen-kuan Yüeh chang* 貞觀樂章.

Yüeh chang 樂章. (725). By Chang Yüeh 張説.

Yüeh chang 樂章. 5 *chüan* (737). By Wei T'ao 韋綯.

Yüeh-fu ku-t'i yao chieh 樂府古題要解. 1 *chüan*. By Wu Ching 吳兢.

Yün ch'üan 韻銓. 15 *chüan*. By Wu Hsüan-chih 武玄之.

Index

275

I-wen lei-chü 藝文類聚 compiled by Ou-yang
Hsün and others including Ling-hu
Te-fen and Ch'en Shu-ta, 85
Imperial Chancellery, see *Men-hsia sheng*
Imperial Library, see *Pi-shu sheng*
Imperial Observatory, see *Ssu-t'ien t'ai;*
T'ai-shih chü
Imperial Secretariat, see *Chung-shu sheng*
Inner Palace affairs, 43–50, 145–6
Inner Palace Diary, see *Nei Ch'i-chü chu*

Jen Sui 任隨, 108
Jih-li 日曆, *see* Daily Calendar
ju-ko 入閤, abbreviated form of *huan-chang
ju-ko*, 36, 37, 55
Jui-tsung Shih-lu 睿宗實錄 by Liu Chih-chi
and Wu Ching, 136–7
Jui-tsung Shih-lu 睿宗實錄 by Wu Ching,
138

K'ai-yüan ch'i-chü chu 開元起居注, 42
K'ai-yüan li 開元禮 compiled by Hsiao Sung
and others, 101, 105, 107, 172, 176, 208
K'ai-yüan Shih-lu 開元實錄, anon., 139
K'ai-yüeh 凱樂 triumphal music, 212
kao 誥 imperial decree, 35
Kao Chih-chou 高智周, 129
Kao Li-shih 高力士, 59, 60, 181–2, 186
Kao Shang 高尚, 46
Kao-tsu Shih-lu 高宗實錄 compiled by Ching
Po, revised by Hsü Ching-tsung under
direction of Fang Hsüan-ling, 123–5
Kao-tsung hou-hsiu Shih-lu 高宗後修實錄
begun by Ling-hu Te-fen, completed by
Liu Chih-chi and Wu Ching, 129–30
Kao-tsung Shih-lu 高宗實錄, various works:
by Hsü Ching-tsung and others (also
entitled *Huang-ti Shih-lu*), 128–9; by Wei
Shu 130; by Wu Hsüan-chih 130; by Wu
Tse-t'ien, 130
k'ao 考 annual merit assessments of
officials, 69; by Board of Civil Office and
formal assessments, 82
K'ao-k'o ling 考科令 Statutes on
Assessment, section of codified law, 82
K'ao-kung ssu 考功司 Department of Merit
Assessments, part of Board of Civil
Office, 66–70
K'ao shih 考使 commissioner for local merit
assessments, 28
K'o-ti lu 科第錄 by Yao K'ang, 90
Ku-chin chao chi 古今詔集 by Li I-fu and
Hsü Ching-tsung, 98
Ku-chin chao chi 古今詔集 by Wen Yen-po,
98

Ku-chin chün kuo hsien tao ssu-i shu 古今郡國
縣道四夷述 by Chia T'an, 229
Ku-chin kuo-tien 古今國典 by Su Mien, 109
Ku-chin shu-lu 古今書錄 of Wu Chiung, 175,
231–2
Ku Hsü 顧虛, 128
Ku-kung lun 股肱論 by Kao-tsung, 99
ku-li 故吏 "former employee," 69–70
Ku-liang chuan 穀梁傳 commentary on
Ch'un-ch'iu, 64
Ku Yin 顧胤 (also written Ku Ssu 顧嗣), 6,
98, 125, 126, 164–6; compiler of *Wu-te
Chen-kuan liang-ch'ao shih*, 164, 166;
compiler of *Kua-ti chih*, 227
Ku Yün 顧允 (also written Ku I 顧裔),
compiler of *Huang-ti Shih-lu*, 128
Kua-ti chih 括地志 compiled by Li T'ai and
others, 227–9
Kuan-hsiang li 觀象曆 calendar by Hsü Ang,
220–1
Kaun p'in ling 官品令 Statutes on Official
Ranks, section of codified law, 230
Kuei Ch'ung-ching 歸崇敬, 89, 211; author
of *Li-i chih*, perhaps part of Yüan Tsai's
T'ung chih, 211
Kuei-shih yüan 匭使院 office for Urns for
Communication with the Throne, 17
K'un-wai ch'un-ch'iu 閫外春秋 by Li Ch'üan,
94
Kung-ch'eng 宮城 Palace City, 17
Kung-sha Chung-mu 公沙仲穆 (or Sha
Chung-mu), author of *[T'ai-ho] Yeh shih*,
157
Kung-yang chuan 公羊傳 commentary to
Ch'un-ch'iu, 64
K'ung Shu-jui 孔述睿, author of Revised
Monograph on Administrative
Geography, 89, 226–7
K'ung Ying-ta 孔穎達, 20
Kuo-ch'ao chiu-shih 國朝舊事, anon., 110
Kuo-ch'ao chuan-chi 國朝傳記 by Liu Su, 110
Kuo-ch'ao ku-shih 國朝故事, anon, may be
identical with *Kuo-ch'ao chiu-shih* 國朝舊
事, 110
Kuo Chih-yün 郭知運, 68
Kuo Hsien-chih 郭獻之, author of *Wu-chi li*
calendar, 220
kuo shih 國史; general term used for all
national records including Veritable
Records and Court Diaries, 124; *see also*
National History
Kuo shih 國史 by Liu Fang, supplemented
by Yü Hsiu-lieh and Ling-hu Huan,
178–87, 207
Kuo shih 國史 (exact title unclear),
compiled by Hsü Ching-tsung, 166

286